SOME SOUTH INDIAN VILLAGES

SOME SOUTH INDIAN VILLAGES

EDITOR

GILBERT SLATER

GYAN

Published by

Gyan Publishing House
5, Ansari Road
Daryaganj, New Delhi-110002
Phone: 011-47034999, 9811692060
E-mail: books@gyanbooks.com

Distribution Network
gyanbooks.com
India, USA, Canada, UK, Australia

ISBN: 978-93-7097-393-0 (HB)

First Published, 1918

2nd Impression 2025

Printed at: Gyan Press, Delhi.

SOME SOUTH INDIAN VILLAGES

Editor: GILBERT SLATER

SOME SOUTH INDIAN VILLAGES

SOME SOUTH INDIAN VILLAGES

EDITED BY

GILBERT SLATER, M.A., D.Sc.

Professor of Indian Economics, University of Madras

1918.

CONTENTS

ILLUSTRATIONS

ECONOMIC STUDIES.

I.—SOME SOUTH INDIAN VILLAGES.

INTRODUCTION.

WHEN in January 1913 Sir Theodore Morison delivered the Inaugural Address of the Madras Economic Association, he suggested that economic enquiry in the Madras Presidency should begin with a sociological and statistical survey of a typical Indian village. Obviously too much stress must not be laid upon the word "typical." No single village can be typical of the Presidency of Madras and the neighbouring States of Southern India. It can at best be typical of a particular district, and long acquaintance with the district is necessary to qualify an enquirer to decide which village is most typical. On the other hand the advantages of the method of study recommended by Sir Theodore Morison are obvious. Villages came before towns, and even in the most industrialized countries, where all economic questions tend to be studied from an urban point of view, it is well to be reminded that the economic life of a town or city cannot be understood without reference to the lands which send it its food and raw materials, and the villages from which it attracts young men and women. The importance of rural activities and of village life in India, in view of the enormous preponderance of its agricultural population over that engaged in mining, manufacture, commerce and transport, is not likely to be overlooked; and least of all in Southern India, which has no coal mines and no great industries like cotton manufacture in Bombay and jute in Bengal.

On taking up my appointment as Professor of Indian Economics in the University of Madras in December 1915, I determined to direct the attention of students towards the study of particular villages. Instead of endeavouring to select typical villages, I made my choice on the simple principle of taking those that were most available. I asked students of the University who were willing to help to make surveys of their native villages during the long vacation. To help them I drew up a "Village Questionnaire"—a book of questions, spaced fairly liberally, interleaved with blank pages.

Some study was necessary in order to decide what questions to ask. In this I was assisted by Mr. E. V. Sundaram Reddi, who accompanied me to his native village of Eruvellipet in the second week of February 1916.

ERUVELLIPET.

The route.—One hundred miles south of Madras on the main line to Trichinopoly, Madura, and the alternative crossings to Ceylon, is the town of Villupuram, the junction for Pondicherry. Here the railway which has been keeping to the west of French territory turns eastwards to approach the coast at Cuddalore; but the high road from Madras, which also passes through Villupuram, keeps its direction a little to the west of south. Eight miles from Villupuram along this road lies Eruvellipet. We left Madras in the early evening, reached Villupuram at night, and went on to Eruvellipet by bullock cart in the early morning.

The country is flat, though the rocky spurs of the Eastern Ghats are visible in the west. The road is a high road in the literal sense, for it has been built up some feet above the level of the surrounding rice fields, which, in the early part of February, were mostly ripening for harvest, though in some spots the harvest had already been carried, and the land was being ploughed for a second crop, and in other places it was still green, and needing water. In the comparative treelessness of the landscape the picottahs stood out conspicuously, with two or three men plodding patiently on the swinging beam that works this primitive pump, alternately towards and away from the wooden pillar, some 15 or 20 feet high, on which it hinges, but always, in either direction, climbing upwards, for the picottah combines the characteristic features of the see-saw and tread-mill.

As is usual with South Indian roads this one has its margin well planted with trees. But whoever was responsible for tree-planting here had views not generally shared by his colleagues in other districts. Though shade was of course the first desideratum, he achieved a secondary object also, instead of the usual banyan or margosa planting coconut palms, mango trees and tamarinds. The right of picking the fruit of these for each mile of road is sold annually by auction, and the proceeds go to the highway fund. This fund apparently needs all the adventitious support it can get, for the road is very bad, in places almost impassable, and, presently when it reaches the bank of the South Pennar river, it presents a hiatus of a mile of sandy track, with, at one spot, a feeble trickle of water just enough to wet the feet of the oxen. A mile or two further on the same phenomenon recurs, where the road crosses the Malattar river, another channel of the South Pennar. Between these two channels, and along the bank of the Malattar, lies Eruvellipet, a village of 1,139 acres and (1911) 1,150 inhabitants.

The River Malattar.—Unpromising as the River Malattar appears, an arid waste of sand, with little vegetation beyond prickly-pear, into which cattle, buffaloes, goats and pigs are turned apparently rather for air and exercise than for any nutriment procurable, it is this river that dominates the life of Eruvellipet. It is a river in spite of its appearance; the water is there, flowing from the tableland of Mysore to the Bay of Bengal, beneath the surface of the sand, and is to be won by digging. Wells in the village if sunk deep enough, are filled by infiltration; the largest of those wells, equipped with an effective pump driven by an oil-engine, supplies a continuous stream of water for the irrigation of about a dozen acres of technically "dry" land. A more important part of the water-supply comes from the bed of the river, and is brought down by what are known as "spring channels" to the village. These streams supply the water used for drinking and domestic purposes, and irrigate a large part of the "wet lands." Every year, in the monsoon, these channels in the bed of the river are partly obliterated;

PICOTTAH AND IMPROVED BULLOCK LIFT, USED IN SOUTH ARCOT.
Photo by Agricultural College.

every year they have to be dug afresh, by the co-operative labour of the villagers. The fact that this co-operative labour is necessary and that it is certain to bring its reward, goes far to counteract the forces, always so powerful in Indian villages, tending towards industrial apathy and excessive conservatism. Perhaps also the racial constitution of the village helps. Though it is, taken as a whole, a Tamil village, the leading families are Telugu-speaking Reddis, immigrants from the north, somewhat taller and larger in frame than the Tamils, lighter and yellower in complexion. The Telugus in their own country are more backward educationally and industrially than the Tamils; but here, like Danes in Anglo-Saxon villages, as a superior caste, speaking one language in their homes, and another in the village, they are the more apt to make the effort to learn English also, and are in fact frequently trilingual.

Besides the water drawn from the River Malattar, the village has a tank (i.e., an artificial lake) that gives a three months' supply of water for the irrigation of the greater part of the wet land. It is fed by the "Reddi channel," about 15 miles long, starting from the River Pennar, but receiving surface drainage on the way. It is now blocked at the head though not being kept in repair, and at present the tank is fed only by the water that drains into the channel during the monsoons. The repair of this channel is locally considered a desirable improvement. The amount of water received by the tank varies from year to year; but the inconvenience resulting is reduced by the fact that some lands can be watered alternatively from the tank and by spring channels.

Cultivation.—Of the total area of the village, 1,139 acres, 722 acres are available for cultivation, 417 acres not. This includes the area of the inhabited village and its two streets, of the tank, of the parts of the river bed and high road within the village boundaries, and of the channels for the distribution of water. Of the 722 cultivable acres 542 acres are officially considered "wet," and pay a kist (land revenue) of Rs. 2,694-11-0 averaging Rs. 4-15-6 (6*s.* 5½*d.*) per acre; 180 are "dry," and pay Rs. 247-14-0 averaging Rs. 1-6-0 (1*s.* 10*d.*) per acre. Where land is let by the immediate holder under Government to a sub-tenant, rents run up to Rs. 40 (£2-13-4) per acre. The use of the land is not strictly according to its official classification. The lands are officially "wet" which can be completely irrigated from the tank and the spring channels; but "dry" land may be adequately irrigated from a private well, and grow rice, and "wet" land may be used for a "dry" crop. In the year of settlement, 1891, 24 acres of "dry" land were under rice, and 28 acres of wet land under groundnut, spiked millet and ragi, which are "dry" crops.

In that year only 656 acres out of a maximum possible of 722 were cultivated, as follows:—

	ACRES.
Rice	499
Spiked millet, ragi and Italian millet	70
Indigo	44
Groundnut	19
Vegetables of various sorts	15
Palmyra and tamarind	9

Since that year, there have been various changes. The total area cultivated has been increased practically to the maximum. Indigo was found unprofitable, and its cultivation entirely abandoned until the effect of the war on the price was realized. In 1916, 25 acres were sown; with a prospect of a further extension in 1917. On the other hand, the area under groundnuts was much increased, and averaged about 50 acres in recent years. Groundnuts are generally shipped from Madras and Pondicherry for export to Marseilles, and on the outbreak of war, the Eruvellipet growers speedily cut down the acreage to 10 acres. Of the wet land about 13 acres is now under sugarcane. Groundnut (combined with another crop) and sugarcane have this economic characteristic in common, they both are valuable crops, but costly to cultivate.

In Eruvellipet the more common practice is to combine groundnut with kambu (spiked millet) or tenai (Italian millet) on dry lands that depend entirely on rain; in the case of dry lands that can be watered by wells, a crop of ragi is raised first, and the groundnuts sown just before the ragi is ready for harvesting. The combination of groundnut and ragi yields a maximum gross produce of Rs. 200 per acre. Groundnut, being a leguminous plant, enriches the soil. Sugarcane may yield up to Rs. 500 per acre, though not more than Rs. 400 has been realized in Eruvellipet, but it occupies the ground for a little over twelve months, and should not be grown on the same land more frequently than once in four years. The extension of either of these crops involves an increased local demand for labour. Other crops that have been tried on a small scale and found profitable are tobacco and Cambodia cotton, the Cambodia seed being obtained from the Agricultural department. Gingelly and indigo is considered a good dry land combination; the gross yield being about Rs. 150 on land dependent on rain, and Rs. 200 where some well water can be applied.

Tree planting and fuel.—In two other ways the practical value of the Madras Department of Agriculture to these villagers is exemplified. On the worst land, sandy spots awkwardly placed for irrigation, casuarina, a fir-like tree introduced by the department from Japan, is grown. Casuarina grows very rapidly and is excellent firewood. It is customary to cut it down five, six or seven years after planting.

He who grows casuarina does a service to the whole community, because the more firewood is available, the fewer varatties are burnt. Varatties are large handfulls of cow-dung mixed with husks made into round flat cakes and stuck on any convenient rock or wall to dry. To a certain extent they are used in preference to wood, where a slow burning fire is required, as for boiling milk when it is inconvenient to watch it; but mainly varatties are used because wood is costly or unobtainable. In treeless districts, like much of the Deccan, practically all the cow-dung that is not required for washing the walls and floors of houses, or for surgical dressings for wounds and burns,* is burnt as fuel. Though the ashes are saved and used as manure, it can hardly be doubted that the loss in fertility from this practice is very great. Even if all the manurial constituents of chemical value remained in the ash

* On the antiseptic qualities of urea, and its value for surgical purposes, vide "Lancet," December 1915.

(which I presume is not the case) its value in building up humus and improving the texture and power of retaining moisture of the soil, as compared with that of dung, is practically nil. But where wood is abundant by far the greater part of the cow-dung is used for manure. There are even some districts on the West Coast where the women are beginning to object to the duty which ancient custom prescribes for them, of picking up the freshly fallen cow-dung on the high road whenever the opportunity offers, and of carrying it home in big handfulls. As ox-wagons travel in unending streams along the roads on the plains of Southern India, the traveller by road has reason to bless this custom, which keeps the road much cleaner, and makes the dust less noxious, than would otherwise be the case. Nevertheless the sight of women walking with the erect and stately carriage which the practice of carrying burdens on the head confers, reaching down a hand adorned with numerous silver rings and a bracelet apparently of gold (actually gilded lac) to pick up the moist dung, does not readily lose its quaintness.

For various reasons the demand for fuel is a growing one. The price of casuarina in Madras was 8*d.* per hundredweight in 1907, and at the time of writing (February 1917) it is 1*s.* 2*d.* per hundredweight. Land under casuarina yields about 5 tons of wood per acre per annum (a casuarina plantation of seven years' growth yields about 35 tons per acre), it requires practically no attention except at the times of planting and felling, and only needs a little irrigation while the trees are very young. The thinnings supply fuel for domestic purposes, and when the trees are cut down, and the roots removed, the land is greatly improved in fertility. Hence a plot of barren land planted with casuarina is a splendid savings bank for a ryot who can foresee a period of heavy expense in six or seven years' time; as, the marriage of a daughter, or the education of a son at the University.

Single transplantation.—The village of Eruvellipet has generally adopted the system of "single transplantation" of paddy recommended by the Agricultural department. All except the poorest and laziest cultivators of rice in the Madras Presidency sow the paddy on comparatively small spots, and transplant it thirty to forty days after sowing. But the customary method in transplanting is to put several plants together into one hole in the levelled mud of the rice field. Experiment has proved that if each seedling is separately planted and all are evenly spaced, there is a considerable saving of seed and a heavier crop. The new method is spreading, but as yet very slowly. Unless the grains are sown thinly in the seed-bed, single transplantation takes more time and labour, and if this is not realized, disappointment follows. The poor ryot, moreover, naturally and properly, refuses to experiment, as he cannot afford a failure, and waits to see with his own eyes that a new method is an improvement before he adopts it. Richer ryots, who can afford to experiment, also can afford to employ hired labour, and they find the coolies whom they employ will not change their methods unless compelled to do so by strict supervision. They want to do their work in the semi-automatic manner attained by unchanging habit, and not to tax their brains and think about what they are doing.

Sugar refining.—The enterprising spirit, however, has its dangers. In 1885 (cir.) two brothers, well-to-do ryots in Eruvellipet, took a leading part with others in the erection of a sugar refinery. They were disappointed in their hope of obtaining a licence for the distillation of arrack, which would have been a profitable by-product; and there was another mill in a village five miles distant which competed for cane. The result was that in 1895 the Eruvellipet company was wound up,* and the mill fell into ruins. One of its two tall chimneys still rears its head, but the other has been pulled down to supply bricks for other buildings, and the two brothers above mentioned having died, left their families encumbered by debt. What followed is rather curious, and throws some light on the economics of the Hindu family system. The dead men had held jointly a holding of 102 acres. One of them left one son, the other four. It was resolved by these first cousins to divide the property, so that each might struggle with his own debts. By law there should first have been an equal division of the holding into halves for the two families, and then the family of four brothers should have equally divided their half among themselves. On the other hand if the ancient law of Welsh gavelkind, which may be regarded as springing from the sense of justice of a people under the patriarchal system, had been applied, there would have been an equal division among the five first cousins. Actually there was a sort of compromise between these two principles. The land was divided into six equal parts, of which the only son took two, thus getting one-third of the whole instead of his legal share of a half, and the four brothers took one part each, thus getting one-sixth each, instead of one-eighth. He who had the larger share was able to clear off his debts; but the four brothers, each with holdings of about seventeen acres, and debts of some thousands of rupees at not less than 18 per cent interest, had a much harder struggle. The most business-like way to deal with such a situation is for the ryot who is so placed to face it immediately and sell enough land to pay off his creditors, as even in the case of a forced sale land will fetch sixteen years' purchase of its annual value and upwards. It is obviously bad business to pay 18 per cent on borrowed money in order to avoid realizing property that only yields 6 per cent. But the land hunger of the Indian peasant is comparable in intensity, being no doubt similar in its psychological basis, to his craving for jewellery. He will buy land recklessly when he gets an opportunity, but he will not sell unless he is absolutely compelled. There are other resources. An unmarried landed proprietor, owning (under Government) seventeen acres, mostly "wet," may hope for a handsome dowry with his wife. His sons may, if he manages to give them an English education, secure a Government appointment, and even, though this is a remote possibility, achieve the magic letters "B.A., B.L." and become vakils. And if one member of the family succeeds in so establishing himself, all the others benefit. Family solidarity in India is a great fact, most important both for good and evil. It is family solidarity that in a country of widespread poverty copes with destitution so effectively as to preclude

* Sugarcane crushing is still carried on, the oil-engine mentioned above drives the mill.

A SPLENDID CROP OF SUGAR-CANE.
Photo by Agricultural College.

a poor law, and to preclude also the formation of the custom of the whip round among workmen for a mate in misfortune from which the British Friendly Societies and Trade Unions developed.

What the "family" means in India may be judged from the following dialogue. I noticed that a friend referred to a fellow caste man, Mr. A.B., as his uncle, but hesitated a little in using the word. So I asked "How is he your uncle, is he an uncle by blood, or by marriage?" He replied, "He is not exactly my uncle. He is related to me this way. My mother's brother was C.D. C.D.'s uncle's son on his father's side was E.F. E.F.'s daughter married A.B.'s sister's son." I commented "That is not a very close relationship." He replied "There is another way in which he is related to me. He married a girl whose sister, G.H., had been married to K.L. G.H. died, and K.L. married subsequently the daughter of the sister of my father's sister's husband." When such meanings as these are attached to the word "uncle," the meaning of "nepotism" in India may be guessed.

A typical holding.—Such a holding as that referred to will consist of a number of small plots of land scattered over the area of the "village" in its wider sense; while all the habitations of the people are congregated together in two spots, which may be termed, respectively, the caste village and the pariah village. The following are the exact measurements of a typical holding of the larger size at the time of the last settlement, 1891, in acres and decimals of an acre:—

1·49, 1·87, 2·31, 6·88, 1·55, 0·83, 1·65, 2·24, 1·44, 1·38, 2·47, 0·41, 0·39, 0·30, 0·32, 0·09, 0·13, 0·28, 0·20, 0·96, 2·51, total 29·70 acres in twenty-one parcels.

The distribution of land in different holdings, therefore, resembles that in English villages containing numerous small holdings in the open field districts before enclosure. There is, however, a marked difference in the shape of the different plots, which, instead of being, as in England, long narrow rectangles, approximate to squares. Each plot of wet land is surrounded by a little embankment, about a foot broad and about a foot high, to keep in or exclude the water, which is turned on or off by temporary openings in the embankment according to the requirements of the crop. These embankments also serve as paths for men and cattle.

Some of the holdings in 1891 were "joint pattas" some "single pattas." The following table gives an idea as to how these were held:—

Joint Pattas.

5	proprietors,	1 holding of	21 plots.
	"	1 "	3 "
4	"	1 "	11 "
	"	1 "	9 "
	"	1 "	7 "
	"	1 "	3 "
	"	2 holdings of	1 plot.
3	"	1 holding of	30 plots.
	"	1 "	13 "
	"	1 "	4 "
	"	1 "	2 "
	"	5 holdings of	1 plot.

Joint Pattas—cont.

2	proprietors,	1 holding of	16 plots.
	,,	1 ,,	10 ,,
	,,	1 ,,	9 ,,
	,,	1 ,,	5 ,,
	,,	1 ,,	3 ,,
	,,	2 holdings of	2 ,,
	,,	5 ,,	1 plot.

Single Pattas.

1 of 112 plots.	4 of 8 plots.
1 ,, 36 ,,	1 ,, 7 ,,
1 ,, 35 ,,	1 ,, 6 ,,
2 ,, 24 ,,	3 ,, 5 ,,
1 ,, 16 ,,	4 ,, 4 ,,
1 ,, 13 ,,	6 ,, 3 ,,
2 ,, 10 ,,	8 ,, 2 ,,
2 ,, 9 ,,	32 ,, 1 plot.

The average area of each plot was just over one acre; and the 656 acres of cultivated land were shared by no less than 165 ryots, which allows a little less than 4 acres for each ryot on the average. This is according to the official survey. At the present day the ownership of land is much more concentrated. The largest of these holdings, that of 112 plots, and another of 24 plots were, in 1891, held by brothers, one of whom was childless, and they both passed to the only son of the other brother. The larger property thus created has been steadily increased by the purchase of more land from small ryots who, unable to make headway against debt, have sold their land and, in some cases, emigrated to Ceylon. Altogether this relatively wealthy man at the time of my visit owned about 400 acres in the village, and about 200 acres in adjoining villages. He cultivated about 200 acres himself, and let out the remainder to tenants. What is let is let to small holders who cultivate by their own labour. The large farm which he keeps in hand he cultivates by the help of 40 "padials."

Padials.—A "padial" is a sort of serf, who has fallen into hereditary dependence on a landowner by debt. In almost every case the original debt was a sum of money borrowed by a landless man to solemnize his marriage or, more frequently, that of a son or daughter, the borrower undertaking to work for the lender, until the debt should be repaid, in return for a certain limited supply of food. Quite recently a lad of 18 borrowed Rs. 25 in cash and grain to celebrate his wedding with due festivity and became a padial. Such a loan never is repaid, but descends from one generation to another; and the padials themselves are transferred with the creditor's land when he sells it or dies. One proprietor informed me that he paid his padials 30 Madras measures of paddy per month per head. At present prices 30 Madras measures of paddy are worth about Rs. 3-12-0 (5*s*.). A Madras measure of paddy weighs 2½ lb., but when husked loses about half its volume and one-third of its weight. The padial's paddy allowance there-

HARVESTING PADDY.

Photo by Agricultural College'

fore works out at about 27 oz.* of raw rice per day; a quantity that the man is probably able and willing to eat himself without assistance from his wife and family. Another landowner gives his padials 22 Madras measures of paddy per month, a daily meal of ragi porridge, and annually two cloths and 18 measures of paddy or some other grain. The family of the padial must help the patron when required, but then extra payment is made. Padials are sometimes required to work with two intervals from 4-30 a.m. to 6 p.m.; but the regular hours of labour are 6 a.m. to 6 p.m.

The one way of escape for the padial from this condition of servitude and poverty is emigration. At Villupuram there are offices of the "Ceylon Labour Commission," which recruits labour for the Ceylon plantations. Their economic condition in Ceylon is vastly improved, and they have opportunities of saving money, and, if they choose, of returning to their native districts and buying land. Needless to say the emigration of padials is discouraged by their creditors. It is impressed upon the padial that it is a point of honour for him never to leave his master; and he is given to understand that he cannot legally do so. In some districts the creditors adopt the device of making the padial sign a fresh document every few years, so that in a court of law it may be made to appear that a fresh debt has been incurred.

Emigration to Ceylon is not on the indenture system, and the emigrant's contract with the planter who employs him is terminable by a month's notice on either side at any time; nevertheless there are some signs that the agitation against indentured emigration to Fiji and other places may be widened so as to check the flow of emigrants to Ceylon.

Debt is an almost universal condition. Landowners and cultivators, large and small, are in debt to one another and to Chettis (a merchant caste) in Villupuram. In some cases the debts are temporary, contracted afresh every year and liquidated when the crop is sold; in other cases they are permanent, either because the debtor cannot pay, or because he prefers to go on buying land with borrowed money or incurring other capital expenditure, to paying off what he owes. The rate of interest may be 24 or 36 per cent, i.e., 2 or 3 per cent per month. It is noteworthy that in many cases the ryots consider it worth while to hold up their crops for a while after harvesting, expecting the rise in price to more than counterbalance the extra interest. One man was pointed out to me as an exception to the general rule of indebtedness—a man who lives on his earnings and within his income. He is a dhobi (washerman) and is said to have over 1,000 rupees saved.

The efficiency of labour.—If labour is extraordinarily ill-paid in South India, it also appears to be extraordinarily inefficient. At Eruvellipet I saw both ploughing and reaping. The reaping in particular is an extraordinary sight. A number of men, clad in loin-cloths only, squat in the field that is ripe for harvesting. At that time the rice stalks no longer stand upright, but are laid before the wind. Work begins at the windward edge. Each man

* The gaol allowance for a man doing hard labour is 25 oz. of ragi flour, rice and pulse combined, 6 oz. of vegetables, ½ oz. of oil, and 2 oz. of various condiments, per day.

has a sickle, about the size and shape of a small bill-hook, but with a serrated edge. He squats on the ground on his heels, holds the stalks that grow from a single root in his left hand, severs them close to the ground with a blow from the sickle in his right hand, then gently deposits the bundle of cut stalks on one side. Then, still squatting, he shifts his position by an inch or two, and similarly deals with the next root. In the course of a day eight men may cut an acre.* In other districts it is the custom for women to cut the corn, and, in Mysore, I was informed, it took fifteen women to cut an acre in a day. But in Eruvellipet the women carry the corn. They collect it into bundles, carry these on their heads along the earth embankments mentioned above to the nearest village threshing-floor which is a small plot of land elevated sufficiently above the level of the paddy fields to keep dry. A man there receives the bundles, shakes out the loose grain, and tosses the straw on to a heap to be subsequently trodden on by oxen to recover the remainder. The rice afterwards has to be husked, by being pounded on the pestle and mortar system. The easier method of doing this is to boil the grain, and dry it in the sun first; but for Brahman consumption the grain is husked without boiling.

The village munsif was ploughing a plot of between one or two acres. He had sixteen plough teams on the job: twelve were at work, four resting. Each plough team was a pair of feeble oxen or of feeble buffaloes, which crawled through the liquid mud, dragging the light wooden ploughs behind them. The treading of the mud by the oxen is as important a part of the preparation of the land as the churning of it up by the plough. It is considered that stronger and heavier beasts would sink too deep in the mud.

Cattle.--The village has about 250 working cattle, which works out at about 5½ acres per plough team, and that means that it is rather short of cattle. As a general rule it is considered that four acres of wet land to a pair of bullocks is the right proportion. Ploughing must be done when the water is available. Eruvellipet, however, with its tank and spring channels, can extend its ploughing season over a longer period than many villages, and can therefore manage with fewer oxen.

Besides the working cattle, the village had about 150 cows and she-buffaloes, and about 180 young animals of these species. Not enough young cattle are raised in the village to maintain the supply of beasts for the plough and for cartage to Villupuram, and the stock is continually renewed by purchase. The imported bulls and bullocks come from Mysore, and are superior to those reared in the village. The supply of milk from the cows is very small. Besides calves and milk, the Indian cow produces manure or fuel, hides and bones; for the sake of these commodities, and to avoid the sin of cow-killing, vast numbers of animals are doomed to drag out a miserable semi-starved existence. In Eruvellipet the dung which the village herd of cows and young stock leaves in the bed

* "Six to ten men, or ten to twelve women will reap the crop. Bundling and carrying to the floor close by, two men and four women. Stacking, if done preparatory to threshing, one man per acre." R. C. Wood, "Notebook of Agricultural Facts and Figures, p. 35."

Treading out the corn (paddy).

Photo by Agricultural College.

of the river is the perquisite of the village potter, who has the special right to collect it for fuel. Goats and pigs are also kept; and one or two donkeys, the property of the dhobis. The goats number about 100; they are valued chiefly for manure: only the low caste people will drink goats' milk.

The caste village.—To a great extent the village is self-supporting. The various sorts of habitations in the caste village and pariah village are made almost entirely out of local materials by local labour. Bricks and tiles are made. There are carpenters, blacksmiths, goldsmiths, schoolmasters and priests; a post office in the charge of the headmaster of the school, and two oil-mills, besides the sugar mill worked by the oil-engine mentioned above. Agricultural implements and carts are made by the village carpenters out of local timber. There is no weaving done in the village, but there is a weaving village a few miles away. Palmyra trees supply toddy and jaggery. Religious festivals satisfy the more imperative spiritual cravings.

Even in this small, almost self-contained, Dravidian community we find two civilizations, both apparently of vast antiquity, existing side by side, and though each for innumerable generations has acted and reacted upon the other, they still remain distinct. On the west side of the high road is the caste village, open, exposed to the sun. One house in it is imposing, with two stories, a flat roof, a covered approach, ornamental iron gates and pillars adorned with paintings. The two parallel streets, running east and west, and connected at the west end by a cross street, are maintained in a fit condition for cart traffic. The houses, some built of brick, some of earth, some tiled, some thatched, have the little pial, or verandah, facing the street, with niches in the walls for lights to burn at nightfall. Built round little courts which are open to the sky, they give seclusion to those who desire it; and, though there are no Muhammadans and no purdah in the village, the women habitually stay very much indoors. At the eastern end of the village, adjoining the high road, are two temples to Siva—one a temporary building which the god is inhabiting, till the other, the new temple, is finished. Here also are the sacred cars in which deities are joyfully conducted round the village during certain festivals, and a great stone lingam, the symbol of the function of generation, and therefore of life. At the west end is a temple of Ganesa, the elephant-headed "belly-god," the god of prosperity, son of Siva. There are two cars, one for Ganesa, used on his birthday, the festival of *Vinayaga Chaturti*; the other for Ponniamman (Kali) on *Tirunal*, a ten days' festival in May.

The Pariah village.—To the east of the high road is the pariah village, with its own architecture and its own temples. It has no streets, only paths worn smooth by the pressure of bare feet. It lies altogether in the shade, in a grove of palms mixed with trees of various kinds. Houses are made of a framework of sticks, the roofs thatched with palm leaves, and the walls also woven, as it were, of leaves and twigs. These dwellings are dark inside, but with sufficient openings to keep well ventilated. The floor is bare earth. There is little privacy here. Men, women and children live in the open air. The one substantial building is a new temple, built at a cost of 300 rupees by the pariahs out of their own funds, to Desamma or Mariyattal, the goddess of small-pox. There is also an open air shrine of Aynar, or Ayanar, who is carved in stone squatting between his two wives Purni and Pushkali, all three being naked except for ornaments and head dress. The two goddesses wear tall sugar loaf erections on their heads somewhat similar to those on Assyrian statues; but the god one of a very different type. There is a Puranic story to the effect that Aynar is the offspring of Vishnu and Siva, Vishnu having temporarily assumed the form of a woman; but it may reasonably be assumed that the cult of Aynar, which is very widely spread in South India, had originally no connection with either that of Vishnu or Siva. The stone on which these images are carved in rather deep relief stands about 10 inches high, and is about 2 feet long. Yet, another shrine, in the form of a sacred margosa tree, the leaves of which are used as a poultice for small-pox, stands in the high road between the two hamlets. As is usual the space in front of the image of Aynar is surrounded with clay figures of horses, whereon the god rides round the village at night, guarding it from evil spirits.

PURNI AYANAR PUSHKALI

Before leaving these village deities it may be worth while to mention that across the river worship is paid to a carved stone figure representing a mythical landed proprietor, whose fields were tilled for him through the night by Kali and her six sisters. One night they took a holiday, and the ungrateful man reviled them next day for idleness. The goddesses promptly killed him for his ingratitude; and in consequence, by a psychological process which I do not understand, he himself became divine, and his image, which juts out amid the sand and prickly-pear of the river bank, is black with ghee. Beside him the goddess Kali herself, represented by a small stone with three red spots on it, presents a very insignificant appearance. Pariahs, like Brahmans, and upper-caste Hindus generally, burn their dead; but priests of village deities, together with carpenters, blacksmiths, and goldsmiths, bury.

Sanitation.—Statistics of births and deaths are recorded in the village, and I found the figures for the three years, 1912, 1913, 1914, available. It appears that actual births and deaths are recorded accurately, though this is far from being the case in all villages. In those three years there were 122 births, an average birth-rate of 35·4, and 93 deaths, giving a death-rate of 27·0. Of the recorded causes of death cholera accounts for 22, small-pox for 1, "fevers" for 35, "other causes" for 38. The high proportion of deaths from cholera seems to be associated with two articles of sanitary faith firmly held in the village, (1) that the water derived from the river bed by spring channels is perfectly safe and pure, and can be drunk unboiled; (2) that the most fitting and seemly solution of one sanitary question is to use the river bed as a latrine. It is probable that both these beliefs are held by other villages on the banks of the river, above and below, and if so, the prevalence of cholera right along its course is easily understood. It goes without saying that the dhobis take the dirty clothes of the village to the spring channels to wash them there by the process of alternately sousing them in the stream and battering stones with them; and that the people who will drink the water further down make no protest.

THE UNGRATEFUL CULTIVATOR

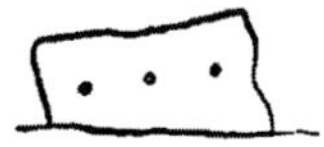

KALI

The school has 67 boys and 7 girls on the rolls, a few of whom come from outside the village. The children are graded in five standards. The headmaster takes standards III and IV; his two assistants, both men, take standards II and III, and the infants, respectively. The villagers' petitions entrusted to me for conveyance to Government were (1) for an English school, and (2) from the pariahs, for a new well.

The common fund.—In spite of the social and religious severance between pariah and caste-man, and the economic severance between land-owner and padial, the general impression made on my mind during my four days in Eruvellipet, was that of a spirit of local solidarity. I heard no mention of what is so frequent, the division of the village into two hostile factions. It was said that the munsif was able to deal with such disputes as occurred. There seemed to be no trouble about the administration of the common fund of the village, the very existence of which is a testimony to the existence of this village solidarity. It is derived partly from the sale of an exclusive right to catch fish in the tank to one villager, and of that to cut reeds, which grow extensively in the tank, and which are valued for thatching, to another. But the greater part comes in another way. I have previously said that the right of gathering fruit from the trees along the high road is sold, in mile sections, annually by auction. The Eruvellipet villagers do not compete with one another at these auctions. They send one representative who buys the fruit on two miles of road which lie mainly, but not entirely, within the village boundaries. Then they have a subsequent auction among themselves, and prices about ten times as high are ordinarily realized. The profit amounts to about 200 rupees per annum. The village fund is used to promote the economic well-being of the village, by religious ceremonies which secure favourable seasons, and by presents bestowed where the giving of presents is deemed a profitable investment.

In some respects the village of Eruvellipet is fairly typical of predominantly "wet" villages in the plains to the south of Madras. In other respects it is exceptional. Unfortunately, in its economic and sanitary weaknesses and defects, in the padial system, the general indebtedness, the bad management of cattle, the prevalence of cholera, it is far more representative than in the enterprise and initiative it displays and its power of combined action.

The population problem.—It will be noted that the density of population in the purely agricultural village of Eruvellipet is no less than 650 per square mile of land of any description, cultivable or otherwise. This immediately provokes the question whether local over-population is not threatening, or already present. There is a natural increase of population, by excess of births over deaths, of ten per annum. If cholera and other preventible diseases were dealt with the natural increase would be greater; for it is difficult to conceive a reduction in the birth-rate corresponding to the possible reduction in the death-rate. Indian families are seldom very large. The period of child-bearing is shorter than in Europe, as, though it begins earlier, it also ends earlier. Occasionally a girl will be a mother when only twelve years old; but very rarely will a woman bear children when past thirty-five, and the average period of fertility can be put at a duration of twenty years. A baby is first fed with other food (rice) in addition to his mother's milk at the age of six months, but the mother continues to suckle him for about two years longer; and the ordinary interval between successive births is three years. Hence the Indian birth-rate per thousand married women is low; it is the fact that all girls are married, almost without exception, either before or immediately after puberty, and that husbands and wives, again almost without exception, are keenly desirous of having children, that causes the birth-rate per thousand

KABALAIS NOT AT WORK. Photo by Agricultural College.

living, to be so steadily maintained at a very high figure. This living, to be so steadily maintained at a very high figure. This attitude of mind is extremely deeply rooted; and while it is, of course, subject to change, such change is sure to be very slow. We are not likely to see any alteration in Indian feelings with regard to marriage and parentage sufficient to diminish the birth-rate appreciably during the next hundred years. On the other hand reduction of the death-rate is immediately possible, and is, in fact, a work which is already in hand, and likely to go forward with rapid acceleration.

Under a steady increase of population an agricultural village has three resources:—(1) an extension of the cultivated area, (2) an intensification of cultivation, (3) migration to less thickly populated areas, or to manufacturing districts; and, in some cases, the possibility (4) of ceasing to be purely agricultural, by developing local manufactures or handicrafts. In Eruvellipet, as has been stated above, the extension of the cultivated area has reached very nearly the maximum possible. Intensification of cultivation also has already reached a very high point, though it is impossible to put any limits to further possibilities.* One effort to create a local manufacture has been made and has failed. Existing handicrafts cater for most of the village demands, and a neighbouring village weaves the coarse country cloths worn by the bulk of the people, and no idea either of extending existing handicrafts or introducing new ones appears to have occurred to any one. For the present, therefore, the natural increase of population tends to be balanced by emigration.

Emigrants' earnings.—The emigration from Eruvellipet and the surrounding district appears to be entirely to Ceylon. There is an office of the Ceylon Labour Commission in Villupuram which does a pretty active business. Money for the passage is advanced to coolies, and they subsequently pay off their debt out of their earnings. On the tea and rubber estates they are housed by the planters, and supplied with rice and other necessaries, and at the end of the month receive in cash the balance of their earnings over the amounts they have drawn. They work in groups under a "kangani," who is both a foreman and recruiter, and who is paid, in addition to his own earnings, a small commission on the earnings of the gang. I am indebted to Mr. N. H. M. Bowden of Trichinopoly for the following statement of the earnings of such a family group during four months, on a Ceylon rubber estate. It will be noticed that all the members of the gang are related to the kangani, and that there are in all eight men or lads and four women, besides some young children who do not earn and whose names do not appear. It has to be remembered, on the one hand, that the money wages stated are in *addition* to maintenance, and, on the other, that the four months are, on the whole, the most favourable in the year. In the driest months the flow of latex diminishes, and in the monsoons the rain interferes with the work of collection.

* For example, if the Reddi channel above mentioned were cleared, so as to bring the flood water in the Pennar river into the tanks dependent on it, all or nearly all the Eruvellipet wet lands could grow two crops, and the silt would add to the fertility of the land.

Earnings Table.

Number.	Names and relationship.	Balance pay paid in cash for				Total.
		Sep.	Oct.	Nov.	Dec.	
		RS.	RS.	RS.	RS.	RS.
1	Ramaswami Kangani	11·37	12·78	14·19	14·40	53·74
2	Ondimuthu, brother of 1 ...	9·37	11·47	8·66	13·01	42·51
3	Colandavale do. ...	7·77	8·05	11·06	8·39	35·27
4	Kandan, cousin of 1	12·71	7·87	8·76	7·41	36·75
5	Suppani, brother of 1	10·47	11·75	11·76	11·53	45·51
6	Thangiah, brother-in-law of 2 ...	8·77	8·95	6·42	14·87	39·01
7	Maradaie, sister of 1	9·39	8·69	11·52	10·72	40·32
8	Mariaie, wife of 2	1·98	1·13	4·86	8·82	16·79
9	Savariaie, daughter of 1 ..	3·45	2·11	4·73	5·29	15·58
10	Marimuthu, cousin of 1	6·01	9·97	10·96	10·59	37·53
11	Payan, do.	1·91	8·37	9·16	6·73	26·17
12	S. Mariaie, wife of 10	3·34	6·59	8·02	·40	18·35
	Total ...	86·54	98·83	111·10	112·16	407·63

Mr. Bowden assures me that this can be taken as fairly typical. Even if these earnings be above the average, it is clear that emigration to Ceylon opens out possibilities of very considerable economic advantage to the landless labourer or peasant with a very small holding and a large family. Indian emigration is a subject of keen controversy and fiery agitation; but the problem is not to be solved by merely keeping the coolie in his native village. One is glad to see that this fact is recognized by the Editor of "The Indian Emigrant."

Indian poverty.—To draw conclusions with regard to the broad economic conditions of life in India from a single village would be foolish; but even a single village may suggest far-reaching hypotheses, which it is worth while to state with a view to subsequent correction or verification.

India was famous for centuries for its wealth. Recent writers, from Lord Macaulay onwards, assure us that India is extremely poor. The official estimate of the average income per head of the whole Indian population in 1898 was only £2, though that was, very probably, an underestimate at the time, and would have to be very considerably raised now. My own estimate for the average income per head in the Madras Presidency in 1916–17 is not less than Rs. 72, *i.e.*, nearly £5. Eruvellipet suggests that, at any rate so far as the Carnatic plain is concerned, the truth is that India is a very rich country, inhabited by very poor people. The real wealth of any country consists mainly in sunshine, either sunshine received directly from year to year, or stored in the form of coal or oil. True, sunshine is valueless without rain, but Southern India has, over the greater part of its area, as a rule an excellent rainfall, though liable sometimes to be deficient, sometimes excessive. Our English arable land will bear a crop of wheat once in four years; the paddy field of the Carnatic bears one, two, and sometimes three crops of rice every year. Other crops are

KABALAI AND PICOTTAH IN SAME WELL.

Photo by Agricultural College.

produced in immense variety and many of these are extremely productive and profitable.

But if the land is extraordinarily productive, labour is extraordinarily unproductive. From a comparison of results in reaping and ploughing it might be estimated, roughly that a week's work by a ryot or coolie in the Madras Presidency is about equal to a day's work by a British agricultural labourer, if unaided by machinery. As in the Madras Presidency, on one crop land the agriculturist works for only about five months in the year, and on two crop land only for about eight months, it would follow that, on the average, the Indian agriculturist during a year does only what would on British standards be one month's work.* This comparison is not quite fair to the Indian worker, as he would doubtless be more expeditious over ploughing and reaping if it were necessary, but the fact remains that the Indian worker earns very low wages, has a very low standard of expenditure, and attains a very low level of efficiency, and these three characteristics of Indian life are so inter-connected, that it is impossible to say which is cause rather than effect. Indian employers do not believe in the Economy of High Wages; and as yet only faint beginnings of trade unionism are to be found among Indian manual workers. Nor does Indian popular religion, which fosters submission, nor popular philosophy, which inculcates the art of abstinence, encourage a revolt against the prevailing conditions. Family solidarity, involving as it does the interdependence of each individual with a large circle of relatives, is not conducive to strenuous individual effort. In fact various strands of economic, social and religious conditions and customs are strangely and deftly interwoven in the web of South Indian life, and low wages, low efficiency, and high abstinence are the ground plan of the pattern.

SALEM.

The next villages I had the opportunity of investigating personally were in the neighbourhood of Salem, a town of considerable importance on the railway that runs from Madras to the West Coast through the Palghat gap between the Nilgiri and Palni ranges. Salem carries on a considerable trade in grain and cotton cloth; it has an extensive weaving quarter and other quarters devoted to cart building and bamboo mat-making. The bamboos are cut on the slopes of the Shevaroys, which form a table land, the top of which is occupied by coffee plantations with the little hill station of Yercaud. Lower hills, mostly very steep and rocky, almost surround the town; one of them being Kanjamalai, which

* Some Indian workers attain a much higher degree of efficiency. For instance there is a caste of navvies in Madras, called Ubravars or Oddars, immigrants from the north, famous as good workers. They work in sets, each set consisting of one man and one woman. Mr. J. W. Madeley, Special Engineer, Madras Corporation, who employs these Ubravars very largely, estimates that three sets will do as much work in a day as two English navvies. Reckoning a woman equal to half a man, this makes the proportion of efficieney 1 : 2½. The same proportion is found to hold between the weavers in the Buckingham and Carnatic Cotton Mills in Madras, and Lancashire weavers. These mills are extremely well organized and use only up-to-date machinery. Boys (half timers), in the spinning sheds, are said to be little, if at all, inferior to their Lancashire rivals. In North India the cases of high efficiency of labour are more numerous than in Madras.

largely consists of iron ores of varying qualities. From Kanjamalai came the material of the Menai Tubular Bridge, built during the period (1829—67) during which Josiah Heath and his successors were carrying on the attempt to establish a great steel industry on the basis of the Kanjamalai ores and charcoal from the neighbouring forests—a splendid failure. In Salem the chief memorial of the work of the Heath Companies is the ruin of most of the local forests. In an "unreserved" forest, i.e., one that is not protected by the Forest Department, there is in any case a struggle between natural recuperation and the destructiveness of the peasants, who require the foliage of the forest for green manure, and are reckless in their manner of collecting it. The balance was upset when wholesale felling for charcoal was resorted to; and when the villagers turned on their goats the ruin was completed. Rocks, prickly-pear, and euphorbia alone remain, except where there are sacred trees or groves. Many of the reserved forests in the neighbourhood are in little better case. They are protected by a few granite posts with the letters "R.F.," and by forest guards, one man to a vast extent of country, and this protection is not always adequate.

Hence in the neighbourhood of Salem the problems connected with the inter-relation between agriculture and forestry are specially urgent. Throughout most parts of South India there is little pasture except common pasture. Working cattle are mainly fed upon straw, and cotton seed in the cotton growing districts; cows generally have to struggle for a scanty living. If they produce but little milk, they yield dung when alive, and bones and hides when they die of disease or starvation. The tendency to overstock, which is general in all countries where pasture is held in common, is specially rampant in South India, where the co-operative spirit and power of organization are specially weak. The improvement of the quality of the cattle is one of the most important lines of advance open to Indian agriculture, and this is as much a question of the improvement of the methods of feeding and the growing of fodder, as of improvement of breeds. Every attempt on the part of Government to protect forests where they are being destroyed is bitterly resented by the neighbouring villages which are accustomed to use these forests as pasture. As long as the forest areas, or other common grazings are available, improvement in methods of feeding are not likely to be adopted. Similarly, it is in most cases much more profitable to grow for green manure leguminous or other crops specially rich in nitrogen, than to gather it from the forest, but as long as the peasant can get green manure, of a sort, which grows wild, he is not to be convinced of this.

MALLUR.

The village of Mallur was selected for me by the Collector, Mr. E. W. Legh, as a typical dry village of the Salem district. It is even more thickly inhabited than Eruvellipet. With a cultivated area (not capable of appreciable extension) of 750 acres only, it has 2,042 inhabitants. The whole village speaks Tamil, and the leading inhabitants are Vellalas, an important cultivating caste, though there are trading and artisan crafts in considerable numbers. The pariahs number 427. There are 16 families of weavers, working mostly with common country looms, though two or three use the fly shuttle, weaving coarse cloths for the Salem market, and earning about five annas per day per loom. Weaving, at the time of my visit, was doubly depressed, firstly by the shortage of dyes and consequently of dyed yarn, and secondly by the fact that plague was raging in Salem, and the market was in consequence somewhat disorganized. The earnings of a weaver were, at that time, scarcely better than those of an agricultural labourer, which also averaged about 5 annas per day. This, so far as my experience goes, is unusual. Elsewhere I have generally found that weavers earn more than agricultural labourers, and this is one of the most striking witnesses to the remarkable vitality of hand-loom weaving in India. It is characteristic that the weaver does not combine his craft with agricultural work.

In addition to the weavers there are in Mallur ten potter families, and masons, blacksmiths, goldsmiths and carpenters, together numbering fifteen or sixteen households. There is a weekly "sandai" or market on a rocky open space adjoining the high road to Salem, at which the products of the village manufacture, together with an immense variety of other goods, are sold.

Mallur tank.—The rainfall in the Salem district is very variable. There has very recently been constructed a great reservoir, the Panamarattuppatti tank, by the construction of an embankment across the outlet of a mountain valley, for the sake of the water-supply of the town. It so happened that the period of construction was marked by a succession of seasons of deficient rainfall. The people of Mallur suffered. They have a tank fed by its own stream from the hills, which should give a six months' supply, and also fill up with water the subsoil into which the Mallur wells penetrate. For several years in succession only a three months' supply was stored. The Mallur people attributed this result to the Salem reservoir and despaired of their tank. It became to a considerable extent silted up. Then rain came somewhat more abundantly, and the tank bund was breached, and even less water was stored. The Mallur cultivators borrowed about Rs. 20,000, which they spent on deepening their wells. They paid about 18 per cent interest. They might have borrowed the money from the Government under the Agricultural Loans Act, at 6 per cent. It is noteworthy that the extra interest they incurred was in excess of the whole of the Land Revenue of the village, which is only Rs. 1,812-13-0. Meanwhile the acreage under paddy had greatly declined, being—

	Acres.		Acres.
1912	239·79	1914	121·25
1913	187·42	1915	55·52

The village has a co-operative credit society of four years' standing, which has lent some Rs. 2,000, of which about two-thirds was outstanding in March 1916. Except for the large recent borrowings, it has little debt. Out of the Rs. 20,000 above mentioned, about half was lent by villagers, the other half being borrowed from Salem money-lenders.

Field huts.—The most interesting characteristic of agriculture in the Salem district is a device for diminishing the inconvenience caused by the intermixture of holdings. In this district proprietors exchange lands with one another, each one being desirous of reaching an arrangement whereby what lands he has in the remoter parts of the village area shall be adjacent to one another, and not scattered in all directions. When this is attained, he builds a "field hut," which may be merely a storehouse for implements and a place for sleeping in the busy season; or it may evolve into a comfortable cottage or miniature farm house. The typical field hut in Mallur is a small building of some 12′ × 15′, of stone walls, with a doorway, and, in place of windows, a space between the top of the walls and the roof, which gives excellent ventilation and sufficient light. It is situated beside the proprietor's well, with a few coconut palms to shade it. Mallur has about twenty such huts, and in five cases the family owning the hut lives in it, having moved out of the village. This looks like the beginning of a transition somewhat parallel to "Enclosure" in England in one of its most important features.

Another feature of Mallur cultivation which can be similarly interpreted is that there is a beginning of pasturage on private land. Ten ryots grow grass on some of their "patta" lands, and the area under grass is 25 acres. No special care is taken of it, and it is not mown nor watered. The proprietors turn their cattle on to these grass lands when it suits them to do so. As they are not fenced, it seems probable that this development would not have occurred apart from the aggregation of plots of land belonging to individual peasants and the building of field huts.

Ownership and cultivation.—There were, in 1911, the year of resettlement, 72 single pattadars, and 60 joint pattas, making a total of no less than 256 separate landowners. Of these 250 cultivate their own land, and the six who let their land (46·46 acres) include three temple priests, two petty officials, and one old woman. The village is therefore one of almost perfect peasant proprietorship; just over two-thirds of the 395 families, apart from the pariahs, own land, and the average size of the estate of each family is 3 acres. Much of the land is good black loam, and where there is water enough two crops of paddy and one of cholam (the great millet), are raised. Groundnut is grown on 85 acres which have the most precarious water-supply; and nearly all the rest of the cultivated area yields two crops of millet (cholam, ragi and kambu) per annum. The stock list reads—

Working oxen ...	308	Donkeys	6
Cows	164	Horses	15
Buffaloes	109	Sheep and goats ...	880
Young of above species.	296	Pigs	200

There is therefore a pair of working oxen or buffaloes to less than 4 acres of land.

*The kabalai.**—The steady work of irrigation, particularly since the deepening of the wells, keeps the working cattle well employed. The wells are worked by the ordinary South Indian bullock-lift, and the kabalai, also used in Mesopotamia, and probably, both in India and in Mesopotamia, of immemorial antiquity. The oxen

* Or *Kamalai.*

work on an inclined plane which slopes downwards from the edge of the well. Descending the slope they drag up the kabalai, then they are made to back up the slope, and the kabalai is lowered to the water level. The kabalai is a big bucket of leather or metal somewhat less than two feet in diameter, continued below in a leather tube about four or five inches in diameter, and between two and three feet long. When the kabalai is being raised from the water, the top of the bucket and the end of the leather tube are level, each being attached to its own rope, and the two ropes being dragged simultaneously by the oxen. But the rope attached to the bucket passes over a pulley about four feet above the ground level, that attached to the tube, over a roller at the ground level. When the oxen are near the end of their run the open end of the tube is pulled over the roller, and as the bucket is raised still higher towards the pulley, the whole of the water in the kabalai is poured out and flows by a prepared channel in the desired direction.

It may reasonably be assumed that this bullock lift has been unmodified for thousands of years. But quite recently a Mr. Ramachandran of Madras has invented an ingenious variation. He increases the steepness of the slope, lays down rails, and puts on them a little platform mounted on low wheels. A single ox takes the place of the pair, and faces towards the well instead of away from it. The platform is attached to the kabalai; the ox has to drag the platform up the slope, then stand on it, and slide backwards down the slope, pulling up the kabalai as he does so. It is said that one ox can thus lift as much water in a day as a pair with the ordinary lift. I cannot at present vouch for the accuracy of this claim, as the one attempt at demonstration which I witnessed was a failure. The framework of the pulley was badly constructed and broke under the strain as soon as operations began.

On the basis of these preliminary inquiries, I drew up a "Village Questionnaire," as a guide to students in the investigation of their own villages; and the following Village Surveys were worked out in the basis of that questionnaire.

The first two were made by students who had taken the degree of B.A. with Honours in History and Economics of the University of Madras, the remainder by students who were preparing for that examination, during the long vacation of 1916, and in some cases revised in that of 1917. Each student chose his own village, it might be his native village, or some other village where he had friends, and where it was convenient for him to spend the vacation.

I am greatly indebted to Mr. R. Cecil Wood, Principal of the Agricultural College, Coimbatore, for most of the photographs used as illustrations. For kind assistance in the preparation of the Glossary I am indebted to Mr. G. A. D. Stuart, Director of Agriculture, Rev. Dr. Chandler, Editor of the Tamil Lexicon, Mr. F. Ware, Superintendent, Civil Veterinary Department, Mr. D. A. D. Aitchison, Principal, Madras Veterinary College, and Mr. T. V. Ramakrishna Ayyar, acting Government Entomologist. The author of the first survey, Mr. K. Ramachandran, died of cholera on 31st May 1918.

GILBERT SLATER.

SCHEME FOR SURVEY OF A RYOTWARI VILLAGE.

General instruction.—Embody in your report the official information which is available, but endeavour also to test its accuracy and to correct it when possible. Throughout use some distinguishing mark to indicate whether your information is derived from official sources. Thus the letter "O" can be used to mark official information, "N" unofficial, and "N & O" official information, confirmed by non-official.

Preliminary—

(1) Survey number of village.
(2) Name of village.
(3) Taluk.
(4) District.
(5) General description of geographical position and position in relation to any forests, rivers, hills, etc., which there may be in the neighbourhood.

A. Population—

(1) Total population of caste village.
(2) Castes.
(3) Number of families and individuals in each caste.
(4) Number of children in families—
  (*a*) Living.
  (*b*) Dead.

N.B.—A good way of getting this information is to ask parents how many children they have had and how many are still alive.

(5) Number of homesteads.
(6) A complete census of ages, if obtainable, is useful.
(7) Give statistics of the births and deaths given in the village accounts, and try to ascertain to what extent they are accurate; and if defective, why so?
(8) Population—men, women and children—of paracheri, given if possible in families, with number of dead in families.

Notes.—(*a*) Endeavour to give, if possible, the population according to the last two or more censuses.

(*b*) Use the figures so obtained to ascertain whether the population is increasing or decreasing, and if so, which sections of the population (caste and sex) show the increase or decrease.

(*c*) State the age you choose to distinguish between children and others. This should be 10 years or 15 years.

B. Land—

(1) Area of wet lands.
(2) Area of dry lands.
(3) Area of lands watered by wells.
(4) Common waste.

(5) Pasture other than common waste.
(6) Woods and forests.
(7) Fruit trees and scattered shade trees.
(8) Tanks.
(9) Wells.
(10) Other sources of water-supply.

Notes.—(*a*) The information under B can mostly be obtained from the village accounts, but some correction may be necessary. Procure, if possible, a copy of the village map. Add, if possible, a classification of wet, dry and well lands according to the amount of land assessment.

(*b*) The statistics under the several headings should be compared with similar statistics for a period anterior to the present by 10 or 15 years. The necessary information can be gathered either by enquiries in the village or from the Firka books of Revenue Inspectors. Such a comparison is important as showing the economic progress of the village and changes, if any, in the methods of cultivation, the standard of living of the people, in cattle rearing, etc.

C. Occupation of land—

(1) Area cultivated by the landowner.
(2) Area sub-let and cultivated by tenants.
(3) Number of cultivating landowners.
(4) Number of non-cultivating landowners and their respective occupations.
(5) Number of tenants who own no land.
(6) Agricultural workers who neither own nor rent land.
(7) Areas of holdings according to ownership.
(8) Areas of holdings according to tenancy.
(9) Rents in money or in kind.
(10) Land Revenue—give total kist of village and amount per acre for different qualities of land.
(11) Particulars of people who combine agriculture with other occupations.

Notes.—(*a*) Give (7) and (8) in as much detail as possible.

(*b*) Under (9) give as full information as possible, both about the sorts of agreements that are concluded between the pattadar and the tenant, and also the amount of the rents, and what extras such as straw, vegetables, etc., are paid in addition to grain or cash rents. If landlord and tenant share the produce, explain how the kist and costs of cultivation are shared, and whether the tenant has all the straw, and endeavour to calculate the actual value of the share of produce obtained by either party. Again, landowners and cultivators usually pay the village servants certain perquisites at the time of harvest, Pongal feast, etc. These should also be noted.

D. Agriculture—

(1) Area under each of the principal crops.
(2) Area yielding one crop per annum.
(3) Area yielding two crops per annum.
(4) Area yielding three crops per annum.

N.B.—Give these statistics for a short series of years.

(5) Customary crop cultivation, of wet, dry and garden lands respectively.
(6) Types of plough used, and the number of acres cultivated per plough in wet, dry and garden land respectively.
(7) Other agricultural implements.
(8) Describe types of pumps or waterlifts used (no elaborate description is needed if they are of common types). Are oil engines used?

(9) Is water sold for irrigation by one villager to others? If so, what price is charged?

(10) Stock—
- (*a*) Working oxen.
- (*b*) Cows.
- (*c*) Male buffaloes.
- (*d*) Cow buffaloes.
- (*e*) Young stock of above species.
- (*f*) Horses.
- (*g*) Donkeys and mules.
- (*h*) Sheep.
- (*i*) Goats.
- (*j*) Pigs.

(11) Are ploughs or carts and bulls hired out? If so, give rates of hire.

(12) Describe the customs with regard to feeding of domestic animals.

(13) Manuring—
- (*a*) What percentage of the cattle dung produced is used as manure?
- (*b*) What quantity of cattle dung is applied per acre of wet, dry and garden land?
- (*c*) How is cattle urine utilized?
- (*d*) Other animal manures.
- (*e*) Green manure—
  Under this head explain whether green manure is grown, or obtained from woods or forests.
- (*f*) Are chemical manures used? If so, how obtained?

(14) Garden cultivation—
Give here any information available not given under other heads.

(15) Chief insect pests and methods of combating them.

(16) Chief cattle diseases and methods of combating them—
Under heads (15) and (16) note particularly whether assistance is obtained from the Agricultural and Veterinary departments.

(17) How and where is wood obtained for fuel, implements, building, etc.?

(18) What is the cost of cultivation per acre of wet, dry and garden land, respectively?

(19) Has there been any recent improvement in methods of cultivation, as single transplantation of paddy, seed selection of cotton, introduction of new crops, etc.? If so, how was such improvement brought about? Are the villagers disposed to adopt new methods if their utility can be demonstrated?

(20) Do the villagers breed their own cattle, or purchase? If the former, give as full an account as possible about their methods of breeding and rearing young cattle: if the latter, state how the cattle are procured, what breeds are preferred, where they come from, what prices are paid, and what becomes of the cattle afterwards.

E. The village—

(1) Area of the village-site.

(2) Localization of castes.

(3) Dwellings of depressed castes.

(4) Types of dwellings, e.g., how many houses are respectively thatched, tiled, and terraced—

(*a*) in caste village.

(*b*) in paracheri.

(5) Gardens adjoining dwellings.

(6) Maximum distance of cultivated lands from home of cultivator.

(7) Unsatisfied demand for building sites.

(8) Site values.

(9) Do the ryots exchange lands in order to get their lands continuous? If so, do they build and use field huts? To what extent are the lands of an average cultivator scattered about in small parcels?

F. Subsidiary industries—

(1) Number of weavers.

(2) Condition of the weaving craft.—What yarn is used? What looms and winding implements? Do weavers co-operate at all? What evidence is there of growth or decay in the weaving industry? Give average earnings.

(3) Is handspinning practised? if not, when abandoned?

(4) List of other crafts in the village giving, when possible, the proportion of working time spent on the craft, average earnings and any interesting features about the craft.

(5) Give any information available showing whether any village industry is developing or increasing; or, on the other hand dying, decaying, or becoming less remunerative.

G. Village trade—

(1) How do the villagers purchase commodities required—

(*a*) for industrial and agricultural use?

(*b*) for their own consumption?

(2) Sale of village produce—

(*a*) Estimate the quantities of village produce sold out of the village.

(*b*) Describe the methods of sale.

(3) Condition of village with regard to local roads, access to main roads, railways and commercial centres.

(4) Extent of co-operation in village trading.

(5) Further remarks.

Note.—Please make a special effort to get an accurate statement of the quantity of agricultural produce that is sent away from the village in an average year.

Also endeavour to ascertain if the poorer ryots sell grain at a low price immediately after harvest, and have to buy it back for their own food or for seed at a higher price later on.

Try also to find what proportion the price the ryot receives for his produce bears to the prices obtained in large markets.

H. Economic condition of village—

(1) Customary rates of wages—

(*a*) in money.

(*b*) in kind.

Note what extra perquisites are given to the labourer in addition to his regular wage.

(2) Current prices of staple foods.

(3) Number of families which have made savings.

(4) Utilisation of savings—

(*a*) Agricultural or industrial capital.

(*b*) In Savings banks.

(*c*) On loans to neighbours.

(*d*) In jewellery.

(*e*) Other methods.

(5) Rural indebtedness.

(6) Number of padials and conditions of their service to creditors, stating amount of wages or allowances of grain, clothing, etc.

(7) Causes of indebtedness.

(8) Proportion of debtors who have liberated themselves from debt.

(9) Is there a co-operative credit society? If so, add a special appendix giving the fullest possible account of its origin, progress and prospects.

(10) Sources and extent of communal income (i.e., income belonging to the village as a whole, and not to individual villagers).

(11) Expenditure of communal income.

(12) Administration and supervision of communal income.

(13) Give any particulars known about selling prices of land.

(14) Estimated annual expenditure on religious festivals.

(15) Estimated expenditure in recent years on new temples.

(16) To what extent is advantage taken of the Agricultural Loans Act, and the Land Improvement Loans Act?

Note.—The following statement will be found suggestive: "In villages interest is a most insiduous poison and the damage it causes is generally not properly appreciated. It is only loans of large cash sums that are regulated by a fixed and reasonable rate of interest such as 9, 12 or 15 per cent per annum. But a good deal of the borrowing in villages is done either in the shape of small sums of money or advances of food grain, seed grain and other commodities on credit, and it is the interest on these latter transactions that proves the most ruinous. If one stayed in a village in a district like South Arcot or Chingleput for a few days and made careful enquiries among the villagers, one will come across many cases in which ryots borrowed a single rupee for seed grain and bought 8 Madras measures of seed with it on the understanding that at the harvest time, i.e., about six months thereafter, the creditor should be paid back the rupee plus three Madras measures of paddy, the money value of which at harvest time is generally 4 annas. In other words, they agreed to pay 25 per cent more for the use of the money for six months. This high rate of interest does not of course prevail all the year round, but six months of such interest are enough to break any ryot's back. Further, all purchases of articles on credit carry very high rates of interest besides giving room to the exercise of much fraud on the part of the lender. Correct and detailed information as regards the rates and forms of interest paid on the several kinds of loans would afford valuable help towards the suggestion of means to overcome the evils of indebtedness."

I. Sanitary condition of village—

(1) Prevalence of malaria.

(2) ,, cholera.

(3) ,, plague.

(4) ,, tuberculosis.

(5) ,, small-pox.

(6) Prevalence of other epidemic diseases.
(7) ,, other endemic diseases.
(8) Estimated rate of infantile mortality.
(9) Snake bites.
(10) Medical assistance available.
(11) Insanitary habits.
(12) Prevalent customs with regard to—
  (*a*) Infant marriage.
  (*b*) Purdah.
(13) Nature and quality of water-supply for drinking and domestic purposes.
(14) Do the villagers bathe and wash clothes in the same stream or tank as that used for drinking ?

J. Education—

(1) Number of schools.
(2) School accommodation.
(3) Educational character of schools.
(4) Number of boys in attendance.
(5) ,, girls ,,
(6) Average duration of school-life.
(7) Percentage of adults able to read the Vernacular.
(8) ,, ,, to write the Vernacular.
(9) ,, ,, to talk English.
(10) ,, ,, to read English.
(11) ,, ,, to write English.
(12) Number of pandits or specially educated persons.
(13) Are there any adults who have learnt to read, to write or to cipher who have lost such ability after leaving school ?
(14) Number of boys and girls who have proceeded to more advanced schools elsewhere.
(15) How have their school expenses been defrayed ?
(16) Have boys from the village who have passed through secondary schools obtained satisfactory careers later on ?
(17) Have any gone to an Agricultural College ?
(18) Have any boys who have received a good education settled down in their own village ? If so, how do they use their education ?
(19) How many books and of what character in the village ?

K. Village administration—

(1) Panchayat.
(2) Village Administration.
(3) Sanitary Administration.
(4) Police Administration.
(5) Contact with higher authorities.
(6) How much crime has there been in recent years ?
(7) Are any of the villagers engaged in litigation and if so, why ? Are any in debt in consequence of litigation ?
(8) Are offences and civil disputes dealt with in the village without resort to the Courts ?

L. History and prospects of village—

(1) What evidence is there to show either economic deterioration or economic improvement in the past?

(2) What opportunities does the village seem to have for economic improvement? Note specially the possibility of extending the area of irrigated lands. Could more wells be sunk with advantage? If so, why are they not sunk?

General.—If opportunity offers illustrate by giving a more detailed account of the occupations, income, expenditure and the general condition of a few typical families. Add any information which appears to be interesting and significant not asked for in this form; as for instance, information as to the decrease of land held by different castes, reasons why people buy land and why they sell it, the emigration from the village either to cities or to foreign countries, why the emigrants go and whether they return, what effect such movements have upon the economic, intellectual and social life of the village; what new expenditure on luxuries or comforts is becoming customary; what other changes there are in the standard of living; and if there is any change in custom with respect to marriages or religious observances.

RAMNAD DISTRICT.

VADAMALAIPURAM ALIAS KONDUREDDIPATTI.

[*By K. Ramachandran, B.A., St. Joseph's College, Trichinopoly.*]

Preliminary.—The village of Vadamalaipuram, comprising the (Government) revenue villages of Kizhātiruttangāl, Mēlāmuttūr and Karseri, the inam village of Nāranāpuram and the zamin village of Vadimitta, is situated in the north-west corner of the Sattūr taluk in the Ramnad district on the banks of the river Arjuna, a tributary of the Vaippar. There are no mountains or hills near it except the Western Ghats, which are 25 miles west of the village. There are no forests in the vicinity except on the slopes of the mountains. The soil is black of the type called black loam, and here and there, especially on the banks of the river, hard rocks are to be found. The rainfall is fair during both the monsoons but the heavier showers are in October. The river is useless for irrigation as its bed is lower than that of the surrounding country. The village has come before public notice in recent times for the excellent co-operative society that it possesses, but it is not without interest in other respects also. It can be taken as a type of the villages in this part of the district within a radius of about 10 miles.

Population.—The population according to the census of 1911 is 780—630 castemen and 150 of the depressed classes. The village is a Nayakar village inhabited solely by one caste except for the paracheri and a few families of the artisan classes which are necessary in every village. One thing that is note-worthy is the absence of a single Brahman family till about ten years ago. Even now it possesses only two Brahman families—a Mahratta Brahman and an Aiyangar. The former is the secretary of the local co-operative credit society, the latter is the teacher in charge of the school. The Nayakars have a priestly class among themselves and so are not in need of the services of the Brahmans for their religious functions. The following is the distribution of the people among the various castes. It is the result of a census taken with the help of the villagers on 4th September 1916.

Nayakars ...	100 families ...	389 persons.
Goldsmith ...	2 ,, ...	11 ,, besides two girls married outside the village.
Carpenter ...	4 ,, ..	17 persons.
Blacksmith ...	1 family ...	8 ,,
Dhobis ...	2 families ...	8 ,,
Barber ...	2 ,, ...	7 ,,
Potter ...	1 family ...	1 ,,
Tailor ...	1 ,, ...	7 ,,
Telugu shepherds ...	12 families ...	60 ,,

Maravars *	...	6 families	...	25 persons
Pandaram (flower suppliers).		1 family	...	7 "
Vellalas (highest sudra caste).		2 families	...	9 "
Brahmans	...	2 "	...	11 "
Panchamas—				
Pallans	...	21 "	...	89 "
Chakkiliyans	...	8 "	...	52 "
Total	...	165 "		811 "

The number of children in the caste village seems to be about 81 and in the paracheri about 20. The death-rate among children of the castemen is about one out of four, five or six children born. The following are some of the persons who gave the facts in their families :—

Males.

(*a*) Krishnama Nayak, South Street, 37 years—

Total number of children born	...	6
Living	...	5
Dead	...	1

(*b*) Venkatarama Nayak, 45 years—

Total number of children	...	6
Living	...	5
Dead	...	1

(*c*) Venkataswami Nayak, North Street, 40 years—

Total number of children	...	3
Living	...	2
Dead	...	1

Females.

(*d*) Naranammal, age 55—

Total number of children	...	5
Living	...	4
Dead	...	1

(*e*) Venkatammal, age 52—

Total number of children	...	6
Living	...	3
Dead	...	3

(*f*) Ramachiammal, age 60–

Total number of children	...	4
Living	...	3
Dead	...	1

In the paracheri out of 29 families, 12 families had deaths within recent times. They had lost 6 males, 6 females and 3 children under 10. There are at present 60 males, 61 females and 20 children in the paracheri.

* A fighting caste, descendants of retainers of Poligars of old, who were feudal nobles subordinate to the Vijayanagar Kingdom, but practically independent. The Maravars are now employed as watchmen or as cultivators, but are famous for robberies and dacoities.

Census of Caste Village.

—	Under 5.	5 to 16.	16 to 25.	25 to 50.	Over 50.
Males	31	49	41	130	50
Females	50	60	51	154	54
Total ...	81	109	92	284	104

There are 105 homesteads (N.O.).

Land. —The soil is black and is divided into three sorts, superior black loam, "Pottal karisal" (inferior black cotton soil) and "Vellai tharai" (red sandy loam).

(1) Area of wet lands—50 acres (N.O.).
(2) Area of dry lands—1,500 „ „
(3) Watered by wells—actually cultivated 500 acres (N.O.).
possibly cultivable 600 „ „
(4) Common waste—Cattle-stand, 1·20 acres (O.).
Threshing floor, 6·37 acres (O.).

The cattle graze in the cattle-stand though there is not much grass there. Besides, they graze on tank bunds, river banks and in fields which lie fallow. There are no woods or forests near the village and even in the village itself there are not many trees. Fruit trees are not found at all, and except for a few margosa trees in the cattle-stand and a few more wild trees bordering the country road that passes through the village, there are no trees worth mention.

Wet, dry or poramboke.	Class and sort of soil.	Taram.	Crops.	Rate per acre.	Extent.	Assessment.
				RS. A. P.	ACS.	RS. A. P.
Wet	...	9	Triple	6 0 0	25	150 0 0
„	...	11	„	4 0 0	25	100 0 0
Dry	Black loam.	2	Double	1 11 0	500	843 12 0
„	Pottalkaraisal	3	Single	1 2 0	1,000	1,125 0 0
„	Vellai tharai.	4	„	0 13 0	500	406 4 0

Water-supply.—Water for irrigation is supplied by two tanks and about 120 wells. The larger of the two tanks is situated to the north of the village and covers an area of 86 acres (O.). It irrigates about 25 acres of land producing paddy, plantains, sugarcane (given up during this year because it did not bring profit), cotton, ragi, cholam and other crops.

The smaller tank is in the north-west of the village, is shallow, covers an area of about 60 acres (N.O.) and irrigates nearly 50 acres of land producing paddy. There are 120 irrigating wells, almost each holding possessing one. There is plenty of water in these wells, most of them having a kamalai worked by a pair of bulls. Some of them even possess a double kamalai. There is water in the river all the year round and in the rainy season the river is in flood. Some of the villagers think that if the bed of the river could be raised, all this water could be used for irrigation. How far the scheme is practicable is for the Government and the Public Works Department to consider. For drinking purposes, most of the villagers use the river water. In addition, there are six wells which are utilized for drinking. Before 1915 there were only four wells, all in the caste village, to which the depressed classes had no access. The result was that these people had to get from the river, about 1½ furlongs off, all the water they required. This hardship was remedied in 1915 by the co-operative credit society, which with the help of a Government grant sank two wells exclusively for the use of the Panchamas, one near each of the paracheris in the village.

Occupation of land.—One interesting feature about the occupation of land in the village is the absence of the system of *kattukuttakai* or sub-letting. All the owners of the land are cultivating landowners and as such are directly interested in the yearly produce of the land. So it is no uncommon sight to see even the richest landowner shouldering a plough and walking to his field in the early morning followed by his workmen, or the owner of the land driving the bullocks round and round on the threshing ground threshing the grain, whilst his paid workmen attend to other business. The number of landowners among the castemen is 107 and among the Panchamas six or seven. One feature that is noteworthy is the fact that there are no holdings larger than 170 acres and only three above 100 acres there being also one of 100 acres. The following is the account of holdings according to ownership:—

Between 1 and 10 acres	... ...	38 holdings	250 acres.
„ 10 and 25 „	... ...	38 „	649 „
„ 25 and 50 „	... ...	12 „	469 „
„ 50 and 100 „	... ...	3 „	211 „
„ 100 and 250 „	... ...	3 „	471 „

The following is a detailed list of the holdings:—

1 of 1 acre.	1 of 21 acres.
5 „ 2 acres each.	2 „ 23 acres each.
4 „ 3 „ „	1 „ 24 acres.
2 „ 4 „ „	5 „ 25 acres each.
4 „ 5 „ „	1 „ 26 acres.
1 „ 6 acres.	2 „ 27 acres each.
1 „ 7 „	1 „ 30 acres.
5 „ 8 acres each.	1 „ 35 „
4 „ 9 „ „	1 „ 41 „
11 „ 10 „ „	2 „ 43 acres each.
4 „ 11 „ „	1 „ 47 acres.
4 „ 12 „ „	3 „ 50 acres each.
3 „ 13 „ „	1 „ 51 acres.
4 „ 14 „ „	1 „ 60 „
4 „ 15 „ „	1 „ 100 „
2 „ 16 „ „	1 „ 141 „
2 „ 18 „ „	1 „ 160 „
3 „ 19 „ „	1 „ 170 „
3 „ 20 „ „	

Most of the villagers own some land at least. In fact buying land has become almost a craze in the village. Many of the villagers possess more land than they can conveniently attend to, and many of them are in debt on account of their lands. Some have even gone to the length of buying land with money borrowed at from 12 to 18 per cent though the yield can never be expected to be beyond 4 or at the most 6 per cent. Even the Pallans and Chakkiliyans invest their surplus money in land. So it is very difficult to find in the village people who own no land except the actual labourers and some of the artisan classes. The Brahman families being only recent comers possess no land in the village. The permanent labourers who work throughout the year under landlords are about 53 in number. They are all males. Temporary labourers who work during harvest and other seasons number about 45 males and 50 to 60 females. The conditions of their service are interesting. The permanent labourers take their meals in their master's houses—three meals a day—and get wages ranging from Rs. 50 to Rs. 60 per annum. As for the temporary labourers, males get daily wages ranging from five annas to eight annas for cultivation purposes; or if it is paid in kind, two Madras measures of grain and one midday meal. Females get about four annas or six annas a day or two Madras measures of grain without the midday meal. Wages have more than doubled in the last twenty years.

Rents are paid in money whether for Government or zamin lands. The land revenue comes to about Rs. 2,625 besides a cess of Rs. 164-8-0.

There are six people who combine trade with agriculture in the caste village. Some of the depressed classes also own land which they cultivate in addition to their ordinary work. Among castemen two are shopkeepers who keep two small shops selling the things that are required for the village such as grocery, condiments, etc. These are small businesses with an invested capital of less than Rs. 100. The daily sales in each of the shops, according to the shopkeepers' estimate, is Rs. 3 a day, and the profit is about 1½ or 2 annas per rupee. Each of them pays a rent of Re. 1 per month.

The other four are dealers in cotton. It is they who arrange to have the cotton in the village sold and they make some profit out of it.

There was a timber shop in the village for a period of two years. It was having a good sale. Timber was sold to other villages for building. Moreover some furniture was also made. I saw the chairs, tables, benches and bureaus made at the shop and the workmanship was good. It supplied all the furniture for the local school and the co-operative credit society. But for want of a good manager who knew the business the shop was closed. The owner expected a large profit from the very beginning and was disappointed at not getting the huge profits of which he had dreamt. Moreover the villagers have very little confidence in trade as a profession. Their idea is to make money somehow and invest it in land so that they may be sure of their capital. Hence even if they start a business their idea is not to continue it, but to make as much money as possible in the shortest time, wind up the concern, buy some land and live on the produce of it. Thus even the shopkeepers are not steady. There have been more than six or seven shops that have been started and wound up within four or five years. The present shops are only a year old. There were two cloth merchants who were selling cloth imported from Madura. But they too have closed their businesses for the past two years. There is one other industry that is being carried on by the women of the village. This is the making of ghee from butter. The village was supplying ghee to the Madura co-operative stores regularly but for some unkown reason it is not doing so now. Yet the women sell it in small quantities even now.

Agriculture.—Agriculture, in fact, is practically the sole industry in the village. Of the 2,050 acres of cultivated land 1,500 acres yield only a single crop per annum. Five hundred acres yield two crops per annum, and 50 acres of land irrigated by the tanks yield three crops per annum. The principal crops and the number of acres cultivated are given below :—

	ACRES.
Cotton and catch crops like malli (coriander) ...	800
Cholam and pulses	300
Kambu	300
Varagu, kudirai-val	300
Ragi	300
Sweet-potatoes, chillies, plantains, brinjals, etc. ...	100
Paddy	50
Tobacco	30
Senna	400

Paddy is very little cultivated except in the tank-irrigated area. Nor is the staple food of the people rice as in other parts of the district. Cholam, ragi and kambu and sweet-potatos form the chief food except for the two Brahman families who take rice purchased from the neighbouring village of Tiruttangal or the town of Sivakasi. Cotton is the chief crop that is grown for the market. Cholam and other food grains are mostly for home consumption and for distribution to the workmen. A small quantity of it, however, is sold when merchants come to the village. When I visited the village some eight years back there were many gardens growing vegetables. Subsequently, I am told, vegetable growing was given up as the soil was found to be suitable for the growth of Cambodia cotton and the latter fetched a far greater price than the vegetables. But this year (1916) the mania is for senna and large plots of land are now covered with senna shrubs. The chief occupation of the people when I visited the village now was the picking, drying and packing of senna leaves. All the available free space was being utilized for the drying of senna leaves. But this speculation has cost the villagers dear, for within the last few months the price of senna has fallen down rapidly from Rs. 180 to Rs. 20 per candy of 375 lb.

The following is the rotation of the crops :—

Three-crop land ...	Keppai—Adi to Kartigai (June-October). Tobacco—Kartigai to Chittrai (October-April). Cholam—Vaikasi to Adi (April-June).
Two-crop land ...	Keppai—Adi to Kartigai (June-October). Fallow—Margali and Tai (November and December). Cholam—Masi to Adi (January-June).

Keppai is a grain like cholam and is used as a staple food by the lower classes.

In lands that bear only one crop the seed is sown just before the monsoon in September. The chief crop in these lands is cotton (September to June).

Agriculture is carried on here by means of the old sort of ploughs. They are all locally made by the village carpenter and blacksmith. The villagers have not yet taken to improved methods of cultivation or improved forms of plough. Besides the plough and the small sickles used for harvesting the villagers possess hardly any other agricultural implements. Almost all the cultivators have a baling instrument called Kamalai made in the village with the help of the local tanner and carpenter. A triangular harrow however is kept by the Co-operative Agricultural Society and is used by the members when needed.

Stock.—The village possesses about 160 oxen yoked to the plough and some 40 more to spare. There are about 100 cows and about 50 of them are possessed by the Pallans. There are also about 120 cow-buffaloes, but only two male ones. These latter are kept for breeding and not for work. There are in all about 100 young stock of all the above species. The village possessed some three or four horses but now there is only one mare. The donkeys in the village number about ten and belong to the washermen. The village possesses about 1,200 sheep and goats and 40 pigs. There are also five sheep-dogs which serve the double purpose of sheep-watching and keeping guard over the village at night.

The villagers get their cattle at the cattle fair held in the neighbouring village of Kanniseri every year. This cattle fair is one of the biggest in those parts and cattle come to it from all over the surrounding country. The village is 4 miles off and many of the cattle that come from the west of the village have to pass through. Old stock is sold at the same fair though it must be observed that the villagers do not change their stock very often. The cattle have full work most of the days. In the early morning at about 6 or 7 a.m. the oxen are taken to the fields. They return only in the evening at about 6 p.m. In the noon they are given about 1 or 2 hours rest when the workmen come home to have their midday meal. They do the ploughing in the ploughing season, but most of the time they are used to draw water. They may have rest when the lands lie fallow, but some of the owners give their cattle on hire to draw carts for either taking the cotton and other produce to the neighbouring towns or for the conveyance of the passengers. The cattle are good.

The working oxen and the milch cows and buffaloes are given cotton-seed in the early morning followed by some fodder. Some fodder is given to them at noon and again in the evening when they return from the fields. The other cattle are given only fodder and no cotton-seed. The fodder is raised by each cultivator from his fields. After the crops, a special crop of cholam is grown for fodder and dried and stored up in stacks for use throughout the year. For the grazing of the cattle some of the families make their own arrangements. The others, however, leave theirs in charge of the village cowherd, who is a Panchama. He has charge of the cattle between the hours of 10 a.m. and 5 p.m. He is assisted in his work by his wife and children. He gets twelve annas (1 shilling) a year for every beast looked after by him and he has the charge of some 100 or 120 cattle. Besides this he is given kanji or rice water from the villagers every day. Moreover the dung that falls on the grazing ground belongs to him and so keen is the competition for the dung that he is able to sell it for Rs. 2 or 3 every month. So on the whole he is well off.

Manuring.—The villagers are keen about the manure and they utilize all that is available. Their chief manure, however, is cow-dung and this they are careful not to waste. About 95 per cent of the cow-dung goes as manure, the remaining 5 per cent being utilized for heating the iron tyres of bandies when they have to be repaired. They do not use cow-dung for domestic fuel as is done in the villages in the southern part of the district. Though they are so very keen about the cattle dung, they do not care at all for the cattle urine. In fact except the small percentage of urine that gets necessarily mixed up with cattle dung in the stalls, cattle urine does not form part of the manure. Even where special cattle stalls have been built no attention has been bestowed upon the storage of cattle urine. Sheep and goats are made to stay at night in the fields and that is all the other animal manure that is used.

Green manure is also utilized to some extent, being gathered from the waste lands near the village. The chief green manures are Avarai, Athalai, Manjanathi and a very small quantity of wild indigo.

There is no garden cultivation at all. No fruit trees are grown. There was a garden some years ago where some flowers were grown by the Pandaram of the village but that too has been brought under regular cultivation now.

The crops suffer often on account of insect pests and diseases. The following are the chief pests that affect the different crops:—

(1) *Kambu.*—The chief insect pest is the *Pachalai* found in different colours which sucks away the juice from the stalks.

(2) *Cholam* (*a*) *Kilipuchi.*—A dangerous insect like the mosquito, black generally, but found in other colours also.

(*b*) *Kuruthupuchi.*—A sort of worm which eats away the stalks when they are tender.

(*c*) *Sendal and Vellaithal.*—A sort of disease which prevents the further growth of the plants.

(*d*) *Mallai.*—A sort of weed which eats away the substance of the crops and thus makes the harvest poor.

(3) *Paddy.*—*Tondaipuchi*, a sort of worm, which enters the stalk when it is tender and prevents the crop from ripening.

(4) *Varagu.*—*Sendal* and *Vellaithal* described above.

Mallai also described before.

(5) *Tobacco.*—*(a) Mallai.*

(b) Sambal disease which turns the leaves grey.

(c) Pandaram.—Another disease that turns the leaves white and makes them wither.

(6) *Cotton.*—(*a*) *Verpulu,* a sort of worm, that eats away the roots.

(*b*) *Kunaivandu* which eats away the plant before it grows big.

(*c*) *Kanjurnoi* makes the plant wither.

(*d*) *Sambal* disease makes the leaves turn grey and prevents the formation of cotton.

(7) *Plantains.*—(*a*) *Mallai.*

(*b*) *Thavalainoi*, a disease that makes the plant wither.

(*c*) *Karugal*, another disease that turns the leaves black and prevents the formation of fruit.

(8) *Chillis.*—(*a*) *Verpulu.*

(*b*) *Suruttai*, a disease that makes the plant wither.

(9) *Sweet potatos.*—*Sevattai*, a disease that turns the plant red.

In spite of the fact that there are so many pests and that these pests appear pretty often, the villagers take absolutely no preventive measures against them. Nor do they seek to remedy it when a disease or pest actually destroys the crops. They take it as their lot and blame their fate, sit with folded hands and give full liberty for the pest to make havoc among the crops. That is what the villagers told me themselves and they look with surprise when they are asked whether they seek no remedy.

Cattle diseases.—Small-pox, cholera and a disease something like fever called *Vethupu* are the chief diseases that affect the cattle.

Horses have a sort of disease called *Pattu.* There are also many skin diseases. In the case of cattle diseases the people have some sort of medicines handed down to them from antiquity. It must be remembered that every household man knows something of medicine and every agriculturist is a veterinary doctor. In many cases these specifics handed down from our ancestors are very good. But still when difficult cases come the villager does not seek proper help. He receives no help from the Agricultural Department for he never applies to it. Again the carelessness and the insanitary habits of the villagers are great breeders and fomenters of diseases, e.g., when I was in the village a calf evidently affected by some skin disease was herded along with the rest and there was no attempt made to separate the affected calf and prevent the spreading of the disease to the rest of the cattle. One or two of the villagers however think of getting help from the Veterinary Department. One of the villagers was talking of taking his mare to the veterinary doctor at Srivilliputtur, a town seventeen miles off.

For fuel the villagers largely use the dried stalks of the cotton plant. As soon as the cotton harvest is over the stalks are gathered and stored up for use by the side of the cholam stalks. This is the chief fuel. Also dried trees, withered branches and twigs broken by the wind are used.

Wood for buildings and making ploughs is got from Sivakasi, four miles off, and other places. One year it was got from the Forest Department through the Co-operative Society. But this was not continued for it seems it did not meet with encouragement from the Forest and Co-operative Departments of Government though Government noted with pleasure the procedure of the villagers.

The present value of land.—Wet Rs. 600 per acre; dry (well irrigated) Rs. 500 per acre and dry (ordinary) Rs. 100. The land is rising in value. This is due to two things. First the villagers are bent on investing all their savings in land and hence there is a large demand for land. Secondly the project of a railway line between Virudupatti and Srivilliputtur or Watrap has made the value of the lands near that line rise. It is probable that the line will pass within a mile of the village and hence the price of land is going up.

The village.—The area of the village site, taking only that portion occupied by the houses and the waste land separating the two portions into which the village is divided, is according to the village accounts 18·4 acres.

The main portion of the village is of course occupied by the Nayakars. Telugu shepherds, Maravars, artisans, dhobis and barbers form a group and live in the north-east corner of the village. The Panchamas live in the north-west and south-east corners.

The dwellings of the people are good. The houses of the depressed classes are decent. In the caste village there are 32 terraced houses, 5 tiled houses and 68 thatched houses. There are about 29 houses in the paracheri, all of them thatched. It must be noted that there has been an increase in the number of tiled and terraced houses within recent years. Six years ago the number of tiled and terraced houses was not more than ten or twelve. The rest have been built within recent years partly to be free from the fear of fire and partly also for the increased social status conferred. The houses are well ventilated—at least better than the average houses in such villages—and many even possess a chimney. The dwellings of depressed classes are not different from those of the caste men except for the fact that they are somewhat smaller in size. There are no gardens adjoining the houses. The familiar Indian sight of a garden at the back of the house is not met with here.

There is plenty of space available for building houses. The maximum distance of cultivated lands from the home of the cultivator is three miles.

Subsidiary industries.—There are no subsidiary industries in the village beyond the necessary artisan crafts needed for repairs. It seems that handspinning and country ginning was practised some fifteen or sixteen years ago. But after the advent of ginning mills at Sattur and Virudupatti these industries have declined. The local *carpenter* makes the ploughs for the villagers and also any repairs. During his spare time he makes country carts. He works about eight hours a day on the average and his earnings come to about Rs. 120 per year. He gets 4 marakkals of paddy for every plough that he makes and 2½ marakkals for every kamalai. (One marakkal = 5⅓ Madras measures; one marakkal of paddy weighs about 13 lb. and yields about 9 lb. of husked rice.)

The *blacksmith* also gets the same rate of wages for a plough and a kamalai. His earnings are approximately equal to the carpenter's.

Washerman.—Each of the two washermen gets 12½ kotahs (value Rs. 125, weight about 31¼ cwt.) of grain per year; and something more than 2 meals a day, for he gets a small quantity from each villager.

Barbers.—Each of the two barbers gets 6¼ kotahs (nearly 16 cwt.) of paddy a year (Rs. 62½) besides a small quantity of food from each house.

Tailor.—12½ kotahs of grain (Rs. 125) and 2 meals a day.

Besides these selling of ghee and letting carts and bullocks for hire may be taken as subsidiary occupations.

Village trade.—The chief items in the village trade are the sale of cotton, tobacco and senna. The villagers purchase the seed they require at Sattur and Virudupatti and sometimes at Sivakasi. As for their implements, the village makes its own ploughs and kamalais. Goods necessary for consumption are bought at Sivakasi.

The villagers take the cotton they produce to Sattur and Virudupatti and sell it to the agents of the many ginning companies that are there. The other commodities are not taken to the market by the villagers but are sold to the merchants who come to the village. Tobacco, senna, chillis and sweet-potatoes are sold to Sivakasi merchants who visit the village regularly.

Every year the village sells 200 candies of cleaned kapas (cotton bolls without seed) average price recently about Rs. 180 per candy, and Rs. 500 worth of tobacco or 400 thulams. The quantity of senna sold cannot be gauged as the contractors make contracts not according to the bales but on the standing crops.

The situation of the village is on the whole good. It is on the country road between Virudupatti and Rajapalaiyam, one of the most important commercial highways. It is two miles away from Tiruttangal, a famous Vishnu shrine to which large numbers of pilgrims resort. It is only 5 miles away from Sivakasi, which is a commercial town containing some of the most wealthy Shanar* merchants. It is only 15 miles from Sattur which is a railway station and contains many cotton ginning mills. It is 11 miles distant from the important commercial town and railway station of Virudupatti. The nearest railway station however is Tulukupatti, 7 miles off. The situation of the village will become much more important if either the railway line to Srivilliputtur or the road from Virudupatti to Rajapalaiyam is constructed.

Economic condition of the village.—*Wages* are now generally paid in money except for some of the old immemorial wages paid in kind to barbers, washermen, etc. The following is the list of current wages :—

	AS.	
Agriculture—		
Men	8	per day.
Women	4	"
Boys	4	"
Carpenters	12	"
Blacksmiths	12	"
Bricklayers	12 to 14	per day.

* [The Shānārs are the most numerous caste in the extreme south of the peninsula. Their special occupation is climbing the palmyra to collect the juice that oozes from the cut stems of the fronds, and palmyra fibre. At this occupation they can only earn 2 or 3 annas per day. The juice can be boiled into jaggery, from which sugar is obtained, or brewed into toddy. They are a rising caste, and very many have become Christians. There is a violent dispute about their social status. Ed.]

The potter and the shoe-maker are paid piece wages

Customary prices.

		RS.	A.	P.	
Cotton—local	...	40	0	0	per bale of 16 thulams.
Cambodia	...	50	0	0	,, ,,
Cholam	...	10	0	0	per kotah.
Kambu	...	10	0	0	,,
Keppai	...	9	0	0	,,
Tobacco	...	1	4	0	per thulam.
Senna	...	0	12	0	,,
Varagu	...	7	0	0	per kotah.
Blackgram	...	4			Madras measures per rupee.
Coriander seed	...	8			,, ,,
Greengram	...	4			,, ,,
Horsegram	...	7			,, ,,

It is very difficult to estimate the number of people who have made savings. For many people have debts and yet the savings of the year are utilized for buying more land instead of paying off debt. Sometimes land and jewellery are bought by contracting a debt. There is no sum to be found under the heading of deposits in the co-operative society's accounts. However it is clear that two families have made savings worth about Rs. 8,000. This sum they have lent to their neighbours for interest. In this connexion it may be noted that in spite of the fact that there is a co-operative society lending at 9 per cent, the general rate of interest is about 15 to 24 per cent for big loans and 48 per cent for small loans. The total debts of all the villagers come to about a lakh of rupees. However they have assets worth Rs. 2,90,000.

The system of Padials exists in the village but there are only eight of them. The Padial is given 3 meals a day and also the usual rate of wages. These wages are credited to his debt and he has to serve his creditor till his wages are equal to the debt. If the Padial breaks the service in the middle the usual rate of interest will be charged on the sum standing to his debit on that date.

There are in the village almost none, at least among castemen, who are not indebted to some extent at least to somebody. The causes of this widespread indebtedness are the desire of the land-owners for lands and buildings. In many cases they borrow the money to buy these things. In the case of buildings it is dead capital and earns no interest. In the case of land the return is so poor that it covers only part of the interest.

The communal income of the village is derived chiefly from a tax called 'Mahimai' upon goods sent away from the village. It is a fixed rate upon each article of trade. The following are the rates for the different commodities :—

Rate of Mahimai.

		RS.	A.	P.	
Cotton	... ...	0	8	0	per bandy load.
Senna	... ...	1	0	0	,,
Tobacco	... ...	0	8	0	,,
Paddy	... ...	0	8	0	,,

		RS.	A.	P.	
Plantains	... ...	0	2	0	per bandy load.
Sweet potatoes	... ...	0	2	0	"
Bulls, cows and buffaloes	...	0	4	0	per head.
Sheep and goats	... ...	0	0	3	"

To this must be added the rent or tax levied on each shop of Rs. 12 per annum.

On an average the income amounts to Rs. 150 or Rs. 200 per annum.

The chief items of expenditure out of this communal income are (1) the celebration of the festival of the God of Tiruttangal temple for one day at a cost of Rs. 50. The temple according to tradition was the halting place of Vishnu on his way from Madura to Srivilliputtur to see the Goddess Nachiyar, (2) charities, (3) maintenance of village roads and conservancy.

The administration is vested in a board of sixteen, appointed by the villagers. They are permanent members, vacancies occurring only through death or grave misconduct, then being filled by co-option.

Religious festivals.—There are two festivals celebrated in the village, one in April, the other in July. The cost of the April festival is borne by six rich landowners each of whom pays a sum of Rs. 20. The July festival is celebrated out of the communal income. The villagers contributed by means of voluntary subscription Rs. 2,000 towards the repairs made in the Tiruttangal temple, in 1914.

Three people in the village took advantage of the Agricultural Loans Act and got loans from Government to sink wells. Two of them got Rs. 300 each and the other Rs. 200.

Sanitary condition of village.—The village is on the whole very healthy. It is on a higher level than the surrounding country so that it is not damp or marshy.

The prevalent diseases there are not many. Indeed the place by itself is not liable to any disease. Any epidemic must be one of importation. Thus for instance about 35 persons were attacked by malaria last year. This was due to the fact that a party of 30 persons went on pilgrimage to a malarial spot called Varisanad Hill in the Western Ghats. They all got malaria and spread it to their neighbours. Cholera was rife in the village some years back. It has disappeared now.

Small-pox prevailed last year. About ten persons got the disease but all of them were cured. Vaccination is accepted and is an ordinary custom.

Plague has not appeared in the village at all. There was one case of death due to tuberculosis during the year. At present however there is no one suffering from the disease.

During the year ten infants were born out of whom two died. There have been no cases of snake bites.

Medical assistance beyond the home recipes known to most Hindu mothers, is not available in the village. The secretary of the co-operative society however keeps some medicines of the ordinary sort, e.g., omum water, plaster, etc. When cholera broke out in the village a few years ago he kept some medicine and distributed it to the stricken people with very beneficial results.

He also cultivated some medicinal herbs for counteracting the poison of scorpion bites.

The habits of the people are not very sanitary. In most houses the cattle shed and poultry are not kept apart from the quarters of the people. Till recently there was no drainage system of the village. The drains used to flow into the pathway and often formed mires stinking horribly. This and the pools formed by the rain water made the pathway look nasty and unfit for use. Only last year the villagers got a grant from Government of Rs. 1,000 through their co-operative society and with Rs. 400 more out of their communal income they constructed a drain through their main street and also a good macadamised road running north to south. The appearance of the village is much better after that and the sanitation also much improved.

There is no difficulty on account of night-soil. There are no privies attached to the houses so that privy scavenging is unnecessary. Men and women go out to the fields.

Drinking water is generally got from the river. Some people however use the six wells that are in the village. One family has improved upon the system generally followed. It had a tube well sunk at a cost of about Rs. 200 which by means of pipes supplies water both for household purposes and for the cattle shed that it has built.

Marriage and purdah.—The marriages are all post-puberty. There was only one pre-puberty marriage in the village and that was the marriage of the son of the Secretary of the Co-operative Society who is a Raoji Brahman. Marriage of girls is generally between the ages of 16 and 25. There is no purdah, and women work as hard as men. It is a familiar sight to see them in the morning hours plucking weeds in the fields or picking cotton, tobacco or senna. They wield great influence at home. One custom peculiar to the village is the system that all the villagers should contribute according to their status towards the expenses of the marriages and funerals in the village. The effect is wholesome. The marriage expenses are not very high and a marriage or death in a family does not mean a huge debt to that family but is distributed among the villagers.

Education.—The village has an elementary school where instruction is free. It is supported by the co-operative credit society. Seven and a half per cent of the net profits of the society goes to the school. Besides this all the members have generously consented to give the dividends they receive from the society for the upkeep of the school.

There are two teachers at present. Instruction is up to the fourth standard and the students are given instruction in the three R's. There is a museum attached to the school. The chief collections there are those of the seeds of different crops. Behind the school there is a small plot of ground which has been turned into the school garden. Here each student is given a plot of ground and he has to cultivate that plot and grow the things that he is asked to grow. The student does all the business in his plot, the digging, planting, watering, etc.

One special feature of the school is the training that is given in co-operation. The boys are given instruction in the management of co-operative societies and a practical way of demonstration is adopted by asking the students to keep a co-operative store where pencils, paper, etc., are sold to the students. The students are allowed to have deposits and to keep credit accounts.

The school is located in a mandapam,* in which some improvements have been made to make it convenient for the class room. Furniture locally made has been supplied. A library is attached to the school which contains about 40 volumes including school texts and novels. Most of them are Tamil works, the only English books being school text-books.

The present school is the improvement of an old pial school that existed in the village. The villagers in the enthusiasm for civic improvement that characterized the few years following the establishment of the co-operative society decided to improve their village school and arranged that a part of the profits of their society should be utilized for this purpose.

There are 25 boys and 5 girls in the school. One or two of them come from the neighbouring village of Petchutrapatti, a mile distant. There are some Panchamas also reading in the school. The attendance is not quite satisfactory as the parents take away the children when there is any work for them in the fields or at home. The average school-going age in the village is 6 to 11.

There are 47 males and 8 females who are literate. Five of the literate males are Panchamas, so that 7½ per cent of the castemen and 3½ per cent of the Panchamas are literate. There are only two persons who can read and write English, the Secretary of the Co-operative Society and one of the school masters. There are very few persons who have specialized in any branch of knowledge. There is a Tamil pandit and an astrologer. The villagers get "New India" and the "Swadesamitran"† for their co-operative society which is also their reading room.

Of the boys who have passed through the school only one has continued his studies further. He is now in the Hindu High School, Srivilliputtur. His expenses are borne entirely by his parents.

The school has been in existence only for the last four years and so it is too early to make any pronouncement on the capabilities of the students that have passed out of it. But it would be much better if parents realized a little more the value of punctuality and regular attendance.

Village administration.—The village administration is conducted by the village munsif, his karnam and a panchayat of 16 persons. The village munsif looks to the collection of revenue and other Government business while the panchayat looks after sanitation, education and other local matters. Most of the panchayat members belong also to the panchayat of the co-operative credit society.

The panchayat holds on the average two meetings every month. Last year the panchayat's activities were specially in the direction

* Rest-house for pilgrims.

† A Tamil daily newspaper.

of sanitation, especially the construction of the road and of the drains already mentioned. The panchayat has appointed a scavenger on a monthly pay of Rs. 2 to keep the streets clean and especially to look after the drains. The drinking water wells are regularly cleansed, the cost of each clearing being borne by the group of people who use the well.

Police administration.—The villagers are not satisfied with the police administration. Especially during last year petty crimes have been very common. During the past four months there have been three thefts and two attempts at house-breaking besides some instances of setting fire to hay ricks. The value of goods stolen amounts to Rs. 500. Not one of the culprits has been caught. Indeed the villagers complain that it is more than two months since any police authority visited the village. These crimes are attributed to persons from outside.

The relation of the villagers to the higher authorities is very amicable. The villagers are however very independent and many of the petty exactions and tyranny that are common in other villages are not to be met with here. The Collector of Ramnad was in the village in May 1915 to open the newly constructed road named after him the Tottenham Road. The Divisional Officer has been to the village twice during the course of the year.

None of the villagers are at present engaged in litigation.

There was a little litigation some years back but after the advent of the co-operative society a new spirit has come over the villagers of not resorting to courts but of having all their disputes settled by their panchayat. Most of these disputes are of a civil nature. Criminal cases have not yet arisen in the village and it remains to be seen whether the parties would be satisfied with the verdict of their panchayat.

The Co-operative Credit Society.—The chief institution which has made the village famous is the co-operative society. The Vadamalaipuram society was the earliest society started in the district and it is accepted as a model by the other societies surrounding it. The high level of excellence of the society is due to its Secretary Mr. Ananda Rao who is the life and soul of the society. It was he who started it and who works zealously for the success of co-operation in the district. He is an honorary organiser and an honorary supervisor of the Madura-Ramnad Central Bank.

There is also a society for the purchase and sale of agricultural implements.

The credit society was started on 12th February 1909 with 13 members and a capital of Rs. 65. The liability is unlimited and the members are jointly and severally responsible for the liabilities of the society. The society is registered for 200 shares of Rs. 50 each, which makes a capital of Rs. 10,000. The society's maximum borrowing power has been limited to Rs. 20,000. The society borrows at a rate not exceeding 7½ per cent. The maximum amount that the society lends to each of its members is Rs. 1,000 at the rate of Rs. 200 per share. The interest it charges on the money it lends is 9 per cent.

The following figures show the condition of the society on 30th June 1916 when the last co-operative year ended:—

Number of members 74.

	RS.
Share capital	1,582
Number of shares	124

Liabilities.

Madura-Ramnad Central Bank	12,478
Vadamalaipuram Agricultural Society	25
Local Deposit	98
Share capital	1,582
Total ...	14,183

Assets.

	RS.	A.	P.
Collections during the year	2,642	6	0
Loans outstanding on 30th June 1916	11,912	0	0
Reserve Fund	933	0	1
Total ...	15,847	6	1

The following is a classification of the loans given during 1915–16 according to amount and purpose:—

	RS.	A.	P.
70 Loans below Rs. 50	1,736	6	0
3 Loans between Rs. 50 and 100...	248	0	0
6 Loans between Rs. 100 and 250	658	0	0
Total 79 loans ...	2,642	6	0

Purpose of loans.

Agricultural	1,484	6	0
Purchase of cattle	506	0	0
Trade	233	0	0
Education	39	0	0
Repair of houses and cattlesheds	150	0	0
Discharge of prior debts	230	0	0
Total ...	2,642	6	0

For reasons explained above there were no loans for marriages.

All these loans were given on personal security. The fault among the villagers is that they do not repay their loans punctually. The loans granted during the last year were however all discharged in the course of the year. The outstanding loans were those that had been lent in the previous years. Two suits were filed during the year against two of the members and decrees obtained. The Reserve Fund of the society is invested in the Madura-Ramnad Co-operative Society.

The net assets of the members amount to Rs. 2,39,168 and the society owns furniture valued at Rs. 180 after allowing for depreciation. The chief articles of furniture are an iron safe and a wooden bureau.

The following are the charges for year 1915-16:—

	RS.	A.	P.
Clerk at Rs. 6 per month	48	0	0
Remuneration to manager	50	0	0
Contingencies	71	2	6
Rent for building	36	0	0
Other items	7	0	0
	212	2	6

The Agricultural Society for Purchase and Sale.—This was started on 13th August 1913 with 24 members and an initial capital of Rs. 24. The maximum share capital of the society is Rs. 1,000 divided into 200 shares of Rs. 5 each. The maximum borrowing power of the society is Rs. 2,000. It has a common-good fund of Rs. 104-15-2, which can be utilized only for the purchase of agricultural implements. It was out of this that the harrow above mentioned was bought. On 30th June 1916 there were 44 members and 121 shares. The capital was Rs. 121. It has a reserve fund of Rs. 40-6-8 invested in the Madura-Ramnad District Bank. The commodities bought by the society during the year were fodder, cotton seeds, and leather for buckets. The following shows the activity of the society during the year:—

	RS.	A.	P.
Stock on hand	322	9	3
Bought during the year	420	1	0
Sold during the year	828	9	4

History and prospects of the village.—According to the villagers, it seems they were more prosperous some fifteen or twenty years back. We know that cotton ginning and spinning were carried on as cottage industries. But this disappeared before the formidable competition of the cotton mills at Satur and Virudupatti. But the poverty of the villagers is due not so much to the disappearance of these industries as to the burden of debt, the debts being to a large extent of their own making for the purchase of land and building of houses. Mostly they borrowed from the Shanars of Sivakasi. The income from the lands and houses is not sufficient to meet the interest on the capital borrowed. Hence they are driven to borrow more and more. The interest on such debts was from 24 to 50 per cent. After the introduction of the co-operative society, these petty loans are advanced to the ryots from the society at 9 per cent. But these loans are sufficient only to meet their yearly agricultural demands and to pay the interest on the old loans. The society is not in a position to tackle the whole debt of the village. Besides these borrowings there is one more cause that has contributed to the deterioration of the village economically. During the last fifteen years the produce of the lands has not been satisfactory. The war has also adversely affected their interests. In 1915 the villagers found that they had no profitable market for their cotton. This year the senna speculation has brought heavy loss to many.

But the condition of the village would have been much worse had it not been for the immigration into the village of Mr. Ananda Rao,

As soon as he came he found that two things must be remedied as early as possible, the indebtedness of the ryots to the Sivakāsi Shanars for petty sums at ruinous rates of interest and the ignorance of the villagers which had induced them to invest their small savings with a chit * secretary whose methods savoured of swindling. For remedying the first of these, he started a permanent fund in the village which lent money to the villagers to repay their petty loans. He put himself in correspondence with the chit secretary and after a good deal of argument and brow-beating succeeded in getting from him the bare capital invested by the villagers with him. The office of the nidhi formed a sort of club and Mr. Ananda Rao took advantage of the opportunity to advise and direct them. Finding that their outlook was very narrow he induced them to subscribe for the "Swadesamitran" (the leading Tamil daily). He used to read out the news and articles to the villagers when they assembled in the nidhi office. The villagers have continued to get the paper since then, though very few of them read it themselves and others only listen when it is read out.

When the co-operative movement was started in India Mr. Ananda Rao induced the villagers to form a society in the village and promised to work for it himself. He has remained the secretary of it since its inception. Most of the improvements in the village like the construction of the road, the drains, the sinking of wells and tube wells are due to his suggestions. But the villagers are very slow to move and do not stick to good principles.

General.—The only other item of interest in the village is emigration. Emigration is chiefly to Colombo, Rangoon, Penang and Devikulam. The following table shows the number of families that have gone to the different places and also the number that have returned:—

Emigration—	
Colombo	3 families.
Rangoon	30 ,,
Penang	6 ,,
Devikulam	4 ,,
Returned—	
Rangoon	10 families.
Penang	2 ,,
Devikulam	4 ,,

Those who returned from Penang came without any savings. Only the following four persons returned with some substantial surplus:—

		RS.
Krishnama Nayakar	about	500
Gopala Nayakar	,,	300
Chinnaswami Nayakar	,,	300
Venkatakrishna Nayakar	,,	700

* [A "chit fund" or "nidhi" or "kuri" is a sort of slate club. The members pay in a fixed sum per month, and the money so collected is given each month to one member to use as capital. The recipient must then give security for the continuance of his monthly payments till every member has had his turn. The selection of the member to take the fund may be made by lot or by auction. In the latter case the *lowest* bidder gets the fund, i.e., the one who is content to receive the smallest portion of it. The remainder is divided among the other members. Ed.]

The following are the family budgets of some of the villagers. They have no accounts and the figures are only rough approximations derived for information taken from the persons themselves. The figures are as far as possible the actual expenses of last year—

(1) *Family budget of Narayanaswami Nayakar*

(the richest person in the village).

Family—			
Parents	2	Daughters	2
Husband	1	Servants	5
Wife	1		13
Sons	2		

Assets—	RS.		RS.
Lands	25,000	*Liabilities*—Debts	1,477
House	8,230		
Moveables	5,000		
	38,230		

Receipts—	RS.	*Charges*—	RS.	RS.
Grain, 100 kotahs	1,000	Grain, 100 kotahs		1,000*
Cotton	1,500	Cotton seed for cattle		500
Tobacco	300	Fodder		500
Fodder	500	Manure		100
Senna	600	Tobacco plants		30
Sale of horse	700	8 servants—	RS	
		Grazers of oxen, 3	150	300
		" of sheep, 3	80	
		" of buffalo, 1	20	
		Household servant, 1.	50	
		Miscellaneous wages		200
		Kist		150
		Repayment of debt and interest		1,500
		Grocery		100
		Clothes		100
		Marriage and other miscellaneous expenses		50
	4,600			4,580

	RS.
Receipts	4,600
Expenditure	4,580
Surplus	20

He has constructed a special cattle shed by converting a house into a cattle shed at a cost of Rs. 4,000. He has 8 bullocks, 4 cows

* For consumption of family and labourers.

(3 giving milk) and 4 cow-buffaloes of which none give milk. The cost of maintaining it comes to Rs. 1,200 per year, as follows :—

	RS.
Cotton seed	500
Fodder	500
Wages of four servants	200
	1,200

(2) *Budget of Alagaraswami Nayakar.*

Family—			
Husband	1	Servants	3
Wife	1		
Mother	1		7
Child	1		

Assets—	RS.		RS.
Lands	9,445	*Liabilities*	4,300
House	4,125		
Moveables	1,100		
	14,770		

Receipts—	RS.	*Expenses*—	RS.
Cotton	420	Grain, 50 kotahs ...	500
Grain, 50 kotahs ...	500	Fodder	200
Tobacco	70	Cotton seed	250
Chillies	40	Wages of servants— RS.	
Coriander seed	60	Agricultural labourer. 60	80
Green gram, 2 kotahs ...	20	Buffalo-herd ... 20	
Fodder	200	Household servant ...	50
Senna	600	Manure	200
Trade	200	Kist	70
Loan	200	Seed for sowing	50
		Cost of oxen bought ...	160
		Repayment of debt and interest	500
		Grocery	75
		Clothes	50
		Marriage	100
	2,310		2,285

	RS.
Receipts	2,310
Expenditure	2,285
Surplus	25

4

(3) *Budget of Lingama Nayakar, Clerk of the Co-operative Society.*

Family—			
Mother	1	Servant	1
Husband	1		
Wife	1		4

Assets—	RS.		RS.
Lands	5,020	*Liabilities*	1,570
House	1,020		
Moveables	350		
	6,390		

Receipts—	RS.	*Expenses*—	RS.
Grain, 30 kotahs	300	Charges for the field (manure, kamalai, etc.).	150
Cotton and tobacco	500	Fodder	110
Chillis	100	Cotton seed	100
Fodder	100	Do. for planting	15
Salary	96	Tobacco plants	20
	1,096	Grain (seed), 2 kotahs	20
New debt incurred in year.	250	Pay to servant including clothes	50
		Temporary coolies and field labourers	200
		Kist	50
		Repayment of loan and interest	400
		Grain	140
		Grocery	24
		Clothes	50
		Marriage expenses	20
	1,346		1,349

	RS.
Receipts	1,346
Expenditure	1,349
Deficit	3

(4) *Budget of Krishnama Nayakar.*

Family—			
Husband	1	Daughters	3
Wife	1		
Sons	2		7

Assets—	RS.		RS.
Land	3,000	*Liabilities*	2,430
House	200		
Moveables	nil.		
	3,200		

Receipts—	RS.	*Expenses—*	RS.
Grain	50	Grain, 15 kotahs	150
Cotton	150	Kist	20
Senna	350	Wages for ploughing ...	30
Fodder	30	Fodder	80
Loan	230	Cotton seeds	70
Trade	100	Manure	50
		Cotton seed for sowing ...	20
		Miscellaneous wages ...	100
		Clothes	50
		Grocery	75
		Marriage expenses ...	100
		Repayment of loan and interest	160
	910		905

	RS.
Receipts	910
Expenditure	905
Surplus	5

The two following are the budgets of Panchamas, one from each of the two sections:—

(1) *Budget of Ammaiyadia Kudumban (Pallan).*

Family—
Husband ... 1
Wife 1
Sons ... ... 3 (eldest 18 years of age).
5

Assets—
Land 3 acres of dry (rain-fed) land.

Liabilities—Nil.

Receipts—	RS.	*Expenses—*	RS.
Earnings of Ammaiyadia Kudumban (six annas per day)	90	Grain, 11 kotahs	110
Earnings of wife (three annas per day)	45	Clothes— Two female cloths, Rs. 6; Two men's cloths „ 4; Boy's clothing „ 10	20
Earnings of eldest son (five annas per day)	75	Grocery	20
Produce of land	27	Feasts	50
	237		200

	RS.
Receipts	237
Expenditure	200
Savings	37

This is a typical Pallan family in which all the members work. Their wages are their only means of living. The three acres of land that the family possesses were bought out of the savings. These people accumulate their savings by either hoarding or investing it with their employers till they get a good sum and then they buy land with it. They are on the whole a frugal people. But the Pallans as a class have a great number of feasts in the year and their expenditure on this score is a big item in their budgets. The three acres of land would produce Rs. 34 worth of cotton or Rs. 20 worth of grain. These two are cultivated alternately and hence the average of Rs. 27 is given as the income from land. The family would have work for twenty days in the month.

(2) *Budget of Perumal Pagadai (Chakkiliyan).*

Family—		*(contd.)*	
Husband	1	Grandsons and granddaughters	8
Wife	1		
Sons (aged 35, 30 and 25, respectively)	3		16
Daughters-in-law	3	Daughters (gone to their husbands' houses) ...	3

Assets—$4\frac{1}{2}$ acres of land.	*Debts*—Nil.

Receipts—	RS.	*Expenses—*	RS.
Grain, 4 kotahs	40	Grain, 22 kotahs	220
Wages for stitching kamalais (on the average six per year), 2 kotahs of grain ...	20	Feasts	10
Miscellaneous leather work.	50		
Wages of labour of three sons	80		
Do. three daughters-in-law	50		
	240		230

Occasionally the villagers give them kanji.

	RS.
Receipts	240
Expenditure	230
Savings	10

Besides the kanji the family get the necessary cloth from the villagers. One other thing that is noteworthy is the absence of quite such a large number of feasts among the Chakkiliyans as among the Pallans.

N.B.—All these family budgets are only approximate. None of the villagers keep regular accounts and hence only approximations are possible.

TINNEVELLY DISTRICT.

GANGAIKONDAN.

[*By P. S. Lokanathan, B.A., St. Joseph's College, Trichinopoly.*]

Preliminary.—Gangaikondan is a big village comprising the subdivisions of Gangaikondan proper, of Vadakkur, Kilur, Aladi Paracheri, Pungan Paracheri, Anaitalai Paracheri and Turaiyur Paracheri. It lies on the right bank of the Chittar river and is on its 18th anicut. This river has its source from the famous Courtallam falls and many anicuts have been built across the river to utilize its water for purposes of irrigation. The village is 12 miles north of Tinnevelly and 2½ miles distant from the railway station which goes by the same name. On the side of the river the soil is rocky, but as we go further away, it is somewhat better but nowhere is the soil very fertile.

Two miles to the south of the village, on the left side of what is known as the Madras Road there lie 1,500 acres of Reserved Forest only very recently handed over by the Government to a Panchayat of six members. There is a large area of poramboke (land reserved for purposes other than cultivation) in the village. The village is ein th plains and no hills are found in its neighbourhood.

The village is under the usual ryotwari tenure of Madras except 536 acres 55 cents which are inam lands (i.e., lands held on specially favourable tenure); but of this only 8 acres 36 cents are wet land; this area belongs exclusively to the temple. The following are the chief inamdars :—

	Extent. ACS.
1. Temples	354·88
2. Dikshadar *	33·96
3. Accountants (Karnams)	28·0
4. Village munsif	44·92
5. Watchman	33·48
6. Barber	12·13
7. Scavenger	22·92
8. Washerman	6·26

All these pay quit-rent of ⅝ of the ordinary assessment. The total revenue from the inam lands is Rs. 280-14-0. The history of the inam rights is interesting, but no old records exist. The people told me that only a small portion now remains out of the vast extent of lands once held under inam rights.

Population.—The total population of the village (including caste village and paracheri) is, according to the census of 1911, 3,495, of whom 1,675 are males and 1,820 are females.

The total population of the caste village is estimated by the villagers as 2,395 persons.

* "Dikshadar" is a hereditary title obtained by performing a sacrifice. Inam land is granted to a "dikshadar" on consideration of his being a guru.

Census figures for the years 1881, 1891, 1901 and 1911 are herewith given—

	Males.	Females.	Total.
1881	1,423	1,438	2,861
1891	1,476	1,476	2,952
1901	1,514	1,551	3,065
1911	1,675	1,820	3,495

The increase in the number of females from 1901 to 1911 is appreciable.

The castes are as follows:—

1. Brahmans	100 families.
2. Pillaimars or Vellalas	31 ,,
3. Maravars	102 ,,
4. Shepherd caste	60 ,,
5. Barbers	5 ,,
6. Oilmongers	12 ,,
7. Betel men	50 ,,
8. Carpenters	6 ,,
9. Blacksmiths	6 ,,
10. Goldsmiths	6 ,,
11. Dhobis	3 ,,
12. Potters	10 ,,
13. The Fishermen caste	20 ,,
14. Tondamans *	3 ,,
15. Pipers	4 ,,
16. Brothel women	2 ,,
17. Kshatrias	3 ,,
18. Muhammadans	5 ,,
19. Kaikolans or weavers	20 ,,

It must be borne in mind that all these are distinct castes by themselves and they have no inter-relation such as marriage, etc., though it must not be forgotten that this does not in any sense stand in the way of active business intercourse. This is also true of the relationship with Panchamas.

I have in a few typical families enquired the number of children living and dead:—

Caste.	Total number of children born.	Dead.
1. Brahman	8	1
2. Brahman	5	...
3. Maravar	8	3
4. Shepherd	7	2
5. Pallan	5	...
6. Vellalan	9	3
	42	9

This shows an average of 7 children per family born, of whom 5½ per family survive.

* A caste of lime burners, who emigrated to Tinnevelly from Pudukkottai. The Raja of Pudukkottai's family name is Tondaman; he is the head of the Kallan (thief) caste.

Including those of the Paracheri there are 729 houses of which about 100 belong to Brahmans.

The population of the depressed classes amounts to nearly 1,100 persons of whom about 530 are males.

These consist of—

—	Number of families.	Number of individuals.	Males.	Females.	Children.
1. Pallans	175	900	250	270	380
2. Eshuvans	8	35	10	15	15
3. Paraiyans	8	42	13	14	15
4. Shanars	8 (1 family alone is 18 in number).	50	20	18	12
5. Chakkiliyans	14	65	22	27	16
6. Kuravans	2	6	2	2	2

The population is no doubt increasing all round but more on the side of females than on that of males. It seems that there is an increase in the population of the depressed classes and also a rise in their standard of living. I have taken 15 years as the differentiating age between children and others.

The Brahmans are deteriorating in numbers and prosperity. Other castemen show signs of progress.

Land.—The area of wet cultivation in the year of resettlement which was in fasli 1318 (1908–09) was 1,022·40 acres but has increased to 1,030·28 last year, thus showing an increase of 7·88 acres.

In the same manner there is an increase in the dry cultivation from 6,069·15 acres in 1908 to 6,107·31 in 1915.

The area of lands watered by wells is only about 45 acres. Wells do not pay the ryots in proportion to the amount of trouble and expense involved. Altogether there are 47 wells of which three have dried up. Five are found in the wet cultivation, the rest in the dry. They are worked by kamalais and pairs of oxen.

There are 23·97 acres reserved as cattle stand and 1,088·65 acres set apart for grazing. The cattle graze on the river banks and tank bunds as well as on the patta lands of dry area.

In the forest Oodai trees (flat-topped acacias) are abundant. There are some trees of margosa and other kinds.

In the year of resettlement (fasli 1318) the area of fruit trees was 6 acres while that of the trees of other varieties amounted to about 39 acres. The fruit trees consist mainly of mango, lime and plantain. There are many shade trees found abundantly on the canal banks and also on the sides of the road. Chief among them are the Banyan trees, the Bassia longifolia, the Terminalia Alata and the Portia trees. There are many trees of the latter kind in the backyards of houses. In addition to these, there are a very large number of coconut and palm trees of which 1,091 are temporarily free of assessment as they stand within backyard limits.

The number of palmyras assessed at resettlement is given below:--

—	Number of rough trees.	Number of smooth trees.	Total.
On patta lands	9,098	9,020	18,118
On assessed waste	19	59	78
On poramboke	2,030	4,103	6,733

There are three irrigation tanks and one canal. Just a mile to the west of the village an anicut has been constructed across the river Chittar. The *Sirukulam canal* has its source here flowing from north-west to south-east of the village; it finds its way to the *Sirukulam tank* which is fed entirely by this canal.

The other two tanks, the *Pallankulam tank* and the *Pappankulam tank* are entirely rainfed. The Pallankulam with an irrigable area of nearly 6 acres is situated on the south-west of the village, on the left side of the main road and its area is only 10 acres. The Pappankulam a little bigger in size with an area of 40 acres is on the right side of the road and irrigates an area of 24·91 acres.

The following table shows the irrigable area of the tanks and total revenue demand:—

	Irrigable area. ACS.	Total demand. RS.	A.	P.
1. Sirukulam tank (fed by the channel).	793·9	4,628	12	0
2. Sirukulam canal	215·13	1,253	1	0
3. Pallankulam tank	5·99	24	0	0
4. Pappankulam tank rainfed	24·91	59	4	0

In addition to the 47 irrigation wells there are about 40 wells used for domestic purposes. Nearly 25 of them are in the Brahman quarters while the rest are distributed among all the others. The well water is somewhat brackish and is used for all other purposes except drinking for which the river water is used.

The river Chittar, being so near, satisfies the people's wants with regard to drinking water. People bathe and wash their clothes in the river itself. Three people have pumps in their houses. On the whole the village has a fair water-supply but in the summer people may experience some difficulty because the quantity of water in the river diminishes considerably and hence the water is not so good.

There does not seem to be any progress in the method of cultivating the fields. The standard of living has no doubt increased as is apparent from the everyday life of the villager just at present, but this is not due to prosperity.

Occupation of land.—Out of a wet area of 1,030·28 acres only about 300 acres are cultivated by the landowners and this is to be explained by the fact that most of these lands belong to the Brahmans. Many landowners, and especially the Brahmans, find it convenient to lease out their lands to tenants. The percentage of cultivating landowners is decreasing while that of the non-cultivating landowners is increasing.

	1907–08.	1912–13.
(*a*) Percentage of cultivating landowners in the district	20·4	11·8
(*b*) Percentage of non-cultivating landowners	0·5	1·1
(*c*) Percentage of cultivating tenants ...	2·7	7·7

I am told that dependence solely on agriculture is not calculated to keep a family out of want. The members of the family must also engage in other pursuits which bring them some addition to the income they get from land. So the landowners find it to their interest to sublet their lands and themselves engage in other walks of life. So far with regard to wet area.

In the case of the dry cultivation, the position is better. Excluding nearly 2,000 acres of dry lands where usually no cultivation is done, more than 60 per cent of the area is cultivated by the landowners themselves (that is, more than 2,400 acres). Thus on the whole 730 acres of wet land and 1,600 acres of dry area are cultivated by tenants.

The number of cultivating landowners is nearly 600 out of a total of 926. Most of the castemen other than Brahmans and all the Panchama landowners cultivate their lands themselves.

The number of non-cultivating landowners is 326 and most of them have some dealings in money—in lending and borrowing and getting some profit from the differential interest. There are a small number of men who have gone out of the village and are employed elsewhere in good positions.

There are fifty tenants who do not own any lands but who cultivate other people's lands.

About a hundred are agricultural labourers who neither own nor rent any land. There are six men employed under landlords rather as domestic servants than as agricultural labourers. They get one regular meal a day with occasional grain or rice entirely at the option of the landlord or at the pleasure of the mistress of the house. Among the actual labourers in the fields are about 45 females who get a money wage of 3 annas a day. The remaining 55 are male labourers who get not less than 5 annas a day. In busy seasons there is a rise in wages by at least an anna a day. At this time of the year when sowing and planting have to be done for the pishanam crop, i.e., the crop sown in September and October, the wages of male and female labourers are 6 annas and 4 annas each respectively. Boys under fifteen years of age are paid at the same rate as females.

Holdings according to ownership.

Extent.	Number of owners.
Under 1 acre	105
From 1 to 5 acres	220
,, 5 to 10 ,, ...	250
,, 10 to 20 ,, ...	100
,, 20 to 30 ,, ...	50
,, 30 to 40 ,, ...	60
,, 40 to 50 ,, ...	50
Over 50 acres	90

But it must be borne in mind that since there are included here the whole of dry lands and especially the 2,000 acres usually lying uncultivated, the extent of holdings appears larger than it really is. Now a person owning some 7 acres of wet land will be better off than one having 15 acres of dry land. Hence a better idea can be got if we confine our attention to wet lands alone and estimate the extent of holdings there. With this idea I made some inquiries in the village, the results of which are shown below :—

Holdings of wet land.

	Number of owners.	Extent. ACS.
Over 100 acres ...	...	...
From 50 to 100 acres	1	80
" 40 to 50 "	...	...
" 20 to 40 "	3	70
" 10 to 20 "	5	60
" 5 to 10 "	40	250
1 to 5 "	210	400
Under 1 acre "	200	120

There are about 350 tenants who cultivate other person's lands in addition to cultivating their own. Of them 175 are families of the depressed classes and the rest are Maravars and Shepherds.

The areas of holdings of wet lands according to tenancy are as follows :—

Tenancies.

	Number of tenants.	Approximate extent. ACS.
Under 1 acre ...	100	70
From 1 to 5 acres	215	400
" 5 to 10 "	30	200
" 10 to 20 "	5	60
Over 20 acres ...	...	...
	about	730

Rents are always paid to the landlords in kind. The amount of rent paid depends on the nature and fertility of the particular land rented and also on the nature of the contract entered into either party. There are various kinds of contract between the tenant and the landlord and four sorts actually obtain in this village—

(*a*) The tenant agrees to pay a certain number of kotas (1 kota = 112 Madras measures, and 1 kota of paddy weighs 2½ cwt.) every year absolutely fixed. Sometimes a proviso is added that in exceptional years—years of very bad harvest owing to want of sufficient water, or crops being damaged very much—some reduction shall be granted. In this village about 10 kotas, value about Rs. 100, for the year is the customary rent charged for a double crop area of 1·68 acres (1 kota of land).* Under this agreement the entire cost of cultivation is borne by the tenant; the seed, the manure, the labour for ploughing, sowing, weeding, planting and harvesting all have to be supplied by the tenant himself. The landlord has simply to pay the kist (about Rs. 11). All the straw is for the tenant.

* [i.e., Rs. 60 per acre. From detailed statements given below it appears that land for senna cultivation pays a rent of about Rs. 28 per acre. Ed.]

(*b*) There is another sort of agreement whereby the landlord receives two-thirds of the actual return for the year. Here almost the same conditions prevail as in the above-mentioned contract except that the landlord has more responsibility. Usually a landowner resident in the village has recourse to this contract, as by persistent supervision he can expect to get a greater return; the tenant's position also is better since the greater total return means more gain for himself. The landlord must see that the tenant cultivates the land properly, sows enough seed, manures the field sufficiently and spends liberally on all necessary items. If the manure is wanting, it is the owner's interest to give the tenant manure and debit it to his account; or if the tenant has no money, he sometimes pays him for necessary expenses and gets it back at the harvest time. As soon as the crop is harvested, a certain amount is set apart for the labour incurred in reaping the fields and the rest divided between the landowner and the tenant in the proportion of 2 : 1. Here also the straw belongs to the tenant, because he does the ploughing. The tenant gets some remuneration for all the work he does for the owner, in addition to some grain or cash he receives occasionally as a present.

(*c*) A third contract prevails by which the landlord gets three-quarters of the actual return while one-quarter is given over to the tenant. Under this agreement, all the manure is supplied by the landlord and the rest, the seed and labour, have to be borne by the tenant. The kist is paid in this as in every other case by the landholder. The straw is for the tenant but a rich landholder is able to exact from the tenant a part, usually one-sixth, of the straw, by threatening to make an agreement with another.

(*d*) There is yet another kind of contract that prevails here by which the landlord pays for the seed, manure and all other cultivation costs except labour, which it is the duty of the tenant to provide. Only one-eighth of the produce is given to the tenant while the rest is taken by the landlord. The straw is divided between the tenant and the landlord.

The total land revenue of the village is Rs. 9,230-12-0, but before resettlement it was only Rs. 8,227-0-0. Hence an increase of Rs. 1,003-12-0. The total revenue of the village for all items together is Rs. 10,575-9-1.

Class and sort of soil.	Taram.	Double or single crop.	Rate per acre.	Extent.
		Wet land.		
			RS. A. P.	ACS.
1. Worst black loam	11	2	5 0 0	215·80
2. Inferior black loam... ...	9	2	6 4 0	610·34
3. Inferior red loam	11	2	5 0 0	105·63
4. Ordinary red loam	11	1	4 0 0	30·90
		Dry land.		
1. Worst black loam	5	1	0 9 0	11·69
2. Inferior black loam... ...	4	1	0 13 0	3·45
3. Inferior red loam	5	1	0 9 0	86·4
4. Ordinary black loam ..	3	1	1 2 0	2,032·93
5. Ordinary red loam	...	...	...	...
6. Worst red loam	6	1	0 6 0	11·46
7. Worst red sand	7	1	0 4 0	4,000·98

There are a few sowcars and bankers. There are two cloth merchants who have each a shop where they sell goods brought from Tinnevelly. The village munsif and the karnam are agriculturists also. The former is the Secretary of the Co-operative Society. There are 12 families of oil-mongers, 50 families of betel-men, 3 of washermen, 3 of barbers, 30 families of shepherds and 2 families of kshatrias (ayurvedic physicians) who follow their respective callings but who also own lands and cultivate them.

Agriculture.

Area under principal crops—

Name of crops.	Average extent cultivated in the following years.			
	1902–03.	1905–06.	1908–09.	1915.
1. Paddy	907	1,068	837	1,163
2. Cholam	325	142	242	448
3. Kambu	1,227	932	892	762
4. Ragi...	358	290	425	70
5. Beans	...	...	...	...
6. Horsegram	149	217	327	}
7. Blackgram	80	84	86	} 257
8. Other pulses	144	34	44	}
9. Sugarcane	1	...	...	½
10. Gingelly	347	178	296	90
11. Castor	38	53	81	20
12. Fruit trees	...	2	6	25
13. Chillis	...	...	...	...
14. Other vegetables	17	19	25	...
15. Senna	Not available	..	...	125
16. Cotton	Do.	...	...	1,050

Customary crop cultivation—

	Time of cultivation.	
	First crop.	Second crop.
Paddy	... June to September ...	... October to February.
Senna	... April to September ...	... ...
Cholam	... (In wet) April to September	... (In dry) October to January.
Kambu	... " "	... " "
Ragi	... (Wet) May to August	... " October to December.
Cotton	... September to February	... ...
Pulses	... September to December	... ...
Sugarcane	... May to March ...	... ...

The ploughs used are only of the common country type. They are locally made. The people have not taken advantage of the foreign ploughs specially recommended for cotton cultivation by the Agricultural Department Farm at Koilpatti.

A plough with a pair of oxen will plough in a single day 40 cents in wet, 60 in dry land (after rain) and about 50 in garden land. Wet land is ploughed three times, dry land twice.

The wells are all worked with a kamalai and a pair of oxen. There are some wells which work with a double kamalai. Once an

A SPLENDID CROP OF RAGI.

Photo by Agricultural College.

oil engine was introduced by a rich landholder but now it is not used. It did not pay—probably for want of being kept in proper order.

Stock—

Working oxen	526
Cows	294
Male buffaloes	43
Cow „	190
Buffaloes under four years	111
Heifers „	214
Others „	80
Horses	3
Donkeys	11
Sheep	2,817
Goats	682
Pigs	about 60
Carts	107
Ploughs	263
Oil mills	4
Looms	11

There are some 20 deer and 10 stags in the reserved forest. A few hares also are often found there.

Ploughs, carts, bulls, etc., are usually hired for ploughing purposes and the rate of hire for a plough and pair of oxen and the services of the ploughman is from As. 6 a day to Rs. 1-4-0 in very scarce times. In October 1916 it was As. 12.

The cows and buffaloes are given rice straw both in the mornings and in the evenings when they are at home and are let out to graze in the poramboke in the interval. If they are in milking at the time, they are given ground cotton seed once a day at least, though some people give it twice. Sometimes cholam stalks are given for them as the main food, this is given once either in the morning or in the evening. Bullocks used for ploughing or drawing water are given straw and cotton seed. They are taken out in the morning for the fields and after some hours of work are given some cholam fodder. Before 3 p.m. they are taken back to the houses where they are treated to cotton seed and straw.

Manuring.—Nearly all the cattle dung available is used as manure except a very small percentage, perhaps about 10 per cent, which is used for cleaning the houses and for fuel.

For wet lands ten cart loads of cattle dung are applied to one acre, though for the pishanum crop five or six cart loads will do since the pishanam crop gets more green manure and sheep dung. For one acre of dry land only about four cart loads of cattle dung are applied. For garden land not less than twenty cart loads are required.

Cattle urine is utilized to some extent jointly with cattle dung. Much however is wasted, for the manure is collected and placed somewhere on the backyard but not covered. The farm of the Agricultural Department at Koilpatti has a good way of utilizing the urine without any waste since they protect it from the sun. Here such a thing is not done.

There is little of other kinds of animal manure except sheep dung. A large flock of sheep is kept for several nights in a field and all the dung is manure for the field.

The usual green manure applied to fields in this village is kulanjai and avarai leaves (wild plants). Green manure is grown to a very small extent, only in the dry lands. Almost all green manure is brought from neighbouring places and people get it in large quantities. In the wet lands one cereal crop is grown and for the other crop cholam is cultivated partly with a view to get the stalks for manure.

Chemical manures used—Nil.

There are three gardens where the following are grown chiefly, mangos, lime trees, plantains and other vegetables. The garden cultivation is not so profitable as one would imagine and an owner of a garden told me that he cultivates it more for the sake of getting the necessary vegetables at his pleasure than for the sake of profit, though he admitted that he might get a profit of about Rs. 75 or 100 per annum from 1½ acres. But for the sake of this small return, he himself and one of his two sons work at it for at least two hours a day. The produce is sometimes stolen, but then its value is recovered from the Maravar caste.

Insect pests and crop diseases.—A green insect called "Aruppampuchi" infests crops on wet lands, dry crops are infested by "Masuran" which eats away the stalks. Kambu and cotton suffer from the same pests as in Vadamalaipuram. Cholam stalks are attacked by two diseases known as "Pothimuzhungunoi" and "Karuppukittinoi," as well as by the Kuruthupuchi.

Prayers and offerings to the gods are the only means of combating these in use.

Cattle diseases—

(*a*) *Kainoi* and *Vainoi* make the tongues sore.

(*b*) *Tavalainoi* attacks the cattle by making it difficult for them to walk since the foot becomes long.

(*c*) *Adiyappan* is a kind of disease which suffocates the cattle.

(*d*) *Vethuppu* is a kind of disease whereby the body of the animal gets heated.

(*e*) *Kazhichal* is a kind of disease almost akin to attacks of cholera on men which kills the cattle in a few days after the attack.

Medicines are given for all these diseases. These diseases do not attack the cattle very often but come now and then. Neither for combating them nor for the pests which destroy the crops, is any sort of assistance got from the Government Veterinary department.

Fuel.—Fuel is obtained from the neighbouring forest. The cotton and the cholam stalks, the palm and dried cow-dung are also used as fuel. When trees are blown down they are put to auction. The villagers are given an opportunity to take for each person from the neighbouring forest so much fuel as can be borne by a single man without injuring the tree. But this is not taken advantage of except by a few.

A GOOD CROP OF CHOLAM.

Photo by Agricultural College.

Costs and profits of cultivation.—The following estimates were obtained from villagers, but their accuracy cannot be vouched for:—

Costs for cultivating an acre of wet land.

	RS.	A.	P.
10 cart loads of cattle dung	10	0	0
Sheep manure	4	0	0
Ploughing expenses	4	8	0
Seed	5	0	0
Green manure	6	0	0
Labour for harvest, weeding, etc. ...	5	0	0
	34	8	0

Estimated yield per acre, seven kotas* of paddy or Rs. 70, leaving a profit of Rs. 35–8–0, out of which the kist of about Rs. 6 must be paid.

Cost of cultivating one acre of dry land (Cholam).

	RS.	A.	P.
Cattle dung	3	8	0
Sheep dung	4	0	0
Ploughing expenses	7	8	0
Seed	1	8	0
Labour for harvesting, etc.	3	0	0
	20	0	0

The yield depends on the nature of the soil, on the amount of the year's rain, hence it is not definite. About nine kotas can be got, worth about Rs. 90. Deducting Rs. 20 for the cost of cultivation and Re. 1 for kist, there remains a profit of Rs. 69. But this is the return for a good year. The profit on dry land is greater than on wet if the rains are good. Taking an average of good and bad years in karisai (black) lands the ryot can expect from Rs. 50 to Rs. 70, whilst in red sand he can get only Rs. 10 to Rs. 20.

Cost for cultivating one acre of garden land.

	RS.
Two full-time labourers	144
Sheep manure	8
25 cart loads of cattle dung	25
	177

A pair of bullocks is also necessary. The yield is estimated at roughly from Rs. 150 to Rs. 250.

* [The inaccuracy which Mr. Lokanathan suspects is evidently to be found in this estimate of yield. It is stated above that the customary rent for such land is two-thirds of the crop, or if there be a fixed grain rent, 10 kotas for 1·68 acres, i.e., 6 kotas per acre. The average yield therefore can hardly be less than 9 kotas per acre (i.e., 2,520 lb.). This is a reasonable crop to expect from land of this sort, viz., well manured black loam wet land, yielding two crops per annum. This would leave a profit of Rs. 55–8–0 out of which the kist of Rs. 6 must be paid. Ed.]

In comparison with the above estimates I am able to give the actual cost incurred by a ryot in 1916 in cultivating 20 acres of senna—

	RS.	A.	P.
Rent	562	8	0
Seed	264	0	0
Cost of picking	175	0	0
Cost of ploughing	120	0	0
Rent for the house (rented for the purposes of drying the leaves)	40	0	0
	1,161	8	0

	RS.		RS.	A.	P.
Sales	1,500				
Estimated value of unsold senna ...	60	Net profit.	398	8	0
	1,560		1,560	0	0

Hence in rent and cultivator's profit the land yields a net return of Rs. 48 per acre.

In 1917 senna became unsaleable for want of freight. Here are the actual expenses incurred by a tenant who rented 8 kotas of land (13·44 acres) to grow senna—

	RS.
Rent	375
Cost of ploughing	70
Seed	35
Cost of watering the land, twice	10
Cost of weeding, twice	20
Cost of picking the flowers	15
Cost of picking the leaves	70
Rent for shed to dry the leaves	15
Minor expenses	10
	620

Crop, 20 candies of 375 lb. of leaves, and 7 candies of pods, worth respectively Rs. 1,600 and Rs. 200 at normal prices, Rs. 1,800 altogether. If the anticipated prices had been realized the cultivator would have made a profit of Rs. 1,170, or Rs. 87 per acre, after paying a rent a little over Rs. 28 per acre. Actually he has no immediate prospect (September 1917) of selling at all.

No great improvement of any sort (in agriculture) is visible. The poorer owners have not sufficient capital. The richer landlords are not inclined to adopt new methods of cultivation. They refuse to imitate the methods actually demonstrated to them by the Agricultural touring demonstrators for the better cultivation of cotton. They have neither secured the London ploughs called the "monsoon plough" nor have they resorted to seed selection of cotton. Much benefit would be derived by them if they at least adopted the system of the agricultural farm for preserving the cow-dung and keeping it out of the sun.

Cattle.—The villagers breed their own cattle but the number bred is not sufficient. So they purchase stock at the cattle fair at Shivalaperi, which is only about 6 miles from this place. The Mysore breed are the ones usually preferred. The price of a pair of oxen varies from Rs. 90 to Rs. 150. After they are bought they are made use of for a period varying from a year to some five or six years according as the oxen are strong or weak. Never do they allow them to get emaciated. As soon as the oxen are found to have outlived their usefulness they are sold though at a very low price.

When a person wishes to breed an ox, he allows the cow to give three-fourths of its milk to the calf. As the calf grows it is given plenty of green grass and also straw. At its fifth year it can be put before the cart.

The rearing of sheep and goats is the main occupation of the shepherds of the village and a large number are reared every year. Though the ewes are milked for medicinal purposes, nearly all the milk is left for the lambs and kids. The young ones are also given the tender leaves of certain trees such as the Ficus religiosa and the margosa.

The village.—The area of the village site is 116·38 acres. The Brahmans live in one street exclusively. On either side of the eastern part of the street live the Pillaimars, the Kshatrias, the pipers, etc. In all cases men of the same craft live in the same street. In Vadakoor, there live Maravars, potters, oilmongers, Pariyans, Chakkiliyans, etc., but they live in different portions of Vadakoor. Except in the Pungan paracheri, where only Pallans dwell, the depressed classes live in the same block along with castemen—only they live a little apart.

The dwellings of the depressed classes are fairly good and they are neat considering their state of literacy and general progress.

The houses are good; even among the Panchamas about 20 out of 220 are tiled; the rest are thatched. Of 520 houses belonging to the castemen about 150 are tiled. In the backyards of many houses are grown vegetables and herbs. Gardens are watered daily in the evening and morning. Such gardens are commonest in Brahman houses.

The maximum distance of cultivated lands from the home of the cultivator is nearly 3 miles. Many landowners have to go about from one corner of the village to the other, a distance of 2½ to 3 miles—because their lands are scattered so far apart.

There is plenty of space left unoccupied. Especially is this the case in the Brahman quarters.

For a house-site of 1,620 sq. ft. the value is Rs. 60 to Rs. 100.

The people sometimes exchange lands in order to make them continuous, but this depends on the condition that both desire an exchange. But they do not build field huts. The number of plots is 1,913. There are 600 plots under ½ acre.

	No. of plots.
Under ½ acre	about 600
From ½ to 1 acre	„ 550
„ 1 to 5 acres	„ 500
„ 5 to 10 „	„ 100
„ 10 to 20 „	„ 100

	No. of plots.
From 20 to 50 acres	about 5
„ 50 to 100 „	„ 5
„ 100 to 250 „	„ 4
„ 250 to 400 „	„ 2
Over 400	...

Here again the inclusion of dry lands accounts for a certain number of big plots of 50 acres and upwards. In wet land the plot is almost always under one acre.

Subsidiary industries.—There are now 20 looms and about 30 persons engaged in weaving. The condition of the weaving craft is not prosperous, though the weavers are better off now than 10 or 12 years back. The yarn used is cotton of very inferior quality, not more than 30 counts. Towels, blankets and female cloths are woven. The latter are used only by the lower classes. I saw samples of the towels and blankets and considering the quality of the yarn used, I must say that the weaving was good. The weavers get a daily wage of about 4 to 6 annas a day. They are exclusively employed in the weaving craft and females also work in it. The females work as agricultural labourers in the fields in the busy times of harvest, etc. There are no fly shuttles; all looms are of the primitive type.

Hand spinning was practised extensively throughout the village some 25 years ago. An old man of the village described to me in mourning tones how once upon a time the industry was thriving excellently well, how the females in every household would get up early in the morning and sit in small parties of five or six and go on spinning. It was the chief occupation of the females of the caste village. It has now disappeared altogether without any prospect of revival. No winding machines are used, and each weaver sets up his own loom.*

Other crafts are only the usual ones belonging to every village. There are six families of carpenters and they get a daily wage of 12 annas. They get employment almost throughout the year. The six families of blacksmiths are better off than the carpenters and all of them are landholders. They also get a wage of 12 annas a day. Their wages depend on the nature and number of implements made. The goldsmiths are paid on the quality of the ornaments they are asked to make and they get about Rs. 15 to 20 each per mensem. The daily wage of a mason is 12 annas; but they suffer from unemployment in the rainy seasons. The potters earn monthly about Rs. 10.

Village trade.—The ploughs and other agricultural implements are all made locally. The carts too are made here.

Seeds are obtained in the village itself except senna and cotton seeds which are got from Sattur or Koilpatti.

There is a fair at Kytar every Thursday. This place is only 7 miles to the north of Gangaikondan on a main road. Hence

* [In the "village" of Ayakudi (20,000 pop.) near Palni, I saw the Muhammadan handloom weavers setting up their looms in co-operation, in groups of twelve, and simple winding machines driven by hand, by which one boy could wind forty shuttles simultaneously with slight exertion. By these means, I was informed, the output of an average day's labour had been doubled, without any alteration in the loom.—Ed.]

TINNEVELLY CART TAKING COTTON TO MARKET—LOAD ABOUT 10 CWT.

Photo by Agricultural College.

transportation is very easy. All the necessary vegetables and some pulses too are got from the fair. For the rest, Tinnevelly supplies every necessary want. There are about half a dozen shops of which two sell cloth and the rest pulses and other things necessary for domestic consumption. Most of these items are brought from Tinnevelly town which is only 11 miles from the village. There is a Railway station only 2½ miles distant by road from the village. Another way shorter by half a mile than the metalled road cannot be used in the rainy season. There is a branch post office in the village.

Sale of village produce.

Name of the particular produce.	Quantity sold to other parts, about.	Where sold.	Ultimate destination.
Paddy	400 kotas	At the spot. Bought by the dealers.	Consumed in the district.
Cotton	200 candies ...	Partly at the spot and partly taken to Tuticorin.	To Tuticorin and abroad.
Cambu	Locally consumed.		
Senna	50 candies ...	Partly at the spot and partly taken to Tuticorin.	London and America.
Cholam	Locally consumed.		
Pulses	Do.		
Ragi	Do.		
Coriander seed ...	50 candies ...	Bought by the dealers at the spot.	Petti and neighbouring places.

The information given above is a rough estimate given to me by some of the villagers and I think it is fairly correct. The senna crop is bought by dealers before it is harvested. Sometimes the same thing is done with regard to the cotton crop also.

The villagers show little spirit of co-operation in the matter of trade. But there is no great necessity for them to combine for trading purposes for the very obvious reason that they have not much to sell outside the village. It is satisfactory to note that even the poor ryots keep the necessary seed to themselves and sell the rest of the produce. This is due to the comparatively low rate of interest prevailing here. Hence the ryots are not in the clutches of sowcars. Except in the case of senna and cotton, the price they receive for the produce they sell is not far less than the current price in large markets. In the case of senna and cotton the dealers get a large amount of profit and this entails a corresponding loss to the ryot.

There is a main road which begins at Palamcottah and it goes straightway as far as Madura and thence to Trichinopoly and Madras. It is called the Madras road. It cuts the main street of the village into two halves, the west street and the east street. There is a bridge very near the village on the river Chittar. There is also a Sub-Registrar's office, for the registration of births and deaths and bonds, mortgages and other legal documents.

Economic condition of village.—One chief peculiarity in this village is the utter displacement of wages in kind by wages in money. The old and time-honoured system by which the villagers used to pay every labourer and artisan in kind has totally disappeared. Even the barber and the washerman get their wages in hard cash. No perquisites are given except certain presents given to them on the Pongal day. The wages of blacksmith, the carpenter and the bricklayer are usually 12 annas a day. The barber gets 2 annas for a shave; half an anna for boys. The washerman is paid from 3 pies to 6 pies for every cloth washed. The estimated earnings of the barber and the washerman are Rs. 10 per mensem. The wages of agricultural labourers are 8, 4 and 3½ annas respectively for male, female and boy labour per day, in busy seasons. In slack seasons only about half these rates. The higher rates can be earned for the sowing season, which comes twice a year, about six weeks each time, and from 2 to 4 weeks twice a year during harvest, i.e., for about 18 weeks in the year in all.

We can estimate the annual wage of a man at about—

	RS.	A.	P.
18 weeks at Rs. 3-8-0	63	0	0
30 weeks at Rs. 1-12-0	52	8	0
4 weeks time lost			...

Total for a steady man Rs. 115-8-0 per annum, and for a family of five, man, wife, 3 children of whom one earns :—

	RS.	A.	P.
Man	115	8	0
Wife	38	8	0
Boy	38	8	0
	192	8	0

To earn this annual wage a man must be exceptionally fortunate in getting employment.

Current prices of staple foods:—

Paddy	Rs. 10 per kota (112 Madras measures).
Cotton	„ 175 per candy.
Ragi	„ 12 per kota.
Cholam	„ 10 „
Kambu	„ 10 „
Coriander seed ...	„ 10 „
Black gram	4½ measures per rupee.
Dholl gram	7 „
Horse gram	8 „
Mochai	6 „

Among the Brahmans very few only—not more than four—have been able to make any savings. Even this has been due not so much to agriculture as to banking. Among other castemen and Panchamas there are almost 10 families of Idayans (Shepherds), 2 of Maravans and 6 of Pallans who have saved quite a considerable sum. The Brahmans are not so prosperous as they once were because they spend largely on marriages and other ceremonies. Such is not the case with others. They can save something if they try their best. The savings of the higher classes are spent partly in jewellery and partly in loans to neighbours. But those of the lower classes are utilized in purchasing new lands, agricultural implements and stock. Neither class invests in savings banks.

Of padiyals there are none in the village. In former times many families of the depressed classes were bought as slaves by Brahmans, and even now the latter have a claim on the services of the former. Services must first be rendered to the master and then only to any other.

The extent of indebtedness is estimated by the villagers to be over a lakh of rupees. I went to the Sub-Registrar to see the actual number of registered documents and the amount of money involved in them. But he told me that since 1890 they had ceased issuing annual statements regarding these documents, and that therefore it would take over a fortnight for him to select from the vast file those concerning this village alone. Hence I was not able to make use of official information, but the estimate of over a lakh of rupees as the extent of indebtedness of this village was confirmed also by the Sub-Registrar.

The causes of indebtedness are many and they cannot be easily found out from registered bonds, because the most false reasons are given there. Brahmans are of all castes the most indebted, the cause being their marriage customs. With very little profit from agriculture, they have to meet all extraordinary expenditure in any year by borrowing. Moreover among the Brahmans there is no difference between the rich and the poor in the matter of diet. The poor spend almost as much as the rich on food, except ghee, which is very costly.

The other castemen and Pallans are in debt only for small sums and mostly for agricultural purposes. The rate of interest is not more than 12 per cent for sums above Rs. 50 and not very high either for very small sums. Hence these people are not so badly off as those of many other districts. Yet there are cases where a debtor not being able to liberate himself from his former debt, seeks for a new loan with even higher rate of interest.

Among the Brahmans, all are indebted to some amount, except three rich families.

The Co-operative Credit Society started on January 30th, 1912, has not been able to cope to even a small degree with the indebtedness of the village.

The society has 250 shares of Rs. 3 each of which only 105 shares have been taken up. No one member can own more than five shares. The society's borrowing power is limited to Rs. 5,000 and its lending power to Rs. 375 to any individual member. A member can borrow only at the rate of Rs. 75 per share. Not more than Rs. 20 can be lent for any ceremonial purpose.

The society lends under the following conditions :—

(*a*) If a member has deposits, 90 per cent of them may be withdrawn.

(*b*) On mortgage property.

(*c*) On personal security of one or two members at the rate of Rs. 75 only per share.

The difference in rate between the society's borrowing and lending is usually ¾ pie per rupee per month.* The reserve fund thus formed has in the course of the last three years amounted to

---

* [I.e., $4\frac{11}{16}$ per cent per annum.—Ed.]

Rs. 200 which is deposited with the Madras Central Urban Bank. The society borrows only from the Madras Central Urban Bank.

The secretary is given an honorarium of Rs. 15 per annum.

Herewith is appended a list showing the number, the amount of loans issued, the purpose of each loan, the time when it was repaid,—for the official year 1st July 1915 to 30th June 1916.

Time of issue.	Lent on what security.	Amount of the loan.	Purpose.	Whether default.
		RS.		
10 July 1915 ...	Personal security.	30	Agricultural use	Paid in time.
13 July 1915 ...	Do.	100	The borrower having contracted to do road repairs for the Local Board borrowed to meet his expenses. Refused to repay.	Default.
9 Aug. 1915 ...	Do.	75	Purchase of seed ...	Paid.
9 Aug. 1915 ...	Do.	75	Agricultural	Default.
30 Aug. 1915 ...	Do.	32	Do.	Paid.
30 Mar. 1916 ...	Do.	50	Marriage	Not yet due.
10 May 1916 ...	Do.	150	House building	Do.
10 June 1916 ...	Do.	26	For the purchase of bullocks.	Do.

The very long interval of inactivity between August 30 to March 30, a period of full seven months, during which borrowing from other sources continued, shows the extent of help which the society renders to its members. On the day I examined the society's accounts (18th October 1916) there was a cash balance of Rs. 150, but the secretary told me that he was going to send the full amount to Madras. He was not prepared to lend to any member.

There are absolutely no communal resources. On certain marriage and festive occasions, a certain sum is set apart for the temple. Further the sum presented on the same occasions to the Loka Guru "Sankaracharya Swamigal" of Sringeri mutt* is duly taken away by some of his servants who come once a year. The sums thus collected for this year are under the custody of a certain respectable person of the village till they are handed over to the authorities of the mutt. A "mutt" is a place where gurus live, something like a monastery.

The price of an acre of wet land ranges from Rs. 1,000 to Rs. 1,400. The price of an acre of good dry land ranges from Rs. 180 to Rs. 200. Fifteen years ago it was only about Rs. 600 for wet and Rs. 120 for an acre of dry land. Thirty years before it was not more than Rs. 100 for an acre of wet land. It is in the

* The thirty-fourth successor of the great Sankaracharya of the eighth century. He lives in Sringeri mutt at Mysore. He keeps up a huge establishment. He helps to maintain the Sanskrit College at Mysore, and gives great sums in charity. Before he dies he nominates his successor. The goddess Saradambal, to whom he makes offerings daily, appears to him in a dream and names the successor. He informs the Maharaja of Mysore, who sends for the successor, and the Sankaracharya imparts certain secrets to him. The Sankaracharya and his successor have to be carefully guarded against poisoning.

memory of many of the villagers that twenty-five years ago when people wanted to do a ceremony costing them Rs. 3, they used to sell one kota of paddy for Rs. 3.

A sum of Rs. 6,000 is spent every year in religious festivals, but this is borne entirely from the temple funds. There are two festivals in the year, one in October and the other in December. The temple is managed by a trustee who is advised by a committee.

No new temples have been built in recent years. There are already six temples of which the Kailasanathaswami kovil is the biggest and the richest. Next in importance comes the Perumal kovil.

Though some wells have been sunk taking advantage of the Agricultural Loans Act, on the whole the conditions and limitations under which the loans are placed at the disposal of ryots are so inconvenient that little use is made of them. The *takavi* loans made use to some extent in making improvements to land.

Sanitary condition of village.—The village is a very healthy one. The Tinnevelly district is one of the very healthy districts of the Presidency, but this village is one of the best in the district. Little disease of an infectious kind exists. Malaria is not prevalent. Cholera comes in occasionally once in eight or ten years. Only two years back, it made its appearance and fifty persons died, mostly of the depressed classes. Plague has fortunately not yet appeared, nor is tuberculosis prevalent.

Smallpox is one of the worst diseases that the district has to face and it comes in at intervals of five or six years. No really effective cure has been found for this disease. Vaccination is resorted to as a preventive, but some people are very sceptical about its value. Some fifteen to thirty persons die on account of its attack whenever it does come.

On an average one infant dies for every five born. This is due, I think, to the want of proper medical assistance during the time of delivery.

Snake-bites are few and far between.

Medical assistance is rendered to the village by native doctors of whom one Pillai, aged almost 85, is the most clever and efficient. There are also two others, a Brahman and a barber, who treat patients. Except for operations on sores and wounds, the medical aid that is at the villagers' command is fairly good. For delivery cases, assistance is sought for from Tinnevelly English doctors. It must, moreover, be understood that every old man and woman in the house is a fact doctor to some extent, and it is a pity that the people of this generation do not care to equip themselves with all that necessary medical knowledge which is so useful in daily life. In past times every mother knew what was best for the child, and what medicines to give and when. Unhappily nowadays young girls with absolutely no knowledge of either native cures or foreign medicines bear children.

The villagers are not of very sanitary habits. The streets are not as well swept and cleared as they ought to be. There are lanes and by-paths where nuisances are committed to a very great extent. Except for this, the village is fairly well off, since there is no drainage problem. Nor have they any difficulty with regard to the disposal of nightsoil, for the simple reason that men resort to the fields or the neighbouring plains and the pigs do the business of scavenging. Women retire in the backyards of the houses, but there too the pigs and buffaloes render uncalled for, though very useful, aid.

The houses of the Brahmans and those of the better castemen are fairly well kept, floors being washed with cowdung water which is considered by Indians to be the best thing for that purpose. Necessarily the Panchama houses are dirty. This is due to their poverty and to the want of proper education in sanitary principles. They wear very dirty cloths and they do not keep their bodies clean.

The Brahmans marry their girls before puberty. Ordinarily the marriageable age of Brahman girls is between 9 and 11. It is very rarely that girls are married after that age though marriages before 9 and 8 are common enough. Boys marry only after their sixteenth or eighteenth year.

In the case of all other castemen and Panchamas post-puberty marriages are the rule, pre-puberty marriages the exception. The girls marry usually from their fourteenth to eighteenth year. The marriageable age among young men is between 20 and 25.

Time was when Brahman boys of 10 and 11 were married to girls of 4 and 5. But happily such early marriages have disappeared from the village.

There is no purdah system. Women work as hard as men and they go about freely outside. The females of the Brahman and other richer castemen do exclusively household duties. Others, especially the Panchama women, work in the fields as agricultural labourers. The shepherd caste women prepare rice from paddy. Even Muhammadan women go outside and do the business of collecting fuel.

Well water is used for household purposes. The well water, though somewhat brackish, is good enough for all purposes other than drinking. For the latter, people use the river water. Three persons have pumps in their houses. The canal (Sirukulam kal) supplies water to the shepherd caste who live very near it.

The people bathe and wash their clothes in the river itself which, as is said above, is used for drinking purposes as well. Even cattle are cleaned in the river. However there is one saving clause here and that is the fact that it is a river and not a tank.

Education.—There are three primary schools in the village, of which the most important is the one managed by the Local Board. There seems to be a possibility of its being raised to a lower secondary school. The other two schools are managed by missions, one Catholic and the other Protestant. The Local Board school is located near the Brahman agraharam and there are no Panchamas studying there. Whether the Brahmans would object to the presence of Panchama children is a question which has not yet risen, because in the other two schools the Panchamas are almost the sole children studying.

The school accommodation is fairly good in the Local Board school and the building is a tiled one. The others are thatched but the accommodation is good. In the Local Board school all classes are seated on benches. English is taught from the third standard.

There are 70 boys in the Local Board school and about 35 in other schools. The number of girls that attend the schools is 35. The average duration of school life for boys is seven years from the 5th to the 12th year, and girls four years, from the 5th to 9th year.

A large percentage of Brahman *male* adults are able to read and write the vernacular; among others about 10 per cent. Among the Panchamas about four or five persons can read and write. About 20 persons can read, talk and write English. There are four persons in the village well versed in Sanskrit and there is one astrologer.

About half a dozen boys go every year to Tinnevelly to further prosecute their studies. But usually they discontinue before completing the school final course. There are only a few persons who have proceeded to more advanced schools elsewhere. One is an overseer at Nagarcoil in Travancore; another is a Nazir at Srivaikuntam. There is a graduate who is employed as an assistant in a High School. Another is a mechanical engineer who had training in Bombay for some years.

No one has gone to an Agricultural College.

No one who has received a good education has settled down in the village.

There is a library in the Local Board school in which are some 50 Tamil books for children, Tamil translations of the Ramayana and Mahabharata, and some maps of the district and the Presidency. Grantham and Sanskrit works are abundant, most of them being in palm leaves. There are also a few Telugu books.

Village administration.—There is no system of Panchayat for the general administration of the village. There is however a forest panchayat consisting of six members to whom is entrusted the task of managing the forest which was once a reserved forest. The committee pays the Government Rs. 300 per annum. This they realize out of the sums collected from the villagers for allowing their cattle to graze in the forest. On an average the committee realizes Rs. 500 a year, and allowing Rs. 150 for the establishment charges such as the pay of the watchmen they get a net profit of Rs. 50. By this the Government too is a gainer, for, without having any responsibility whatever, it realizes an annual income of Rs. 300.

The administration of the village is carried on by the village munsif and the karnam on behalf of the Government.

The streets are swept by the village scavenger who is given some lands at a quit-rent of five-eighths of the ordinary assessment. He is further paid a small sum by the temples at the times of religious festivals. He cleans the street on behalf of the temple.

There is a police station with five constables and one head constable. Till recently there was a Sub-Inspector of Police in charge of this station, but now it is merely an outpost of the station at Sivalapperi. Except very small thefts which are detected and punished at once, there occurs no crime whatever. The village is free from crime because, no doubt, of the presence of the police in the village.

There are however 15 or 20 suits filed every year, but all of them are civil suits and a sum of Rs. 2,000 to Rs. 3,000 is involved in the suits. There is unhappily a growing tendency among all borrowers to delay payment till the creditors go to court.

None are in debt because of litigation.

All disputes are decided by going to court. There is no co-operation among the villagers. Compromises are so difficult that ultimately people settle the dispute by appealing to the courts. The village munsif has some small jurisdiction in deciding certain disputes, but even there the people appeal against the village munsifs more often than not.

History and prospects of village.—There is no doubt that reviewing the economic condition and prospect of the village we find visible signs of retrogression. The old cottage industries which were the chief occupation of females and which contributed on no small measure to the material prosperity of the villagers have entirely disappeared. It cannot be said that the lands have shown signs of exhaustion; far from it. On the contrary if the villagers of this place take to better habits of cultivation and adopt some of the suggested measures of improvement demonstrated to them by the Agricultural farm at Koilpatti, the lands will pay them far better than now. The real cause for the poverty of the agriculturists lies elsewhere. Hand spinning which was a very big industry in this village some 25 years back has totally been abandoned.

There is already a large number of emigrants going out of the village in search of employment.

A few persons with English education have gone elsewhere and are employed in various capacities. There are some thirty Pallans and Maravars who have gone to Colombo and are working there on the tea plantations. Some of them have returned and they have made some small savings. Some six oilmongers have gone to Penang and after trading in oil there for some years have returned with a capital of about Rs. 1,000.

Family budgets.—(1) *Brahman, wife and two children.*—The account here is fairly correct because the gentleman keeps accounts.

Income.

	RS.	RS.
Paddy, 30 kotas	300	
Cholam, 7½ ,, ...	75	
Straw, fuel, palm trees	60	
Gingelly	15	
	450	
Less cost of seed, etc.	120	
		330
Interest on loans lent out	200	
Less interest on money borrowed	80	
		120
Total income ...		450

Expenditure.

	RS.	A.	P.
Paddy, 12 kotas *	120	0	0
Blackgram	5	0	0
Greengram, dholl and other pulses	5	0	0
Salt	5	0	0
Dried chillis	7	8	0
Tamarind	1	8	0
Assafoetida, coriander seed and spices	10	0	0
Gingelly-oil (24 measures)	18	0	0
Castor-oil	1	8	0
Coconut-oil	4	8	0
Minnai-oil	3	0	0
Ghee	18	0	0
Milk	24	0	0
Curd and buttermilk	12	0	0
Sugar...	11	8	0
Coffee beans	9	0	0
Vegetables	12	0	0
Fuel	25	0	0
Cloth (both himself and his boy)	9	0	0
Female cloths (three)	24	0	0
" for a girl	5	0	0
Barber	2	0	0
Washerman	2	0	0
Vessels, purchasing of new, repairing, etc. ...	20	0	0
Four birthday ceremonies	12	0	0
Special offering every month to the temple ...	11	0	0
Anniversaries (four)	22	0	0
Other important religious occasions	18	0	0
Fees for the education of his boy	24	0	0
House repair (whitewashing, etc.)	8	0	0
Beds	2	0	0
Female servant	12	0	0
Journey and travelling expenses in the year ...	25	0	0
Kist	45	0	0
Charity	12	0	0
Total ...	410	0	0

Saving, Rs. 40.

(2) *Pallan, a tenant owning no land, cultivating three acres of wet land.*—Family consisting of man, wife, two children (a boy of about 14 years old and a young boy).

Income.

	RS.
Four kotas of paddy, net return from his land ...	40
Income from his labour during the year	42
Wife's wages	25
Son's wages	10
The son gets also from his employer two meals per day.	...
	117

* [This works out at 6 lb. of raw rice per day, a large allowance for such a family.—Ed.]

Expenditure.

	RS.	A.	P
Ragi, cholam and paddy	42	0	0*
Salt	1	0	0
Tamarind	0	8	0
Dried chillis	1	0	0
Other items	2	0	0
Oil of all kinds	3	0	0
Cloths	8	0	0
House repair	2	0	0
Ceremonies	12	0	0
Implements	3	0	0
Drink (toddy)	20	0	0
Dipavali, Pongal festival and other occasions ...	10	0	0
Fish	5	0	0
Washerman and barber	2	0	0
Small luxuries such as travelling, etc.	2	0	0
Total ...	113	8	0

Saving, Rs. 3-8-0.

This second budget cannot claim as much accuracy as the first, but it is probably approximately correct.

* More food is consumed which does not come into the budget. The man and wife are not supposed to get their meals given them, but actually they do get some food where they work. [The sum indicated would not allow more than about 2½ lb. per day of the cheap cereals.—Ed.]

TANJORE DISTRICT.

PALAKKURICHI VILLAGE

(*By K. Soundara Rajalu, Christian College, Madras.*)

Preliminary.—Palakkurichi is in the Negapatam taluk, Tanjore district. It is watered by one of the branches of the river Koleroon, itself the largest channel of the river Cauvery. The river Kaduvayar runs about 3½ miles to the north of the village. There are neither hills nor forests in or around the village. The whole Tanjore delta, formed by the river Cauvery, and intersected by the numerous channels which distribute its waters for irrigation, forms a vast, level, fertile area, the site of a very ancient civilization.

Population. –The total population of the caste village is 421, of the paracheri 430.

The following is the number of families and individuals in each caste :—

Caste.	Section.	Families.	Individuals.
Brahmans ...	Smarthas	2 families ..	6 individuals.
	Aiyangars	3 ,, ...	11 ,,
	Total ...	5 ,, ...	17 ,,
Non-Brahmans.	Nayudus (Kammas *)	28 ,, ...	147 ,,
	Pillais (Saivites)	2 ,, ...	9 ,,
	Non-Saivite Sudras	17 ,, ...	83 ,,
	Dhoby	1 family ...	9 ,,
	Barber	1 ,, ...	7 ,,
	Goldsmith	1 ,, ..	8 ,,
	Carpenter	4 families ...	23 ,,
	Blacksmith	2 ,,	13 ,,
	Tree-climber	2 ,,	12 ,,
	Christians	1 family ...	4 ,,
	Muhammadans	2 families ...	12 ,,
	Drummer	1 family ..	6 ,,
	Chettiyars	2 families ...	12 ,,
	Cowherds	6 ,, ..	29 ,,
	Oilmonger	1 family ...	3 ,,
	Oddans	5 families ...	27 ,,
	Total ...	76 ,, ...	404 ,,
Pariahs ...	......	96 ,, ...	430 ,,
	Grand total ...	177 ,, .	851 ,,

* The Kammas are a class of Nayudus; they speak Telugu and are mostly to be found in the northern part of the Madras Presidency (Kistna, Guntūr and Gōdāvari districts), but they are also found in Tanjore, Coimbatore and Tinnevelly. They were originally a warrior caste, but now cultivators.

Lands.—The village lands have an area of 1,238·12 acres, of which 951·99 acres are wet land, 91·77 acres dry and 194·36 acres poramboke, which includes tanks, ponds, village-site, roads and common pasture. There are no lands watered by wells. There are no woods but about half a dozen coconut topes.

The village threshing floors are nineteen in number, and there are four fairly large sheep-folds.

There are two tanks about 12 feet deep, each about 2½ acres in area, which always contain water, besides an innumerable number of small ponds. There are no permanent wells in the village, but in summer the villagers dig temporary wells in their fields adjoining the village site for drinking purposes and for domestic use. There is no other source of water-supply.

Occupation of land and Agriculture.—There are 132 owners of land in the village, and all except five of them cultivate some at least of their own land. Of the remaining five one is a guru, one a temple priest, and the other three are widows. More than three-quarters of the cultivable land is cultivated by the owners. There are 19 cultivating tenants who own no land, and ten who own small holdings and also rent land.

Rent is invariably paid in kind, the rate varying according to fertility, facility of irrigation and convenience. The rent per acre for the best land is about 360 measures of paddy, worth about Rs. 40; the average rent for all land rented in the village is equal to about Rs. 30. The owner pays the kist. The total kist for the whole village is Rs. 4,903-11-0.* About half the land can yield two crops per annum but many cultivators are too indolent to grow two crops.

Stock.—The village possesses—

Working oxen	191
Cows	124
Male buffaloes	8
Cow do.	51
Horse	1
Donkeys and mules	...
Sheep	70
Goats	357
Pigs	...
Carts	29
Ploughs	91

The ploughs are all ordinary country ploughs.

Straw is given to bullocks, cows and buffaloes at all times and in all seasons; grass in the months of November, December, January and February. Bran and gram are used for feeding bullocks that draw carts, at the rate of two measures per day. Buffaloes are given bran and oil-cakes.

Manuring.—Very nearly 40 per cent of the manure used is cattle dung. Much of the cattle urine is wasted; but in the summer when there is no cultivation cattle are made to lie down in the fields. And recently people have come to understand the

* This works out at an average of Rs. 4-11-0 per acre of all cultivated lands, wet and dry, the fertile wet land paying a little more than Rs. 6 per acre.

UPROOTING PADDY SEEDLINGS FOR TRANSPLANTATION.

Photo by Agricultural College.

value of cattle urine and they have devised means to direct it to the dungpit or dunghill.

Green manure is obtained from trees, and avarai, wild castor and adatudai * are grown for green manure.

In addition, the silt deposited in the tanks, and dug out when they are dried up, is much valued as manure. There is also an old river course, now dry, passing through the village, and the silt from this is also used.

Plantains, lime trees and mango trees are grown in gardens besides many kinds of vegetables such as chillis, brinjals and drumsticks. In some gardens, flower shrubs and crotons are found.

For insect pests and plant diseases no remedy is possible or conceivable to the villagers; many look upon the havoc wrought as punishment from Heaven.

The chief animal diseases are *Adappan* (heart failure with a sign in the neck), *Santhadappan* (heart failure with a sign in the legs), *Vekkai* and *Kunnal* (cold and fever). All these diseases are very dangerous and fatal; antiquated remedies are applied, but nine out of ten animals attacked succumb to these diseases.

Wood is obtained for fuel and implements from the trees grown in the village. For building, in addition to the timber obtained in the neighbourhood, teak is purchased from Negapatam, which is less than eight miles distant.

Village.—In the caste village the different castes are located in different streets. The area of the village site is 41 acres, half an acre per homestead, and every house has a good-sized compound. Out of 81 houses, 39 are tiled, 1 terraced and 41 thatched.

The paracheris are built at a furlong distance from the caste village connected only by the small narrow earth banks which separate one plot of wet land from another. All the houses are thatched; they are exceedingly small and crooked. Recently rich individual landlords, in consequence of the trouble and expense of supplying their pariah padials with bamboos, palm leaves, etc., for the repair of thatched houses, are proposing to build tiled houses for them, something like barracks. In some neighbouring villages, which belong to very rich proprietors, they have already built tiled houses in the paracheri, and in this village one proprietor has made arrangements to do so.

Building sites fetch from Rs. 1,000 to Rs. 2,000 per acre.

The maximum distance of any plot of land from the home of the cultivator in the village is one mile. The intermixture of the holdings is a considerable inconvenience. One man reaps earlier than those who hold adjoining plots; he cannot graze his animals on the stubble till his neighbours have reaped. The conditions of water-supply also may compel a man to grow the same crop as his neighbours, when he would prefer to grow another. In consequence, the villagers have adopted a system of mutual exchange of lands called "Parivarthanai," by which plots of equal value are exchanged in such a way as to give the various owners as many

* [Tamil for "sheep-not-touching," a plant which sheep and goats will not touch, identified by Mr. P. F. Fyson with Adhatoda Vasica, Nees, the Justicia adhatoda of Linnæus. It is grown on tank bunds, and also used for fences. It has a very bitter taste. It must not be confused with *āḍuḍiannāpālai*, the "sheep-not-eating-plant." —Ed.]

contiguous plots as possible. But when this is done, the proprietor does not build a field hut.

Parivarthanai is a difficult process, because in order that the two proprietors may agree to exchange it is necessary to have equality in value, taking into consideration area, fertility, distance from the village, irrigation facilities, and other convenience. The rich proprietor will frequently refuse to exchange in such a way as to convenience a small neighbour: and the small proprietor is very much at the mercy of a rich man who holds adjoining land.

Padials.—There are about 120 padials, who are compelled to give personal service to proprietors in return for payments in kind. The usual daily wage for a padial is one Madras measure of paddy, worth (retail price) two annas. For a free labourer the daily wage is four annas or two Madras measures of paddy. In addition the padial is allowed about a quarter of an acre to cultivate for himself. In harvest he gets about 2½ measures for every kalam of 24 measures he reaps. Out of this, one measure is set apart and is given to him in the months of October, November and December. Women of padial families are paid a little more than half a measure of paddy per day. The status of padials is more or less like that of territorial serfs in England in the twelfth and thirteenth centuries. They are transferred with the land.

Village trade.—Rich people purchase articles of consumption in Negapatam; the poor in the weekly fairs in the neighbouring villages of Velanganni, Kottur and Kilayur, and retail shops in the village.

Negapatam is seven miles distant by a good road, Velanganni three and a half miles by an inferior one. The nearest railway station is Kivalur, eight miles away.

Paddy is the product of the village agriculture which is sent to market. About 8,000 kalams* is sent away annually. The selling price of land varies from about Rs. 150 to Rs. 1,000 per acre.

Sanitary condition of village.—The village is free from malaria and plague, but suffers sometimes from cholera and smallpox. About four infants under one year on the average die annually. Infant marriage is rare, and purdah is not observed, even by the Muhammadans. The quality of the water-supply is bad. In the winter the tank water is used for drinking and domestic use as well as for other purposes; in summer the poor have to rely on temporary wells. There are, however, some wells supplying very good water, and rich and well educated people use filtered water for drinking purposes. The chief insanitary practices to be noted are the disposal of nightsoil and sullage water on the land immediately surrounding the inhabited village, and sleeping in closed rooms without windows.

Education.—There is a school (unauthorized) in the village attended by 36 boys and 4 girls. There is only one teacher and he has no recognized qualifications. The rich send their children to school in the adjoining towns. In Negapatam there are two secondary schools; in Mannārgudi, 35 miles distant by rail, there are two high schools and a first grade college; in Tiruvālūr, 16 miles distant by rail, a high school.

* [215 tons, at present prices worth about Rs. 20,000.—Ed.]

Transplanting paddy, crop of sunn-hemp grown for green manure in back ground.

Photo by Agricultural College.

In the paracheri only two adults can read and write Tamil, but 98 per cent of the adults in the caste village can. Five per cent of the adults can read and write English, and two per cent can also talk it. Three Brahmans and one Nayudu rank as pandits. Four boys of the village are preparing for Matriculation in the University. One of the villagers subscribes for an English daily-newspaper, two others for Tamil newspapers and magazines. There is in the village a branch of the Theosophical Society which has a collection of about seventy religious books.

Village administration.—The head constable in Velanganni has the general supervision of the police administration, which is directly in the hands of a constable and two assistants, assisted by the village munsif and karnam, who are appointed by the Local Government and supervised by Taluk and District officers.

There is no officially recognized village council or panchayat. But in practice this old institution persists. The richest and most influential landowners in the village, including the munsif, constitute a non-official panchayat board, which practically settles all disputes arising among the villagers, manages communal affairs, administers communal income, supervises large undertakings, such as temples, roads, tanks, dams, etc. If disputes arise between two villages, the panchayats of both the villages confer and settle differences.

By way of common income, about Rs. 50 is obtained from fish in the tanks, about Rs. 10 from market and stallage dues, and about Rs. 10 from fines. By far the greater part of the communal expenditure is met by direct contributions. About Rs. 2,000 is annually spent on religious festivals, and in the last six years Rs. 8,000 has been spent in rebuilding temples.

History and prospects of the village.—Until lately the village was deteriorating in fertility. Evidence from tradition shows that the whole village was for generations in the hands of large landlords who did not take any interest in maintaining the full productivity of the soil, and who consequently did not manure adequately. Irrigation facilities were also lessened by limiting the water-supply to this village, and directing the surplus to water the lands in adjoining villages newly brought under proper cultivation. Both of these defects are now being remedied.

But in another direction the village has improved. Up to the seventies there were no cart roads; palanquins, asses, mules and boats were the means of communication. The village roads, though not yet in a thoroughly good order, have improved the mental, moral, social and economic conditions of the village, and enabled it to get the advantage of its proximity to the coast towns of Velanganni and Negapatam.

About ten years ago the four carpenters of the village combined in order to start the making of carts, which were previously purchased from a distance. They sell carts at Rs. 60 each, and earn about a rupee a day each, in a working day of about seven hours. They have not yet obtained a high reputation for workmanship.

Recently also two landowners have taken up cattle-breeding, and have collected herds of about a hundred cows each. They breed the best variety of Tanjore ox "jadi madu," or "kalai"; a medium sized, very active animal, with the following five characteristics (1) a white spot on the face, the size of the palm of a hand, (2) white tail, (3) white hoofs, (4) spotted body, (5) a big hump. They obtain from Rs. 150 to Rs. 300 for their best bulls. Other cattle are brought at the cattle fairs of the district.

Emigration.—Emigration to Indian cities seldom occurs, but emigration of padials or poor tenants or peasant proprietors to foreign cities, such as Colombo, Rangoon, Singapore and Penang, is common. As these people do not go there with any capital, they seldom make profits, and as many of them go there through emigration depots they return poorer and emaciated. But their account of their wanderings and experiences in such foreign places (which have a halo of romance about them) usually induces people to try their chance and thus causes a general unrest in the village and its neighbourhood. One boy of 20, of a respectable Nayudu family, emigrated out of love of adventure and dissatisfaction with his home, and has not been heard of since. Several young men have emigrated from the few Muhammadan families in the village and they send money home regularly.

The typical Nayudu.—The Nayudu caste is the most influential in the village and it is they who own most of the lands, and their individual holdings are fairly large. In a typical family, the oldest man is one of the non-official panchayats of the village. He is very influential among all classes, both high and low, rich and poor. His opinions are often much valued. He has one or more brothers (the joint family system being the recognized institution) and one or more sons, all living under the same roof. The old man is obeyed by all. His will (which will be always in deference to the wishes and will of his grown up juniors) is practically the law within the family. Women, mostly illiterate, are in complete obedience to men. Of course grandmothers are respected for their grey hairs and accumulated experience which is commonly astounding. The old man in the household is in most cases an easy-going gentleman having no work to do, but chatting away his time, or adjusting the communal matters of the village or busying himself with matters of litigation. Perhaps he is the accountant of the household. His juniors are as it were the stewards of the household, and the supervisors of the lands.

The typical family will have two or more male servants, one being the cart driver, and a female servant, or a boy, doing miscellaneous and domestic services. The family owns one or more bullock carts or carriages for the purpose of making journeys.

The headman of the family is the recipient of all honours and he attends the marriage of a respectable and influential person. For other marriages, the juniors are sent as a matter of course.

The family gets an income to the extent of Rs. 2,000. Of this Rs. 150 will be spent for ordinary festivals, Rs. 100 as donations to the poor, or to some communal undertakings such as temples, chatrams, etc.; Rs. 500 will be spent for food and clothing; another Rs. 300 as land revenue. The balance is the annual saving which is spent on jewellery, marriage expenses, etc., so that the landlord, or more properly the farmer, does not find himself rich. Hence the adage, "*Vuzhugiravan kanakkai parthal uzhakku kooda minjathu,*" "An agriculturist's accounts if seen, one ollock does not remain" (one ollock of paddy is about a quarter of a pound).

Green manure on paddy land.

Photo by Agricultural College.

The Nayudus are a very thrifty people, but for unnecessary litigation. They do not ordinarily launch their capital into doubtful enterprises. They are emphatically not a trading class. By custom and instinct they are agriculturists. They know of no other occupation or trade, and this is owing to their extreme conservatism and to the joint family system which has a strong hold on them.

These things kill the individual initiative and enterprise and sap the vitality of the community as a whole. They think and pride themselves upon the thought that agriculture is the noblest, the least harmful and the most independent of all professions. Education they do not want—at any rate higher education, for this higher education involves dependence, absence from the common hearth and consequent anxiety and care on the part of the elders.

This conservatism is their main strength as well as their main weakness. It serves as a strength in so far as it keeps them aloof from the ultra-materialistic tendencies of the cities and in so far as it prevents them from becoming bankrupt through doubtful enterprises. Their conservatism is their main weakness, inasmuch as it keeps them behind, notwithstanding the progressive movement of the times. Not only the Nayudu caste but village is in this backward condition.

The villagers are a simple, goodnatured, uninterfering and amiable people with no interest either in politics or sociology. To them their respective families are everything and the community or country nothing.

In these circumstances the feature of almost permanent ownership of land is not surprising. They do not ordinarily sell their land except for debts. But they buy lands wherever and whenever possible.

NORTH ARCOT DISTRICT.

DUSI.

[*By P. Krishnama Acharya, Christian College, Madras.*]

Preliminary.--The village of Dusi in the Cheyyar taluk, North Arcot district, is the headquarters of the Deputy Tahsildar, the Sub-Magistrate and the Police and Abkāri Sub-Inspectors of the taluk. It is what is termed a '*firka,*' a subdivision of a taluk, and it is shortly to become the centre of an office of the Sub-Registrar of Assurances.

The village occupies an area of nearly seven square miles. No forests are situated near it. It is situated on the southern bank of the river *Palar*. But the lands of the place are not directly irrigated by water from that river. It is about 30 miles from the sea-coast.

A hill about five miles long is situated on the western border of the village. This hill is attractive as forming the eastern bank of the *Dusi-Mamandur Lake,* which is considered the biggest in those parts, occupying an area of more than 25 square miles, and supplying 36 villages with water for irrigation. The irrigation arrangements are under the supervision of the Subdivisional Engineer of the place. In winter, when the lake is full, it is very picturesque, and the few Europeans stationed in the neighbourhood enjoy boating on it. There is a channel connecting the River Palar with it, whereby it is filled whenever there are floods in the river.

Without any great claim for excellence in regard to natural scenery, it can safely be said, that the village has a peculiar simplicity and charm of its own which is alike attractive and interesting.

Population.—The total population of the village is 1,266 individuals in 251 households. There are nearly half a dozen castes in the village, such as Vaishnavite Brahmins, Saivite Brahmans, Sudras or Vellalas, Padials or Goundans, the carpenter and other artisans, and Muhammadans.

Number of families in each caste—

Vaishnavite Brahmans ...	64	families.	
Smartha Brahmnas ...	2	„	
Vellalas	16	„	of whom one or two are landowners.
Padials ... ... about	150	„	
Artisans	5	„	
Muhammadans	11	„	

These are the main castes, though there are other subdivisions. On the average there are about six persons in each family.

There are 89 living children in the 66 Brahman families alone.

According to the statistics of last year there were 23 births and 11 deaths. As every one in the village is expected to register any birth and death in his house within three days of its occurrence, to the village munsif, under pain of punishment for default, and as the village is divided into two hostile factions (one street against another), and members of either faction are ready to inform against members of the other, it is probable that the official record is accurate.

There is no pariah village adjoining the caste village and attached to it.

Land.—There are 517·35 acres of wet land, 221·13 acres dry, 1,180·53 acres of common pasture and waste. There is no land watered by wells, and no woods and forests, but there are scattered over the village about 2,826 trees (fruit and shade). Of the fruit trees the most important are mango (300), pomegranates (42), coconut palms (576), plantains (142), and tamarinds (618) which is a most useful tree, supplying the sour fruit essential for cooking purposes. The rest are shade trees. Chief among them are margosa, aswatha and pursa. The coconut palms are mostly leased out for drawing toddy.

Water-supply.—Two tanks are situated in the western part of the village, and the water is used for drinking purposes. The tanks are small in area, each occupying an area of 1,500 square yards at the most. One bank of one of the tanks is situated a small antiquated temple of Hanuman, and on its other bank is situated the Police station of the place.

No wells are sunk for irrigation, but there are 40 wells adjoining houses for the purpose of supplying water for drinking.

There is a small lake or tank in the village, about a mile long and about 150 yards broad (its bund is about two miles long) for the exclusive use of the village. It is used for irrigation, bathing, etc. There are also two channels in the southern portion of the village. They are used for irrigation and drinking. The last and largest source of water-supply for the village is the *Mamandur Lake*, which has been mentioned before. In the hill adjoining the lake are several caverns, mandapams and temples, all ancient and each of them having an interesting and ancient history of its own. These are places of interest which have a deep meaning to the archæologist; and these places are held in sanctity by the people of the neighbouring villages. People within a radius of about ten or twelve miles go there on pilgrimage.

Occupation of land and Agriculture—Tenancies.—Three-fourths of the land is let by the landowners on the "varam" or share system. One-fourth is let on lease. Under "varam" the tenant does the work under the personal supervision of the landowner. The tenant has to sow the land and reap the harvest for the landlord and in return for his work throughout the year, he gets a certain proportion of the produce. There are three landowners of the place who do not reside in the village but are employed in other parts of the Presidency. The lands of these also are managed and cultivated by their relatives in the village, who pay the kist and the tenant out of the produce and hand over the remainder to the owner either in paddy or its money equivalent. Again there are others who, too indolent to look to the cultivation personally, entrust their land to tenants who have to put in at their own cost the manure, the plough and oxen and other requirements for the cultivation of the land, and pay the landlord a fixed and arranged portion of the produce.

This is what is called the "kuthakai" system. Here the tenant is free from the landlord's interference during the period for which the lease is taken. The lease is taken generally for one year and it may be renewed year after year. The landlord is at liberty to increase or reduce the amount of grain which he may claim at his tenant's hands when he renews the lease. But the increase or reduction must not be made during the term of the lease. The lease is annual and renewed from year to year.

The landlord is again at liberty to evict or change any tenant, and the tenant to leave the landlord at the end of the harvest season, in June, the Tamil month *Ani.* There is no account in the official records as to the area of land under each of the leases.

There are 57 landowners who let land on "varam," and about 410 acres of wet land are so cultivated.

There are about eight non-cultivating landowners, and they are employed variously. One is an Assistant Inspector of Salt and Abkāri Department, another is a District Munsif, some are employed as petty officials in Madras. These eight landowners hold about 100 acres of wet land, and lease it on the "kuthakai" system.

All the non-Brahman population, excepting six persons who belong to five different families, are tenants of the Brahman landlords of the place. They own no land in the village.

The dry lands are sometimes planted with groundnuts, but usually used for grazing only; being practically used as common pasture though owned by different persons. The cultivation of groundnuts was very profitable during the five or six years preceding the outbreak of the war, a large quantity being exported. But the trade having decreased owing to the war, the cultivation has almost entirely abandoned in this village.

The rents paid by the tenants are always in *kind.* Under the "varam" system, where the landlord supplies everything and the tenant supplies only labour, the tenant is entitled to one-sixth of the produce. Under the "kuthakai" system where the tenant supplies everything and cultivates the land at his own cost, the tenant will have to pay to the landowner 10 to 15 kalams* for every crop on every acre of land which he has taken on lease from the landlord. The amount of rent varies according to the fertility of the land.

The selling price of wet land varies from Rs. 1,500 to Rs. 2,500 per acre, the price depending on the fertility of the land, its accessibility from the village, and its proximity to the source of irrigation.

Land revenue—

		RS.	A.	P.
The land revenue for the dry land	... ...	260	10	0
" for the wet land	... ...	5,069	7	0

The land revenue for wet land ranges from Rs. 10 to Rs. 12 per acre,† this difference being due to the classification made by the

* [One local kalam = 12 local marakkals = 48 Madras measures = 120 lb. and at present wholesale prices is worth about 5 rupees. The non-working landowner therefore receives from Rs. 50 to Rs. 75 per acre in rent, or from five to seven times the kist.—Ed.]

† [Since the total revenue for 517·35 acres of wet land is Rs. 5,069-7-0, the average per acre must be just under Rs. 10. The average per acre for dry land is only Rs. 1-3-0 (1*s.* 7*d.*).—Ed.]

Settlement Department according to the fertility and accessibility of the land.

Of the two lakes which supply water for irrigation, the Mamandur lake supplies water for raising two crops every year with certainty. Therefore the assessment of the lands under the ayacut (irrigable area) of this tank is compounded, i.e., the assessment for first crop plus the assessment of the second, which is always half of the first, is totalled together and something is deducted from the total and the balance is fixed as the compounded assessment for two crops. In the case of the smaller tank which gives water only for one crop every year with certainty in normal years, only a single crop assessment is fixed, and half of that assessment will be levied for a second crop whenever it is raised but not otherwise. In the case of compounded lands, the Government foregoes a small portion from the total of the first and second crop assessment, whereas the ryot on the other hand undertakes a certain risk in paying the compounded assessment, as soon as the first crop is raised, whether the second crop is raised or not. The second crop might be lost either through want of water-supply or negligence of the tenant. In the case of single crop lands, single assessment is paid, and a second crop assessment only when a second crop is raised *with the water from the tank.* But the ryot is not compelled to pay for a second crop when he does not use the tank water. Nor is he compelled to raise a second crop even when there is water in the tank.

If the dry lands are cultivated with Government water, a separate water charge is levied. But if such irrigation causes diminution of water-supply to registered wet lands, the ryots are imposed a prohibitory assessment and at times are even prosecuted.

Cultivation.—All the wet lands are used for the cultivation of paddy. The dry lands are used either for cultivation of groundnuts and at times gingelly or sesamum, or as pasture.

Eighty-three acres yield one crop per annum; 435 acres yield two crops per annum, one being harvested in May and June and the other in December or January.

The old-fashioned Indian wooden plough drawn by two bullocks or buffaloes is used.

It is not customary to transplant paddy. The usual method is to sow the seed broadcast in well ploughed land. After some time the weeds, which grow along with the crop, are all plucked out. But in 1916 one enterprising villager read some of the suggestions of the Agricultural Department and tried to apply them to his own land. He replanted the young plants in another well-ploughed field. Each plant was planted a yard apart from its neighbours to give it space to take root and grow well. This, of course, leads to an economy in the amount of seed. He used only the chemical manure of Messrs. Parry & Co. The paddy grew about 5 feet tall, taller than the growth in the neighbouring fields. The sight of the field itself was interesting. It seemed one big dark mass. But after the harvest he complained that the produce of his fields was not in proportion to the labour and money he bestowed upon them. That method of cultivation was abandoned. If he has been successful others might have copied him.

I do not know wherein the defect lay, whether in the field or the suggestions or in his work itself.

Live-stock.—The village has—

260 oxen,	2 horses,
200 cows,	5 donkeys,
84 bull buffaloes,	98 sheep,
92 cow buffaloes,	64 goats, and
455 young of above species,	17 pigs.

The villagers both buy and breed. They rely mainly on the cattle they breed themselves; not many are bought. They buy the more valuable oxen for road work. The quality of the cattle is pretty good, but the animals are usually small and light. Oxen and buffaloes are fed with straw and powdered husks. Cows are fed with grass, oilcake and cotton seed. Donkeys are fed on the waste lands. Horses are fed with grass and gram; the sheep and goats feed upon the leaves of plants. The pigs live upon refuse; they are not particularly cared for; powdered husk is their favourite food. Each family engages a cow-boy to look after the cattle. He is paid a small wage.

The chief cattle diseases are—Rinderpest or Komari, and Bad Tongue or Navuri. Assistance is obtained from the veterinary surgeon resident at Vellore, the headquarters of the district.

Manuring.—About 10 per cent of the cattle dung is used for fuel, the rest for manure, and this constitutes 80 per cent of the manure used; the remainder being manure from other animals, particularly pig manure, silt from the lake, and green manure. Green manure is not grown, but leaves of plants are brought from neighbouring villages that have woods, and fetched in carts and used. Some landlords use the chemical manure sold by Messrs. Parry & Co.

There are two kinds of worms which destroy the paddy crop. They are the tail worm and Thalpuchi. These insects are killed by sprinkling lime-water over the crop as soon as there is a suspicion of the ravages of the insect.

Wood for building, making carts and implements, and fuel, is obtained from trees growing within the village. About four acres are planted with casuarina, a new departure of the last ten years. The wood is sold in Conjeeveram.

The village.—The village occupies an area of 28 acres 55 cents. Brahmans live in the western part of the village. This portion is called the "agraharam." The other castes live together and form a sort of semi-circle round the Brahman quarter, on its east, north and north-west sides.

Most of the village houses are thatched. There are 180 thatched houses, 64 tiled houses and 7 terraced.

Every house has a small garden attached to it, situated within the house compound and occupying the rearmost portion. The gardens are used for the cultivation of vegetable plants and small fruit trees. The chief plants cultivated are brinjals, pumpkins, drumsticks, beans, bandaikkai and chillis. The chief fruit trees are guava, pomegranate, plantain and coconut. These are in short the plants cultivated in the gardens adjoining houses.

It costs a man about Rs. 1,500 to build a house on a site 30 feet broad and 150 feet long, the house itself occupying about one-third of the area. This sum includes the cost of the site which might be valued at about Rs. 500.

The maximum distance of cultivated land from the home of the cultivator is two miles.

The tenants exchange lands in order to get their lands contiguous, if these lands belong to the same pattadar. Pattadars' lands are usually scattered, and they do not exchange for this purpose.

Subsidiary industries.—There is no industry at all in the village excepting agriculture and the minor crafts of the carpenter and the other smiths.

There are no weavers in the place. In some adjacent villages, the whole population carry on the weaving industry and they supply the neighbourhood with cloth. It should be noted that villages generally are not self-sufficing, but supplementary to one another. This is the case with the villages that constitute the Dusi-Mamandur Union. Dusi itself is mainly a Brahman village, and the Sudras who reside there are forced to devote their whole time to the cultivation of the land, and there is no industry within it.

The chief crafts are—(1) carpentry, (2) smithy, (3) washerman and (4) barber. The carpenter earns Rs. 5 a month, the smith about 8 annas a day, the washerman about Rs. 4 a month and the barber about Rs. 15 a month. The barber is also the piper of the village, and the native doctor, and heals wounds by means of herbs. The barber women are the midwives of the village.

"*Inam*" *lands.*—In the olden days instead of money payments, lands termed inam lands were assigned for services in the village like those of the smiths, the washerman, the barber, the village officials and menials and the village pandit. Each of these men had certain duties, that of the pandit being the recital of Vedas. The holders of these lands had to pay the Government only quit-rent, i.e., only about 3 annas in the rupee on the full revenue assessment on the land. To compensate for this loss in revenue, the Government raised a village cess of one anna in the rupee from every householder. The village officers like the monigar and karnam are now paid salaries by the Government and in consequence the cess is abolished and the inam lands have been resumed by the Government. The recital of the Vedas having now ceased those lands have also been resumed. For their services to Brahmans the craftsmen like the washerman and the barber are paid in money. The Sudras, on the other hand being very poor, do not pay the craftsmen in money, but the craftsmen go to their houses daily both morning and evening and collect from the Sudras morsels of food from every house. In return for this, the washing and shaving are done for the Sudras gratis. It might be noted here that the poverty of the Sudras, coupled with the fact that both the men and women have to go and work daily for their livelihood explains the custom of Sudras cooking only at night. In the morning they take what is left of the previous night's meal. But the fact that in most cases the Brahman landlords of the place give their tenants food almost daily goes a large way in minimising this difficulty. The Brahmans, in addition to the payment in money, give to the craftsmen a small portion of the produce during the harvest season. This free gift is thrown out to the craftsmen in order to serve as an inducement for them to remain in the village itself without migrating to another village in search of a better livelihood. At present all the 'Inam' lands have been resumed by Government, and the full assessment is levied on the lands.

In the two villages of Abdullapuram and Iyangulam, each about one mile distant from Dusi, the former being included in Dusi Union, the population is mainly engaged in weaving, the people being indeed hereditary weavers. Both men and women work at their handlooms from morning till evening. The poorer weavers go to Conjeeveram every evening with their daily turnout and sell to the traders there so as to use their earnings for next day's bread. Each weaver will on the average earn nearly twelve annas profit a day. Only handlooms are used, and it is noteworthy that the handloom industry is thriving well in these parts. Also in the village of Pillaipalaiyam, five miles from Dusi, about 2,000 families carry on this industry. Hand spinning is still practised, though machine-spun yarn is used to a large extent, bought from the Choolai Mill in Madras, and to some extent also from Bombay. With encouragement this industry might become more profitable and extend its production.

Village trade.—The chief commodities bought for agricultural purposes are (1) the chemical manure sold by Parry & Co., (2) rock salt, (3) pig-manure.

The inhabitants of the village have to purchase all articles necessary for food excepting rice and tamarind. The chief among these are:—salt, chillis, pepper, asafoetida and all kinds of pulse.

The chief produce sold by the villagers is paddy. They do not convey it to the market. Corn dealers from abroad come with bandies and gunny bags and pay for the paddy and then take it to the market to sell at a profit. Each landlord retains as much paddy as is necessary for his own consumption and sells the rest to the corn-dealers for money.

To the west of the village and a furlong from it runs the main road that connects Wandiwash and Conjeeveram, the two great commercial centres of this part. Wandiwash is 24 miles from this village and is connected with it by the splendid main road. Conjeeveram is about four miles from this village and has the same easy conveyance. Conjeeveram is the largest town of the Chingleput district. It is a great commercial centre, a revered place of pilgrimage attracting lakhs of devotees every year, and the largest railway station on the line connecting Arkonam and Chingleput. Thus this village has a great convenience in commercial dealings by being near Conjeeveram. Conjeeveram is the railway station for Dusi.

Economic condition of village.—The inhabitants of the village have an understanding as to the price of corn at every season, and no man will sell his corn at a lesser rate. The usual price is between Rs. 35 and Rs. 50 per bandy of 10 kalams or 120 marakkals.

Wages.—Servants of the household receive wages in kind. The cart-driver will receive about twelve marakkals* per month. The

* [Worth about Rs. 5.—Ed.]

cow-boy will be paid about four marakkals per month. But in the case of the other men such as the barber, it depends upon the will of the payer to pay the wage in money or in kind. The servant will have to take it. Anyway, the remuneration of the servants is but scanty, whether paid in money or in kind. The servants do not grumble, for they oftentimes obtain everything they want as a free gift from the landlords who are always very kind to their servants. When employed on business other than agriculture and by other persons a male servant will receive 6 annas daily, a female 2½ annas and a boy 2 annas.

Almost all the landlords have made savings. About 20 per cent of the savings is utilized as agricultural capital, about 10 per cent in savings banks, about 50 per cent on loans to neighbours, the rate of interest being about 12 per cent per annum on promissory notes, and about 5 per cent on jewellery.

Nearly all the landlords are rich and they are not indebted to anybody. They have lent money to the ryots, who in return promise to be their tenants under the usual conditions, till they are in a position to redeem themselves from their bondage.

There are about 280 *padials*, i.e., ryots. The ryots are not bound to perform any service to the creditors except that they have to pay the interest for the money borrowed at a rate ranging from 10 or 12 per cent either in kind or in cash. But in the case of servants, such as the cart-driver, etc., the servants enter into an agreement with their master when borrowing, to consider the debt as discharged after serving for a certain number of years or by a small periodical reduction from their monthly wages.

If the servant has a large family and his wages are too small to suffice for his livelihood, he has to borrow again from his landlord. And as the landlord is always a kind creditor, the servants prefer to borrow from the master rather than from a stranger. In most cases the servant is often excused by his master from paying the debt.

Only a very few, less than one-tenth of the landowners of the village can be called in any sense debtors. These have got into debt through gambling and vice, and are pretty sure never to liberate themselves.

Communal income and administration.—The *fish rent*, i.e., the rent paid by the contractor who purchases the right to fish in the lake for one year, is one of the sources of communal income. Another source is the price obtained from the herd who is allowed to feed his geese on the lands of the villagers after the harvest. These geese belong to a neighbouring village. Again there are groves, the produce of which is sold and the sum divided among the villagers.

The extent of the communal income for the village is Rs. 2,000 per annum.

A portion of the money is spent on the festivals during the year. A smaller portion is spent in digging canals which have silted up.

The money is received by the village monigar, or the most influential ryot of the place, and after the expenditures are met, any remainder will be equally distributed among the villagers.

The annual expenditure on festivals is about Rs. 200. During festival days, the villagers arrange for a series of dramas, the expenses of which are met from the communal income. There are numerous cheap festivals for the different deities during the year.

The cost of the festivals is partly met by raising subscriptions from every householder in the village. The costliest festival is the *Chaitra Pournami*, which falls in April. Thousands of devotees come here to worship Sri Devaraja, who is taken in procession here on that day all the way from Conjeeveram. The *Abhishekam* or *Tirumanjanam* * that is performed, that day, to him in Iyangulam is both sacred and grand. This festival costs the villagers about Rs. 200, and they consider the occasion worth spending even more.

There has been no expenditure in recent years on new temples.

Sanitary condition of village.—The general sanitary condition of the village is good; cases of persons suffering from malaria are few, ill-health itself is rare. Cholera visits the village perhaps once in five years and its victims are few in number. There are no cases of plague. There are about five cases of tuberculosis. Though many are attacked by smallpox it seldom happens that even one or two cases become fatal. About half a dozen infants die per year in their first years.

No case of snake-bite has proved fatal, at least during the past two years. But there are about a dozen cases of snake-bite every year.

All diseases are treated successfully by the native doctors with the help of herbs. The percentage of cures through such means excels the cure through even English medicines in every variety of treatment, whether surgical or medicinal. In the case of snake-bites, the person bitten is cured by the mere pronunciation of certain mantrams; it is not a superstition to be lightly spoken of, is the actual case. And all men are cured of their poisonous wounds generally by means of these mantrams, the pronunciation of which itself has some scientific effect.

Everyone, whether he is a Brahman or non-Brahman, especially the former, rises up early, goes inspecting the fields and bathes in the channel water at 6-30 or 7 a.m. Every man washes his own clothes, and so he always wears very clean though cheap clothes. The tenant of course has to work in the fields before he can bathe and so he is unable to follow the habit of an early bath. The roads are kept clean by the servants of the houses. The houses are all washed early in the morning. The only bad practice is that every man keeps a store of manure in the backyard of his house, but it is kept at a distance. Even the cow-sheds are always washed and kept clean, without any traces of dung or urine which are all deported to the store of manure. Straw is thrown down on the ground for cattle to eat. The straw which the cattle do not eat, and which is trampled on and fouled with dung and urine is removed in the morning.

Drinking-water is got from the channels. The channel water is free from any mud or dirt. It is healthy and sweet. The villagers also bathe in the same channel. But as the water is flowing, bathing and drinking the same water is not considered insanitary. Drinking-water is also taken from the small lake of the village. The water is good for drinking. For domestic purposes water is

* [The pouring of water, milk, oil and other liquid offerings over the image.—Ed.]

drawn from the wells which are situated in the backyard of most of the houses.

Some decades back, infant marriage was frequent and the father of the bride in return for some remuneration in the form of cash gave his daughter in marriage to anyone of his own caste. Now the people have become more advanced, and the girls are married after their tenth and before their twelfth year. The bridegroom gives jewels to the bride and the father of the bride often gives the bridegroom a small dowry, especially if the bridegroom is young and educated. In most cases the consent of the girl and boy also is taken. The marriage is performed at the cost of the bride's father.

Education.—There is only one school in the village, a small building situated at the end of the Brahman quarter of the village, capable of accommodating about 150 children of various castes studying up to the fourth standard. Arithmetic, kindergarten, nature study, vernacular and a little English are taught. It is a primary board rural school maintained by the villagers out of fees with the help of a small Government grant. The teaching is done by a master and his assistant who are matriculates and who have received training in the Government Training School, Saidapet. The master is paid Rs. 20 and his assistant Rs. 15 per month. It was at first a free school, but now a small fee is charged.

There are about 61 boys and 22 girls attending the school this year, aged from five to ten years.

In the Brahman quarter more than 60 per cent of the inhabitants both male and female read and write the vernacular. Among the non-Brahmans about 25 per cent of the males are able to read and write the vernacular. No non-Brahman female can read. About eight or nine individuals can read, write and speak English.

There is only one pandit in the village who is well versed in the Vedas and other Sanskrit books. There are about three persons who have taken the degree B.A., and are employed elsewhere. Twenty-four boys have proceeded to advanced schools elsewhere, but no girls.

The school expenses of those who have taken up higher education are necessarily paid by the parents of the students; and as I have expressed already, all the landowners are rich and can afford to send every one of their sons to receive higher education.

Of those who have passed through Secondary schools there are about half a dozen Government servants (District Munsif, Deputy Collector, Salt Inspector, etc.). Some are continuing their education. One is in the pass B.A. course and another in the Honours, about two are in the Intermediate. The rest have discontinued and are quietly reposing in their village homes. It is a credit to the village that one of its sons is the State pandit in Mysore and is considered a profound scholar of Sanskrit.

There are about 200 books in the village; all religious, either written in Sanskrit or Tamil. The villagers are all very orthodox.

Village administration.—There is no regular panchayat system in the village to settle disputes.

In the matter of the *collection of revenue,* the landlords pay their revenue or the Government kist to the karnam of the place. He is the village accountant. Above him stands the village monigar or the headman of the place who gives the account to the

Revenue officer. He also settles small disputes among the villagers. Over him again is his superior, the Revenue Inspector, who is also resident in the village and who is responsible to the Government to the correct collection of the Government kist.

As regards judicial administration there is the Sub-Magistrate of the village who settles all criminal disputes. The civil disputes are settled by the Deputy Collector of the district who frequently visits the place but whose headquarters is at a village a dozen miles from Dusi.

The *police* of the place again look after law-breakers and other men who disturb the peace of the village. These are also subject to the Sub-Magistrate of the place.

The sanitary convenience of the place and the keeping of good, clean and well lighted roads, are controlled by the "Union." The union is something like a small municipality. It comprises seven or eight neighbouring villages in addition to Dusi. The chairman is chosen by the Collector of the place from among a list of the influential inhabitants of the place submitted by the Sub-Magistrate. The members are elected by the inhabitants. The number of members is fixed. The union levies a small tax on all householders. With this money it meets the expenditure on sanitary and other conveniences for the people of the villages.

Irrigation is looked after by the Subdivisional officer of the place.

The people and the loacl authorities are always in touch with the higher authorities as they prove an appellate body over the decisions of the smaller authorities.

There have been few crimes committed in the village and the police have no hard task.

The disputes in the place are in many cases settled only in courts. The nearness of the court in the village induces every man to think that he has suffered much through his neighbour and to have recourse to law against him for imaginary offences.

Till recently the Sub-Magistrate's Court was held in the *chavadi* (the office of the village monigar) which is in the middle of the village; now a special building has been constructed at the western end of the village at a cost of Rs. 24,000, and the Sub-Magistrate's Court and the police station have been removed to it. A public choultry for travellers and officials on circuit is now being finished. Another important work which strikes the eye of the visitor is the beautiful gravelled road across the Palar which was constructed at the cost of a lakh of rupees.

APPROACH TO THETTUPALLI.

Photo by E. Krishnamurti.

CHITTOOR DISTRICT.

THETTUPALLI.

[*By E. Krishnamurthi, Christian College, Madras.*]

Preliminary.—Thettupalli, belonging to the Punganūr Zamindari in the Chittoor district, is situated in a valley, surrounded by some rocky, and some gently sloping hills on three sides within a radius of 1½ miles, and on the north by hills more distant. The hills are not cultivated. Some have grass, some scrub jungle, some thick forest, about ten miles away there is dense jungle with tigers. It is on the same level as the Mysore plateau, about 2,000 feet above sea-level.

The total population of the caste village is 149—men 43, women 43, children 63 (36 males, 27 females).

Castes 11.—Brahman, Komati (Vaisya), Kapu (cultivators), Balija (cultivators), Dhoby, Karamala (Blacksmith), Boya (cultivating low caste), Yekili (low caste Muhammadan), Kummara (Potter), Muhammadan, Dommara. The Dommaras are travelling pedlars who also cultivate and manufacture country carts.

Caste.		Brahman.	Komati.	Kapu.	Balija.	Dhoby.	Karamala.	Boyas.	Yekili.	Kummara.	Muhammadans.	Dommara.
Number of families		2	2	4	4	2	1	8	1	1	2	2
Individuals ...	Males.	1	2	6	4	4	1	13	1	2	3	4
	Females	2	1	4	7	4	3	11	2	2	2	4
	Children under 12.	3	5	8	6	9	1	12	4	3	7	4
	Total ...	6	8	18	17	17	5	36	7	7	12	12
Children living under 12 ...		3	5	8	6	9	1	12	4	3	7	4
Dead		...	...	2	6*	4	...	8	2	...	4	3

* All the six belong to one family. Seven were born, of whom 6 died and the remaining one is a baby 3 months old.

Castes.	Brahman.		Komati.		Kapu.		Balija.		Dhoby.		Karamala.		Boyas.		Yekili.		Kummara.		Muhammadan.		Dommara.		Total.		Grand total.
	M.	F.	M.	F.	M.	F.	M.	F.	M.	F.	M.	F.	M.	F.	M.	F.	M.	F.	M.	F.	M.	F.	M.	F.	
Under 1 …	…	…	…	…	…	…	…	2	…	…	…	…	1	…	…	…	…	…	…	1	1	…	2	3	5
1—5 …	2	…	2	…	1	1	1	2	2	1	…	1	3	2	…	…	…	1	…	1	…	1	11	10	21
5-10 …	…	…	1	…	3	…	…	…	3	1	…	…	…	2	…	…	…	1	1	…	…	1	8	5	13
10-15 …	…	…	…	1	3	…	1	…	…	1	…	1	1	1	1	…	…	1	…	…	…	…	6	5	11
15-20 …	…	…	…	1	2	…	…	1	…	1	…	…	…	3	…	…	…	…	1	1	…	…	3	7	10
20-25 …	…	…	…	…	…	…	…	1	1	1	…	1	3	4	…	…	1	…	2	…	…	1	7	8	15
25-30 …	…	1	…	…	1	…	…	1	…	…	1	…	…	…	…	…	…	1	1	…	…	1	3	4	7
30-35 …	…	…	…	1	…	2	1	…	1	1	2	…	3	1	2	…	…	…	1	…	2	…	12	5	17
35-40 …	…	…	…	…	…	…	1	…	…	…	…	…	1	…	…	…	…	…	1	…	1	…	4	…	4
40-45 …	…	…	…	…	2	1	…	…	…	1	…	…	…	1	1	1	…	…	…	1	…	…	3	5	8
45-50 …	1	…	…	…	1	1	…	…	1	…	…	…	2	3	1	…	1	…	…	…	…	…	7	4	11
50-55 …	…	…	1	…	1	…	1	1	…	…	…	1	1	1	…	…	…	…	…	…	…	…	4	3	7
55-60 …	…	1	1	…	…	…	1	1	…	…	…	…	1	…	…	1	…	1	1	…	…	2	4	6	10
60-65 …	…	…	…	…	…	…	…	1	1	1	…	…	2	…	1	…	…	…	1	…	…	1	5	3	8
65-70 …	…	…	…	…	…	…	…	…	…	…	…	…	…	…	…	…	…	…	…	…	1	…	1	…	1
70-75 …	…	…	…	…	…	…	…	…	…	…	…	…	1	…	…	…	…	…	…	…	…	…	1	…	1

M. = Male. F. = Female.

The population of the paracheri is—men 13, women 12, children 19; 44 in all in 30 homesteads.

—	Family No. I.	Family No. II.	Family No. III.	Family No. IV.	Family No. V.	Family No. VI.	Family No. VII.	Family No. VIII.
Men …	1 (age 60)	1 (age 45)	Age 2 {20, 16	1 (age 60)	1 (age 35)	1 (age 50)	Age 5 {55, 30, 27, 25, 20	1 (age 56).
Women …	1 (age 36)	1 (age 30)	3 {50, 16, 13	1 (age 50)	1 (age 20)	2 {35, 35	1 (age 12)	2 {40, 35
Children ..	6	2	…	2	…	3	…	6
Number dead.	…	3	…	…	1	…	…	…

Land.—There is jungle all round the village, where the cattle belonging to the village are allowed to graze on paying grazing fees to the zamindar.

There are five tanks. Out of these only two are of some size. The rest are small tanks. Even in the big tanks the water stored is sufficient for only one crop.

There are about 20 wells. Water is lifted up in most of them by means of the picottah. Four of the wells have been dug out of hard rock.

KABALAI AT WORK, THETTUPALLI VILLAGE.

Photo by E. Krishnamurti,

There are no other sources of water-supply. There are no streams or rivers belonging to the village. There is one at some distance, but its water is used to irrigate lands belonging to adjoining villages.

According to assessment—

Wet lands.			Dry lands.		
Rate per acre paid to zamindar.	Extent.	Revenue.	Rate per acre.	Extent.	Revenue.
RS. A. P.	ACRES.	RS. A. P.	RS. A. P.	ACRES.	RS. A. P.
8 14 3	4·89	44 3 9	2 1 9	11·11	23 7 2
7 12 6	1·57	12 8 2	1 10 9	4·65	7 11 1
7 6 6	0·86	6 6 6	1 7 3	2·91	4 3 11
6 10 9	1·11	7 7 2	1 3 7	13·95	17 6 7
5 8 11	8·35	48 12 4	1 0 0	3·41	3 7 7
4 7 2	58·60	266 6 1	...	...	...
				Total ...	442 0 4

Inams.

Dry lands.			Wet lands.		
Rate per acre.	Extent.	Revenue.	Rate per acre.	Extent.	Revenue.
RS. A. P.	ACRES.	RS. A. P.	RS. A. P.	ACRES.	RS. A. P.
2 3 1	1·06	2 3 3	10 15 0	3·46	39 5 10
1 10 3	15·52	20 9 4	8 12 0	5·69	61 5 8
1 6 9	7·90	11 3 8	7 10 6	4·54	34 15 2
1 3 2	3·58	4 4 11	5 7 6	0·85	6 5 0
				Total ...	180 4 10
				Other lands ...	442 0 4
	Grand total of revenue received by zamindar ...				622 5 2

Occupation of land.—A very small area, 62½ cents of dry land, and 31 cents of wet, belongs to the zamindar himself and is cultivated by a tenant. Such lands are called "kanagi." The rent is Rs. 1-5-2 for the dry land and Rs. 2-11-0 for the wet land.

There are eight ryots who hold land under the zamindar, of these six cultivate their holdings, and two, of whom one is the karnam of the village, let their land to sub-tenants who pay in shares of the produce.

There are thirteen sub-tenants who own no land.

In cultivating paddy, ragi, cholam, sazzulu, and other such grains, half of the produce generally goes to the cultivator, and the other half to the zamindari tenant who lets out his land, all the straw going to the cultivator only, who supplies himself with all the necessaries for cultivation.

But in some cases the zamindari tenant (the pattadar or inamdar) himself supplies one pair of bulls, and ploughs the land, while the cultivator simply helps him in his work. In that case only one-sixth of the produce is given to the cultivator. If the zamindari tenant supplies two pairs of bulls, one-eighth goes to the cultivator.

In the case of sugarcane, the cultivator gets 1½ shares and the zamindari tenant only one. If the sub-tenant cultivates on contract, the cultivator must give two maunds of jaggery for every 2½ cents of land planted with sugarcane.*

Of the agricultural families, all the males cultivate some land and also work for hire. There are two females, however, who do not cultivate, of whom one lives on charity and the other by working as a coolie.

Of the lands which are called "Sirkar" there is only one kind of ownership and holders of such land are called pattadars.

As regards lands designated "inam" lands there are slight differences. The inamdars pay, instead of the full rent, what are called quit-rents and road-cess.

There are five villagers who combine agriculture with other occupations. One is a blacksmith, the other a potter, the third prepares combs, and two others are dhobis. The sub-tenants mentioned above also do the work of coolies between harvest and sowing time.

Agriculture.—All dry lands yield only one crop per annum. Wet lands yield two crops. No land yields three crops.

For millets and pulses, the land is ploughed after a shower of rain when it is soft. Generally June or July is seed time. After a time when the plants sprout up the fields are weeded. After that four or five good showers of rain are needed. Then when the corn is ripe, it is cut and piled in bundles. The bundles are trod upon by bulls and the corn drops out.

For paddy the harvest time is November for the first crop, for which seed is sown in June or July; April and May for the second crop, for which seed is sown in December or January. When there is sufficient water the paddy fields are flooded with water and then ploughed till they become miry. Afterwards, green leaf manure (generally kanaga leaves) and animal manure are spread and well trodden in. Before planting paddy is steeped in cow-dung water in pots, which water is renewed every day. After four or five days the plants sprout up and then they are removed from the pots and placed in the prepared fields. After they are thus planted the fields are again flooded with water. But the water is allowed to remain for a day only. The next day it is let out and the fields are allowed to dry for three days when the plants are of some size. From that time onwards till the corn is ripe water is allowed to flow freely on the fields. When it is ripe it is harvested. Then it is cut, heaped in bundles, struck against a bed of rock when the grain falls out which is all collected and taken home.

Sugarcane.—The land is well ploughed, but unlike paddy is not made miry at first. Long trenches of comparatively little depth are made by means of the ploughshare. Then the field is well manured, and water is let in till it becomes miry. The sugarcane already cut in small pieces is planted in these trenches. No water is let in on that day. After an interval of three days water

* [This must be taken to mean, not the Railway or Bengal maund of 82⅓ lb., but a local maund of 26 lb. very nearly. The rent in jaggery is therefore nearly one ton per acre, worth about Rs. 150.—Ed.]

AGRICULTURAL IMPLEMENTS USED IN THETTUPALLI.

Photo by E. Krishnamurti.

is again let in once in three or four days. After a comparatively short space of time when the plants have grown, the heaps of earth separating the two rows of plants are made higher and broader. From that time onwards water is let in once in three or four days till the crop is full. After three months when the cane has grown, two or three stalks are bound together by means of its dried leaves. When the stalks are still higher once more they are tied together at the top. Then long rods with forked ends are planted in the ground and long bamboos are laid in a line with the trenches, resting in the forks and the canes are tied to them. In this way the binding goes on for about eight or nine months as the stalks grow longer and longer. When they are full they are cut and removed. The crop is carried about one year or a little more after the cultivator starts getting the land ready. The country wooden plough is used for all purposes, the other implements being yoke, picottah bucket made of leather and sometimes of iron, *yetham-bana,** *palikimanu*, *guntaka*, *gorru*, *palikiguntaka*, *mamoti*, reaping hook, shorthandled hoes.

Stock—

Working oxen	45	including paracheri.
Oxen not in a fit condition to work ...	65	
Male buffaloes	6	
Cow buffaloes	15	
Young stock of above species up to a year old	59	
Horses	...	
Donkeys and mules	4	
Sheep	47	
Goats	8	
Pigs	18	
Cows	85	

The cattle are of the well-known Punganur breed, rather light, but quick and active. The villagers breed cattle, and buy and sell in the cattle fair held annually in Punganur.

Manuring.—Most of the dung, about 90 per cent, is used as manure, the rest being utilized for household purposes.

Cattle urine is allowed to run to waste. The dung of goats, sheep, pigs, donkeys is used as manure.

Except the leaf of the kanaga tree, no green manure is used. This is obtained from topes planted many years ago. Sometimes it is taken on contract from the zamindar from the jungle all round.

There are practically no gardens, all the lands being used to grow grain. It is only now that beginnings are being made. Small plots of land are being planted with mango-grafts. The karnam of the village started this.

Insect-pests.—*Thellachida* affects generally paddy crop, eats away the leaves and stalks.

Pethachida affects all crops; consists of innumerable kinds of insects, eating away all the leaves.

Aggijadyam.—Paddy turns a vivid scarlet.

Kondapurirogam.—The worst pest affecting rice. The whole crop is consumed as by fire. The long stalks get shrivelled up to a ridiculously small length. To get a crop is impossible when once this sets in.

Locusts.—These destroy the crops.

* Vide p. 105.

The people think that these are all visitations of goddesses and accordingly offer a sheep, or pig, or a white hen or cock as a sacrifice.

Cattle diseases—Kurama.—The ox or cow when it suffers from this refuses food, shivers, suffers as from cold. *Domma*—Shivering, swelling of the stomach and purging. *Chalidomma*—Swelling starts at some portion of the body, extends to the neck and proves fatal. *Nalupu jadyam*—Purging and dying. *Gundasala*—The heart bursts in this. *Musara*—Ulceration all over and refusal of food.

Medicines are prepared out of omum, assafœtida, turmeric, pepper, onions and like articles and some medicinal herbs found in woods and forests.

Up till now no assistance has been given by the Agricultural department.

Fuel is obtained from the jungle near by. Wood for building and implements is obtained from the Avulapalle forest, a magnificent forest abounding in good game, belonging to the zamindari itself. The distance from here is about a dozen miles.

The village.—The depressed castes live in circular thatched huts. Everything is dirty inside and out. The dwelling is circular consisting of but one room which serves for all purposes. Generally the diameter of the house is about 22 feet.

There are thirty houses in the caste village; three are terraced, none tiled, one earthen-roofed, all the rest thatched.

The ryots occasionally exchange lands to get their lands continuous. Field huts are used only at harvest time.

Subsidiary industries.—There are no weavers at all now. Handspinning was once practised when cotton was raised locally, but abandoned about thirty-five years ago, because cotton is no longer raised.

Crafts.	Working time.	Earnings.	Remarks.
Blacksmith ...	About 75 per cent.	Rs. 40 or Rs. 50 per annum.	He does not work every month. It is at harvest times that he gets mamuls called *thiripamu* and *mera*. These amount to about three or four putties; 1 putti = 160 Madras measures [i.e., 400 lb.—Ed.]
Dommara ...	Almost always.	Rs. 15 or Rs. 20 per annum.	Makes wooden combs.
Potter	Do.	Rs. 70 or Rs. 80 per annum.	Not only sells to others, but also gets the same mamuls as the blacksmith from the ryots at harvest time.

Village trade.—Wood required for agricultural and industrial purposes is purchased in the forests belonging to the zamindari above mentioned. Iron implements are purchased in Punganur, or Chouldepalli.

The nearest market is Kandur, a village 3 miles off.

Whatever is grown in the village and required for household purposes is retained by the villagers. The rest is all sold.

There is a local road which passes by this village running from Somala to Kalikiri. This local road connects with the trunk road running from Punganur to Chandragiri. The nearest railway

Oil mill in Thettupalli.

Photo by E. Krishnamurti.

station is Kalikiri, at a distance of 10 miles. The nearest commercial centres are Kandur and Kalikiri, where grain, tamarind and jaggery are sold in large quantities.

Economic condition.—The customary rates of wages are—in money—men 3 annas per day; women 2 annas per day; in kind—three measures of paddy or ragi per day and a small quantity of food in the afternoon. The measure is half a Madras measure.*

Or a man may be given two annas and a meal.

Current prices—

Rice	8 local measures for a rupee
Ragi	10 " "
Sazzulu	10 " "
Cholam	9 " "
Tamarind	As. 2–6 per viss.*
Jaggery	As. 6 "
Chillies	As. 8 "

The village debt is estimated at Rs. 2,000.

There have been no good rains for the past three or four years and consequently there have been successive failures of crops. The ryot has therefore been obliged to borrow money for buying bulls, and grain, and to enable him to pay his rent. For these reasons there is much indebtedness in the village.†

There are only two families who have liberated themselves to a small extent from debt once incurred.

There is no Co-operative Credit Society.

Wet lands sell at Rs. 400 to Rs. 1,000 per acre, dry lands at Rs. 40 to Rs. 60. It is only recently that the prices have gone up. Formerly they were selling at a lower rate, the maximum rate being about Rs. 500 per acre. The rise in price is due to the fact that there are more ryots than land and demand is unsatisfied.

Expenditure on religious festivals.—At one annual festival, called Paleti Gangamma Jathara, about Rs. 60 or Rs. 70 are spent. Nothing has been spent on new temples in recent years and no advantage is taken of the Agricultural Loans Act.

Sanitary condition.—Neither malaria, cholera, plague nor small-pox are prevalent. For ordinary ailments people get themselves treated by two native doctors in Kandur, two others in Somala at a distance of 4 miles and one other there in the village itself. For more serious diseases people have recourse to the hospitals at Sodam at a distance of 12 miles, or at Vayalpad or Piler, at distances of about 20 miles.

Though there are two Muhammadan families they do not observe purdah.

Night-soil is not allowed to accumulate in the village, but the sullage water is allowed to sink into the ground in every house. In some houses there are cesspools where this collects, and pollutes the air around.

For drinking purposes water is got out of a well about half a furlong from the end of the village nearest to it. For other domestic purposes, only two houses, one Brahman and one Kapu, have wells in their backyards. All the others get water from the well above mentioned for all purposes. The water in the two wells mentioned is brackish.

---

* It follows that one local measure of paddy weighs about 1¼ lb.; of rice, ragi, sazzalu or cholam about 1¾ lb. A viss in Madras is a little over 3 lb.—Ed.

† In 1917 there were good rains—vide under Gownipalle, Festivals.

Education.—A day school has recently been started with 40 on the roll, 25 average attendance. Most of the pupils come from other villages. Three adults are able to read the vernacular. Eight can write their signatures. The karnam alone can read and write well. About five or six have learned to read and write but have lost the ability latterly. No one knows English.

There are about 50 or 60 books, all in Telugu. Of these about seven or eight relate to the Hindu Law and to village administration. The rest relate to the Puranas.

Village administration.—There is no panchayat.

There is a monigar and a karnam and two talaiyaris. The karnam keeps the accounts of the village, and the monigar is the village magistrate and collects the kist. The talaiyaris are the servants attached to the village. There is no sanitary administration.

The nearest Police station is situated at a distance of 12 miles in Sodam, which station was formerly at Kandur.

In recent years there has been practically no crime. About five years ago there was a murder, never detected.

For the present there is only one case belonging to this village pending judgment at the Sessions Court, Chittoor. This is about a land dispute.

Ordinarily disputes are settled here in the presence of the monigar, karnam, and some leading men of the village.

History and prospects.—There has been economic deterioration due to the scarcity of rains and the consequent failure of crops. The ryots have been impoverished and consequently obliged to get into the clutches of creditors.

For the present there does not seem to be scope for economic improvement. The tanks are all getting silted up. The bunds are getting decreased in height. Recently one bund burst. The persons concerned are very poor to bear the cost of repairs. But if the repairs are executed then there might be some improvement and the area of irrigated lands might be extended.

More wells could be sunk with advantage. They are not sunk owing to lack of funds with the ryots. People sell land owing to the fact that by doing so only they can support their families and themselves. Land is bought by well-to-do persons as a sort of investment and also because it is sometimes had at a price lower than its right worth.

In recent years there has been no emigration at all. But about ten years ago two persons of Yekili caste emigrated to Natal. They have not since returned. Their emigration was due to their failure to get a living here.

Such movements have generally no visible effect on the life of the village.

Another interesting point is that smelting ovens are seen all round the village in a state of ruin. It seems that formerly (about thirty or forty years ago) iron ore found all round the village was smelted here locally, and that this was sufficient for the local demand. But now no such practice exists. However iron is still found in the shape of filings in large or small quantities round about. Moreover this iron is held to be of good quality. More detailed information can be had from the North Arcot District Manual, wherein it is mentioned.

VILLAGE OF THETTUPALLI.

Photo by E. Krishnamurti.

MYSORE.

GOWNIPALLE.

[*By E. Krishnamurti, Christian College, Madras.*]

Preliminary.—Gownipalle, Srinivaspur taluk, Kolar district, Mysore, is situated in a low marshy district.

It has no forests or even jungle—only thick under-growth. No big rivers—only a stream about a furlong from the outskirts of the village. No hills near by. But about nine miles off there is a very big hill clothed with forest and abounding in good game.

Population.—Total population of caste village 417—men 119, women 133, boys 77, girls 88; homesteads 116.

Castes.—Brahman, Komati (traders), Dhobis, Kammala (black-smith), Bōya and Yekili (agricultural labourers), Kummara (potters), Muhammadan, Barber, Besta (labourers), Edigi-Gandla (oil-mongers), Sāthāni (non-Brahman temple servants).

Number of families and individuals in each caste—

Caste.	Brahmans.	Komati.	Dhobi.	Bōya.	Yekili.	Kummara.	Barbers.	Besta.	Kammara.	Edigi-Gandla.	Sāthani.	Muhammadans.
Number of families.	11	...	..	14	1	1	5	6	1	1	2	30
Males ..	16	6	6	10	...	1	8	6	1	1	2	44
Females ...	24	10	6	13	1	2	7	6	1	3	...	45
Children. Boys ...	13	6	2	9	..	3	3	8	1	3	1	23
Children. Girls ...	15	7	4	8	...	1	4	7	2	2	3	25
Total ...	68	29	18	40	1	7	22	27	5	9	6	137

Paracheri—Population.—Total 126—men 41, women 40, boys 20, girls 25. Number of families 31.

Statistics of births and deaths—

Year.	Population.				Total.	Births.	Deaths.				Total.
									Children.		
	Men.	Women.	Boys.	Girls.			Adult males.	Adult females.	Males.	Females.	
1912	212	210	125	122	669	22	2	5	4	...	11
1913	192	201	111	120	624	24	25	13	6	6	50
1914	180	193	107	106	586	14	10	6	3	3	22
1915	160	174	97	113	544	26	2	2	4	1	9

Land—

	ACS.
Wet land	141·30
Dry land	304·29
Land watered by wells	52·19
Common waste	451·35
Pastures other than waste	898·14
Woods and forests	

There are two tanks, *Kodipalli cheruvu* and *Varadarajulu kunta.* The first is sufficiently deep though not extensive, and the water stored in the tank is sufficient for two crops. The surplus water is allowed to collect in another small pond. There are fourteen wells, all built round with stone; and one stream when in flood affords an additional water-supply.

Classification of lands—According to assessment—

Wet lands.		Dry lands.	
Rates.	Acres.	Rates.	Acres.
Rs. 4-0-0	18·38	Re. 1	304·29
Rs. 5, Rs. 5-8-0	32·38	......	...
Rs. 6-0-0	21·24	......	...
Rs. 7-0-0	20·35	......	...
Rs. 8-0-0	7·37	......	...
Rs. 9-0-0	1·10	......	...

Occupation of land.—Of the dry land 109·02 acres, of the wet land 31·50 acres are cultivated by the landowners, the remainder, viz., 32·28 acres of wet land, and 272·79 acres of dry land are sublet and cultivated by tenants.

There are about 25 non-cultivating landowners. Some hold Government posts, about 12 are engaged in trade; there are between 30 and 40 tenants who own no land, and the agricultural workers who neither own nor rent land number men 113, women 47.

There are two kinds of ownership, inam and patta. All sirkar lands are held by pattadars. The area of holdings of inam ownership is 127·38 acres. The rest of the cultivable land is held by pattadars. Inamdars pay only quit-rent and road-cess.

There are only about half a dozen pattadars. One family alone owns 97·15 acres of wet and 143·14 acres of dry land.

Rents.—There are no cultivators who pay a money rent. Everything is paid in kind. The usual arrangement is that the cultivator himself supplies all that is necessary for cultivation, and out of the produce one-half goes to the landowner and the other to the cultivator. There are no other conditions of contract. But when sugarcane is cultivated the landowner gets only one-fourth of the produce.

The whole land revenue comes to Rs. 1,034-7-0, out of which the revenue from the inam lands alone amounts to Rs. 154-3-0.

Some of the villagers are engaged in trade side by side with agriculture. Others are potters, dhobis, in addition to being cultivators. Some hold Government posts. Some are contractors.

Agriculture.—Area under each of the principal crops :—

	ACRES.		ACRES.
Paddy	123·17	Ragi	171·9
Sugarcane	4·21	Cholam (for cattle) ...	4·27
Coconut topes ...	2·11	Sazzulu	0·27
Other fruit trees and scattered shade trees	11·21	Chamulu	6·36
		Gram	8·30
		Dholl	6·31
Betel gardens ...	1·4	Groundnut	12·15
Plantain	4·22	Castor seeds	2·4
Mango	1·0	Other crops	18·10

Out of the dry land, nearly 250 acres yield only one crop per annum, about 60 acres two crops. Almost all of the wet land yields two crops. There is no land yielding three crops per annum.

The methods of cultivation are the same as in Thettupalli in the Chittoor district of the Madras Presidency.

Implements.—In one house only an iron plough * is used. The rest use the country plough made of wood.

Other agricultural implements used are yoke, picottah, *yethambana*, hoe, *guntaka, donthi, pandluminu, gorru, palikiguntaka, mamoti*, scythe and other minor implements.

The *gorru* is a seed-drill, with a bowl to put the seed in, and bamboo tubes to distribute it. The *guntaka* is a six-bladed harrow, the *palikiguntaka* a twelve-bladed harrow. The *donthi* is a log of wood with twenty wooden teeth, each 5 inches long and half an inch thick, with a curved contrivance at the end of the handle which the driver holds against his stomach. It is used for powdering the soil. The *pandluminu* is a variety of the same.

Stock—

Oxen	144	
Cows	111	
Male-buffaloes	...	
Cow-buffaloes	5	(These do not thrive well here).
Young stock of above species.	103	
Horses	4	
Donkeys	15	
Mules	...	
Sheep	27	
Goats	14	
Pigs	4	

In the mornings cows are fed with grass, gram well pounded with the addition of water and rice bran. Then they are let out to graze in the fields. In the evening they receive the same as in the morning and oil-cake. They are also fed with rice straw and ragi straw. Sometimes cholam also is used and its stalks.

Bulls receive almost the same as cows, but are given less of green grass. Gram is fried and made into flour and then used; also Bengal gram and oil cake.

[* The Mysore State Department of Agriculture manufactures and sells cheap and handy iron ploughs. The general use of these would be of immense advantage on dry land.—Ed.]

Horses are fed on grass and gram chiefly, sometimes also on oats and bran.

Manuring.—Nearly 90 per cent of the cow-dung is used as manure, the rest being used for household purposes.

Almost all the cattle urine is allowed to run to waste except trifling quantities used for household purposes.

The green manure chiefly used is the leaf of the Kanaga tree. Generally all kinds of green leaf are held to be good manure. This is obtained chiefly from the surrounding jungle, licences being obtained on payment of a fee to the Maharaja's Government. Sometimes topes are planted for the purpose.

No other kinds of vegetable manure are largely used. In some cases, for instance in the cultivation of sugarcane, the refuse left after the oil has been squeezed out from the fruit of the Kanaga tree is used.

Insect-pests and cattle diseases and the method of combating them are the same as in Thettupalli.

The village.—The village occupies an area of 9·36 acres. The tendency is for the members of one caste to congregate together. For example all the Muhammadans live in one part of the village together. The Komatis live exclusively in one street.

The depressed classes live in dirty and squalid huts of but one room.

There are in the caste village 85 thatched houses, none tiled, 63 terraced; in the Paracheri, only thatched houses 31 in number. There are no gardens adjoining any of the dwellings. The fields lie adjoining and surrounding the village. The most distant field lies about three-quarters of a mile off.

There is a great demand for additional building sites.

If land is obtained direct from the Government a fee of ½ anna per square yard is charged, payable on sale. If dry land is acquired for the purpose from pattadars, the value ranges from Rs. 100 to Rs. 150 per acre. It is only near this village that the value is so low. Further up the value goes up to nearly Rs. 300 or Rs. 350.

Subsidiary industries.—There are only two pariahs who weave at all. They use two handlooms.

No hand spinning is practised. Yarn is bought ready made. The other crafts are—

Crafts.	Average time.	Earnings per year.	Remarks.
Blacksmith.	The major part of the day.	About Rs. 300 a year.	He receives customary mamūls. At harvest time gets about 10 puttis of paddy. There are also inams in his name.
Potter ...	The major part of the day and almost throughout the year.	About Rs. 100 a year.	Do.
Carpenter ...	For the major part of the year.	About Rs. 150 a year.	No mamūls.

Village trade—Purchase of commodities by the village.—Wood for implements is got from the forests already mentioned. Iron implements are bought chiefly in Chintamani, about 18 miles off, and also at Srinivasapur, about 14 miles off.

Articles of consumption are bought at the weekly fair held here on Tuesdays, also in Chintamani, Kothakota and some other places.

Sale of village produce.—The quantities produced here are: paddy 500 puttis,* ragi 200, † sugarcane to the value of about Rs. 1,500, other millets and pulses to the value of about Rs. 1,000.

Out of this whatever is required for household purposes is retained. The rest, more than 50 per cent, is sold away. The nearest market is Chintamani. Sometimes the grain is transported to Bangalore also.

There are about three local roads, one from Gownipalle to Addegal, a village 4 miles off, one from the village to Manchinillakota, a village 6 miles off, and the other up to Todigol, 6 miles off. Another short road running for three miles runs up to the Mysore frontier. On the other side is British territory and there is no road further up. The local road to Tadigol connects with the Bangalore-Cuddapah road. The nearest commercial centres are Chintamani and Bangalore, accessible by the said road. The nearest railway station is Srinivasapur, about 14 miles off, reached by road.

The fair that takes place here every week is a big affair. People from very different parts come here. The fair is nominally held on Tuesday, but it generally extends from Monday to Wednesday. The chief business is carried on in stock, especially sheep and goats. Business in these is carried on to the extent of Rs. 4,000. They are chiefly sent to the Kolar Goldfields for slaughter and consumption.

Economic condition of village.—The customary rates of wages, in money, are from 2 to 3 annas per day, for a man; and 1½ annas for a woman; in kind, 2 seers of ragi, or 3 seers of paddy to a man, 1½ seers of ragi or 2 seers of paddy to a woman.

The current prices of staple foods are—

Rice	8 Mysore seers for a rupee.
Ragi	28 " "
Sazzulu	20 " "
Cholam	14 " "
Tamarind	Re. 1 for a maund.
Jaggery	Rs. 2 "
Chillis	Rs. 4-8-0 "
Dholl	8 seers for a rupee.

About four or five families have made savings to the extent of Rs. 5,000, but on the other hand others have contracted debts to the extent of Rs. 10,000. Owing to scarcity of rains and failure of crops the people have been obliged to borrow heavily to meet current and occasional expenses.

There are practically no families who have liberated themselves from debt. While paying off old scores they borrow in new places.

There is a co-operative credit society. The capital is subscribed in shares of Rs. 10 each payable in twenty monthly instalments.

* [Weight about 89 tons, value about Rs. 10,000.—Ed.]
† [Weight about 48 tons, value about Rs. 4,000.—Ed.]

Money is lent at about 9½ per cent interest per annum. The registered capital is a little over a thousand rupees. There are forty-six members. There is a Secretary, a President, and a Treasurer, all honorary posts.

Dry land sells at from Rs. 100 to Rs. 150 per acre; wet land from Rs. 400 to Rs. 800. There has been a rise in prices owing to the increased demands for land and insufficient supply.

Under the Mysore Agricultural Loans Act loans nearly to the extent of Rs. 1,200 have been taken up at 4 per cent interest per annum from the Mysore Government.

Festivals.—A great festival is held at irregular intervals in honour of the goddess Gangamma, the tutelary goddess of the village and its fields and crops. There was a celebration in 1911, and another, prompted by a succession of bad seasons, in 1917. This last was celebrated from the 22nd to the 29th of April. The inhabitants of sixteen villages took part, every family making some contribution, and some 10,000 people congregated in Gownipalli. An image of the goddess is made of rice-flour, copying the silver image in Punganur. It shows only the neck and head, wearing a lofty head-dress. Before this image some 2,000 victims are sacrificed. The first sacrifice is that of a male buffalo; this takes place at midnight, and is followed by that of two or three goats. In the following morning 21 buffaloes are sacrificed. Throughout the festival there is great rejoicing and weird dancing at night, with *kolattam,* short sticks held in the hands and beaten together. Finally the goddess is carried in procession, with drums and cymbals, to the water and thrown in, and there she dissolves. This year there have been good crops and all the tanks are full. The animals sacrificed, in addition to male buffaloes and goats, are rams and cocks. The Brahmans take no part in this festival. The village officers make money out of it, the patel may get Rs. 30 or Rs. 40.

Sanitary condition.—Malaria is always prevalent. The water for drinking purposes is bad and the village is situated in a low marshy place. Two years ago the village suffered from cholera. There were about fifty deaths. It is free from plague. This year (1916) there was an attack of small-pox, with some deaths. In disease people get themselves treated by native doctors. The nearest hospital is at Srinivaspur, but no advantage is taken of it, as they regard it as most unsatisfactory.

All kinds of filth and dirt are allowed to accumulate in the courtyards of the houses. Cattle are housed there only and people sleep near these places. This is to a great extent minimized among the Brahmans.

No infant marriages are allowed in Mysore. The bride must be at least eight years old and the bridegroom sixteen years.

All Muhammadans observe purdah.

Water for drinking purposes is found in abundance. All the Brahmans drink water got out of wells in their backyards. Others drink out of a well about half a furlong from the village and out of the stream aforesaid. Almost all the water is fresh. But it has a tendency to bring on malaria.

Education.—There is one school, but the accommodation is insufficient. The classes, about seven in number, are held in two

SUGAR-CANE CRUSHING.

Photo by Agricultural College.

rooms. The school buildings have been erected at the cost of the villagers. Efforts are being made to provide more accommodation. The school trains pupils for the Kanarese Lower Secondary Examination and instruction is given in Kanarese. Now efforts are being made to open classes in English and also to open a school exclusively for girls. There are about fifty boys in attendance and about fifty girls. School is held from 6-30 to 10-30 in the morning and from 2 to 6 in the evening. No time is allowed for play at all. Instruction is in Kanarese, although the language the people speak is Telugu.

The number of persons who know how to read the vernacular is 131; fifteen or sixteen can read and write English.

There are about thirty or forty books almost all in Sanskrit and Kanarese.

A night school has recently been opened. It has twenty on the rolls, mostly adults. Average attendance five.

Village administration.—There is a panchayat composed of five members. The main work of the panchayat lies in the field of village improvement in the different branches of education, sanitation, etc.

There is a patel and a shanbhog. The shanbhog's duty lies in keeping the village accounts. The patel is concerned with the general oversight of the village and the collection of revenue. There are four servants, two for police purposes and the two others concerned in the collection of revenue.

Sanitary administration.—The panchayat is concerned with the sanitary administration of the village. The panchayat holds meetings when occasion arises and takes steps to improve the sanitation of the village. Every Monday each family supplies half a day's labour, compoundable by a money payment of an anna. This does what is needful for the sanitation of the village. The panchayat exercises a general oversight in these matters. The Sanitary Inspector and the District Health and Sanitary Officer inspect the village often.

There is a police sub-station with a daffadar and five police constables. During nights, three other men watch the village; their services are purely voluntary and unpaid.

The higher authorities are the Amildar, Assistant Commissioner, and the Deputy Commissioner. The Amildar is the only official with whom there is contact at all often. The others visit the village about once or twice in a year. There is a resident shaikdar or revenue inspector.

Crime.—There have been practically no crimes punishable with capital punishment hitherto. Whatever crime there has been consists only of burglaries and minor thefts. These too are rare. For the past six years there has been only one burglary (in 1916); valuables were lost to the value of Rs. 150.

No villagers are engaged in litigation. Almost all civil disputes are decided in the village itself by the panchayat.

History and prospects.—There has been economic deterioration due to the scarcity of rains and the consequent failure of crops. The ryots have been obliged to borrow and this is very well evidenced by the amount of rural indebtedness. No remission is allowed by the Government for waste lands. An economic enquiry is held by the village officers every year and a report is sent to the Government.

There is scope for improvement on a large scale if only ryots are prepared to start with a large capital and adopt modern methods of agriculture. There does not seem to be any possibility of extending the irrigated lands. Almost all available land has been used up, and brought under cultivation.

The condition of tanks and wells has been improved of late. More wells could be sunk with advantage, but are not sunk owing to lack of funds.

The barbers, dhobis and others are tending to lose their lands owing to their pernicious habit of drinking. People sell land in order to pay off old debts. Loans are given only on mortgage of lands. The chief purchasers are money-lenders.

There has been no emigration. But two Muhammadans are at the front as sepoys. About a hundred belonging to this particular taluk are in the army and most of them are at the field of operations.

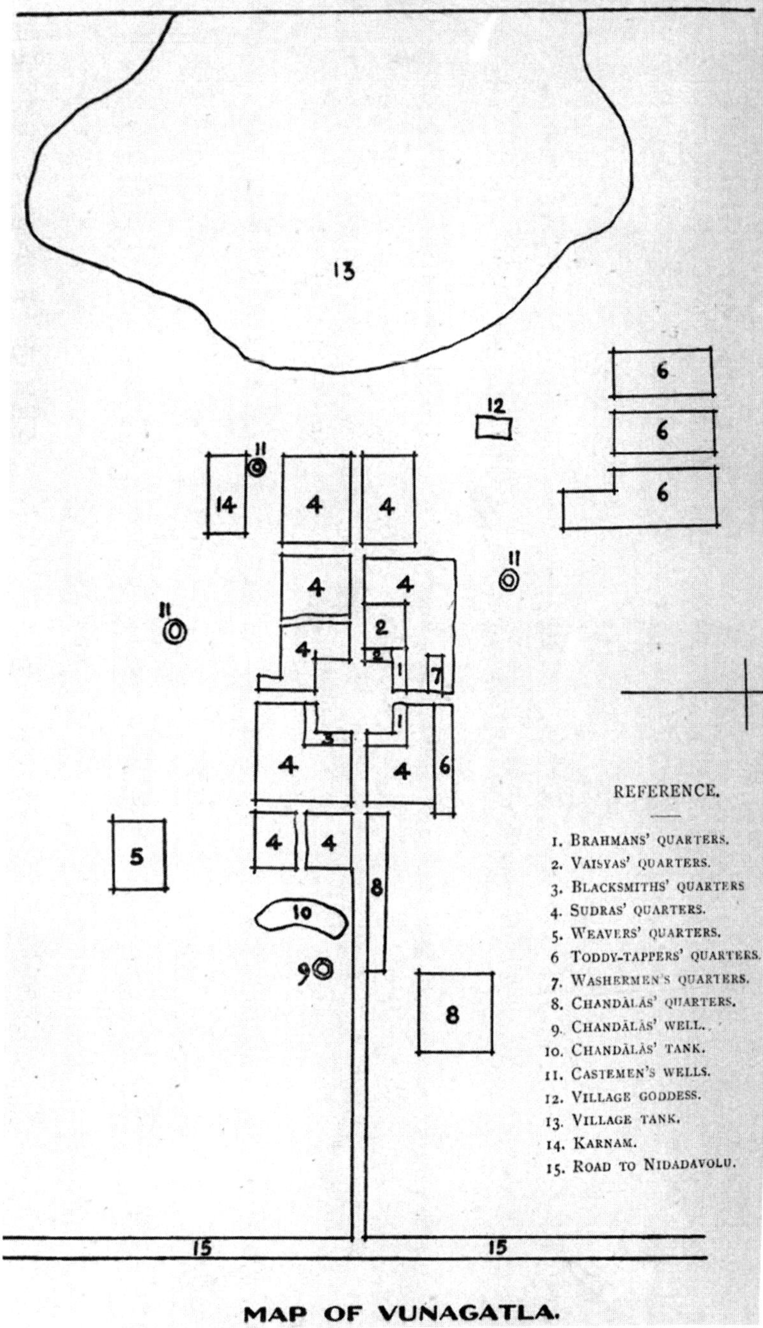

MAP OF VUNAGATLA.

KISTNA DISTRICT.

VUNAGATLA.

[*By K. S. Narayana Murti, Christian College, Madras.*]

Vunagatla, in the Yernagudem taluk of the Kistna district, is an upland village, four miles distant from Nidadavolu, an important centre of railway and river traffic. On one side it is bounded by the high road from Nidadavolu to the Gōdāvari Agency, on the other by a great sandy tract filled with palmyra trees. The climate is extreme, the unbearable heat of summer being followed by the excessive rains of the rainy season, and the extreme cold of winter. It is a purely dry village, depending entirely on the annual rains.

Population.—The population has been increasing steadily since the first census.

Census.	Population.	Census.	Population.
1871	1,237	1901	2,150
1881	1,567	1911	2,519
1891	2,017		

Brahmans and Vaisyas are increasing, and so are the Sudras, who are temperate and simple and hardy in habits. The rate of mortality is high among the Pariahs and washermen and other low castes.

The official figures of births and deaths cannot be entirely relied on. They are, for 1911—15, as follows:—

Births.

Year.	Males.	Females.	Total.
1911	33	52	85
1912	55	49	104
1913	49	49	98
1914	48	52	100
1915	41	52	93

Deaths.

Year.	Cholera.	Small-pox.	Fevers.	Respiratory diseases.	Other causes	Men.	Women.	Children under 14.	Total.
1911	226	...	42	...	28	71	88	137	296
1912	...	...	48	...	47	30	24	41	95
1913	...	...	62	3	2	18	20	29	67
1914	6	8	62	4	18	33	40	25	98
1915	...	112	41	17	13	53	49	81	183

The figures for deaths are in general accurate, according to information collected in the village, with the exception of the deaths in the cholera epidemic of 1911 and the small-pox epidemic of 1915. In the latter, according to non-official information between 80 and 85 children died, and 160 persons in all. The record of births appears to be very defective.

By the 1911 census there were 396 homesteads; there are now 430 to 440, there being many recent extensions of the inhabited village into the fields on the north and south.

An approximate statement of the population according to caste is as follows:—

	Adults.	Children.
Brahmans	25	13
Vaisyas	55	40
Sudras, Kammas	225	220
" Kapus	275	240
Carpenters and silversmiths	33	24
Weavers	26	22
Barbers	10	4
Washermen	100	150
Toddy-tappers	283	305
Shepherds	52	33
Potters	4	2
Muhammadans	5	1
Oil-mongers	11	5

Land.

	Acres.
Wet land	Nil.
Dry land, cultivated	1,545·27
Land watered by wells	7·40
Common waste	145·36
Pasture other than common waste	415·82

Most of the land is cultivated by the pattadar, but 226 acres are sublet to tenants. There are about 350 agricultural workers who neither own nor rent land.

The following are the principal crops:—

	Acres.
Paddy	166·39
Cholam	468·88
Kambu	73·68
Gingelly	194·74
Horsegram	151·34
Ragi	...
Chodi	1·90
Korra	6·10
Chillis	0·67
Jute	1·80
Tobacco	1·34

Land is assessed for revenue at the following rates:—

	Per acre.		
	RS.	A.	P.
Best black clay	1	12	0
Best black loam	1	10	0
Best red loam	1	10	0
Best red sand	0	10	0

Sandy tracts with palmyras fetch a rent of Rs. 10 per acre, without trees, Rs. 2 or 3 only; black clay Rs. 15 to 16 per acre.

The black clay land sells at about Rs. 350 per acre, the red sand at about Rs. 150. But the price has fallen now owing to two bad harvests.

Stock.

	By official information.	Non-official.
Working oxen	539	800 about.
Cows	412	600 ,,
Male buffaloes	6	14 ,,
Cow buffaloes	184	200 ,,
Young stock—buffaloes	208	250 ,,
Do. cows	637	650 to 700
Horses	...	...
Donkeys and mules	...	...
Sheep	58	61
Goats	225	200
Pigs	100	...

According to the census of 1900 and 1910 they were—

	1900.	1910.
Bullocks and he-buffaloes	650	545
Cows	580	412
She-buffaloes	171	184
Young stock	802	845
Sheep and goats	778	283

The straw of cholam and paddy is reserved for the summer feed of cattle; in the rainy season the green grass of the common pasture is available. Each ryot reserves one or two fields for pasture for his cattle. In days of heavy work, the bullocks are given cooked horsegram mixed with the husk of paddy, and the fine dust from the grain which is mixed with it in husking. Cotton seeds are also cooked and given for food; and oil cake, especially for milch cows. Ryots who have insufficient pasture send some of their cattle to the Agency tracts for the three months, July to September; they are charged Rs. 3 or 5 per pair.

Only about 50 per cent of the cattle-dung is used as manure, the rest is used for fuel. The average ryot applies six to eight cart-loads of dung per acre; besides the manure of the cattle kept in fields at nights. He accumulates a stock at home throughout the year and applies it at the end of the year to the fields.

No green manure or chemical manure is used.

Garden cultivation has been tried as an experiment with water-supply from a well, lifted by a water pump got from Bombay. Lemons and plantains are planted. The pump required some slight repairs, which were delayed for want of a mechanic near by. The garden too has not yet proved to be decidedly profitable; and all the villagers laugh at it as an innovation.

Cost of cultivation.—The following is an account of the expenditure for ten acres of an average ryot, obtained from four ryots.

8

No exact accounts are possible, for the ryots do not keep any record of them.

Items.	RS.	A.	P.
2 Bullocks, for keep... ... ... (The figures given by the four ryots were Rs. 75, 80, 90, 80; two cows also are maintained out of this.)	80	0	0
2 annual servants (Rs. 50 and Rs. 25 respectively)	75	0	0
1 plough, its necessary implements	2	0	0
" charges for making it	2	0	0
Seed for two crops	28	0	0
Coolies to weed two crops	40	0	0
Coolies to harvest it (some say even Rs. 20) ...	15	0	0
Government tax at Rs. 1-12-0 per acre	17	8	0
Rent, if the land is leased, at least	100	0	0
Perquisites at harvest time—			
to the head servant one bag	7	0	0
to the second servant half a bag	3	8	0
to the village barber three or four seers (at 8 seers per rupee)	0	8	0
to the washerman...	0	8	0
to the shoemaker, 16 or 20 seers	2	8	0
to three village servants, 2 seers each	0	12	0
To manure the fields in summer with rented flocks of sheep and goats, as is the custom, for eight or ten days at an acre a day; the tenant takes three-fourths of the milk on such days ...	35	0	0
Other agricultural implements (even higher) ...	5	0	0
Other repairs of the field, such as digging up the soil, etc.	5	0	0
Total expenses foi ten acres ...	424	4	0

During the last two years there were excessive rains; crops failed badly; there was double the expenditure for useless plants; the cultivators had to sow three times, so that the average expenditure for seed was trebled. Such extraordinary expenditures are frequent. But assuming the season is favourable the utmost that the cultivator can get is—

	RS.	A.	P.
40 bags of paddy at Rs. 4½ per bag	170	0	0
20 bags of gingelly at Rs. 7½ per bag	150	0	0
30 bags of cholam at Rs. 6¼ per bag	187	8	0
20 bags of Bengal gram at Rs. 8-5-4 per bag ...	175	0	0
20 bags of red gram at Rs. 7½ per bag	150	0	0
Black gram	8	0	0
Total ...	840	8	0

The average crop is Rs. 560 or Rs. 600 per annum. The cultivator can moreover earn in summer 90 or 100 rupees by letting out his cart to convey jaggery.

The area of the village-site is 33 acres 32 cents. The dwellings of the depressed castes, about 125 in number, are crowded together on the northern and north-east sides of the village. On the northern side, but apart from the village, crowded together in irregular muddy streets of obnoxious smell are the houses of the washermen (70 houses) and the toddy-drawing class (150 in number). All are thatched with palmyra leaves. It is difficult to go into the midst of these huts because of the bad smell.

There are 271 houses in the caste village according to official information, actually 350; 125 in the paracheri.

The village is rather crowded and there is no space for gardens. There is much demand for building sites. There are extensions on the north and south sides into the fields. Some houses contain even two or three families crowded together. From Rs. 2 to 3 per square yard is paid for house-sites. Some of the cultivated land is distant 5½ miles from the home of the cultivator. A hereditary disposition to hate changes, as well as party feelings, and suspicions of inequalities, prevent the ryots from exchanging to get their land continuous. Field huts are used, but mostly for the working seasons only, and are not permanent.

Subsidiary industries.—At the time of the 1891 census there were 69 weavers; in 1901, 17; in 1911, 12; now there are only three. Foreign yarn of 10, 20 and 40 Nos. is purchased from fairs held at Nidadavolu, four miles off. The cloth woven is a very rough sort, used by the very poor classes; 75 per cent of the people prefer and use foreign goods. The implements are of the ordinary country type and of primitive nature. There is no co-operation among the weavers. They are unable to face the mill competition. As they find little demand for their goods, they are frequently forced to go away as agricultural labourers, and practise weaving only as a hobby for leisure hours. A weaver with five sons, as a rule, sends four of them to agricultural work and only one to his own industry. Till 10 years back 95 per cent of the population used to wear the village cloth. Now 75 per cent prefer and use foreign clothing. Two weaving families recently went to Rajahmundry as factory coolies. Ten years ago, many women of low castes used to practise handspinning. A little cotton was grown in the village up to 1912, but latterly it was sold for higher prices than the spinners could pay.

Economic condition of the village—Rates of wages.—Labourers are employed for the day or for the year. In the latter case Rs. 25 per annum is paid to boys and Rs. 50 per annum to men. For daily labourers the wage is three to four annas to men; 1½ to 2 annas to women; 1 to 1¼ annas to children; this may be paid in grain or money, or half in money and half in grain. The only perquisites are at harvest time. Thus for each crop, the yearly labourer receives 8 or 12 seers; on the whole 1 bag nearly. In festivals, they are given only meals and nothing more.

Current prices—

	RS.	A.	P.
Paddy per bag of 166 lb.	5	8	0
Cholam "	9	1	6
Gingelly "	12	8	0
Red gram "	8	6	0
Kambu "	9	6	0
Soap nuts "	7	8	0
Ghee, per tin...	18	0	0

Rural indebtedness.—One of the greatest curses that an Indian village suffers from is the indebtedness of its inhabitants. Almost every family in our village has some family debt or other, whether it has property or not. Capitalism and money-lending are the chief occupations of the rich, the result being wealth heaped on wealth on the one hand, and poverty heaped on poverty on the other. I can count six families that were once financial magnates of the village, now reduced to absolute poverty.

The chief causes of indebtedness are—

(1) Expenses for the bare maintenance of the family. Many of the poorer classes contract debts simply because they must live and they must eat.

(2) Expenses for marriages, etc. Such ceremonies are performed only when crops are good. It is not however an exaggeration to say that ryots overstep the limits of their resources and contract debts on such occasions.

(3) Emergency expenditure such as sickness of long duration, which is of frequent occurrence and costly in character.

(4) Agricultural expenses.

(5) Expenses of litigation. Such debts run to even Rs. 9,000 or Rs. 12,000. Seven or eight families have left the village, because of such debts, going to the Gōdāvari Agency to earn a living.

(6) The accumulation of smaller debts already contracted, by means of compound interest, into very large amounts, finally ending in mortgaging and then selling off of any hereditary property.

(7) The underlying cause is that most people depend every year on the yearly crops; when the crops fail or when an emergency expenditure comes up, they borrow.

The most common forms of debt are—

(1) Promissory notes executed on good security at a fair rate of interest, as Re. 1-8-0 or Rs. 2 per cent per month. These are not many in number.

(2) Mortgages of land and other property.

(3) *Jettis*, i.e., debts contracted mostly for agricultural purposes to be paid back in the shape of grain when harvested. The creditor in this case pays at the rate of Rs. 40 or 45 per candy, while the market rate will be Rs. 75 or 80. This kind of debt is common in agricultural seasons; and four or five months is the duration of the loan.

(4) A poor man will borrow, say one rupee, and promise to pay it back three months hence. He will have to pay back one rupee plus one *kuncham*, i.e., 4 seers of grain (i.e., 6 annas). If he fails then (as they generally do), he will have to pay Re. 1 plus 8 seers of the next crop and one quarter anna, and so on.

(5) *Paddus.*—The money-lender lends money at Re. 1-8-0 per month per cent to a poor peasant, and says "If you do not return it by the Pongal, I will charge compound interest." In most cases they defer the payment to three or four years, and in some five or six years, owing to failure of crops, or, in some cases, mere neglect.

A ryot having five children and 12 acres of land borrowed Rs. 150 at Re. 1-8-0 per cent five years ago, to marry his eldest son. Two months ago, he handed over his 12 acres of land to the merchant, because he found it impossible to repay the debt. This is a common case.

ROOFING A HUT WITH PALMYRA LEAVES.

Photo by Agricultural College.

The result is that many families that were once rich are now reduced to absolute poverty. The rich few are becoming richer. But 65 to 75 per cent of the population are in debt. Of these 25 to 30 per cent have hopes of clearing it off in three or four years by mortgaging their lands. The rest, 35 to 40 per cent, are not able to escape easily out of debt. The pity is that these classes do not hesitate to contract debts at first, and then they are not in a hurry to return them soon, and small sums accumulate into large amounts.

Trade.—The villagers purchase commodities for industrial and agricultural purposes from weekly fairs held at Nidadavolu and from Rajahmundry; for consumption, partly from weekly fairs at Nidadavolu and partly from the local traders. The amount of village produce sold was approximately as follows:—

	1916-17.	1915-16.
Soap nuts	250 bags.	500 bags.
Horsegram	200 (or 250) bags.	400 „
Gingelly	220 bags.	850 „
Red gram (this is mostly retained for local use).	50-60 „	100 „
Bengal gram	25-30 „	100 „
Ghee	50 60 tins.	50-60 tins.
Cholam (this is retained for local use; no crop this year).	...	50 bags.
Black gram	20 bags.	12 „

Jaggery trade.—The most noteworthy feature of the village is the jaggery trade, carried on during the summer season. Nearly half the field area of the village consists of dry sand, filled with palmyra trees. These trees are rented out to the toddy tappers, who have to pay from Rs. 15 to 20 each in rent. One man can draw toddy from about 60 trees. Some 1,000 to 1,200 of these tappers come from the different taluks of the Kistna and Gōdāvari districts to this village in summer; while 200 to 225 go from the village itself. These people settle in the fields in the three summer months during which the fields lie waste, and draw toddy from 5 to 10 a.m. and 3 to 7 p.m. They have to climb the tree and suspend pots, lined with lime, beneath the cut ends of the stalks of the fronds of the palm from which the juice (toddy) flows. But for the lime the toddy would immediately begin to ferment. The women at home boil the toddy till it is condensed into jaggery.

Part of the jaggery is sold to the direct agents of Messrs. Parry & Co., who have opened an extensive business in these parts and invested a large capital. These agents of the company purchase jaggery with the company's money and get a commission at the rate of As. 2-6 per bag. They send it to Samalkot, where the company converts it into sugar.

The remainder is sold by the tappers to private capitalists and retail traders, who purchase the jaggery in the fields and sell it again to the company's agent in the village. They receive no commission, but make a profit in three ways: (1) There is a difference in the cost per candy between the prices in the fields (i.e., near the tappers' huts) and in the village. (2) The traders lend money to the tappers in times of need and get "Jattis" executed, promises by which the tappers agree to repay the money in the shape of jaggery at a reduced price, generally 13 to 15 rupees per candy, while the market price in summer will be Rs. 23 to 29 per candy. Last year, owing to the appearance of a competing company, Messrs. Simpson & Co., the price was, Rs. 35 to 42 per candy. No interest is charged for such debts. (3) They invariably use false stones in weighing the jaggery in the fields, while in the village the company's stones are used. This results in an enormous profit.

With these three sources of profit, the private capitalist is able to realize a profit of Rs. 5 at least per cart (of 8 bags) while daily he sends 3 carts at least to the company's agent. The total export of the village during the summer will be from 17,000 to 20,000 bags; this year (1917) it is 18,000 bags, i.e., 6,000 candies.

The rich capitalist makes the largest profit out of this trade. Many of the villagers are now a class of capitalists, great or small. Many that were poor three or four years ago are now able to invest a few hundreds and start independent businesses in this line. There are three people who invested about Rs. 30,000 each this year.

The toddy tappers are not materially better off. As a class they are only a little above the level of absolute poverty, while individually, there are only four or five who own a property of Rs. 500. Though their gross earnings are from Rs. 20 to 25 for the three months, the net income will be Rs. 6 to 8 only.

The village barber and washerman earn at least Rs. 30 to 35 during the three months. The lime dealer earns 50 to 60 rupees. The Pariahs who carry firewood get wages at the rate of 4 annas to 6 annas per day. Owners of carts get rent at the rate of Rs. 2 per turn to carry jaggery from the field-huts to Nidadavolu, the headquarters of the company. Makers of tin-pots, used in boiling the toddy, get 100 to 150 rupees. Pariah women prepare baskets of palmyra leaves to hold the jaggery, for which they are paid Re. 1 per 100. Brahmans are employed to prepare the accounts and are paid Rs. 10 per mensem.

Besides these payments for services rendered (which are in the shape of jaggery in most cases) there are certain extra perquisites or "mamuls" which the toddy tapper is compelled to pay. These illegitimate exactions mount up to thousands of rupees. The village servants also get presents, while the coolies are profited by carrying rice or other articles to the fields. There are many small shops opened by retail traders in the fields themselves for the benefit of the tappers; while the performance of two or three dramas, based on some popular mythological story by country actors is not of rare occurrence.

The effects on the village are innumerable and many sided. One of the greatest difficulties for the Indian labourer is want of proper employment; it is no exaggeration to say that many families are reduced to poverty, simply for want of sufficient local demand for their labour. This village is to a certain extent relieved of this anxiety during a season when, the fields being fallow, they have no agricultural occupation to attend to. Many a poor family would have long ago left the village but for this attraction. Industrially, it has raised the efficiency of every craft, by providing it with more work to turn out. While in all the other seasons the whole village is entirely agricultural in character, in summer it can be said to be industrial and commercial in tone.

Socially, it increases drunkenness in the lower classes; and I find more crimes in summer than in other seasons.

But it has turned the honest and sympathetic ryots into greedy money-lenders and capitalists. It has increased the lust for gold. True that the poorer classes have an opportunity of clearing off their family debts; true that they find sufficient food to eat in summer at least; true that there is more money in the village now than 20 years ago. But equally is it true that there are more debts now; that the gulf between the rich and the poor is widened more and more; that the once poor are now poorer and the once rich now richer. There is greater struggle, greater competition, and greater rises and falls of life.

Economic history of the village.—When compared with fifteen years ago, the village has, on the whole, progressed economically. True that estates once united are now split up into fragments; and that the once poor have now become poorer. True that there are cases where people borrow money and purchase land with it; and then sell it again to clear off that debt some years later. Still the village has improved. There is increase and improvement in agriculture. Many fields that were once forest are now brought under cultivation. There is more money in the village now than 20 years ago, more produce is now exported from the village than before. The introduction of the railway near by has revolutionized the commercial condition of the village. Prices have risen both of the commodities produced and of land in general, three or four-fold. There is a greater inflow of foreign goods into the village. Kerosene oil has completely driven out castor oil. There are sixteen Japanese wind-proof lamps in the village. The standard of living has decidedly been raised. Among the lower castes to eat solid food was a luxury; conjee, prepared of korra and ragi, was the food for all the lower castes, including Sudras. Now they all eat rice and cholam and wear better clothing. But the money is ultimately finding its destination into the hands of the rich money-lenders. Formerly there was enough corn in the land and there was a sort of self-sufficiency. Now there are more debts, consequently more ruin of families with the higher rates of interest, and greater servitude and misery.

If the Government were to open a sugar factory and utilize the jaggery, both the Government and the villagers would be profited. Wells can be very profitably sunk in the fields. But the ryots never do it, though it costs only Rs. 200. A ryot is prepared to spend even Rs. 1,500 in litigation but not Rs. 200 for a well in his fields, even though he is rich and knows that it is profitable. By example they may improve.

The Brahmans have almost lost their former property for want of any profession, while they incur heavy expenses for marriages, etc. Only one family is now well off. The Vaisyas too have lost their former lands by litigation, marriages, and other expenses. On the whole, the Sudras have grown richer, both with agriculture and the jaggery trade, and the rise of prices for their produce. The weavers, washermen, the Panchamas, many of the Sudras, are growing poorer; they are selling off the little lands they have for debts and other expenses.

Lands are sold chiefly to clear off old debts, though there are some cases where profits tempt people to purchase or sell. The poorer classes, when they find that their debts have overgrown their income, generally hand over their lands to the lenders of money.

Emigrants leave the village for two reasons:—(1) indebtedness and (2) want of sufficient work and means of living. As previously stated two families of weavers have gone to Rajahmundry for factory work, and one family of Komatis to the Gōdāvari Agency. Some of the Panchamas and toddy drawers go to Rangoon, Moulmein, Singapore, and formerly went to Natal and the Transvaal. They return at the end of 1½ or 2 years. Some have made a little profit by going out, but not much. One effect of such emigration is to prevent people from lending money freely to all. The poorer classes do not get loans so easily now for want of security.

Sanitary condition.—There is no malaria. Six years ago there was a heavy attack of cholera, the number of deaths being between 150 and 200. It was impossible to keep any accurate account. Two years ago there was a serious attack of smallpox, when about 160 adults and children together died. It is significant that among Brahmans not a single person was attacked by either of these diseases. Among the Vaisyas the number of deaths was 5 and 3, respectively, among the Sudras it was 50 from cholera, 60 from small-pox. All the rest of the cases were in the lower castes. The death-rate of the children was far greater than that of adults.

The village statistics show 480 children born in the five years from 1911 to 1915, 321 under 14 years of age dying during these years. The record of births is probably very defective, but the rate of mortality among infants and young children is certainly terribly high. There is no effective medical assistance available. The quack doctors of the village are merely deceitful and ignorant and practice the trade with no schooling or knowledge. Men following various occupations, who do not earn much at their proper calling, are the doctors of the village, who administer red or black powders to the patient one after another, call the fever this and that, starve the patient for 15 or 20 days, keep him in comfortable delusions all the while, and having made up 20 or 30 rupees send him to an untimely grave. The villagers prefer to entrust their lives to these doctors than to risk them in the hands of an English trained doctor. The hospital assistant near by has not won a good name for English medicine.

The wife of the barber is the nurse for all cases of pregnancy, and the general authority on all cases of feminine complaints.

For want of education, people do not observe the elementary principles of sanitation. For instance in times of epidemic diseases they do not isolate patients. They spread the disease by cleaning all kinds of cloth in village tanks. They do not reveal the disease immediately after the attack. They keep the patients in crowded houses and move and eat and sleep very close to them. Even for ordinary fevers, the patient is starved for 5 or 6 days, so that he will be weak and useless for work for a number of days afterwards.

The poorer classes are often subjected to disease for want of healthy and sufficient food, and clean surroundings. Every poor man has two or three cattle at least; and their huts being crowded, with limited space, it happens generally that the cattle are kept very close to the human inmates. Rubbish and cow-dung are stored up in front of the houses, while in rainy seasons the whole becomes a stagnant pool of water, rubbish and cow-dung.

The houses of the Pariahs are filled with an awful smell of skins, bones and putrid flesh. The insufficiency of food that they suffer from tempts them to fill their bellies with toddy and other stimulants that ultimately ruin their health.

The Sudras are perfectly temperate and simple in habits and food. The "twice-born" castes are bound to marry their girls before twelve. The lower castes are not bound to do so. But the Sudras and lower castes actually marry their girls at a very early age, both to satisfy the anxiety of elders and for fear they may not have the money afterwards. I know a case in which a girl two months old was married to a boy of two years, the boy dying a year later of cholera. They maintain strict widowhood like the Brahmans. There is no purdah.

The villagers bathe and wash clothes and also wash their cattle in the same tank as that used for drinking.

Education.—There is one school; its accommodation and equipment being a rented house, an atlas, a globe, text books, some pictures of common objects, civics primers, dumb-bells, a black board, a desk, benches for boys to sit upon.

Elementary education is given up to the fourth standard, in the vernacular, in history, arithmetic, geography, civics, etc. This education is most unpractical and incomplete and ill-suited to the villagers, who do not proceed to college classes. It does not enable them to read good books in Telugu or to learn even the elementary principles of sanitation. They are never made to feel that they are citizens of a world, or an empire, or a province, outside the narrow bounds of their village.

Attendance—	Boys.	Girls.
1913	19	4
1914	9	3
1915	45	12
1916	54	8
1917	48	6

About 30 per cent of the adults can read the vernacular; two persons can read and talk English. There is a noted musician in the village but no other pandit. Not less than 25 or 30 per cent of those who have passed through the school have lost their capacity to write or cipher after leaving. One boy has proceeded to the Mechanical Engineering course in the Victoria Technical Institute, Bombay; another to the Arts course in the Madras University.

There are 90 to 100 books, of which 70 are owned by Brahmans, made up of novels, dramas, puranas, the Mahabharata and stories. Among the Sudras, a development of literary taste, though in a very small degree, is perceptible. There are many devotional songs and lives of Telugu saints, while stories of the epics rendered into songs and recited by "Bhagavathars" are very frequent. The latest innovation is the introduction of dramas. Novels are still a rarity, as well as histories. No newspaper comes to the village.

The village has no temple except that of the village goddess. Her festival is celebrated with much slaughter of cattle and goats given by their owners whenever there is an outbreak of cholera or small-pox; or, failing these, once in four or five years. The cost is from Rs. 100 to Rs. 150, largely spent on drink. The priests of the goddess are low caste people, chiefly the washerman caste. They get new cloths as presents. The whole celebration is barbarous and repulsive.

The village administration.—There is no panchayat in the village. The village officers consist of a karnam, a munsif, and three servants. The karnam keeps the village accounts, while the munsif collects the revenue and attends to small criminal cases. The munsif does not generally care to try civil cases even within his province; they all go to the District Munsif's court.

Nobody attends to the village sanitation, though the munsif is expected to do so. The villagers too do not care to help him in his work. The Sanitary Inspector comes once in a year, and quietly goes away with satisfactory remarks from the easy chair in his note book. He being the one officer for two or three taluks, cannot pay much attention to one taluk in particular; besides he also has engineering work.

The police station is seven miles away. When crimes of extraordinary nature take place, the munsif reports the same to the police, who come and conduct enquiries. Most of the crimes are hushed up. Police enquiry is a sham. So is the night patrolling, which is the duty of the village servants.

The munsif is expected to hear petty crimes; but many cases that might have been decided here go to the Magistrate's court. Many crimes have been left undetected, and the criminals unpunished, crimes which were horrible and plainly proved. As locally interpreted, the effect of the Evidence Act is such as to render the most proved case null and void for "want of proper evidence." When a murderer once escapes easily from punishment, another is at once encouraged. All the villagers know that it is these considerations that encouraged a man engaged in litigation to murder another who was about to give evidence against him. That case went unpunished. Such is the case with most murders. In fact, most men engaged in important litigation are afraid for their lives in this village. In three years there have been four murders in the neighbourhood of the village, two killed in connection with litigation and two in connection with robbery from the person.

There is much litigation. About 45 cases are filed every year. Of these twenty to twenty-five will be for non-clearance of debts, and fifteen to twenty for land disputes. The villagers do not seem to show any hesitation or fear in resorting to the courts. The half educated Brahman in the village, acting as an agent for a vakil, with no other profession, tries to earn his livelihood by creating enmity and disputes among ignorant families and dragging them to the courts. Thus several families which were once considered very rich have been ruined. One family of Komatis, for example, with a property of about Rs. 20,000, was sued by some relations for a partition of the estate. The Vaisya refused all compromise in the earlier courts, pursued the case at enormous expense through the three courts, till he finally lost the whole estate in the High Court. In the end, the family of twelve children, with not an inch of land for support, and no means of liquidating the debts contracted for the court expenses, have sold their big house and gone away to the Agency tracts as beggars to fill their bellies. There are many families in the village similarly ruined.

THE COCHIN STATE.

WATAKANCHERY (TALAPILLI TALUK).

[*By S. Subbarama Aiyar, Christian College, Madras.*]

An absence of villages, as they are to be found in the east of the peninsula, is a characteristic of Malabar generally, including the States of Travancore and Cochin and the Malabar District of the Madras Presidency. The Malayalis are averse to having their houses congregated together. But the Taluk of Palghat is an exception. It is situated in the gap between the Nilgiris on the north, and the Palnis and other high ranges on the south, and is the natural line of communication between the west coast and the eastern plains, utilized by the South Indian Railway. All the villages in the Palghat taluk are designed in a manner that suggests that the original immigrants, coming from the east, were accustomed to an intense form of corporate life. They have a scientific and regular plan, and the description of any one of them will serve for all.

The Brahmans live in closely packed houses and their colony is called a '*gramam*' or '*agraharam*.' There is invariably either a temple at one end, or the streets of the *gramam* radiate in all directions from a temple in the midmost place. There are also wells in the street common to all the villagers. There is scarcity of water in summer in almost all the villages of Palghat as they are situated on a high level and rocky ground. The *gramam* is surrounded by the *tarai* in which all the other castes live. Artisans and agricultural labourers live there in houses built singly, but the weavers generally inhabit hovels built in rows. People of the same caste and profession congregate in particular blocks of the *tarai*. The *tarai* is occupied by the richest janmi as well as the poorest day labourer. The *tarai* has its own *kavu* or temple in which the low caste people conduct their worship. The *gramam* with its adjoining *tarai* is set up on rather elevated ground in the midst of paddy fields or on the slope of an adjoining hill so that every available acre of land may be cultivated. All houses in the *gramam* are built in the same way. From the street you step into a verandah whose extent corresponds to the whole width of the house; hence into a small room, the *neli*, to the right of which is a granary. The *neli* leads you into a rectangular hall, in the middle of which is a yard exposed to the sky. To the right of this is another big hall separated from the other by a long window crossed by beams. The store-room is on the street side of this, the kitchen on the back side. The kitchen has a verandah abutting on the garden. A cow-shed is erected at the other end of the garden. The house may or may not possess upstairs rooms; these usually adjoin the street.

In that part of Malabar in which Watakanchery is situated the general plan of the Palghat type of house is followed, with modifications, by the *Tamil* Brahmans. The Malayali Brahmans, known as Nambudris, and the Nayars, have their houses surrounded by big compounds. Entering from the compound you step into a portico which thrusts itself forward from the general structure of the house.

From the portico, you go direct into a big hall in the middle of which is a big yard paved with granite ; this yard is exposed to the sky. On one side of the hall—right or left—are situated two or three rooms, from one of which you are taken to upstairs rooms which are also connected with the portico. On the portico side of the hall are the kitchen, bath-room, and a few more rooms which are utilized for various purposes. In another place of the compound is an outhouse in which Brahmans are asked to perform worship.* Near this house is a tank and a well. The house itself possesses a well near it for the exclusive use of the inmates.

But educated Nayars now-a-days build their houses on different plans.

Preliminary.—Watakanchery is a Government division, rather than a true village, being marked out merely for convenience of revenue assessment. It stretches from east to west a distance of nearly four miles along the foot of a hill. A water-course which runs from east to west forms the northern boundary; the maximum distance from north to south is nearly a mile and a half. The whole area is 3,692·64 acres (nearly 5½ square miles). It is an area containing a few groups of houses intersected by paddy fields and "parambas," i.e., land on which paddy cultivation is not undertaken.

Watakanchery proper, or the town of Watakanchery, as it is called in the village accounts, is at the easternmost boundary of the Government village area and is the headquarters of the taluk containing all the public offices. Two tracts of land, one inhabited by Mappillas (Muhammadans) and another by Syrian Christians (locally known as Nasranees, i.e., Nazarenes) are included in the "town" of Watakanchery from the contiguous areas of the adjoining Government villages on the north and south respectively. Its area is 1½ square miles.

The Taluk of Talapilli contains 74 such "villages" divided solely for revenue purposes. In the "town" Brahmans live in great numbers, while the lower castes occupy the rest of the village area. This block I shall designate Watakanchery (T) and the whole area Watakanchery (V) in the following.

Population.—Watakanchery (T) has about 2,000 inhabitants; Watakanchery (V) about 4,000. Watakanchery (T) contains within its limits three religions—Hindus in the centre and Mappillas (Muhammadans) and Christians to the north and south, respectively. Among the Hindus the Brahmans form the majority in the "town," while there are a few "vocational" castes such as barbers, goldsmiths, etc., and a few Nayars. Though the term "castes" is in strictness to be applied to Hindus alone the Mappillas and Christians are regarded as two other castes. The Mappillas and the Christians cannot touch the Hindu caste-people without polluting them, while there are castes within the Hindu fold itself, such as carpenters, goldsmiths, masons, Cherumas (vide below), Eluvas, etc., who are kept at a distance of a specified number of feet by the higher castes. There is a full and interesting study of the tribes and castes in Mr. L. K. Anandakrishna Iyer's "Cochin Tribes and Castes." The Hindus however form the majority.

---

* [In Nayar houses, I am informed by Mr. L. K. Anandakrishna Iyer, this shrine is sacred to the cobra, to whom worship must be given by a Nambudri Brahman, as otherwise the Nayars are bitten. This belief may be the cause of the subjection imposed on Nayars by Nambudris, particularly in relation to Nayar women.—Ed.]

Court-yard of Nambudri house.

Photo by G. Slater.

There are 440 houses in the "town," and more than double that number in the whole village. The statistics of births and deaths are kept separate for the part of the village outside the town and the town; they stand thus for the last five years:—

Years.	Village.									Town.								
	Births.				Deaths.					Births.				Deaths.				
	Hindus.	Muhammadans.	Christians.	Total.	Hindus.	Muhammadans.	Christians.	Total.	Infants.	Hindus.	Muhammadans.	Christians.	Total.	Hindus.	Muhammadans.	Christians.	Total.	Infants.
1910 11	93	10	23	126	60	8	5	73	33	86	17	23	126	54	21	5	80	39
1911-12	75	6	29	110	71	6	24	101	38	86	34	23	143	83	17	19	119	57
1912-13	40	7	7	54	33	4	6	43	17	72	24	17	113	66	13	18	97	48
1913-14	50	5	6	61	43	2	5	50	17	66	22	23	111	64	8	24	56	37
1914-15	35	3	4	42	20	...	6	26	6	49	27	17	93	29	6	12	47	15

"Infants" include all under the age of three.

The figures for the "town" can be taken as fairly accurate while those of the village cannot be relied on; for the village officers rarely take the trouble of entering the latter correctly, while every dweller in "town" is made to tender accounts of births and deaths on penalty, and these are also within the close purview of the village officers. Note especially the rate of infant mortality in both the town and village. Nearly 50 per cent of the deaths occur among the infants.* Muhammadans and Christians, who are invariably engaged in petty trade, are more numerous in the "town" than in the "village."

Paracheri.—The Pulayas (Cherumas and Paraiyas) in the State and of Malabar form a category by themselves. The State made an enquiry into their social and economic condition last year which I here utilize. There are nearly 300 Pulayas in the village. They are more or less serfs attached to the soil. They are agricultural workers only, and have no sort of proprietorship in the land. They are paid daily wages in kind and that in very low measures. The following is the daily rate:—Men 2 edangalis † of paddy per day; women 1½ edangalis of paddy, boys 1 edangali. In addition, 5 edangalis of paddy are given to men and 4 edangalis to women on certain festive days in the year, and once a year every male and female member of the family is presented with a pair of cloths ‡ 2 yards and 3½ yards respectively by the master. The men plough, tend cattle, water the gardens, gather fuel, etc., while the women pluck the paddy seedlings to replant them, and do

* [The figures show an average infantile death-rate of 284 per 1,000 births for the area outside the "town," and of 336 for the "town"—Ed.]

† 10 Cochin edangalis = 1 para = 8 Madras measures. [Therefore 1 edangali of paddy weighs 2 lb.—Ed.].

‡ These cloths are nearly one yard wide.

work connected with the harvesting, separating the paddy from the stalks, etc. They are employed as a rule throughout the year by their masters; in leisure days however they are paid a little less than the stated wage.

They take kanji (rice boiled in water) and toddy in the morning, toddy in the afternoon, cooked rice at night; they eat also fish and flesh. They behave well, are obedient and honest and loyal to their masters, very earnest about their work, but are completely illiterate. There are no schools for them in the village. They worship spirits in the shape of stocks and stones; and on the occasion of the festivals of their Gods and Goddesses they take a good dose of toddy and with drums and bugles and priests dance in the premises of the 'temple'.

There are sub-divisions among the Pulayas, Cherumas, Paraiyas, Nayadis, Malayas and others, who form separate castes among themselves and are restricted in their intercourse with one another.

The Cherumas dwell in colonies of two or three families each, in low, small thatched huts near the land of their masters. It must be admitted that they are not treated properly by the high caste Hindus, though they form the backbone of agricultural labour in these parts. They are low paid and underfed and treated with contempt and sometimes with harshness by the other castes and their masters. It is a wonder that they still cherish obedience to their masters and earnestness in their work. There are a few who try to get rid of the yoke by running away, but the majority are contented and stay with their masters. They are experts in practical agricultural work and can face any sort of weather.

Land and Occupation of land—

	ACRES.
Area of wet lands	653·24
,, dry lands	937·21
,, lands watered by wells	...
,, common waste	18·81
Pasture other than common waste	33·94
Woods and forests	1,912·35
Fruit trees and scattered shade trees ...	301·48

There are altogether five public tanks in the village, most of which are not used for irrigation purposes at all, but for bathing, which is done by all at least once a day. There are no public wells. The cultivation of rice solely depends on the rains of the South-West Monsoon (June—September) which are copious, and of the North-East Monsoon in November. Every house however contains a well, from which water is drawn for drinking purposes and for watering the compound gardens in the summer. Water can be obtained at a very slight depth in most parts except at the foot of the hills. The sides of the tanks, usually not very large in size, are paved step by step with granite or laterite stones by which people can step down into the water for bathing. Water is lifted from the wells by means of pots for drinking purposes, but for watering gardens lifts of various sorts are used.

The water wheel, which costs about Rs. 35, is very rarely used except in *kol* fields where water has to be lifted out of the land,

GUEST CHAMBER OF NAMBUDRI HOUSE.

Photo by G. Slater.

The mhote too is seldom seen in these parts. The more common sorts of water-lifters are (1) an oval shaped bamboo-basket (costing about As. 2); (2) a wooden groove provided with a handle, costing about Re. 1; (3) and a frame-work consisting of two long bamboos, one small and another big in size balanced on a horizontal beam which is supported by two vertical poles; a picottah is attached to the small-sized bamboo and is drawn up and brought down by one or two persons standing opposite each other on two planks thrown across the middle of the well. The whole frame together with the picottah costs about Rs. 2. The oval shaped basket and the wooden groove are used to spread water from water courses and not from wells. Two persons, generally women, stand opposite each other on the side of a watercourse and pull the basket towards themselves by means of ropes tied round its 'ears' after filling it up with water; the extreme ease and facility with which they carry on the operations, often to the accompaniment of a snatch of song, is wonderful. The wooden groove is allowed to swing on a string and is moved to and fro by a person holding the handle.

The classes into which wet and dry lands are divided, the extent of each and the amount of assessment are subjoined.

Classes.	Wet lands.										Dry lands.				
	Single crop.					Double crop.					Single crop.				
	Area.		Assessment.			Area.		Assessment.			Area.		Assessment.		
	ACS.	C.	RS.	A.	P.	ACS.	C.	RS.	A.	P.	ACS.	C.	RS.	A.	P.
I ..	35	65	116	7	9	320	74	1,527	5	5	301	48	261	11	3
II ...	4	56	15	10	9	59	72	210	6	3	12	69	3	12	8
III ...	16	0	36	0	7	39	73	114	6	0	212	60	77	5	7
IV ...	21	37	39	9	8	15	51	34	11	2	68	39	17	10	3
V ...	109	59	147	9	11	11	5	17	12	11	207	53	44	6	8
VI ...	18	6	34	10	10	1	24	3	2	5	56	49	3	13	8
VII ...	...		...			...		...			78	3	37	0	3

The selling prices of cultivable wet land in the village are approximately Class I Rs. 1,500, Class II Rs. 1,000, Class III Rs. 800 Class IV Rs. 500—600, Class V Rs. 500.

The land is classified according to tenure as follows:—

I. 'Pandaravaka Verumpattam' (Sirkar) non-favourable tenure.	Nilams (wet land) (A. 86·73). Parambas (dry land) (A. 210·88).	109 pattadars.
II. 'Pandaravaka Kanam' (Sirkar) favourable tenure.	Nilams (A. 2·19) ... Parambas (7 cents) ...	4 pattadars.
III. 'Puravaka' (outside Sirkar).	Nilams (A. 563·61) ... Parambas (A. 711·80)...	54 pattadars.
IV. Inams (gift tenure).	Nilams (71 cents) ... Parambas (A. 14·47) ...	6 pattadars.

The revenue paid to the State varies according to the nature of the tenure. It is only the "Pandaravaka verumpattam" lands which pay the full pattam or share due to the State. The Pandaravaka verumpattamdars have full rights to the soil of the lands they hold and their rights remain undisturbed so long as they regularly pay the State revenue, but the rights to metals and minerals are reserved to the State.

In *Pandaravaka kanam*, the land is held on a lease in consideration of a sum of money supposed to have been advanced to the State, and consequently a certain amount is deducted from the State demand on account of interest on the amount advanced. Before the new settlement was made in 1905 it was the custom to renew the lease every twelve years on the renewal of which the kanamdar was to pay over 20 per cent of the kanam amount, plus half of the full pattam (rent) for one year and a fee of 5 per cent of the kanam amount or Rs. 3-2-0 (whichever is greater) for issuing a fresh renewal. But this practice is now done away with and the tenure is for all practical purposes the same as Pandaravaka verumpattam tenure with this difference only that from the assessment due thereon a deduction of one-third is made.

In Puravaka lands (literally lands which are outside) a third party called the Janmi is recognized as holding proprietorship and therefore entitled to share the produce with the cultivator and the Sirkar. The tenure is assessed by the Sirkar in the case of nilams at half the rates fixed for Pandaravaka verumpattam nilams and in the case of parambas at one-fourth.

Inams are personal grants or grants made in some cases for the performance of certain specified services in religious institutions, etc., and in others for services rendered on some previous occasion or for some other similar reasons either absolutely or on certain specified conditions. The deductions range from free assessment to one-third of the Pandaravaka verumpattam assessment.

In all these cases of tenure a royalty cess of six pies per rupee calculated on Pandaravaka verumpattam assessment is payable to the Sirkar.

The *Janmis* of Puravaka land let their land under different tenures, viz., verumpattam in which they make full assessment; kanam and inam they treat as favourable, but the rates are not so fixed or settled as those of the Sirkar's tenures. The leases of the kanam * lands of the janmis are also renewed for twelve years, the janmi collecting certain dues from their tenants for the renewal of the same. The title of the tenant of such lands is precarious for the kanamdar can be evicted on the janmi paying back the kanam amount † at the end of the lease of twelve years. This state of affairs was unsatisfactory, and the State Government has recently passed a Bill called the "Cochin Tenancy Bill" of 1914, an extremely moderate measure indeed, passed in the teeth of much opposition from the Janmis. The Regulation intends "to make better provision for the payment of compensation for the improvements made by tenants, and provide for the speedy realization of rent and other customary dues, by investing the District

* [Kanam = lease. Kanamdars = leaseholders.— Ed.]

† I.e., the amount the kanamdar has deposited with the Janmi at the time of taking up the lease.

GROUP OF NAMBUDRI BRAHMANS.

Photo by G. Slater.

Munsifs and District Judges with summary jurisdiction in the matter." The provisions in the regulation apply only to "Kanam tenants who, by themselves or through their predecessors in interest, have uninterruptedly held the holding for a period of not less than thirty years prior to the coming into force of this Regulation," and provide some restrictions on the part of the landlord in matters of renewal of kanam holdings, and ejection of kanam tenants; and dispense altogether with the right of *Melkanam*. The Puravaka janmis in Watakancheri number 54, of whom a few are Nambudri Brahmans, the others being of various castes. The Nambudris are the big landlords.

These janmis also are in some cases the custodians of "devaswoms" (literally "wealth of the gods"), lands belonging to the local temples; these are treated by them just like their janmam lands, but they keep separate accounts for the same. The Sirkar also manages devaswom lands and there is a department in the State which manages the affairs of the temples and the property belonging to them.

Of the total number of landowners (about 150), only 34 with an area of 194·44 acres cultivate their own lands. The rest sublet.

Of the non-cultivating landowners a few are big janmis like the Nambudri Brahmans and the Paliath Atchan. The Nambudri Brahmans pursue no occupation but that of living in strict conformity with the duties of a Brahman. They study the Vedas and live a pious and cleanly life. Western civilization and ideas have not penetrated to them. They maintain the joint-property system in which the whole property descends to the eldest male member. Only the eldest male is allowed to enter into legal marriage, but he can marry two or three women; the rest keep Nayar females as their mistresses.*

The "Paliath Atchan" possesses much land in the State. The head of the family lives in a place near Cranganore. He manages his estates through departments and officials like the Sirkar. He is the biggest landlord in the State, and a powerful hereditary chief.

The small landowners who do not cultivate their lands pursue occupations like retail trade, Government service, law, etc. These generally sublet their lands to tenants who own no lands and try to exact from these latter as much rent as possible. There are also agricultural workers who neither own nor rent land; the caste of "Cherumas" belongs to this class. Also a few of the low castes, the Mappilas and in some cases the Christians,—male and female—engage themselves in such work. They are low paid. Formerly these wages were in kind, but money wages have begun to prevail; but for harvesting work wages are invariably paid in kind, the worker receiving one para of paddy for every six gathered in.

The rents of paddy lands are paid in kind.

Agriculture.—Paddy is grown on all the wet lands. Out of the seasons, the cultivators also grow to a small extent such grains as gram and peas in the paddy lands. Area under paddy—653·24 acres.

---

* [This phrase must not be understood to mean that such Nayar women are maintained in any way by their Nambudri paramours. They depend on their own family property, which descends in the female line. The children of Nambudri Brahmans and Nayar women are reckoned Nayars, and are members of the joint family of the mother, and entitled to maintenance from that family property.—Ed.]

Area yielding one crop—205·23 acres.

Area yielding two crops—448·01 acres.

There are a few acres yielding three crops, but only two crops are assessed.

There are different kinds of paddy, each having different periods of growth, and specially suited to particular soils. The fields are manured and in some cases slightly ploughed just before the rains in summer. The south-west monsoon usually begins in June and lasts for four months. As soon as the rain comes, lands are ploughed and paddy is sown in particularly favourable areas. Then all the fields of the farmer are well ploughed and manured; the seedlings are replanted over the whole area after a growth of twenty-eight days. Some kinds of paddy grow for sixty days, others eighty and ninety days. The system in which no replantation takes place is also in much vogue. The fields are protected from animal or bird pests; after a period of at most three months the paddy is mown by agricultural workers who separate the paddy from the stalks.

Another crop is also generally sown during the north-east monsoon season (October and November) which usually gives rain for about one month.

The ploughs used are primitive and old-fashioned. The furrowing is done in this wise:—a flat piece of iron sharpened at one end is attached to a wooden frame with a handle; this handled frame is attached by means of a pole to a yoke which is placed on the neck of a pair of oxen or buffaloes; the worker then holds the handle and drives the oxen round and round the field until the whole field is well furrowed over. This is done *before* the heavy rain, when the ground is softened, but not under water. The sod is then crushed by means of sticks, this being generally done by females. The women walk in a row, beating the sod to and fro with heavy sticks held in one hand. After the field has been well watered by rains it is once more worked over by means of a log of wood (levelling board) drawn by oxen.

The other agricultural implements used are the sickle, a big knife and spades.

Stock.—The following is the official census of the stock:—

Working oxen	245
Cows	289
Male buffaloes	361
Cow buffaloes	20
Young stock—	
Calves	169
Young buffaloes	7
Horses	2
Donkeys and mules	22
Sheep and goats	583

Oxe are used to drag carts, and for ploughing the fields. Most of the oxen here appear to be lean and weak; especially those used in ploughing. Cart-drawing oxen are better.

Cows are used for milking only, though the Muhammadans of the locality are not averse to eating beef now and then. The milk, buttermilk and ghee of the cow are in great demand especially among the Brahmans who cannot do without them; the lower

LEVELLING BOARD AT WORK.

Photo by Agricultural College.

castes very rarely use these products. The cows too are not brought up on a scientific basis, and are consequently of a weak build and generally yield from 4 nalis * to 6 or 8 nalis of milk per day.†

Male buffaloes are used in ploughing and sometimes to draw loaded carts. These too are of weak build.

Cow buffaloes are used mostly for milking, but sometimes in ploughing. The milk they yield is greater in quantity but inferior in quality to that of the cows.‡

Very little care is taken of the young of the above species. The young calf or calf-buffalo is not usually reared with the object of getting strong or vigorous oxen or buffaloes, but allowed to grow haphazardly. Some die off young, and especially the buffalo-calf since the buffalo can be milked without its young and not so the cows.§ The official figures in this respect (vide above) are instructive. The usual practice is to buy cows or buffaloes from a fair for milking purposes and to dispose of them, buffaloes especially, unless needed for ploughing, when the milk dries up.

The only use to which the horse is put is to drive jutkas, but as jutkas are rare in this village, horses are seldom seen here.

Donkeys and mules too are few.

Sheep and goats are used for their mutton which is in demand among the lower castes, but more for their milk, which is considered to be medicinal.

Pigs are reared for their flesh by the local Christians; the Muhammadans consider it to be a sacrilege even to utter the name.

Cows, oxen and buffaloes are made to stand in stalls, two or more being allowed to be in the same stall. Bundles of rice straw form the chief food, but green grass is used during the rainy season. Rice dust and poonac (copra from which the oil has been extracted) mixed in water is given. Cows are let loose during the daytime under care of a keeper to feed in the fields or near the hills.

Cattle-dung mixed with cattle urine is used as manure in the paddy fields. This is scattered in the fields during the hot season (April-May). The percentage of cattle-dung will approximately be 25 per cent of the total manure used. Dung is also used as fuel. Women are becoming averse to making varatties and use more wood.

Sheep dung is sometimes used.

But green manure consisting of leaves of certain plants and trees is scattered in the fields after they have been well ploughed in the first fall of the monsoon rains. Green manure is never grown, but is obtained from the neighbouring hills.

Every house without exception has a compound big or small surrounding it in which there are coconut palms, arecanut palms, mango trees, jack fruit trees, plantains, etc., and sometimes pepper. During the hot months (March-April-May) vegetables

---

* [1 nali (nari or nazhi) = ¼ of a Madras measure and very nearly = 9 fluid ounces or nearly half a pint.—Ed.]

† I.e., one or two quarts of milk per day. A Madras cow yields up to five quarts per day.

‡ [I.e., it is less valued. Buffalo's milk is very rich.—Ed.]

§ [It is a fact that an Indian cow refuses to give milk without the calf. If the calf dies the dairyman stuffs the skin and makes an imitation calf. This serves the purposes.—Ed.]

useful for cookery are watered and grown in the compound itself; while during the rains also vegetables are grown, such as brinjals, lady's fingers, pumpkins, peas, etc. During summer the trees and vegetables in the compound are watered from the well which is a special feature of every house.

Insect-pests.—The *caterpillars* of certain moths ate away this year (1916) the tender blades of the paddy as soon as they cropped up from underground. This appeared at the beginning of the sowing season (May) and lasted for a week or two. Farmers here say that these have not appeared for years past. When I wrote to the Agricultural Superintendent of the State at Trichur he suggested the following remedy: "Dig a trench ½ foot wide by 1½ feet deep along the four sides of a field where these insects would fall in their travel from field to field, but would not be able to get out of it."

A kind of fly or flea is said to eat away the juice of the rice at the stalk of the paddy as soon as it reaches the milk stage.

Cattle diseases.—Sore feet. The feet are well washed with hot water, and turpentine, teak-oil, or cashewnut oil is smeared in the sore; the animal is also made to stand in a muddy place into which the leaves of a certain tree are strewn.

Mouth disease. Pig-ghee or bear-ghee is smeared on the tongue.

Swelling in the belly. The animal without any apparent cause falls down and dies. No medicine is applied in such cases.

Malignant sore-throat and cow-pox are also common.

An Agricultural Department for the State has been established recently at Trichur with a model farm attached to it. The present Superintendent is an England-returned Cochinite. Help is often derived from here, but the farmers themselves are shrewd in practical agriculture.

Timber.—Wood for fuel, implements, buildings, etc., is obtained from the neighbouring hills and forests. The taluk of Talapilli is full of forests especially on the eastern side. Nearly 43 per cent of the area of the State is forest and its timber is even exported to foreign parts. The Forest Department is a source of income to the State.

Coolies carry faggots of fuel on their heads from the neighbouring hills for sale; sometimes the people get cart-loads; a decent head-load now costs nearly 4 annas and a cart-load from Rs. 2–8–0 to Rs. 3; prices were much lower a few years back. A full head-load is divided into smaller bundles before being sold, and a woman may get six or eight annas for a bundle as heavy as she can carry.

Durable building materials are got from the forests and timber depots, but mango-planks, bamboos and jack-tree planks are also used.

Houses.—Houses are not built in rows. Every house is surrounded by a compound hedged round by bamboo. Such compounds are intersected by lanes. Rice-straw is used in thatching houses; tiles are replacing thatch but the majority of houses still are thatched. No terraced houses can be seen in these parts where the monsoon rains pour down with full force.

HUT NEAR TRICHUR, COCHIN STATE.

Photo by G. Slater.

Site values of land for building are getting higher and higher in the 'town', chiefly because the Shoranur-Cochin Railway now runs through this place, the principal offices of the taluk are here, and a high school has just been opened. Rs. 500 per acre may be paid in the 'town'; Rs. 50 to Rs. 100 in the rest of the village area. But the best wet land fetches up to Rs. 1,500 per acre. Cultivable land fetches far higher prices than building land, because only land unfit for cultivation, of which there is enough, is used for building.

The practice of exchanging lands is unknown. Generally, though not always, holdings are continuous. Field huts, built in the midst of their fields, are often used by big farmers. The seeds, the harvested paddy and other crops, the stock, the implements, etc., are kept there.

Subsidiary industries.—Weaving is not practised. In the north-eastern part of the State, however, handloom weaving of an exquisite sort and also of a rough character is practised.

Mat-weaving of an exquisite pattern out of certain reeds duly coloured is practised by a set of people locally known as 'Koravas.' The condition of these men, however, is miserable. They have no capital, no organization or culture, but usually make their wares to order, though now and then a few enterprising middlemen avail themselves of these people's skill. They talk a jargon of Tamil and Malayalam, and their females, like gipsies, beg from house to house and profess themselves to be adepts in palmistry. They make mats costing from Re. 1 to Rs. 15 or Rs. 20. They yet live from hand to mouth; and I have my doubts whether they will be able to keep up their skill unless knowing people help to raise their economic condition.

Every village moreover contains within its borders the following castes who follow their hereditary crafts:—the Marasari (carpenter), Kallasari (mason), Tattan (goldsmith), Musari (brazier), Kollan (blacksmith), and Tolkollan (leather-worker). There are a few families of each of these castes in Watakanchery also. "As their services are much in requisition and as they earn better wages than unskilled labourers, they are still engaged in their hereditary occupation. The first five groups are socially in a par with each other. They all interdine, but do not intermarry. But the Tolkollans are considered inferior in status to the rest and cannot touch them without causing pollution, probably on account of their work in leather which in its raw state is considered impure. Polyandry of the fraternal type was prevalent among them, several brothers marrying one wife and the children being treated as common to all. This practice however is fast dying out, if it has not already done so." (Census Reports.) One special feature in the caste-hierarchy is that these people are made to stand at a specified distance while approaching the higher castes (24 feet is the rule).

These castes minister to the every day needs of the community, executing their work generally to order. As they are very poor, they cannot afford to work on their own account on a commercial scale. The village usually contains a recognized *desa-asari* (village smith) to whom the farmers pay a certain amount of paddy at the harvesting season of the year for the repair of their implements. None but the village-smith is entitled to this dole. These may entertain apprentices from their own caste-people, though the father is usually the teacher of his children in the hereditary caste. A good workman can earn from about 8 annas to 10 annas per day.

Village trade.—Iron ware used for domestic utensils and for agricultural purposes is got from Trichur, the nearest town. There are however a few retail shops in the 'town.' All articles of consumption are bought from retail shops, the retail keepers themselves getting their wares from either Trichur or Palghat.

Rice is the principal commodity. Arecanut and to some extent pepper and bamboos form important items of sale. There is a fair half a mile to the north of the 'town' which meets once a week (every Wednesday), for the sale of arecanut and pepper. Merchants from various parts of Malabar and even from the east of the Ghats come here to buy arecanuts. Vegetables and sundries also are exposed for sale for the use of the villagers only.

The main metalled road which passes from Shoranur to Trichur passes through the middle of the 'town.' Another road from the west touches the main road to the north of the 'town.' The Shoranur-Cochin Railway touches this place. The commercial town of Trichur is only ten miles to the south.

Co-operation in trading as well as in most other affairs is conspicuous by its absence. A Registrar of Co-operative Societies has recently been appointed in the State, and, I am told, gave one or two lectures in the place, but nothing came of it. I have hopes that a co-operative credit society will be started within a few years. I may mention that such credit societies have been opened in three places in the taluk and are receiving much help from the State. The co-operative principle as yet is not extended to trading, but with the development of knowledge and culture this may come.

Economic condition—

Statement showing wages (in *money*) for the whole State.

Workers.	Minimum.		Maximum.		Maximum in villages.	
	RS.	A.	RS.	A.	RS.	A.
Carpenters	0	6	1	0	0	8
Blacksmiths	0	6	0	12	0	8
Masons	0	6	0	14	0	8
Bricklayers	0	7	0	12	0	8
Sawyers	0	10	1	0	Piece-worker.	
Coolies –						
Male	0	4	0	10	0	6
Female	0	3	0	6	0	3
Boys	0	2	0	4	0	2

To Cherumans payment is made in kind (see above). Also wages are paid in kind to agricultural workers in the village area especially during the harvest season.

Labour cost of cultivation of one acre of paddy.

For this area 8½ paras * of seed will be used.

Nature of work.	Rate of wages.	Total number of days.	Total amount of wages.	In kind or money.	Remarks.
			RS. A.		
Ploughing ...	3 as. or 3 ed. of paddy per half-day.	25	4 12	Both customery.	The ploughman works only during the first half of the day. He is expected to plough three times over an area of one para of seed capacity in a half day; and the land requires nine ploughings.
Plucking for replanting.	5 as. or 5 ed. of paddy per day (piece-wages).	8	2 8	Do.	Women chiefly employed. One person plucks one para-seed-area per day and is paid 5 ed. of paddy.
Replanting.	Earns 5 as. or 5 ed. of paddy per day (piece-wages).	4	1 4	Do.	Half the labour of plucking.
Weeding ...	4 as. or 4 ed. of paddy per para.		2 2	Do.	Only when transplantation does not take place.
Water-inspection.	4 as. per day ...	for 3 months.	1 13	Do.	One person can supervise 12½ acres.
Safe-keeping of matured paddy.	4 paras of paddy (Rs. 2) for 15 days.	15 to 20	2 0	Do.	At the period of harvest he is paid in kind.
Harvesting (including mowing, thrashing, etc.).	For every six paras of paddy gathered one para is paid.				Women chiefly engaged.

Note.—The yield per para is 10 to 20 fold †; and in specially favoured lands even more. In this table the price of 1 *edangali* of paddy is taken to be 1 anna (which was the market rate 1916-1917).

Statement showing the prices of staple food-grains in the Cochin State for the year 1915-6.

Articles.	Prices per maund of 82⅞ lb.					
	1914-5.			1915-6.		
	RS.	A.	P.	RS.	A.	P.
Rice (husked)	6	8	11	6	5	10
Wheat	5	14	1	5	15	11
Peas	5	10	6	5	12	1
Dholl	6	8	11	7	5	2
Gram	3	8	0	3	10	7
Gingelly	9	9	7	8	6	1
Green peas	3	5	11	5	7	5
Bengal gram	5	15	2	5	15	9

* [Approximately 180 lb., an excessive quantity. "Transplanted, 20 lb. in 7 cents of land will plant up one acre. But this seed-rate is usually very largely exceeded, up to 150 lb. per acre being used" Wood, Notebook of Agricultural Facts, p. 52.—Ed.]

† [I.e., 16 to 32 cwt. per acre, worth about Rs. 50 to 100. With the lower yield the net return is Rs. 31 per acre, with the higher Rs. 75, from which cost of seed must be subtracted. —Ed.]

The families which have made savings are very few in proportion to the population both in the 'town' and in the village area. There is a big Nambudiri janmi in the village. He owns very much land which he has sublet and holds the custody of much devaswom land. As the partition of family property does not exist in a Nambudiri family, their property only increases. The joint property system also obtains among the Nayars, but the Nayar families which are well-to-do and have made savings could be numbered on the fingers. The majority of them are poor and many of them occupy themselves in work for wages. The Brahmans other than Nambudiri Brahmans follow the divided property system.* I can only count four or five families which possess wealth to the value of Rs. 10,000 and above and only one or two which have Rs. 20,000. Most of the Brahmans are comparatively poor. Some are engaged in Government service for a paltry pay of Rs. 20 per month or less, and few are able to save much out of this pay.

No more capital is invested in agriculture than is absolutely necessary from year to year, as for replenishing the stock, implements, etc., and clearing the fields of rubbish and making it ready to receive the rains. Bunds are also constructed, to store water in the water course which runs on the north of the village area, by persons whose lands lie near it, but these dams last only during the summer. A few indeed improve their land by digging it, and one or two have made new fields on land previously waste. About one-tenth of the savings could be said to be utilized in these ways. No one invests his earnings in savings banks.

Lending to neighbours is *the* form of investing one's savings, until they come up to a round sum which can be invested in landed property. A few people in the town take advantage of others' difficulties to lend money at exorbitant interest. Many are in debt.

All castes and conditions of men try to accumulate their savings by subscribing to a *kuri*. A *kuri* serves the purpose of a savings bank. There are three chief kinds—*bhangati-kuri*, auction-*kuri* and lottery-*kuri*. The first prevails among the lower castes and consists of small subscriptions. The *kuri* is started by a *kuri-muppan* (stake-holder) with a certain specified amount as principal, each member subscribing an equal amount. The stake-holder is entrusted with the task of giving a dinner to all the members, each member contributing two or four annas for the purpose. On the day appointed for the *kuri*, the members bid down the amount and the bidden amount is collected from each of the several members and paid to the bidder. Auction-*kuri* is similar to this, but the dinner is dispensed with and the *kuri* deals with large amounts subscribed by well-to-do men. In a lottery-*kuri*, a number of persons agree that each should subscribe a certain sum of money by periodical instalments and that each in his turn, as determined by lot, should take the whole of the subscription for each instalment, all being returned the amount of their subscriptions and the common fund being lent to each subscriber in turn.

Every decent householder among the Brahmans spends some money (at least Rs. 60) on gold ornaments for his wife or other female relatives. The other castes rarely use gold ornaments or jewellery of any cost.

* [I.e., on the death of a man his property is equally divided among his sons.—Ed.]

Savings are not invested in industrial undertakings, there being no openings for the same.

On the question of rural indebtedness, its causes and extent, much can be written. There has been, I am told, an enormous increase in indebtedness among all classes. Nearly 75 per cent are in debt, especially so the poor agriculturists. The great proportion of small landholders and agricultural workers, the want of diversity of industry and occupation, the rise in the price of commodities, the high usurious interest which a few take for money advanced, the substitution of money for kind in taxes, the high cost of education, lower and higher, to which Brahmans resort now-a-days, the high value which people set on Government service, however small the pay, all these are working, some generally and others in particular cases, to cause and perpetuate rural indebtedness. Co-operative credit societies could do much to help the people out of it. I may also mention that litigation is also responsible. For every paltry difference resort is had to the Munsif's or the Magistrate's Court, as there are no other means of settling such differences. There are nearly twenty-five vakils or pleaders in the Munsif's Court alone who cast nets to earn something by favouring the litigious spirit. Among the Brahmans the 'dowry system' is working some mischief. Every girl has to be given in marriage before her twelfth year and the bridegroom demands a good round sum. Social reformers condemn the system. A redeeming feature of it, viz., that that sum is a substantial help to the bridegroom's costly higher English education is not wholly to be forgotten; and no Brahman stops his education until thrown out by the University or money ceases to be forthcoming.

The proportion of debtors who have liberated themselves from debt may be estimated at nearly a fourth.

Communal village life is unknown in the 'village.' The Brahmans in the 'town' try to revive a 'Samooham' (gathering) but with no success so far. There is no communal property. Separate individual life is the order. The local Muhammadans and Christians keep up a kind of unity within their 'castes' because of their religion and Church. The Hindu temples in the village are managed by the State Government. For every slight improvement in the village the people have to approach the Government. For example, the local tank has been in ruins for the last three or four years; the Government of course helps the people, but the tank is not yet repaired because of official delay and when it is actually done, as was done once a few years back, the contractor earns a good round sum as profit and the work is not properly carried out.

Temples and festivals.—The annual religious festival in the local temple at Watakanchery town which lasts for five days is conducted by the Government. Rs. 128 and 128 paras of paddy (24 cwt.) are spent; a contractor bids for the sum and he conducts the festival.

The people of the village themselves conduct an annual religious festival at a temple nearly three miles to the north by collecting subscriptions. They spend nearly Rs. 300 on the occasion. It is pleasant to witness a procession in Malabar. So many elephants are ornamented and made to stand in array. The number of elephants depends upon the depth of the purse. Drum-beaters beat the drums according to their 'science' for two or three hours. The figure of the God or Goddess is taken on the back of the middle elephant in the row. There is a display of fireworks at night.

A few temples in the village are managed by private people or Janmis, usually Nambudri Brahmans. Such temples have landed property managed by these Janmis who generally make use of the profits. Recently the Government has been trying to encroach upon the temple properties in its capacity of *melkoyma*; this is very much resented by the Nambudri Jánmis.

The common people as a rule have no part or lot in temple management or expenditure.

State loans.—Only one person in the village has borrowed from the Government a loan of Rs. 400 to be paid back in ten instalments of Rs. 40 each with interest at 5 per cent. The small landholders do not approach the Government for help; the mediocre landholders rent their land to others; while the few big ones have money of their own if they want to make any improvement. The fact is that agriculture is routine work with many people; no permanent improvements are thought of by the majority.

Sanitary condition.—Plague and tuberculosis are not heard of. Malaria only affects those who resort for agricultural purposes to the foot of the hills four or five miles east from the village. Attacks of cholera frequently occur among the local Muhammadans, who are as a rule quite insanitary, poor, living in low and ill-ventilated thatched huts or hovels; one is sick of the stinking smell when one approaches their huts. The local Christians, though equally poor, are better in this respect. The houses of most of the Brahmans and the majority of the Nayars are decent. The hovels of the lower castes and working men again are poor and insanitary. As the houses are not built in rows, but separate, each having a compound big or small, epidemic diseases such as small-pox when they come at all are easily avoided. But the case is different in the quarters of the Muhammadans and Christians, who build their houses in streets.

The chief endemic diseases are fever, rheumatism, attacks of bile.

There are plenty of snakes in the village everywhere. One sometimes hears of deaths caused by snake-bites. There are however a few who pretend to cure snake-bites by incantations aided by medicines.

There is a Government free dispensary established in the 'town' where the Apothecary is a Sub-Assistant Surgeon. But most people resort to native (ayurvedic) physicians or vaidyans. Ayurveda, or the Hindu science of medicine, makes use of vegetable drugs both in the raw and dried state. The physician comes to your house and prescribes a certain mixture according to the directions laid down in his code which he has committed to memory in the form of verses. The drugs can be got from the market, or from a neighbouring hill, or even from one's own compound.

This science is handed down from father to son in certain families in Malabar who form even now some of the most distinguished native physicians in Malabar. Even in a petty village there will be a specialist for diseases of children, an eye specialist, an ordinary vaidyan who cures all common diseases, and a *mantra-vati* (hymn-chanter) who pretends to cure diseases by chanting certain hymns within himself, and who is believed in by the masses. There is also a *visha-vaidyan*, or expert in curing snake-bite, in some villages.

The Sub-Assistant Surgeons in charge of Government hospitals are, I am afraid, affected by red tape and carelessness born of security of employment and income.

In rural parts especially I am pained to note that their treatment is getting discredited, for the apothecaries take little pains to know the exact nature of the diseases of the poor persons who resort to the hospital and to prescribe proper medicines for the same. There are of course noble exceptions to this, but it is deplorable that there should be any irregularities at all in this most humane of all charities. The native vaidyans, on the other hand, have a local interest, their families living in the village for generations together and they are very keen to keep up their reputations; while the Government Surgeon is a bird of passage, who comes and goes, none of the villagers knowing whence or whither.

Malayalis, as a rule, are very clean, most of them bathe twice a day; their clothes are kept neat and clean. But there is much scope for the spread of modern ideas on sanitation in very many fields. At child-birth the mother is usually kept in the worst possible room in the house. Children too might be brought up in a more sanitary environment; the education of females on these matters is a very crying necessity. It is also deplorable that Brahmans are gradually neglecting the morning-bath and exercise on which their ancestors insisted. The local Muhammadans are extremely insanitary. They are filthy, their children are filthy, their habits too are filthy.

The habit of keeping the stock very near the house should be avoided. Again except in well-to-do Nayar families kitchens are in the houses; they should be in a different building.

Among the Brahmans, a girl has to be married before the age of puberty, generally 12. Among no other caste is this compulsory, though a few people, including the Indian Christians, marry their girls before puberty. These Christians are generally converts from low caste * Hindus, and change of religion has not changed their custom in this respect.

The local Muhammadans do not, as in the east of the peninsula, observe purdah; their women freely talk to any person, work for others as coolies and stir abroad. Most of them are converts from low caste Hindus, and so there is no fanaticism, nor such strict observance of the rules of Islam as elsewhere. Nayar ladies are quite free, and among them descent in the female line (Marumakkattayam) prevails. Brahman ladies (not Nambudris) can go out, and be seen by others, but they are subject to their husbands and are not allowed to speak to Brahman men, and Brahman men are not allowed to speak with the women. A newly married Brahman bride is neither allowed to see nor to speak to her husband until she actually joins her husband after the nuptials. But these

---

* [M. L. K. Anandakrishna Ayyar, Cochin State Anthropologist, informs me that the Syrian Christians of Cochin are mainly the descendants of converts from *high* caste Hindus.—Ed.]

women can speak to other caste people, male or female, without breach of decorum. Purdah is observed among the Nambudri Brahman women.

Every house contains a well from which water is taken for drinking and domestic purposes. Water is specially good in the village since the ground forms a good filter. Wells are generally not very deep. Few people boil the water before drinking. Generally a raised mound is erected round the well to keep bad water out; nevertheless, during the rainy season water from the compounds runs to the wells with the result that the wells get extremely muddy, but the water is used without compunction by the people. Tank water is used only for bathing.

Education.—There are only three schools in the whole village, one for boys which has this year (1916) been raised to a high school, a Church school for Christian boys, and a vernacular school for girls up to the primary standard. The high school is a spacious building recently constructed at a cost of nearly Rs. 20,000. There is a prescribed code of study, and pupils are prepared for the School Final Examination which is conducted by the State. Brahman girls never attend the school after the age of 12. But all of them learn now to read and write the vernacular which is Malayalam in these parts, though the language the Brahmans use in their houses is Tamil, with an intonation markedly changed from the Tamil in the eastern parts. I subjoin below the strength of the respective classes in the high school and the girls' primary school. The Church school is maintained by the Christians in their church for their exclusive use. It is classed as a primary school.

Sirkar High School, Watakancheri.

	Hindus.			Muhammadans.	Christians.	Total.
	Brahmans.	Nayars.	Other castes.			
Form IV	17	7	3	...	1	28
,, III (a)...	9	7	3	...	2	21
,, ,, (b)	10	9	3	...	3	25
,, II (a)...	13	11	1	...	3	28
,, ,, (b)	8	17	12	...	2	39
,, I (a)	11	7	4	...	2	24
,, ,, (b)	10	9	3	...	2	24
Standard IV (a)	7	10	4	1	2	24
,, ,, (b)	10	7	5	...	1	23
,, III (a)	10	20	6	1	1	38
,, ,, (b)	16	12	6	3	2	39
,, II (a)	6	10	9	...	6	31
,, ,, (b)	7	15	7	...	3	32
,, I (a)	16	16	2	...	3	37
,, ,, (b) ...	11	11	6	2	4	34
Infants (a)	9	13	8	4	6	40
,, (b)	9	18	6	1	6	40
Total ...	179	189	88	12	49	527

Note.—The Muhammadans are very backward in point of education. So too the lower castes of Hindus.

Sirkar Girls' Primary Vernacular School.

	Hindus.			Muhammadans.	Christians.	Total.
—	Brahmans.	Nayars.	Other castes.			
Standard IV	1	10	2	...	...	13
„ III...	10	3	2	..	5	20
„ II (a)	14	6	1	...	1	22
„ (b)	7	6	1	...	10	24
„ I (a)	15	10	6	...	3	34
„ (b)	2	19	2	...	13	36
Total ...	49	54	14	...	32	149

Nearly 75 per cent of the adults know how to read and write the vernacular, but those who know how to read and write English may be about 2 per cent. There are no pandits worth the name, nor specially educated persons, except the Nambudri Brahmans who study Sanskrit and the Vedas, but they are extremely exclusive and never mix with any people high or low. Their manners and customs would form an interesting study by themselves.

The number of boys (of girls there is not one single instance) who have advanced to more advanced schools elsewhere are only a few. What with the poverty of the people and what with the rigour of the examinations only a few, perhaps fifty, in the place have been able to reach the Matriculation standard, and of these only 7 have been able to graduate, of whom two are B.L.'s. One is studying for medicine as an Hospital Assistant.

The school expenses are usually met by the students' fathers, and in the case of Nayars, uncles. But a father's purse, as I pointed out already, is not very deep. Of the seven graduates mentioned only three were able, with difficulty, to meet the high costs of modern education. The remaining four were assisted by their wives' dowries or by their fathers-in-law.

The choice of career for a candidate who has passed his Matriculation or Secondary School-leaving Certificate is very limited. Most of them engage themselves in the Government service for salaries sometimes as low as Rs. 9 per mensem, but more often Rs. 12 or Rs. 15 to start with, as clerks, teachers in the lower standards, etc. No one sees any other opening so sure and so lasting. In my judgment the modern literary education which stops with the Secondary School-leaving Certificate is not of much use. The student's energy is damped when he enters the world with his Secondary School-leaving Certificate, at least that is my experience in my village. But it is good perhaps that education is becoming less and less useful as an opening to lucrative employment; but the authorities also, in my humble opinion, should change the character of education or so modify it as to make it less literary and more technical, so that an anxious father may not look forward in vain to his son getting into some employment however mean or undignified.

Of the two B.L.'s I mentioned, one is the District Magistrate in the State, another is a Pleader; of the graduates one is in the Government service in British India on a pay of Rs. 35, and the rest are still continuing their further studies.

Except the Royal Readers and text-books which pupils buy for their school course there are not very many good English books in the village. A few of us have tried to start a reading-room and library for the English-reading public, but it is only a beginning. But good Malayalam books are common.

No description of village-education would be complete without noting those silent yet effective forces of culture which make a Hindu home what it is, so sweet, so hospitable, and so pious.

The village is often visited by a troupe of 'players' who put on the stage Puranic stories in the form of pantomimes and *natakas* or dramas. The celebrated Malabar pantomime is known as *Kathakali*. A big landlord, or ruling chief, forms a troupe of players and sends them abroad, just after the rainy season is over. This troupe comes to a village, and a well-to-do and influential man in the village is expected to make arrangements for a performance. The expenses of the troupe for that day together with a small donation, which seldom exceeds Rs. 10, are to be paid by that person, and the villagers can witness the performance free of charge. The reputation of the man who has started the troupe, generally a big zamindar or a ruling chief, goes a long way in canvassing persons willing to meet the expenses of the play in a village. Sometimes the pantomime takes place in the local temple and the *devaswom* authorities are bound to meet the daily expenses of the players. This troupe travels from place to place and returns at the end of the season to the place from which it started and the members engage themselves in their respective occupations, generally agriculture, or as servants to the landlord who formed the troupe. The same round is repeated in the next season.

There are also various ways of teaching broadcast the Puranic lore such as *chakiyar kooth, ottam thullal,* etc.

In a *chakiyar kooth,* the *chakiyar* recites certain Sanskrit *slokas* illustrative of stories from the Puranas and interprets them with wit and humour in such an excellent fashion that there will not be one in the audience who does not stretch his sides with laughter. In an *ottam thullal,* the person recites with appropriate gestures verses composed in short Malayalam metre dealing with Puranic stories. These are usually performed on the occasion of festivals in temples.

The above institutions are indigenous to Malabar. Among the Tamil Brahmans, a travelling *Sastrigal* often visits a village and reads Puranic stories in Sanskrit in the local temple and interprets them in Tamil so that the men and women in the village may understand them. At the time of his departure a decent sum is subscribed and paid to him.

In every decent home, a member of the family reads stories from the Puranas to the other inmates in the vernacular. All the people listen with rapt attention and sometimes engage in a lively discussion. Tamil Brahman ladies usually learn by heart Puranic stories in the shape of songs which they recite every morning and evening and also in the leisure hours of the noon. I have often noted with interest the way in which even apparently illiterate people discuss among themselves the philosophy of life as preached in the Hindu sastras.

Village administration.—Panchayats were only introduced into the State in 1913. His Highness granted it as one of his boons during the celebration of his sixtieth birthday. "It is also my wish to revive, in commemoration of this occasion, the old village panchayat system which, I trust, will give facilities to the people to settle several matters of each village easily and quickly amongst themselves and give them some training in the art of self-government. It may also afford them better opportunities of representing their wants and grievances to the Darbar." With this Proclamation of His Highness the Raja begins the definition of the constitution and powers of the Village Panchayat Regulation.

Constitution.—Five members of whom the chief village officer of a revenue village (called locally "Parvathiakaran") is an ex-officio member. The rest are now nominated. It meets at least once a month.

POWERS.

I. *Administrative.*—(1) Maintenance and repairs of all minor irrigation works (i.e., works which do not require professional skill) below the cost of Rs. 500.

(2) Maintenance of road avenues.
(3) Maintenance of water-sheds.
(4) Prevention of epidemic diseases.
(5) Clearing and repairing of public wells and tanks.
(6) Formation of Co-operative Credit Societies.
(7) Improvement of public lanes and canals.

II. *Judicial.*—Civil disputes up to Rs. 50 with or without the consent of the parties, and up to Rs. 200 with the consent of the parties.

The judicial portion of the Regulation is still in abeyance and has not been brought into force in any panchayat in the State.

Even the administrative portion is applied only in three places in the taluk, since the rest have not sufficiently responded to the scheme. Watakancheri is still without a panchayat, though it is the headquarters of the taluk.

For executive work every taluk is under the direct administrative supervision of a Tahsildar (Revenue officer) who is also the Chief Treasury Officer. Until recently he was also a Magistrate, but this function is definitely taken away from him. Below him are Revenue Inspectors and village officers. The taluk in question, which has 74 villages, has 4 Revenue officers and more than 30 village officers. Watakancheri with an adjoining village is under a "Parvathiakaran" who collects the revenue and who has a clerk under him. This "Parvathiakaran" is paid Rs. 12 per month and his clerk Rs. 9. The revenue inspector supervises the survey work and collection work, and checks the village accounts. There are also a Munsif's Court and a Magistrate's Court in the village for the settlement of civil and criminal disputes.

Each taluk in the State has, as a rule, one Sanitary Inspector. The village officers should bring to the notice of the Sanitary

Inspector the outbreak of any epidemic. He makes tours in the villages; the two vaccinators in the taluk are under him. These vaccinators have to make tours in the taluk according to a programme previously laid down by the Sanitary Inspector. Public wells, tanks, cremation grounds, markets, cart-stands, etc., are also under his supervision. All towns which have no town-councils (and our town has not) are under health-officers, the Sub-Assistant Surgeon acting as the Health Officer. He attends to lighting.

Police.—Police administration is under a Sub-Inspector who has constables under him. He is under a Divisional Inspector (of whom there are three in the State) with a Superintendent of Police above him. There is, as a rule, one Sub-Magistrate for each taluk.

The official figures for the detection of crime are available only for a division of which there are three (A, B and C) in the State, and not for a village. The figures for the C Division, in which my village lies, are as follows:—

Cases.						Persons.						Property.					
1913-14.			1914-15.			1913-14.			1914-15.			1913-14.			1914-15.		
Charged.	Detected.	Per cent.	Charged.	Detected.	Per cent.	Tried.	Committed.	Per cent.	Tried.	Committed.	Per cent.	Lost.	Recovered.	Per cent.	Lost.	Recovered.	Per cent.
												RS.	RS.		RS.	RS.	
165	143	86·6	96	77	80·2	240	192	80	149	91	61	3,762	1,146	30·46	4,372	2,208	50·50

History and Prospects of the village.—I see no signs of economic improvement in the past; nor is there much deterioration worth speaking about. There has been, however, an increase in population in recent times. There has been no diversity of occupation. The same routine of paddy cultivation goes on with the old primitive tools and implements. Much capital is not invested even for agricultural improvements for the excellent reason that the small landholders who form the majority cannot afford to experiment on a grand scale, and the few big landholders are sleeping partners distributing their holdings to small men for rent. Nevertheless there are opportunities for economic improvement. The establishment of co-operative credit societies is an urgent need. An "Agricultural Society" consisting of members of the occupation could be conveniently started to diffuse modern scientific ideas in agriculture by distributing pamphlets in the vernacular and discussing questions of importance. A little more attention could be given to the rearing of agricultural stock and the use of agricultural implements. As irrigation does not depend for the most part upon wells in our parts, there is no use in multiplying them.

People buy land because land is the best form of investment

in their opinion. There are no other investments so secure, and a little land will feed a man and his family even when he is indisposed to work. Again, a certain amount of prestige is attached to a landed proprietor especially when he is a big one, though there is not such adoration as can sometimes be observed in the attitude of the common people towards the Government officials big and small.

There has been a certain dislocation in the labour market on account of the emigration of certain classes of workers to the rubber and other estates recently established in some parts of the State and elsewhere. Their low wages, their low social position, the baits employed, somewhat nefariously, by the recruiting agents, and the grandiose hopes which the workers entertain of the unseen, have all combined to deplete the village of a certain class of workers from agriculture. The wages not only of agricultural labourers, but of all classes of workers, carpenters, masons, bricklayers, coolies, etc., have gone up. Few of the emigrants have returned, and those who return are certainly not very desirous of going back.

Manual labour is still looked upon as derogatory, and a well-to-do high caste man labouring upon his own compound or his own fields or allowing either his sons or relatives to do the same would be looked upon with contempt. High caste men have always to employ low caste people for any and every work, agricultural or domestic. Skilled work such as carpentry, blacksmithy, masonry, etc., is invariably performed by the particular "castes", which are hereditary and exclusive in character. These occupy a low position in the Hindu hierarchy of caste, but not so low as that other kind of agricultural labourers whom I called "Cherumas" or Pariahs, who occupy the lowest place of all. Each is respectful to his superiors andsomewhat exacting to his inferiors, but there is nothing like hatred or dissatisfaction with one's lot in any of the castes. They take it as Nature-given and the social organism works in a smooth fashion, each man having his own work and his own aspirations. Judging from the present state of affairs it is impossible, and I think undesirable, to unsettle this order of things. There is scope however for the diffusion of education and knowledge, for the opening of a diversity of occupation, for infusing better ideals of social life and joint work, for improving agriculture and removing rural indebtedness and providing means of its non-recurrence in the future. But all this requires enlightened and sympathetic workers.

MALABAR DISTRICT.

GURUVAYUR (PONNANI TALUK).

[*By V. Lakshmana Aiyar, Christian College, Madras.*]

Preliminary.—Guruvayur is situated in the southern part of the Ponnani taluk, and is only 2 miles distant from the Arabian Sea. It is close to the backwater which extends from the northern point of the taluk to Cochin and Travancore. To the east it is only 3 miles distant from the State of Cochin. It is 14 miles away from the capital town of the taluk through which flows the chief river of Malabar. No forests can be seen throughout the whole taluk. The whole taluk is one red sandy mass with no waste lands, no mountains or hills. The chief crop of the village and perhaps of the whole taluk is coconut.

Malabar land tenure.—The system of land tenure that obtains in Malabar is entirely different from that of other districts. No doubt the theory that the Government is the legitimate owner of all the land in India and the people hold the land from the Government to which they pay a rent or tax, obtains its full significance here also. But there is an intermediary landlord, between the Government and the actual occupier of the land. How this intermediary landlord arose requires some explanation.

The origin of Malabar according to tradition is that a demi-god Parasurama reclaimed from the sea the portion of land extending from Gokarnam (Bombay) to Cape Comorin and from the Western Ghats to the sea. This demi-god having killed 21 times all the Kshatriyas, and having surrendered to Rama all his possessions after trial of battle, wanted a place to live in. He ordered the sea to recede and thus formed these lands. Malabar is a portion of that land. What historical facts are concealed in this tradition it is not easy to know but it may be guessed that in the general organizing of the Deccan, a certain number of Aryans * crossed the Western Ghats and reclaimed the lands from forest and wild beasts and made it habitable for civilized men. They may have dominated the original inhabitants by their superior civilization and Parasurama may have been the leader of that little band of Aryans. The tradition says that the demi-god gave all the lands he created to 64 Brahmans who became the leaders of the 64 villages into which the whole of the land was divided. These 64 Brahmans formed the original Malabar Brahmans or Nambudris, and they formed an assembly and decided matters of common concern. Individual villages decided their own matters and in every discussion of their affairs the Brahmana was the president and his opinion had perhaps the force of law. The whole village belonged to him and he was the Uralla or the chief man of the village. As time went on the one important family extended its branches and each branch had an equal voice in the affairs of the village. The one became many. I shall refer later to the remnants of this constitution of the village.

* [This hypothesis is ingenious, but not, in my opinion, probable.—Ed.]

Each village belonged to the Brahmana family and its branches. They might sell the land and yet they retained a certain right over it. The soil was still theirs, but the products belonged to the buyers, the trees, houses, everything standing on the soil. The right of the original family is called the janmam right, i.e., the right of inheritance from the family to which Parasurama gave the land. Every year this janmam-holder receives a certain sum from the occupier. This janmam right can also be sold, or the janmi may lose the right if he fails to exercise it every twelve years. In such ways the janmam right has in some cases passed into the possession of other castes, but the Nambudri Brahmans are still the chief janmis. It is said that no Sudras held janmam rights before the general confusion due to the invasion of Tippu, when powerful individuals usurped the right. In other cases the Brahmans themselves gave up the janmam right in favour of temples, friends, Sudra wives, or through immoderate living. The selling or leasing of the right to occupy the land must be renewed every twelve years according to the present law. If this is not done the janmi loses his right, and deeds executed by him cease to be valid. This he will never do. So what is generally done is that the janmi at the end of twelve years asks the lessee (or "kanomdar") to give back his land, offering him the value of what stands on the land at the end of twelve years. The kanomdar is helpless. He has worked during the time, by planting trees, building houses, etc. He has not yet enjoyed the result of his labour. The janmi is now offering a very low price. If the kanomdar does not accept it he is dragged to the court, and the court fixes a price according to the Tenants Improvements Act. He must accept the price and give back the land, or make terms with the janmi. The janmi demands a heavy fine for the renewal of the lease. The possessor compares the demand with the work he has done and the annual value of the land. If he thinks it beneficial to him to keep the land for another twelve years after paying the demand, he pays it; otherwise he gives back the land. Sometimes a different person comes to the janmi and bribes him to give the land to him, and offers the actual possessor the value of the products. In spite of the fact that the occupier has worked there twelve years he is now deprived of his home. This is done in so many cases that it is a real grievance to the people.

The result of this system of land tenure is that the agricultural population has no inducement for work, for tenants do not know whether they will retain the land after twelve years or whether the janmi will deprive them of the same. Suppose the kanomdar has worked tremendously and increased the capital invested in the land tenfold, from Rs. 100 to Rs. 1,000. What is the result? The janmi sees the land producing enormously. He knows that the possessor will be very unwilling to lose the land. To the extent of that unwillingness he raises the demand for money to renew the lease. He knows that instead of Rs. 100 he can now demand Rs. 200 or 300 or 500 or even 900 (not of course Rs. 1,000). This is actually done. The possessor cannot but give the money, with the consolation, if it is a consolation at all, that for tenfold work, he gets the opportunity to enjoy one-tenth of the product of his labour. There is yet another danger for a hard worked man, for his neighbour seeing the improvements resorts to bribery in order to get the land.

Further this system results in the disregard of agricultural principles. Supposing only ten coconut palms should be planted in a certain portion of land, the possessor actually plants fifteen or sixteen because at the end of twelve years he will get the value of fifteen or sixteen trees according to the Tenants Improvements Act. If he is content with planting only ten according to agricultural principles, he gets only the value of ten. For many years past there has been no attempt towards scientific cultivation, as a consequence of this, in the whole of Malabar. It is impossible to do so. Disregard of science means gain; regard for it means loss. There is an evident deterioration in the production of the land in Malabar due to absence of security, and disregard of science. Lands which brought a gain of Rs. 1,000 do not now bring even Rs. 400 or Rs. 500. An improvement in this system of land tenure by means of legislation would evidently increase the fertility of Malabar.

Population.—Total population 7,596.*

Castes and individuals in each caste—

Name of caste.	Families.	Members.
Nambudri or Malabar Brahmans	36	146
East Coast Brahmans or Brahmans who have emigrated to Malabar from the east ...	107	653
Nayars and their sub-sects	382	1,305
Tiyyas and their sub-sects	437	2,461
Muhammadans	331	2,307
Christians	118	592
Artisan castes, etc.	17	117
Total ...	1,428	7,581

Number of children under ten in families—Living 3,490, dead 928.

Number of homesteads—1,290.

	1915.	
	Births.	Deaths.
Boys	178	76
Girls	158	80
Total ...	336*	156*

The following table of deaths may be useful:—

Children between ages	0—10	87*
Between ages	10—20	2
,,	21—25	8
,,	26—30	8
,,	31—35	6
,,	36—40	4

* [Birth-rate ... ... 44·2 per thousand.
Death-rate ... ... 20·5 ,,
Death-rate for children 0—10 ... 259 per thousand births.
Density of population ... ... 3,231 per square mile.—Ed.]

Between ages	41—50	11
,,	51—60	9
,,	61—70	9
,,	71—80	10
84 years of age	... ...	1
92 ,,	... ...	1
		156

It is to be noted that infant deaths are more than half the total deaths and number 87 out of 156 last year.

This information is not fully accurate because the people do not report births and deaths generally to the village officials and consequently they have to ascertain the facts by inquiring and it is possible that some births or deaths escape their notice. The ignorance of the people and the unnecessary fear of post-mortem examination in the case of deaths explain their silence. Probably a considerable number of infant deaths escape report.

Paracheri.—Three families, 15 members.—7 women, 8 men.

Number of dead for the last ten years—

Family No. 1	7
,, ,, 2	5
,, ,, 3	4

The village lana—

	ACS.
Garden lands	$792\frac{1}{2}$
Wet lands	$360\frac{3}{4}$
Dry ,, ...	$135\frac{3}{8}$
Government lands	$14\frac{1}{3}$
Inam lands	$201\frac{3}{4}$
Total ...	$1,504\frac{17}{24}$

There are no waste lands.

The principal fruit trees are mangoes, jacks, plantains, and there are not many though sufficient for the village consumption.

There are tanks and wells in plenty. Drinking water is got from wells; and the tanks are used for bathing and for agricultural purposes.

Occupation of land and Agriculture.—The number of kanomdars in the village is 385. The large kanomdars do not generally cultivate the land themselves.

The land is divided into small strips, each strip containing from 50 to 1,000 coconut palms. The large kanomdar takes his residence on one of these strips, and he himself cultivates the particular strip where he is, and gives to small tenants the remaining strips belonging to him. Consequently only about 180 acres of the whole village are cultivated by the large kanomdars. In addition to these lands three kanomdars cultivate all of their land. Two are Muhammadans and one a Tiyya. The area belonging to these three kanomdars is about 134 acres. The remaining land, 1,200 odd acres, is given to tenants to cultivate. There are also between 200 and 300 small kanomdars belonging to the agricultural classes, who hold land insufficient for their maintenance and also cultivate the lands of big kanomdars. A number of the big kanomdars who live in the village also possess lands in the neighbouring villages. In the centre of the village a very sacred and important temple is situated. It has existed for nearly a thousand years, and it is believed by all the people of Malabar that many miracles have from time to time happened there. Many rich devotees have granted lands to it, and it is now the most important landowner of the village, possessing the janmam right over nearly 200 acres of land, all leased to kanomdars. A large part of the temple land is not taxed by the Government, but a low amount fixed by the Government is collected by the temple authorities for its maintenance. This kind of tax is called *Sarvamanyam.* The temple is now managed by the Court of Wards. It belonged to the Zamorin, who handed over his estate to the Court. The Zamorin is the head of a tarwâd* of about 300 members, being the oldest man. Hence when he succeeds he is too old to manage well.

It has been stated that the chief kanomdars excepting three cultivate only the small stips of lands that they occupy and leave it to others to cultivate the rest of their lands. They do not follow any other occupation, but lead an idle life, collecting money from their tenants and lending their money to the poor on security of ornaments and other things. The tendency is for every man who has money to be a money-lender. The sowcars are money-lenders by profession, but every man who has money, instead of depositing it in a bank, lends it to others on high rates of interest. The landowner, the vakil, the official or any other class forms no exception to this rule. Only the traders use the bank.

There are 525 tenants not possessing kanom rights who hold land under kanomdars, and 54 agricultural workers having no land and not renting land. The largest tenant is a Tiyya occupying 80 acres.

Rents are paid both in money and in kind. The chief crop of the village is coconut, but nearly one-fourth of the area is under paddy cultivation. Rents of the coconut areas are paid in money, and those of paddy lands in kind.

Land Revenue.—Rs. 6,411-7-0. This is small because of the exemption of temple lands.

The paddy fields all give two crops per annum. When once a coconut is planted, it lasts for nearly 100 years.

Implements.—There are 542 ploughs in the village, all of the primitive type.

The other implements used are—

(1) the levelling board,

(2) a long stick for powdering the soil,

(3) a short iron instrument somewhat in the shape of a knife for sowing the seed and transplanting,

(4) a rather long handled mamoti, a broad plate of iron sharp at one end and joined to a big stick at another somewhat perpendicularly,

(5) sickles,

(6) big rods used for winnowing the paddy and for separating the grain from the straw,

---

* [i.e., a Nayar family community, having inheritance in the female line. Such an estate is the joint property of all the *female* members of the family and their descendants, the male members of the family also having a right during their lives to support from the family estate, but not transmitting any right to their children.—Ed.]

(7) pestle and mortar for husking rice,

(8) (for coconut cultivation) a long broad knife with blade and handle each 1 foot long (this serves all purposes),

(9) an implement intermediate between an axe and mamoti, with a thick sharp blade, and a fairly long handle, used for cutting wood, etc.,

(10) a basket, with ropes attached at both sides, worked by two men, to transfer water from a tank or from one field to another,

(11) a form of picotah, worked by a man standing on a platform inside the well, with his hands,

(12) the ordinary bullock lift,

(13) a sharp rod fixed in the earth for removing the outer cover of the coconut,

(14) ropes tied circularly for the purpose of climbing the coconut tree.

Stock—

Working oxen	922*
Cows	220
Male buffaloes	503*
Cow „	221
Young stock	1,103
Horses	7
Donkeys and mules	...
Sheep and goats	1,305
Pigs	20

There are 112 carts.

The cattle are fed on dry paddy straw, coconut fodder, waste powdered rice mixed with water, and grass in the winter season. The feeding of cattle is very carelessly done. They keep their skins and bones only.

Manuring.—Cattle dung is used for three purposes :—

(1) For cleaning the whole house. Hindus believe that the sprinkling of cattle dung water purifies the house. Consequently, every day every house is thus cleaned.

(2) For fuel. Chaff mixed with straw and dung is dried and burnt for culinary purposes. All the dung from cows kept by the non-agricultural classes (nearly every family of means keeps a cow for milk) is used in the above ways.

(3) The dung produced among the agricultural classes is used for manure, not for paddy or coconut, but for the cultivation of vegetables. Very little dung is used for the cultivation of chief crops. The wastage is also large. Perhaps one-fourth of the total dung is used for manuring vegetables. All the rest is used as stated above or wasted. A small portion of the cattle urine is collected in pots and used as manure for vegetables, but nearly all is wasted.

Fish and muddy water are used as manure for coconuts, but not to a very great extent, and only by the three rich kanomdars who themselves cultivate. Some also use salt for manure, when they plant coconut. This is very advantageous, and sometimes

* [This shows the very high proportion of one working ox or buffalo for each acre of cultivated land, a proportion accounted for by what is stated about the condition of the animals.—Ed.]

leads to the tree fruiting within two or three years, instead of four or five. The leaves that fall from the trees in gardens are used as green manure in the paddy fields and coconut gardens. No such thing as growing green manure is known. No wood or forest is near so that the people may bring the leaves.

In fact very little manuring takes place in the village. What is actually done in the cultivation of chief crops is to plough the land. Every year much is drawn from the soil, and nothing is returned to it. I have stated above that lands which returned Rs. 1,000 a year do not now return more than Rs. 400 or 500. The two most potent causes for this deterioration are the system of land tenure and the absence of manuring. Perhaps the second is the result of the first, but I think the want of agricultural knowledge is the cause of the want of manuring and scientific cultivation.

Wood and fuel.—The outer cover of the coconut, the leaves of the same, mango trunks, serve for fuel for the whole village, and they are obtained in plenty, but the price is rising with the general rise of prices.

Wood for implements, building, etc., is obtained from Cochin State, brought in carts drawn by oxen or buffaloes.

The village—Houses.—For buildings granite is obtained from a place four miles distant, mortar is prepared in the village, mud from the village itself, tiles from different places, the least distant being twenty miles away, for thatch the leaves of the coconut are used, iron things are bought in the bazaar. The houses in the village are all isolated from one another. Every part of the village is inhabited except the paddy fields. However, at the present day traders have a tendency to build their houses as near the road as possible and form streets. The people also have a tendency to live as near the temple as possible, and this has resulted in the formation of four streets, surrounding the temple on all the four sides. These streets form also the bazaar of the village. There are here about 100 houses.

The lands adjacent to the temple are occupied by Brahmans and Nayars. Any other place can be occupied by any family. The houses of the low castes, high castes, and of otheir religions are intermingled. The same garden may be occupied by Muhammadans, Hindus and Christians, and they all live very amicably as if they belonged to one and the same religion.

The Pariahs, whose families are only three in number, occupy certain portions of the land of a big landlord. The landlord gives the Pariahs free houses and a certain allowance a month. He thinks it incumbent upon him to protect and maintain them. Their huts, though small, are yet tidy and neat. The allowance that was freely given them has now become a right. They follow certain industries and go to rich men's houses to beg twice a month, and they are given a certain quantity of rice.

There are 977 thatched houses, 313 tiled houses, no terraced houses.

Crafts and industries.—There are seven families of weavers consisting of 39 members, i.e., 14 men, 12 women, 13 children under fifteen years. They have been in the village from times long past. They weave a cloth 1 foot wide, $1\frac{1}{2}$ yards long, and this is used as undercloth. They also at times weave a cloth $\frac{3}{4}$ or 1

" RATANAM ", A FORM OF WATER-LIFT (TIRUVALLUR).

Photo by Agricultural College.

yard in width and 1½ or 2 yards long. They find it difficult to maintain themselves with this work and also rent small plots of land, and some possess land. They use the unimproved hand-loom. There is no co-operation among them. They sell their cloth in the adjoining market of the village and do not care to send it to other villages. At times they take orders. They do not spin but buy inferior yarn from the market which gets its supply from Bombay through Cochin and Calicut and at times Ponnāni.

Other crafts.—

Sawyers	4	families.
Carpenters	11	,,
Copper workers	1	family.
Iron workers	2	families.
Goldsmiths	7	,,
Masons	10	,,

These give their whole time to the craft.

Native umbrellas and baskets are made by all Pariahs.

Rope-making—thick as well as thin—is carried on by nearly all the women of the Tiyyas and their sub-sects. Some women are wholly engaged in this work and they sell their ropes in the market themselves. The Pariahs make a peculiar kind of rope from grass, which is used for tying calves, and as reins for bulls. The rope is good and strong. They sell a rope for a measure of rice.

Leather work is done by one family which also practises agriculture.

These craftsmen have existed from times long past with no change in their condition or tools. There is no co-operation among them. Their capital is only their tools. They get sufficient work for their maintenance. There is no improvement with regard to their designs except in the case of the goldsmiths whose work is daily increasing and who are the only craftsmen who invent designs. The condition of blacksmiths is getting worse on account of the importation of foreign iron goods. His only work now-adays is to fit things, not to make them as of yore. He does not now make the nails, screws, iron bars, locks, knives, etc. These are bought from the bazaar and he fits them. But he makes all the tools necessary for other crafts and for agriculture. The same is the case with the coppersmith, but he gets sufficient work as people desire to get valuable vessels made in their presence. But his condition may be regarded as precarious. There is no change in the other craftsmen.

Coir rope-making is the chief source of income for all the low caste women. They beat the soft cover of the coconut, after it is well soaked, into fibre, and twist it into strands, and the strands into ropes, in their hands. The rope is sold to the local shop-keepers daily. Some women themselves take the rope to the local fairs. Their work is increasing.

The other industry followed by a great many people is coconut oil-pressing. The whole Christian community with some others subsists on that work. They become tenants to big kanomdars and sometimes buy coconuts from others and extract the oil and sell it in the local market. Some big shopkeepers collect the oil and send it in large quantities to Cochin whence it is exported. One machine mill is already at work in a place eight miles from the village, but the primitive oil mill is chiefly used, worked by two oxen. It is very cheap. Perhaps two rupees would be enough excepting for the oxen.

The village trade.—The chief articles consumed are rice, fish, vegetables, cereals and spices. The price of the total quantity consumed in the village may be estimated at Rs. 2,50,000, the total sales of the shop being Rs. 3,50,000, of which one lakh is to outsiders.

The quantity of produce taken to the market is not very great. The rice and cereals and spices necessary for consumption come from Palghat and consequently must be bought from the bazaar All other articles that are necessary, e.g., vegetables, fish, salt, chillies, oil, straw, fodder, fuel, etc., are brought to the house by petty traders or by the actual producers. In addition to this there is a weekly fair where local produce to the value of about Rs. 1,000 is sold weekly. A smaller quantity, which may be estimated at Rs. 36,000 per annum, is sold to shopkeepers and they sell to other villages. The people sell to shopkeepers only when they cannot sell in any other way, for the shopkeepers offer only a low price.

The main road comes from the Cochin State and passes through the northern and the western side of the village and bends and passes through the southern side. One branch road runs from the west and passes through the centre and ends at the eastern extremity of the village. The road system is not satisfactory. Other branch roads are wanted and those that are made have not been repaired at all for many years, though tolls are collected. People once complained of this to the Taluk Board but to no effect, although thousands of pilgrims visit this place every year on account of the sanctity of the temple. There are numerous by-ways.

The nearest railway stations are Pattambi, Trichur, and Watakkancheri, each twenty miles away. People go to Trichur by boat through the backwaters, and the steam boat that runs from Ponnāni to Tirur is availed of by many and it is cheap. There is backwater communication to Ponnāni and Cochin.

Copra, coir, etc., are taken or sent to Cochin and the people get in return rice, cloth, and cereals and other luxuries. Fish can be got from the sea, which is very near the village. The fishermen go every day in the morning and return in the evening.

Economic condition of the village.—Wages for artisans are always paid in money; for agricultural work both in kind and in money.

Money wages.—The ordinary labourers are always paid in money. In short all those kinds of labour which do not immediately bring fruit to the owner are paid in money. A labourer, for a full day's work, is now paid four annas; five or six years ago three annas. For short work such as carrying weights, etc., the wage is fixed for the moment and will vary according to the distance they have to go, etc. Generally two annas must be paid for one mile as an average. For carrying a bag of rice a high wage is demanded because of high weight.* Woman's labour costs three annas per day now, formerly 2½ annas, a boy's labour 2½ annas now, formerly 2 annas.

Carpenters get six annas a day, boy carpenters three annas, formerly four annas and two annas. Other artisans such as black-

* [160 lb.—Ed.]

smiths, masons, etc., four annas a day. But a skilful artisan earns 6 annas a day. But these people do not generally work at the customer's house, but they are given orders for the things and when they bring them are paid the price. Sometimes they are given the metal and the wages for each particular kind of work.

The making of ornaments is one of the weaknesses of Indians and consequently goldsmiths are in no difficulty to get work. In Malabar in former days costly ornaments were confined to Brahmans, but nowadays all classes are imitating the Brahmans in that respect. It is to be deplored. The number of goldsmith families has steadily increased from two to seven within ten years. They are always given the metal and given the wages for the particular kind of work, ranging from Re. 1 to Rs. 30 for the most complicated work which may employ one man for a whole month. A ring may cost Rs. 2 in wage. The same is the case of coppersmith. The wages depend upon the art and the size of the vessel. A big vessel may fetch him Rs. 20.

In kind.—The chief labour of the agricultural classes for which wages are paid in kind is the climbing of coconut trees and felling the fruit, and the sowing of paddy. One coconut is given if a man climbs four trees. An ordinary man can climb forty trees a day and he can earn ten coconuts, which according to the present price may bring him 8 annas. This has been the custom for a long time and this rate of wage has shown no sign of improvement since the labourers themselves do not demand more; because the price of coconuts has steadily increased and with that rise their wages also must rise.

The sowing of paddy is generally done by women who receive as wage one-tenth of the quantity of paddy sown.

It may be remarked here that throughout the whole of Malabar the Pariyas and other untouchables such as Cherumas, Nayadis, etc., are always paid 2 Edangalis of paddy for men (1½ Edangalis for women) whatever kind of work they do, per day. This has been their wage from time immemorial.

Current prices of staples.—A bag of rice containing 8 paras * costs Rs. 12-4-0, if of inferior sort, Rs. 10. Fish 1 pie † for five small fishes, salt 2 annas for 1 Madras measure.

It may be noticed here that the Muhammadan and Christian labour costs more than the Hindu labour, since those two classes can perform a greater quantity of work because of their superior physical strength.

Savings and debts.—The number of families which have made savings may be estimated as between 75 and 100, of whom ten to fifteen may be Muhammadans, fifteen to twenty of lower castes, and the remainder of higher castes. But the persons who have lost their money are very numerous, probably between 200 and 300. Some lost through trade, many through litigation. But the primary cause of loss of property is the peculiar tenure of land as explained above. Perhaps all or nearly all the savings of the higher classes are used as loans to neighbours. The amount may be estimated at Rs. 50,000.

About Rs. 2,000 a year is spent on jewellery.

The estimated income from land and from other sources for this village is Rs. 2,50,000 a year for a population of 7,596, out of

* [180 lb.—Ed.] † [12 pies = 1 anna = 1 *d.*—Ed.]

which Rs. 6,411-7-0 goes as land revenue and another Rs. 3,500 as income-tax to the Government, leaving Rs. 2,40,000 for the village. There are 385 landowners and these people get Rs. 90,000 a year for their land. The amounts earned by the great merchants may be estimated at Rs. 25,000, and this amount is shared by nearly 100 families. This amount largely comes from parts outside the village and by exportation of coconuts. The profits these people get from the village itself are not calculated under this heading since it forms no income to the village. But that may be estimated at Rs. 5,000 only. Thus all that remains to the agricultural classes after deducting the incomes of the landowners and traders, is about Rs. 1,25,000 which must be shared by 805 families of 6,000 people, an average of Rs. 20-13-9 per head per annum. The total earning of an agricultural family on an average comes to nearly Rs. 146 a year or Rs. 12-2-8 a month or As. 6-6 a day. Taking a rough estimate of what a family has to spend according to the present standard of living, which is in itself a low one, we may estimate the expense of a family to be at 10 annas a day. From personal experience I have found that the cost of giving artisans working in the house the one meal a day which is customary, is 2 annas per man; we made no difference between their meal and ours. Something, but not much, can be saved on this in quality, and, making all allowances for children, I infer that a family of seven members will have to spend at least 10 annas a day for food or Rs. 228 a year. Making an allowance of Rs. 20 for clothes and for religious and social functions—it is only a small amount for a year—they will have to spend Rs. 248 a year for food, in order to maintain their body and soul without suffering, leaving out of consideration luxuries, pleasure, etc. What do they get now? Only Rs. 146. So what they get is sufficient only for one meal. I was told by the carpenters and blacksmiths who worked in my house that they could not provide themselves with meals during the nights and what they do is only to drink rice water, and even that very rarely. They manage with the meal given from the house and what they get as wage is spent on their wives and children with a small saving for contingencies. This economic suffering is the main cause for the physical deterioration in India, and this is the cause of infant mortality, and this accounts for much of ignorance and filthy and insanitary habits, since with every one first food, then other matters. The case of agricultural people is much worse than artisans; they are paid lower and they are rarely given the one meal in addition as are the artisan class. Ordinary labourers if they do not get work have to starve literally.

It is evident from the previous statement of facts that no money can be saved at the present time by the tenants for agricultural capital, or for manure. Further there is no organized industry of any kind. The oil-pressing and rope-making industries, which are the most important, are carried on with primitive tools which require no capital. It has been already stated that the landowners get Rs. 90,000 a year, of which they spend for their maintenance a sum of nearly Rs. 40,000. The remaining Rs. 50,000 are spent on loans to neighbours, jewellery, house-building, education of their children, charity, religious and social festivities such as marriage. Loans to neighbours take away more than half, education nearly Rs. 10,000, and the rest for the other expenses. Money-lending forms their chief profession. These landowners do not lend to the agricultural classes but only to the well-to-do and that in a lump sum, such as Rs. 1,000 to Rs. 5,000 or even Rs. 10,000. The chief purposes for which the well-to-do borrow are (1) to displace tenants by paying off the cost of improvement as explained in the introduction on land, (2) in the case of Brahmans for marriage of their daughters, (3) to rich debauchees, and they are not very few, on mortgage of their lands, thus in the end taking away the mortgaged land, (4) to big merchants who carry on the export trade in oil and coconuts and others who are engaged in trade.

The passion for jewellery which in former days was present only among Brahmans in Malabar—not so in other districts—is unfortunately spreading among other classes too, and a large amount of money is yearly spent on it. At the present time every man of means will have at least Rs. 200 worth of ornaments and, in a rich man's house, Rs. 5,000 or Rs. 10,000 is the usual amount. The total amount of jewellery may be estimated at Rs. 1,00,000. This is the much talked of 'hoarded wealth' of the village, though the jewels are in daily use and not hidden. Nobody has hidden anything.

It is not possible to get the exact amount of agricultural indebtedness. I have already stated that the landowners and other rich persons do not lend to the agricultural classes. But who lends to the agricultural classes? The sowcar or the professional money-lender, the middle class man who is not rich but just earns enough for maintenance and some small saving. The number of professional money-lending shops is twelve, and a large number of persons of the middle class are also engaged in the same occupation. A rough estimate of the amount of money lent by the people may be made by a reference to the account books of these money-lenders. They have together lent about Rs. 1,50,000. The money lent by others must amount to more, since they are more lenient than the sowcars, and only when the poor cannot get money from others do they apply to the sowcar. It has been probably estimated at two lakhs.

A little explanation of how money is lent may not be out of place here. Suppose a man wants to borrow Rs. 50. The interest that is demanded is 2½ per cent per mensem; there is deducted from the amount lent an allowance called the bank allowance, generally 10 per cent, and also six months' interest or Rs. 6-4-0. So the amount actually paid to the borrower is only Rs. 38-12-0 and he executes a promissory-note for Rs. 50. If a man actually wants Rs. 50 he must incur a debt of Rs. 65. By the third year the man must pay the whole amount and the interest. By that time the total amount would have reached nearly Rs. 90. The poor man is not able to pay the money since the very purpose for which he borrowed is to maintain himself and not for productive purposes. He rewrites the note. For what amount? Rs. 65 plus interest for 2½ years plus compound interest plus bank allowance plus six months' further interest plus a commission (which is a new innovation since last year) mounts up to nearly Rs. 125, i.e., nearly double the original amount. In three years he has paid six months' interest and yet he has to pay double the amount he borrowed. This is an ordinary case, but interest at the rate of 3 or 3½ per cent per mensem is not uncommon.

Very few of the poor once in debt ever release themselves. On the other hand the number who are in debt is increasing from year to year. Any amount of money that is in the possession of the money-lenders is absorbed in no time. In the last five years the number of money-lending shops has doubled and their funds invested by this means have trebled. There is yet a demand for money which is unsatisfied.

Another method of supporting, as it were, the poor, is to lend the seed for sowing on the promise that for every 100 measures lent they will return after the first crop, i.e., after four months from the time of lending, 120 or 130 measures. This means an interest of 60 per cent per annum. The cultivators do not as a rule save their own seed, because when they have no means of living they natually use their seed for food. I am told this is the case with every paddy cultivator excepting the three rich agriculturists who are landowners. It must be confessed here that without such borrowing the cultivation itself could not at present be carried on.

The village is free from padials. The debtors only pay interest, but in the Palghat taluk the system of padials survives.

The causes of indebtedness are not far to seek. Economic backwardness is the primary cause. Waste of money on drink and evil habits is not uncommon. In some cases debt is due to ambitious schemes which fail. Excessive display in marriage is not common in Malabar as in eastern districts. Non-Brahmans, especially the castes below the Nayars, pay only Rs. 20 or Rs. 30, according to their means, to the bridegroom, and sometimes not even that. Another Rs. 25 will raise a marriage above the ordinary level. Taking into account that a marriage will be performed in a family only once in five or six years this expenditure of Rs. 50 or so cannot be deemed great.

The ordinary labourers, who number about 500, maintain themselves by their daily work and they are never in debt. It is the agricultural classes and those who are engaged in petty trade that are in debt. The only asset of the tenants is that they have to pay as advance one year's rent to the landowners and they receive for the advance 6 per cent interest. Even this is paid in some cases by borrowing.

There is no co-operative credit society in the village.

Communal life.—The Brahmans of this village have formed themselves into a society for mutual aid and convenience. This organization of the society is on the model of the old village republics. It exists for social purposes only. Two persons are elected biennially to look after the affairs and the income of the society. Every house is represented by its head in the village assembly and that assembly elects the persons. The sources of income to the society are—

(1) the interest on the already existing property which is about Rs. 3,000;

(2) for all social functions such as marriage, etc., the society as a whole has a claim for a fixed sum. The total income from these two sources may be estimated at Rs. 350.

The duty of the society is to appoint the village priest, village barber, village trumpeter and other persons essential for the performance of social or religious functions.

The whole income is spent on the worship of God. The particular ways in which it should be spent have been fixed long ago, and comprise a special feast for the Brahmans once a year, provision of a burial-ground and other public and necessary places for Brahmans as a whole, and the performance of *puja* during one month in a year.

The two elected administrators spend the money as explained above, keep the accounts, and are responsible for the whole income. This organization is seen throughout the Brahman community in Malabar. It may be regarded as a survival of the village communal organization, the political functions of which disappeared with the advent of British rule.

The lower classes have appointed a family to settle caste questions and questions of excommunication, adultery, etc., and this family has been exercising this power from time immemorial. The family still holds the power and the verdict which the head-man of the family pronounces about such questions is tacitly accepted by all.

Religious festivals are performed by the temple, and the temple *in practice* belongs to the Zamorin. It is managed by the Court of Wards at the present time, along with the Zamorin's estate. The income of the temple is the offerings of the devotees who chiefly come from distant places. The festivals which the temple performs will in a year cost more than Rs. 2,000. In addition offerings to the temple from the village itself will amount to more than Rs. 3,000.

The above statements of indebtedness, communal income, etc., are based on careful inquiry with well-known persons and the village munsif, and are given in round numbers as accurately as possible.

Sanitary condition.—Malaria, plague, cholera, smallpox and consumption are absent from the village.

The ordinary diseases of the village are fever, dysentery, elephantiasis and such like diseases. Infantile mortality is high. Out of 156 deaths 87 are infant deaths. The deaths are high among the poor, particularly the Hindu poor. It may be people cannot afford to bring up their children decently. The mothers must work for the maintenance of the family before many days have passed after child-birth. I know of a Tiyya family in which seven out of eleven children born died before they were three years old. Moreover they cannot afford medical help and they implore God to help them and resort to quack doctors. The prevalence of early marriage may be cited as one of the causes for physical deterioration. But the most potent cause especially in the case of the higher classes is the ignorance of the mothers. Domestic hygiene is a sealed book for them. Their habits are not quite sanitary.

There are no venomous snakes.

There is a hospital very near the village. But the chief medical help is from the native doctors who practise privately. There are two great medical experts in the native system but there are also a large number of quacks. The experts have a tremendous business but the quacks do some injury too.

Wearing unclean * cloths, not keeping the house neat, using the same plate for food for the whole family, are some of the insanitary habits of the poor and the lower classes. But the higher classes are very neat and Malabar is famous for its neatness. People bathe every day.

* [I.e., unclean according to the Malabar standard of cleanliness, which is very high. —Ed.]

Marriage customs.—The custom of marriage before puberty is prevalent among Hindus, excepting Nambudris and Nayars. The Nambudris or Malabar Brahmans can give their daughters in marriage at any time they like or not marry them at all. Only the eldest male member of a Nambudri family can marry in his own caste. All the other sons keep Nayar women as mistresses. The eldest member can marry more than one wife, but many women of necessity have to remain unmarried.

The case of Nayars is entirely different. They follow a different system of inheritance, i.e., descent through the female. The result of this system is that the female is at full liberty to choose or to divorce husbands as she likes. The man also has the same liberty. As a consequence of the different systems of inheritance their marriage custom is also different. Before puberty some person closely connected with the family ties the sacred string round the neck of the girl. This custom is purely formal and does not make them husband and wife. Nowadays this formal business is done by the mother of the girl at the temple in the presence of God. After puberty the man who really wants to marry the girl (he must be of the same caste or some one belonging to a higher caste, preferably a Nambudri) comes and performs the real marriage. This real marriage is binding only so long as he and she will. Divorce can be had at any time by a mere word. The woman can marry again. The death of the man does not make the woman a widow. There is no widowhood for Nayar woman. In fact there is no marriage among the Nayars. What actually happens is that somebody comes and lives with a woman for a time, then leaves, and both live with others. The only restriction is that two men cannot live with one woman at the same time, but one man can cohabit with any number of women at the same time. The children born of such unions inherit the propertyof the uncle since the descent is by the female line. Nowadays there is a strong opinion against this system and the descent from father to son is advocated by the educated few, and the proposed regulations in Cochin are attempts to make marriage binding and permanent and dissoluble only under certain circumstances, widows being still allowed to remarry.

With regard to all other Hindus, marriage before puberty prevails. But among the lower classes widow-marriage is allowable, money for a bridegroom is not demanded, and even polyandry is prevalent among certain sections of the Tiyyas. But only brothers can share a wife. A brother can marry his widowed sister-in-law. *Divorce* is allowed in cases of serious infidelity but divorced men and women can marry again.

The purdah system is followed by the Nambudri women alone in Malabar. They cannot see men. Whenever they come out they hold a big native kind of umbrella to hide their faces and come to the temple, etc. The ideas about the purdah system among them are changing nowadays and the abandonment of the system is hoped for in a few years. The Nambudris are also advocating changes in their marriage customs.

The property of a Nambudri or Nayar family cannot be divided among the family sons. The eldest has the right to manage the property and enjoy the profits. The other members of the family have a right for maintenance only. When the eldest dies the next to him in age comes to the position. Inthe case of a Nambudri the brother or son, in the case of a Nayar the sister's son succeeds. The Travancore and Cochin royal families and the Zamorin family descend in the female line.

Water-supply.—Drinking water is supplied by the wells. Every house has one. The sinking of wells is easy here since the soil is loose and there is no rock and the height above the sea level is not much. Wealthy people build the well with granite, others leave it with mud banks. The labourers dig their wells themselves as it involves only two days' work. The wells never dry up. There are three public wells and two temple wells besides. Indeed the scarcity of water is not felt at all. But for bathing purposes the water in the tank is bad, and some people use well-water for the same. The quality of the well-water is fairly good.

Education.—There are seven schools of which one is a secondary school managed by the Taluk Board, one is a Government Girls' School and the other five are elementary schools, one being Muhammadan. There are 680 boys and 185 girls in attendance.

The education imparted is fairly satisfactory, special stress being laid onthe vernacular. According to the educational curriculum prescribed by the Director, the geography of the district, a little Indian History, a good training in the vernacular, a little Arithmetic, and the beginning of English by teaching the alphabet and small words, are all taught in the school.

Eighty per cent of the men and fifteen per cent of the women can read and write the vernacular; about two per cent can read and write English, and somewhat fewer speak it.

Forty boys have left the village and had a college course, and there is one girl matriculate.

About 20 boys after undergoing a little commercial training at Calicut have gone to Bombay and other commercial centres for employment.

It may here be mentioned that emigration to Ceylon is frequent. Emigrants return after three or four years, and remain in the village for one year, and again go to Ceylon. Nearly 150 have gone within recent years.

The only library in the village is the secondary school library which contains nearly 200 books, all juvenile. Five or six private persons possess some books. Some are lawyers and their books are connected with law. Others have only novels. Nobody takes study seriously. Nobody is interested in Science as a subject. This lack of enthusiasm for knowledge makes the Indian less original and less artistic. I know nobody in my village who has designed new arts or invented anything at all. This lack is everywhere visible in India and seen even among students who do not care to know anything more than those things which are prescribed for the examination. This fundamental weakness must be shamefully confessed, but there are signs of change in the right direction.

Village administration.—The head of the village is the *adhigari* or the village munsif. He is the representative of the King-Emperor. He collects the revenue, looks after the affairs of the village, has the jurisdiction over minor civil and criminal cases, controls the roads, Government lands and trees and other public places—in fact he represents every function, in a greater or lesser degree, of the King-Emperor, and is the guardian of the public peace. He must initiate everything for the village, but the final sanction of his proposals rests with the Collector.

Above the village munsif is the Revenue Inspector who looks after the work of four or five village headmen. He has revenue functions only. For other purposes the Magistrate is the immediate superior of the *adhigari*. Next comes the Tahsildar, then the Sub-Collector, then the Collector.

Criminal cases are tried by the Magistrate. The Civil and Criminal Courts are situated in the village itself.

A story is told in the village that a poor agricultural man was asked by another, when the Collector had come to the village in one of his tours, whether the Collector or the *adhigari* was the superior officer. He replied, "I don't know, but the *adhigari* is richer, since he receives money yearly from us." The adhigari's *pay* is only Rs. 7 per mensem.*

The jurisdiction of the adhigari with regard to the criminal cases lies only in cases of petty thefts and nuisances, and in civil matters when the amount under dispute does not exceed Rs. 50.

Panchayat.—There is a judicial panchayat for civil cases in which the amount under dispute does not exceed Rs. 50, or Rs. 200 if both the parties agree. This was introduced three years ago as a tentative measure, but it has proved a success in spite of its drawbacks. The jurisdiction of the panchayat courts extends to four or five villages; and the personnel of the court is a non-official president nominated by the Government and the adhigaris of the villages. Nearly 500 civil suits of a minor character were tried last year. The introduction of this system in small cases has caused enormous saving to the parties since the expenditure is small. There is no necessity for a stamped paper, etc. This institution is an advance in the right direction, but the personnel needs change, since they are all the Government representatives and consequently the people have no part to play in the constitution of the court.

There is no administration of sanitation. It is left to take care of itself. In theory there is a rule that the roads must be swept once a day and some coolies are appointed for the purpose, but the work is practically neglected on account of lack of supervision.

There is a Sub-Inspector of Police and under him a head constable and constables. The people can easily get the help of the police.

A large percentage of population is engaged in litigation. There are three reasons:—(1) The Muhammadans are addicted to litigation with regard to the partition of their property. In fact no partition takes place without having recourse to courts. (2) The peculiarity of land tenure has been already described. (3) The indebtedness of the poor and their inability to pay. The result is the majority of the population are litigants.

Sometimes compromises are arranged by a gentleman in whom both the parties have faith. There is no compromise committee for the purpose, but the people fearing the expenses of the law courts sometimes settle matters among themselves by means of a third person. Such cases are rare.

[* The point of this story is that, in the Madras Presidency the Collector is the chief District officer. The Collector of Malabar, for example, rules over a population of close on three million people, subject to the Government in Madras.—Ed.]

KOTHACHIRA DESAM (PONNANI TALUK).

[*By A. Krishna Wariyar, Christian College, Madras.*]

Preliminary.—This desam is situated about 13 miles south-east of Ponnani, a small thriving town at the mouth of the river of the same name, a Muhammadan centre and the headquarters of the taluk. The visitor to Kothachira leaves the train at Pattambi, the nearest railway station and after a six miles walk along the Pattambi-Chowghat road turns to the left and by a footpath over a rising eminence descends into the paddy fields. A two miles walk southwards through these fields will bring him to the borders of the Kothachira desam.

This desam is a completely rural area and there is nothing of interest in the place. The shortest distance from the nearest river (river Ponnani) is 5 miles. Hills and forests are not rare since the desam enjoys proximity to the Akalanum (east) and the Mattur (north) hills.

The term 'desam' literally means a piece of territory. The desam is the political and social unit in Malabar, and is the nearest equivalent to the villages of the east. The chief differences, however, are—(1) the village organization, in its entirety, is not found here; (2) the village has no particular site. The population is distributed throughout the desam area, each individual landholder having his home and family compound often in the midst of his lands and gardens and separated far from his neighbours.

Population.—The population of this desam according to the censuses of 1891 and 1901 was as follows:—

Year of census.	Number of inhabited houses.	Total population.			Religion.			Occupation.				Population per 100 acres of occupied land.
		Males.	Females.	Total.	Hindus.	Muhammadans.	Others.	Landholders.	Labourers.	Weavers.	Others.	
(1)	(2)	(3)	(4)	(5)	(6)	(7)	(8)	(9)	(10)	(11)	(12)	(13)
1891 ...	295	898	985	1,883	1,678	204	1	767	563	...	553	221
1901 ...	312	961	1,047	2,008	1,808	200	...	559	378	...	1,071	236

The report of the last census (that of 1911) is not obtainable. My enquiry gives the following results:—

Number of houses 333.

Males ...	1,216	Hindus ...	1,990	Landholders ...	442
Females ...	1,107	Muhammadans.	327	Labourers ...	518
		Others ...	6	Weavers ...	...
				Others * ...	1,363
Total ...	2,323		2,323		2,323

* Including all who have no regular occupation, children, women of higher castes, old men, and even a good many young men belonging to joint families.

The increase in the number of families must not be taken for a sign of prosperity. I have sought out its causes. It has both a social and an economic cause. The breaking up of the old 'Tharvads' into small homesteads, owing to want of harmony among the members, mismanagement of property due to ignorance and rank illiteracy, growing indebtedness of the once rich Tharvads to the local money-lenders or the landlord, are the causes of the downfall of the great Tharvads of old which half a century ago were gracing this desam; the stories yet current in those parts of men of high worth and talents who belonged to them, and the occasional ruined foundations of their family houses alone remain. Indeed joint families have almost all broken up and the Tharvad properties all absorbed by the local 'Jenmis.' The people are day by day being reduced to want and dependence on the landlord and the creditor.

The desam cannot be called a 'caste' desam strictly speaking. There are no separate quarters allotted on the basis of caste difference. In spite of the rigorous observance of the 'system of pollution' between caste and caste, peculiar to the Malabar country, all castes hold lands, work, and have families promiscuously throughout the land. For example, every landholding farmer, who is usually a Nayar, has in his family precincts (indeed far enough away to be out of reach of pollution) small homesteads of his labourers who are generally Cherumas or Pulayas * by caste.

There are—

3	Brahman	families	...	24	individuals.
3	Ambalavasi	„	...	36	„
137	Nayar	„	...	956	„
85	Tiyya	„	...	584	„
80	Cheruma	„	..	390	„
24	Muhammadan	„	...	27	„
1	Christian family		...	6	„

The *Tiyya* class includes the families of the artisans—'Asari' (carpenter—two families), 'Karuvan' (blacksmith—one family), 'Kollan' (shoemaker—two families), 'Thattan' (goldsmith—one family), 'Mannan' (washerman of the lower class—one family), 'Panikkan' (stone-mason—one family).

Children living	... ...	642	
„ dead	... ...	188	Born within the last ten years.
„ born lifeless	... ...	67	

Children below ten are alone included in this. This has been ascertained by enquiry among the mothers.

Homesteads number 266. The homesteads of the villagers are miserable looking and squalid, frequently being only mud hovels of eight by five feet, more or less. Not more than 40 houses out of 333 are houses worthy of the name. The rest are simply hovels, often the very picture of poverty and famine.

* Between these two depressed castes there are only minute differences.

The statistics of births and deaths of this desam are obtainable only for the year 1915. They are given below:—

Births.

Males	... ...	50	Hindu	... ...	84
Females	... ...	43	Muhammadan	...	9
		93			93

Deaths.

According to age—

Lifeless deliveries	... ...	7
Below one year	... ...	9
Between 1 and 10	... ...	13
" 10 and 20	... ...	1
" 20 and 30	... ...	7
" 30 and 40	... ...	3
" 40 and 50	... ...	...
" 50 and 60	... ...	3
" 60 and 80	... ...	5
		48

According to sex and castes—

Males	... ...	24	Hindus	... ...	43
Females	... ...	24	Muhammadans	...	5

There is no paracheri in the strict sense of the term. The depressed classes, mostly Cherumas, are still in a state of semi-serfdom, depending for everything on their landlords and masters.

Land.—The area of the desam by settlement is 1,803·40 acres. This desam together with Mattupalli, Peringode, Pillakkattiri, Tolukad, Mathur, Alikara, Kuttanad, Perumannur and Chalisseri desams formed the old revenue amsam of Kothachira. Now Kothachira revenue amsam includes only Kothachira, Mathur and Peringode desams.

The areas under each description of land—

—	Wet.	Garden.	Occupied dry.	Unoccupied dry.	Unassessed.	Inam.	Poramboke.	Total.
	ACS. C.	ACS. C.	ACS. C.	ACS C.	ACS. C.			ACS. C.
Private Jenmi.	445 27	209 43	197 16	935 71	..	...	...	1,787 57
Government Jenmi.	...	...	...	...	...		...	...
Unregistered lands.	...	...		...	15 83	...	...	15 83
	445 27	209 43	197 16	935 71	15 83	..	...	1,803 40

The desam contains 130 survey fields in all. The settlement was first introduced in this desam in fasli 1313.

The following table shows the nature and extent of the holdings and revenue as given in the 'A' register of the village:--

Holdings and Revenue.

Fasli.	Occupied area.								Deduct waste remitted.		Remainder charged.			
	Wet.		Garden.		Dry.		Total.							
	Extent.	Assessment.	Extent.	Assessment.	Extent.	Assessment.	Extent.	Assessment.	Extent.	Assessment.	Actual cultivation.	Waste charged.	Total extent charged.	Assessment.
(1)	(2)	(3)	(4)	(5)	(6)	(7)	(8)	(9)	(10)	(11)	(12)	(13)	(14)	(15)
	ACS.	RS. A.	ACS.	RS.	ACS.	RS. A.	ACS.	RS. A.			ACS.		ACS.	RS. A.
1313	445·27	2,226 5	209·43	502	197·16	157 14	851·86	2,886 3	...	...	851·86	...	851·86	2,886 3

Fasli—*cont.*	Second crop.		Miscellaneous revenue.	Total ryotwari demand excluding waste remitted.	Deduct remission other than waste already shown in column 11.			Net demand for the year.	Amount collected within year.	
	Extent.	Charge.			Occasional remission other than for waste.	Other remissions and deductions.	Total.		Arrear.	Current.
	(16)	(17)	(18)	(19)	(20)	(21)	(22)	(23)	(24)	(25)
	ACS.	RS. A.	RS. A.	RS. A.		RS. A.	RS. A.	RS. A.		RS. A.
1313	8·96	13 11	96 5	2,996 3	...	851 12	851 12	2,144 7	...	2,144 7

The ryots mostly depend on the mercy of the monsoon for the watering of fields. But throughout the summer season beginning from the end of December to the end of July, watering is carried on from wells and tanks, especially in the case of garden cultivation. Tanks and wells are not sufficient and those existing are not deep enough and frequently dry up towards March.

The chief crops cultivated are coconut, arecanut, paddy, gingelly, pulses, horsegram, plantain and jack.

Pasturage is obtainable for the cattle on the unoccupied dry lands. Water for the cattle is obtained from channels, private tanks and wells.

There is hardly any public tank. One stream (channel) flows along the northern boundary of the desam during rainy seasons when the fields become flooded. But its utility is limited since with the summer the whole channel is dried up. There are private wells in all gardens and sometimes in the fields of corn. But they are shallow for the most part and the water-supply is inadequate. The ryots who are wretchedly poor cannot afford to utilise modern progress in the field of well-boring, nor are they conversant with such developments.

There are woods and forests near the desam as we have before mentioned, but they are of no practical use to the people. The forest, which is outside the boundary limit of this desam, is under Government supervision and people are not allowed to cut trees. Other resources of the forest, moreover, are hardly taken advantage of, partly by the general apathy of the cultivator for improvement and partly by its being situated sufficiently far to dissuade them from incurring the necessary loss involved. At the same time it is in a way an influence to the ryots' detriment, for tigers, boars, etc., which the Akalanum and Mattur hills breed occasionally, make nocturnal depredations on the ryots' stock and corn fields. The peasantry are helpless against these enemies.

Occupation of land.—The private jenmam ryotwari holdings during the year of settlement (fasli 1313) are classified as follows:—

Pattadars paying	Number.			Extent.		Assessment.	
	Single	Joint.	Total.	ACS.	C.	RS.	A.
Re. 1 and less	2	...	2	...	50	1	8
Rs. 10 and less but over Re. 1	7	2	9	7	71	33	14
" 30 " " " 10 ...	3	2	5	18	21	96	7
" 50 " " " 30 ...	1	...	1	7	8	37	5
" 100 " " " 50 ...	...	...	...	...	...	...	...
" 250 " " " 100 ...	...	...	...	...	...	...	...
" 500 " " " 250 ...	1	...	1	99	56	401	13
" 1,000 " " " 500 ...	...	...	...	...	...	...	...
Over 1,000 ...	1	...	1	718	80	2,315	4
Total ...	15	4	19	851	86	2,886	3

Out of 851·86 acres no less than 818·36 belong to the two jenmi landlords. There are no occupants of Government jenmam ryotwari land in the same year.

Almost all kanomdars are themselves cultivators. The two jenmis, who are Brahmans by caste, and nearly 10 other families who come immediately below in the caste scale, are prohibited from cultivation by their social status, and hence have let or sublet their lands to tenants of lower castes.

The landholders themselves, who are in a minority, are fast disappearing. They are chiefly owners of small strips held for the most part by a kanom tenure from a jenmi. The growing indebtedness and the consequent process of alienation of lands which are now going on will ere long reduce these people to the rank of landless labourers. But the landholders must be distinguished from land owners. Strictly speaking those who own land are the pattadars who possess jenmam pattas and those few who hold from them lands on kanom tenure. The ownership of the kanomdar is very precarious, since for the most part the kanom being a small amount, and there being no governmental regulations against the arbitrary action of the jenmis, the kanomdars are at the mercy of their jenmis. The ancient right of usage of lands enjoyed by the people is now being sought to be taken away. · The jenmis are oppressive in many ways. All storts of excuses are eagerly clutched at for extorting money from the tenantry. Besides the very high rate demanded at the time of a renewal of tenure (usually these tenures are held for 12 years), there are exactions on the occasion of a death, marriage or other religious festival in the jenmi's household, and fines often in amounts more than Rs. 100 are levied right and left for silly reasons. Various instances have come within the personal knowledge of the writer. One family had to return some lands two years ago to the jenmi because when the term expired and when application was made for a renewal, the fee demanded was so high that 12 years' profit from the land could hardly equal the amount. One man was fined Rs. 100, because he refused to pay 2 annas as a subscription for a religious festival which the jenmi was then conducting. Another case of arbitrary oppression was recently reported to the writer by the sufferers. The jenmi was contemplating a pilgrimage and all tenants were asked to give Rs. 10 each for it within 24 hours! These are actual cases. Up till 1916 no man other than the two jenmis was allowed to tile his house, to build an upstair building, or a gateway; even now it is rash for the ryot to ask for such permission. No woman is allowed to appear before the jenmi with covered breast, no man should approach him with more than single cloth wound round his waist, which should not fall below his knees. Even in these days of British rule these things are in actual existence! I have said so much to give an idea of the relation between the landlord and the tenant in this part of the country.

There are two other dangers to which the landholder is constantly exposed which need mention here, i.e., melcharth, and the recent policy of the jenmi to convert kanom holdings into verumpattam. Melcharth is the jenmi's right to make over by promise at his will to a higher bidder any portion of his land which is being enjoyed by the kanomdar under him on the strength of his right for the land for twelve years. This is constantly exercised by the jenmi and it has a very bad effect both economically and morally over the agricultural population. The other danger is of more recent origin and is the result of the panic created among the jenmis of British Malabar on the passing of the Jenmi-Kutiyan

Harvesting paddy in North Malabar, fields still wet.
Photo by Agricultural College.

regulations in the sister states of Cochin* and Travancore, which have placed a decided check on the arbitrary dealings of the landlord over the tenant in those countries. The fear of governmental interference in the near future to regulate the relations of the landlord and the tenant (for it is well known that this problem is an old one in Malabar, and even as far back as 1885, the popular administration of Mr. Logan had made a draft regulation on the same subject which was only abandoned for want of adequate support by the country and which formed the basis on which Cochin and Travancore could afterwards proceed) has stimulated the process of converting kanom lands into verumpattam, i.e., tenure at will. By this the jenmi has a double advantage. The lands are under his direct ownership, and as they are given to cultivation by annual contracts, he can at any time refuse, withhold or do what he likes with his lands. The lands also being as it were put to auction, will produce a higher rate of income than would be the case by giving it on kanom tenure. There is also a recent tendency on the part of the jenmi to raise the kanom amounts because in Cochin and Travancore this is made the basis for the regulation of rent. Till now the policy was to give lands on a nominal kanom, the advantage being in the facility with which they might reclaim the lands at pleasure.

The Cherumas (the submerged class) are the agricultural labourers who neither own nor rent land. They work for their masters who give them a meagre allowance of 2 edangalis, i.e., 1/5 para (the standard measure) of paddy. With this he supports his wife and family. They are attached to their masters and loath to leave them.

Rents are always paid in kind and are high enough particularly in the case of annual holdings. Eighty per cent of the produce will go as rent to the landowner. The sole advantage for which tenants take up lands are, they say, (1) a few days' maintenance after the harvest, (2) the possession of straw, and (3) employment. But sometimes they have to pay rent in money and this is chiefly in seasons of crop failure. This is met in these ways:—(1) Direct borrowing, (2) profit of garden cultivation and (3) the institution of chit-fund,† which is widely prevalent among them.

The barber and the washerman of the desam are illustrations of how customary occupations are modified by practical necessity. These people, while they perform their traditional occupations to the society and receive for it the fixed remunerations, have long taken to agriculture as their chief source of income. And they are among the chief farmers. There are two manufacturers of

* Vide p. 116.

† [A chit-fund is similar to our Slate-clubs. The members meet periodically, usually every month, and each pays a defined sum into the fund. If it be an 'auction-chit,' the money so collected is given to the member who, not having received it previously, offers to give back the largest amount, e.g., if there be Rs. 100 in the chit, one member may offer to take Rs. 75 only. The remaining Rs. 25 is then divided among the other members. Security is then taken from the recipient of the Rs. 75 that he will continue to pay his monthly contributions till every member has had his turn. In the other variety of chit, the monthly sum is ballotted for. It is the same as Kuri, described on p. 124.—Ed.]

toddy and jaggery and three carters who are mainly agriculturists.

The revenue for the year 1915-16 was Rs. 3,175-10-3. The assessment for fasli 1312 for the Amsam of Kothachira was Rs. 6,519-2 4. By settlement (fasli 1326) it is Rs. 11,228 7-0.

Agriculture.—We have mentioned elsewhere the names of the chief crops. Out of these, the two staple products are paddy and arecanut, the former being a field cultivation and the latter garden. The mainstay of the bulk of the population is arecanut. Every household of any worth is surrounded by an areca palm garden.

The method of cultivation pursued in both these is of an antiquated character.

1. *Arecanut.*--Mature fruits are selected for seeds. They are kept in pots and watered for one year. Next year they are planted and within a year and a half or so, they grow into young plants. Then they are transplanted into the gardens where they have to be grown. They are planted in parallel lines, the distance from one another varying from two to three yards. The plants are at first placed in pits measuring a cubic yard. Some cow dung and ash manure are put, and a watering is given on alternate days in the summer. During the monsoon they are left to themselves. When the plants grow up into trees, the pit is filled up and a shallow basin round it made just to contain a few gallons of water. These are renewed every year in the beginning of summer, small channels are cut across the gardens to bring water to the root of every tree, water-lifts are erected and regular watering begun. This will continue until the advent of the monsoon.

2. *Paddy.*--On the first shower of the monsoon, fields are given a hasty ploughing and seeds are thrown. A fortnight of average showers helps healthy sprouting and the ryot prays for similar weather for another two fortnights to come. By this time, they have grown up into healthy plants. Between the second and third month of their growth, they are carefully unrooted and planted in plots prepared by ploughing for the purpose. Between the fifth and sixth month after sowing comes the harvest. If there is a second crop, the land is again prepared for sowing immediately after harvest and the whole process repeated. For this crop, the ryot depends on the north-east monsoon which gives two months of heavy rain from the middle of November to the middle of January. After this harvest the fields lie fallow for a period of two or three months.

A table given in the next page will show the areas under single and double crop, different soils, and the nature of the assessments on each. (The information is taken from the village accounts.) The assessment given herein is the revised one after the re-settlement.

Classification and Assessment.

Description of soil.	Wet.						Garden.					Occupied dry.				
	Taram.	Whether single or double crop.	Rate per acre.	Area.	Assessment.	Jenma-bhogam.	Taram.	Rate per acre.	Area.	Assessment.	Jenma-bhogam.	Taram.	Rate per acre.	Area.	Assessment.	Jenma-bhogam.
(1)	(2)	(3)	(4)	(5)	(6)	(7)	(8)	(9)	(10)	(11)	(12)	(13)	(14)	(15)	(16)	(17)
			RS. A.	ACS. C.	RS. A.			RS. A.	ACS. C.	RS. A.			RS. A.	ACS. C.	RS. A.	
Red loam, VII-1 ...	...	...	...	...	...	...	2	6 0	1 49	8 15	...	2	1 8	1 10	1 11	...
	...	...	...	...	...	...	3	5 0	4 24	21 3	...	...	...	...	...	...
VII-2 ...	2	1	5 0	8 97	44 14	..	3	5 0	0 75	3 12	...	3	1 0	52 46	52 10	...
	...	2	6 4	205 46	1,284 2	...	4	4 0	24 95	99 13	...	...	...	...	...	...
	...	...	...	...	..	...	5	3 0	33 18	99 8	...	...	...	...	...	...
	...	...	...	...	...	...	6	2 0	73 71	147 5	...	...	...	...	...	...
	...	...	...	...	...	...	7	1 0	13 75	13 12	...	...	...	...	...	...
VII-3 ...	3	1	4 0	33 76	135 1	...	5	3 0	15 67	46 14	...	4	0 12	11 394	85 7	...
	...	2	5 0	95 82	479 3	...	6	2 0	18 28	36 9	...	...	...	...	..	...
	...	...	...	...	...	...	7	1 0	21 56	21 9	..	...	...	...	...	...
VII-4 ...	4	1	3 0	50 60	151 15	...	6	2 0	0 60	1 6	...	5	0 10	19 50	12 3	...
	...	2	3 12	10 57	39 10	...	7	1 0	0 80	0 13	...	...	...	...	...	...
VII-5 ...	5	1	2 0	33 29	66 12	...	...	...	...	...	..	6	0 8	2 62	1 5	...
	...	2	2 8	0 59	1 8	..	...	..	...	.	...	...	...	...	...	...
Red sand, VIII-3	4	2	3 12	6 21	23 4	...	7	1 0	0 55	0 9	...	5	0 10	6 28	4 0	...
VIII-4	...	...	...	...	...	..	...	..	...	...	...	6	0 8	1 26	0 10	...
Total ...	...	...	...	445 27	2,226 5	...	...	...	209 43	502 0	...	...	...	197 16	157 14	...

On registered double crop land, the charge for the second crop has been consolidated at one-quarter of the single crop assessment. For occasional second crop on land assessed as single crop, the charge will be one-half the single crop assessment.

The stock as ascertained by personal enquiry are as shown below. The account of the stock of Kothachira was not obtainable from the village officials, for it is lost. I have tried my best to make the statement complete and exhaustive. But this is a period of extreme fatality to the stock in these parts. Daily one or more are dying. In a single family there died twenty within forty-five days leaving only one or two pairs. The numbers are—

Bullocks	240	
Cows	403	
Buffaloes	287	
Young stock	374	under 4 years.
Goats	712	
Ploughs	414	
Carts	5	
Oil mills	4	

A comparison with the figures for the census of 1899-1900 for the whole amsom of Kothachira (the three desams of Kothachira, Peringode and Mattur) shows an all-round decrease of about forty per cent. I believe the causes of this great reduction to be partly a succession of very bad seasons for stock, and partly selling off under pressure of poverty.

Cattle feeding.—Bullocks and working oxen and buffaloes, besides being left to graze on the unoccupied dry lands and on cultivable areas when they are lying fallow, are given straw and 'kanchi,' water mixed with the dusty part of rice and 'punac' or oil-cake. For cows and young stock only straw is given besides grazing. Goats are simply left to graze. Straw is given to the above working stock after they are housed in their sheds for the evening. The 'kanchi' water is given in the morning just before leading them into fields and in the afternoon after their work is over. They are led to be washed after field work. Bullocks and buffaloes are the working stock.

The breed.—The cattle are very second rate in their breed. The most healthy working oxen grow to a height of from three to three and a half feet and their strength is not half as much as the oxen employed by the firms of Madras. The cow is a pitiable thing ordinarily two to three feet high and milking on an average from a half to one Madras measure per day.* Comparison, it need hardly be said, with Madras cows is odious. They can be milked for only six months. The best come into milking again within a year, but many only within two years.

Manure.—Almost all the cattle dung is used for manure. One per cent perhaps goes for purposes of washing floors, etc. The cattle urine is allowed in some places to flow into the dung-pit, but no systematic attempt is anywhere made to utilize it to the best advantage. Besides this, burnt ashes and green manure are in common

* [A Madras measure is 62·5 fluid ounces = 3⅛ pints. A fair Madras cow in full milk yields about 3¼ Madras measures per day, i.e., 5 quarts.—Ed.]

use. No other manure is used. Green manure is not grown but is got from somewhere or other according to circumstances. Varatties are not made. Wood fuel is the only sort used.

Insect pests.—Of these, the most ruinous is the "Chazhi" the terror of the ryot. The chazhi is a small insect of the locust species half an inch long which in millions appear in a few seasons and spread desolation in the paddy fields. Two remedies are current against this pestilence: (1) catching them directly by drawing a cloth (which serves the purpose of a net) attached to two handsticks over the crops and thus killing them; (2) but by far the most efficacious remedy in the estimation of the cultivator is the putting of a talisman in the fields which a local conjurer (Mandravadi) has prepared for him. What chazhi is to paddy "Mahali" is to the arecanut, the only difference being that in this case nothing is believed to be possible to combat the calamity.

Cattle diseases are (1) hoof disease, (2) Koraladappan (swelling in the neck), (3) Thada (mumps), (4) obstruction of urine and dung, (5) sudden epileptic attacks, and other diseases whose causes and cure are unknown to the peasant. Poisoning is sometimes done by Paraiyas of neighbouring desams for the sake of getting the flesh. For beef is eaten only by this lowest class and when cattle die they will be called to remove the carcase. A number of cattle are annually destroyed by tigers also which often venture into the sheds of the peasants. Talismans and offerings to deities are conceived to be the only remedy.

No assistance is obtained from the Agricultural department, nor any from any veterinary doctor.

Wood is commonly got for all uses from private trees; but the forest also supplies sometimes wood for small necessities. For building purposes, wood is purchased—not from any fixed place.

Houses.—The depressed castes have miserable hovels for their houses. A mud wall of five feet height with a ruined roof which can protect the inmate neither from sun nor rain is the order of the day.

Except the palatial family homes of the two jenmis, there are no tiled houses. Terracing is not customary here. All other houses are thatched, and thatching is always of straw.

Most houses have gardens surrounding them, where arecanut trees, plantains, mango trees, jack, etc., are grown. They are joyful to look at.

The maximum distance of cultivated lands from the home of cultivator is one mile.

An acre of land costs from Rs. 200 to Rs. 300. But purchases on jenmi tenure are worth above Rs. 500. But it is impossible to acquire jenmam property except for jenmis; for the jenmis are jealous guardians of their lands and never sell lands once acquired. Direct threatenings and indirect intimidation are used by them to obtain the jenmam right of lands if held by any lesser landowner.

Subsidiary industries.—Neither weaving nor spinning have ever been practised in this desam.

Other crafts—

1. Arrack and jaggery making.
2. Ironsmith.

3. Goldsmith.
4. Leathersmith.
5. Carpentry.
6. Masonry.
7. Oil pressing.
8. Making of bamboo mats, baskets, etc.
9. Trade in rice.
10. Butter and milk trade.

In arrack preparation two men (Tiyyas) are engaged, but they are also agriculturists and not more than two hours are spent on an average by them on their particular profession. They cut two or three trees daily and from the toddy thus got jaggery or arrack is made. The profit according to their own version is not more than three annas per day. The ironsmith, goldsmith, leathersmith, carpenter and stone mason are whole-time workmen. The ironsmith finds employment in making or repairing agricultural implements. Nothing above this is known to him. The goldsmith's work consists mainly of making ornaments for the jenmis. He is an expert as far as such ornaments are concerned. But beyond these customary works his genius does not go. The leathersmith gets hardly any orders for his work, but his wife supplies chunam* to the country whereby the family maintains a precarious existence. Carpenters and stone masons have work in some seasons. For example, in the ploughing time or the beginning of the watering season, the former has busy calls from every family for the repair of a plough, a water lift or the like. The stone mason wanders to other parts of the country in search of work. He has no work here. The average rate of wages for these is four annas a day and one meal. Goldsmiths' and ironsmiths' remuneration is based on the quality and quantity of their work. None of these have continuous employment for the whole year. Owing to this cause, out of the two families of carpenters consisting of ten members of workable age, eight migrate usually to Calicut where they get twelve annas wages per day. They pay occasional visits to their homes, stay there for a fortnight or so, and then again go.

The oil presses find ten or twelve days' work each year after a gingelly crop is cut.

Mat and basket making is the indoor industry of the Cheruma women. They help their husbands in the fields in minor works but sometimes are also employed on independent wages especially during harvest and sowing time. Their spare time is employed in this industry. These mats and baskets are made of split bamboo. They are rough productions.

There is a curious industry carried on by some Nayar men and women which illustrates the plight they are in. Each of them has a capital of two rupees. They go out with this ten or sometimes fifteen miles away and purchase paddy for this sum where it is sold cheaper by four nazhis (one-tenth para) a rupee. Next day it is boiled, dried and made into rice. On the third day it is carried to Kunnankulam or Guruvayoor, villages eight or ten miles to the

* [Slaked lime for chewing. It is spread thinly on betel leaves, which are folded when put in the mouth.—Ed.]

west, and sold there. The profit of the bargain is four annas. Twelve families subsist on this trade.

Buttermilk, ghee and butter are made and sold by some families. But this is not a steady trade. It is dependent on cows giving birth.

Village trade.—The volume and the extent of village trade is limited; the wants are few and easily satisfied. Paddy seed for cultivation is not purchased but borrowed from the landlord at an interest of sixty per cent. The amount borrowed with the interest thereon is annually given back to the landlord and again borrowed at the sowing season. The borrower is bound to return paddy fit for seeding.

Other commodities useful for agriculture, such as ropes, vessels used for lifting water, etc., are purchased from the little town of Kunnankulam, eight miles off and belonging to the Native State of Cochin. There is a big bazaar at Kunnankulam where almost all necessaries and luxuries are sold. But the usual market for the village trade is that held on every Thursday at Chalisseri, a large village three miles to the west of Kothachira. People take areca, paddy and other vegetables to this market, get these sold there and with the money thus obtained purchase necessaries; sometimes articles are directly exchanged for paddy. The chief necessaries usually purchased are salt, fish, oil, kerosene, chillis, onions, and cloth to wear. Men and women wear simply one *mundu* around the waist. Hence little clothing is required.

Chalisseri is in a way an important place. Much trade in areca is carried on here. The agents of the areca traders of Chalisseri come to each family and purchase directly the quantities each has to sell. The quantity conveyed to market by the ryot himself is not very great. The selling price of areca varies from three to five rupees per tulam (= 25 lb.) according to time and circumstances. The arecanut traders of Chalisseri are absolute masters of this business and often impose their own terms upon the cultivator. After being cut and dried areca is exported by the former into the districts of the east. The best areca grower has sold nuts worth Rs. 400 a year.

The road that runs from the Pattambai railway station to Chowghat passes through Chalisseri. This is the nearest road to Kothachira people. It winds near Kutnad and thus runs parallel to the northern and western boundaries of Kothachira at a distance of two miles from each. A by-road cut from the western arm of the main road to the house of one of the jenmis at his own expense, has long been out of use and is not adapted for public purposes.

The idea of co-operation is unknown. A public road opened along the private footpath that runs between Karuvathur, a village six miles to the east of Kothachira, and Chalisseri, would be of immense use to the public of these parts. Much traffic is carried on along this footpath between these places specially on market days. It would run across Peringode and along the boundary between Mathur and Kothachira and thus benefit all these desams.

Economic condition of village.—The economic condition of this desam is rather discouraging. The people are deep in debt, are overworked and underfed and ground down by a double tyranny, the tyranny of the landlord who is also the money-lender, and the tyranny of deep-rooted custom in all their lives and walks.

Wages are paid both in money and in kind; more often in kind since they find it more to their immediate advantage. The rate of wages is two annas six pies or its equivalent in corn at the standard price, for an unskilled labourer; and four and at times five annas for skilled artisans.

The price of paddy varies in different seasons. In the harvest season and sometimes after it, the price ranges between 2½ and 2 paras a rupee. But towards June and July the price goes up to between 1 and 1½ paras a rupee. This is the only food which can be called staple. In times of scarcity the poorer people depend on jack fruits, mango and fish, of which the latter alone need be purchased, and that is cheaper than other foods.

Excepting the jenmis who are large zamindars, there are but six houses which have made savings. The bulk of the families are unable to liberate themselves from the grasp of the creditors.

The capital saved by these families is employed in lending to the needy agriculturists. A microscopically small amount has gone on jewellery among these middle class families, but with the jenmi the case is different. It looks as though the capitalist knows no way to employ his capital except lending to neighbours.

Debt.—The extent of indebtedness cannot be definitely ascertained by enquiry. But from what I have been able to gather from the accounts of two capitalist families, I have been able to make an almost correct estimate of the state of things with the agriculturist. Ranging from Rs. 10 to Rs. 800 one family account consists of the names of thirty debtors from Kothachira. These are all standing debts and the interest on these varies from 9 per cent to 12 per cent. Twelve per cent is the current rate of "polite" interest, as people call it. But there are capitalists who lend money even at 24 and 30 per cent in the neighbourhood. The capital thus employed, however, is not the result of direct saving but is ancestral property bequeathed by their fathers, who were the heads of a jenmi family.

Thus we find that capitalists who have money at all to lend, have got the money by other sources and not by saving. The agriculturist has many difficulties to meet with. He has no land and not enough stock and implements. His family is large and the expense is ordinarily far beyond his income. From his field cultivation, after all expenses have been deducted, he gets very little for himself. The rents are very high. The capital employed in stock is vital to him and yearly his lot is to lose by death of cattle either by disease or by wild beasts. Last year there were two cases of the latter. Those who have garden cultivation have this profit to utilize. But the majority own no gardens. The population has grown but not the means of subsistence, and no family except the few named find it possible to maintain their family purely from the proceeds of their toil. Thus they incur debt, but debt once incurred hangs heavy on the debtor. Not only is he unable to find means to pay the high rate of interest on the previous year's debt, but he must borrow at all costs again if he is to avoid absolute starvation of his family. This is regularly continued. Litigation follows and an additional and unprofitable expense is thus laid on his head. Law interferes and whatever property he has is lost. But the law does not kill the people, and so long as they live, they have to keep their body and soul together. Thus year by year, the rich become richer and the poor poorer. The process is continuing at a fast rate and the people do not realize it. They are too ignorant and attribute everything to their fate and God's will. To add to these evils, in some years crops fail and there will be utter starvation. Thus the causes of indebtedness are—

(1) High rent.
(2) Population beyond means of subsistence.
(3) Lands limited in area.
(4) Absolute dependence on land of the population.

There is no instance of debtors who have entirely liberated themselves from debt in this desam. There is no co-operative society.

Sanitation.—In regard to sanitation, thanks to the peculiar customs of Malabar, the evils arising from the rigour of social rules are absent. Infant marriage and purdah are both absent. There is no problem of the disposal of night-soil here, for there are large unoccupied areas whither the people resort, while the women have latrines far out in their back compounds. As for insanitary habits, they are not addicted to any similar to what are found elsewhere. All bathe once a day in tanks or streams. There is neither much smoking or snuffing, but there is chewing (betel and tobacco and lime and arecanut all together) among all people, but not to such an extent as among people in Madras, etc. Drinking is a real evil among the Cherumas, but this is chiefly due to lack of proper food of other sorts. Several of them when asked why they drink have given the same unanimous answer, that "while stomach calls, one must respond, else not hear at all." The latter is of course the cheaper course.

Good and clear water for drinking is easily got from private wells.

But with all these, the figure for the year of deaths from diseases and infant mortality is not encouraging.

The list contains the account of only one year that of 1915-16. But it still speaks for itself.

Kothachira.

Ages of dead.	Number according to age.	Fever.	Dysentery.	Tuberculosis.	Diarrhœa.	Dyspepsia.	Hysteria.	Karappani (skin blotched).	Other causes.
Lifeless birth	7	...	...	...	...	...	...	...	...
Below 1 ...	9	...	3	...	...	...	4	2	...
Between 1 and 10 ...	13	4	3	1	...	...	4	1	...
" 10 " 20 ...	1	1	...	.	...	...	...	...	...
" 20 " 30 ...	7	3	...	1	1	...	...	...	2
" 30 " 40 ...	3	3	...	...	...	...	...	...	...
" 40 " 50 ...	...	...	...	...	...	...	...	...	...
" 50 " 60 ...	3	.	1	1	1	...	...	...	...
" 60 " 80 ...	5	...	1	1	1	...	...	...	2
Total ...	48	11	8	4	3	...	8	3	4

Peringode.

Ages of dead.	Number according to age.	Fever.	Swelling.	Tuberculosis.	Diarrhœa.	Dyspepsia.	Hysteria.	Skin blotches.	Other causes.
Lifeless birth	4	...	...	...	...	...	...	...	...
Below 1	9	...	1	...	4	...	3	1	...
Between 1 and 10 ...	5	...	1	...	...	3	1	...	...
" 10 " 20 ...	...	...	...	...	...	...	...	...	...
" 20 " 30 ...	...	...	...	...	...	...	...	...	...
" 30 " 40 ..	4	...	1	...	2	...	...	...	1
" 40 " 50 ...	1	...	...	1	..	...	...	...	...
" 50 " 60 ...	2	...	...	2	...	...	...	...	...
" 60 " 80 ...	5	...	...	1	...	...	...	...	4
Total ...	30	...	3	4	6	3	4	1	5

Mathur.

Ages of dead.	Number of dead according to ages.	Dysentery.	Diarrhœa.	Hysteria.	Tuberculosis.	Rheumatism.
Below 1	2	...	1	1	...	...
Between 30 and 40	1	...	...	...	1	...
" 50 " 60	3	1	1	...	...	1
" 60 " above ...	5	...	5	...		...
Total ...	11	1	7	1	1	1

Education.—There is one elementary school in the amsam, but it is situated in Peringode desam. It is maintained by a wealthy jenmi of Peringode, who is not an enlightened man. It was started two years ago. It has a good building and sufficient accommodation for the children now on the roll. There were a large number at the commencement of the school when there were enthusiastic teachers who knew the value of education. But they were dispensed with as they soon got into the bad books of the jenmi by their independent attitude. Since then there has been a regular decline in attendance. The maximum limit reached was 210. But now the number on the roll is 103—84 boys and 19 girls. The school is now under weak hands and highly mismanaged. The masters are not efficient and their methods of teaching antiquated. They are themselves people whose knowledge is highly limited. Reading and writing the vernacular, simple rules of arithmetic, and geography are taught.

Five per cent of the adults are able to read the vernacular; four per cent to write it. There are only two people able to read, write and speak English, two brothers.

Besides the English books belonging to the English-speaking brothers, 12 other families own a total number of 16 vernacular (paper) books. They are all puranic stories. There are 30 palm-leaf manuscripts in all, which either are puranic stories or deal with such subjects as conjuring and black arts. There are also some Vedic manuscripts in the family of the jenmi.

Village administration.—There is no panchayat. The village has a Government official "Adhikari" who collects the revenue. He has also given a little civil and criminal authority which however is rarely made use of. There is another official "Menon" who is the surveyor and assessor of taxes on lands, etc.

There is practically no sanitary administration. Sometimes a vaccinator visits the country and gets some children vaccinated.

There is a Police station at Chalisseri which has jurisdiction over this place. Weekly or monthly one constable pays a visit and makes a report that the king's peace is kept scrupulously.

The Tahsildar or the Revenue Inspector or a Land Records Inspector may sometimes pay a visit to the amsam officials, but he sees none of the people.

For some time past, thefts have been increasing in this desam. A few youths, born and bred up in rank illiteracy, are straying away from the path of righteousness, and the poor man's property is becoming insecure. Recently this has come to the notice of the police and they have begun to have a watchful eye over some of them. But none of these have been yet of a serious nature.

There are a small number of law-suits against the ryots by the jenmis at all times, but over and above this there is not much litigation. But recently however there arose two law suits between ryots which were the result of bad blood and high words.

Small cases were dealt with satisfactorily by the village munsif this year.

History and prospects of the village.—Centuries ago, as far back as 1,800 years, this desam must have formed a part of the famous division of Kutnad. The name of the once historic land of Kutnad, which at one time covered the whole of the Mid-Kerala, is now confined to the little desam that lies contiguous to Kothachira. The ruins still traceable on the plains below the Kutnad hill, of temples and a fortress, and the large number of ruined walls seen in the vicinity, suggest the existence of a flourishing city in this spot in the past.

But about Kothachira in the more recent past. The country must at one time have been governed by local chieftains from whose hands the Brahman jenmis who now hold the lands got them with the advent of the age of Brahmanic dominance. There are families which still hold the name of "Naduvashis," i.e., the governors of the country, who are now labourers and landless ryots. They still cling with faith and reverence to their old traditions and ceremonial forms which they practised when they were masters of the country.

But within the past few generations itself there has been a great economic change noticeable. There are old men still living who can attest to the state of things thirty or forty years ago. From them, we hear the rise and fall of some of the families. Those were farmers who owned vast extents of lands, which were cultivated by means of their own capital and stock. These families yet survive, but have scattered hovels to live in and are reduced to the rank of landless cultivators, entirely dependent on the landlords for subsistence.

There is however ample scope for economic improvement if some of the standing evils be removed. First of all must come education and enlightenment among the masses, for which nothing short of free and compulsory education can be of help in view of the poverty and the rank apathy of the people. A law must regulate the relations of the jenmi and kudiyan (tenant) which would deal successfully with the problem of oppression of the weak by the strong, and the absolute economic and social servility of the one to the other. Agriculture must be improved and co-operation stimulated. The indebted classes must gradually be liberated from the coils of the money-lenders and landlords, either by means of loans on nominal interest or otherwise. The public must be educated in the modern developments of agricultural science as well by example as by precept. They must also be initiated into the advantages of co-operation and mutual help. The operations of the savings banks, assurance societies, agricultural loans, etc., must be brought into more intimate reach of the ryot. Deeper and more wells should be dug and irrigation works also introduced. Roads and other public ways must be opened into the hearts of these sequestered areas. Boys and girls must be educated and trained to be good industrious men and citizens. In short, a strong movement must be started to awaken the people from apathy into activity, from thraldom into self-help and self-reliance, from illiteracy into enlightenment.

For all these, none but the landlords can take the best initiative. Therefore education must first of all be given to them. Now they belong to a class which is the most conservative, the most dominant, the richest and the most oppressive in Malabar. By education, they must be brought round to a sense of justice, brotherhood and philanthropy. They are orthodox religionists who spend days and nights in ceremonials and chanting of vedic lore. But they do not know what their chants mean and do this because their forefathers did so. This cannot make men cultured and helpful to society.

These are some of the reforms that have to be undertaken and some of these have to come from the people themselves, but there are others which the Government alone can deal with effectively.

APPENDIX.

I. A Possible Improvement.

By deepening the stream that flows in rainy season along the northern boundary of this desam, the lands that lie along them which now yield only a single crop can be made double crop lands.

II. Emigration.

There are five men in Ceylon working as labourers and sending small sums to their aged parents. These return at intervals of two or three years. There is also the annual emigration of the carpenters to Calicut.

III. A Typical Family.

The family is not composed of a husband, wife and children. The people follow the 'Marumakkattayam' form of inheritance, i.e., inheritance along the line of the nephew. Thus the family consists of an aged mother or grandmother and her sisters and brothers, the sons and daughters of these sisters and their progeny, and so on. The eldest male member is the 'Karnavan,' the guardian and manager of the family, all the rest are 'Anandravans' who pay allegiance to the head. The male members of one family marry the females of another and vice versa, but each lives apart and they only join occasionally. The system, however, is rudely breaking up under modern conditions.

VATANAMKURUSSI VILLAGE (WALLUVANAD TALUK).

[*By N. Sundara Aiyar, Presidency College, Madras.*]

Preliminary.—The village lies in the interior of the district, thirty miles west of the municipal town of Palghat on the high road that passes from Palghat to Ponnani. It is to the north of the railway line passing from Calicut to Palghat, and about equidistant from the two railway stations of Shoranur and Pattambi on that line (South Indian Railway). It is fifty-four miles south-east (by railway) of the port of Calicut, the capital of the district.

The village is more or less surrounded by low hills on all sides, and there is a small forest to the east of it. A portion of the village has for its southern boundary the Bharata Puzha (called the Ponnani river, because it joins the sea at Ponnani). The river is of little use for navigation, since it is in flood during the rains and almost dry in summer. The railway passes through the village, for about a mile, though the nearest railway station is 4½ miles distant. The trunk road from Palghat also passes through the middle of the village. The village is roughly in the shape of a triangle with its apex to the north and the base on the south. Being in the midst of hilly country, dry soil abounds in the village, though the few wet acres are comparatively good.

Population.—The total population of the village in Census years was as follows :—

Year.	Occupied houses.	Males.	Females.	Total.	Hindus.	Muhammadans.
1891 ...	322	1,055	1,134	2,189	2,116	73
1901 ...	369	1,130	1,187	2,317	2,226	91
1911 ...	398	1,210	1,270	2,480	2,373	107

The figures include those of an adjacent small village, of which the total population in 1911 was 124, all Hindus.

There are Brahmans and Sudras, the latter split up into a large number of sub-castes and sects like the Nayars, Nambiyars, Menons, Chettis, etc., and the lower classes like the Thiyyas, or Ezhuvans, and the depressed classes of Cherumas, Pariahs and Nayadis. Nayars predominate in the village. There are a few Muhammadans, but no Christians at all.

Of Brahmans there are ten families comprising 60 individuals resident in the village. There are two families of Nambudiri Brahmans with some 30 members.

The great majority are Nayars, of whom there are about 150 families with nearly 1,500 individuals. Cherumas may number between 300 and 400, the Thiyyas or Ezhuvans about 500. The chief minor sub-castes in the village are Chettis (34), Kunparars (Potters, about 50), Asaris (Carpenters, 28), Karuvans (blacksmiths, 21), Thattars (goldsmiths, 19), Panans (makers of bamboo and palm leaf umbrellas, 29), Masons (13), Pariahs (42), and five families of Mannans, washermen of the lower classes, who also make mud walls, engage themselves as herdsmen and act as Pujaris, i.e., perform priestly functions for the lowest classes. There are also in the village a few families of Ambalavasis (about 35 persons) who rank above the Nayars and perform menial and other functions in temples, and also practise Ayurvedic medicine.

Births and deaths.—The village register gives the following statistics of births and deaths for the year 1915 (as far as I could ascertain, a normal year).

Births.

	Males.	Females.	Total.
Hindus	37	41	78
Muhammadans	2	1	3
	39	42	81

Deaths.

	Males.	Females.	Total.
Below 1 year	8	2	10
Between 1 and 5	1	4	5
„ 5 and 10	4	1	5
„ 15 and 20	2	1	3
„ 30 and 40	2	2	4
„ 40 and 50	3	...	3
„ 50 and 60	2	2	4
Above 60	3	4	7
	25	16	41

Causes—

	Males.	Females.	
Fever	7	6	Causes are not accurate.
Dysentery and diarrhoea ...	11	6	
Respiratory diseases ...	6	4	
Injuries	1	...	
	25	16	

The figures seem to be fairly accurate, though not quite so. The death rate seems to be too low compared to the birth rate. But the figures are admittedly incomplete as is seen from the remarks made upon the register by the supervising authority. The deficiency is probably in the record of *deaths of young children*.

The causes of this defect are (1) registration not being compulsory; (2) indifference or ignorance of village authorities and of villagers who hardly seem to realize the importance of registration; (3) the villagers' suspicion of registration; they do not know its object.

There is no Paracheri strictly so called as in villages of eastern districts. There are scattered dwellings of depressed classes, Cherumas and Pariahs. There are five families of Pariahs, consisting of 13 men, 13 women and 16 children. Of the men two have gone for work to the Kolar Gold Fields and one to Wynaad. The proportion of children to adults is much smaller among the Cherumas and Pariahs than among the Brahmans and Nayars.

Land.—

	ACS.
Wet land	681·07
Occupied dry land	231·12
Unoccupied dry land	1,221·92
Garden land	109·59

Woodlands cover an area of about 150 acres. Shrubs and thickets, as well as rank undergrowth are found almost everywhere. Big trees, scattered and in groves, are also abundant.

Fruit trees and scattered shade trees are abundant. Among the former may be mentioned the mango, jack, coconut and areca-nut palms, the palmyra palm (yielding toddy), etc. There are numerous kinds of shade trees, many of which can be used as timber. Among timber trees specially may be noted the teak and the jack-tree.

Tanks and wells are very numerous. Wells indeed are too numerous to be enumerated. Every house has one or more and there are several in the fields, about one in an acre. There are more than 50 tanks, though some of them are mere ponds, dry in most months. A few tanks yield water unfailingly for irrigation on a small rate. They may be 6 to 20 feet deep and of varying lengths, from, say 10 to 100 feet. Some are of irregular shape. The wells are either circular or rectangular and from 10 to 40 feet deep--often deeper still. If circular their diameter measures from 5 to 10 feet and if rectangular they are from 6 to 10 feet broad and 8 to 16 feet long. A few are dry in summer, but many wells yield an abundant and unfailing supply of water for domestic and agricultural purposes.

There is a small channel passing through the village which is full during the rains, but mostly dry in the hot months. A dam is however put across it in some places and the scanty water stored up for future use. But there is not any very considerable quantity.

Occupation of land.—Most of the cultivated area is sublet to tenants. This is characteristic of Malabar, where most of the landlords do not themselves cultivate the land, but let it to others on short leases of 12 years called *kanom* leases. The kanom lease-holders in turn sublet the land, though a few of them actually cultivate it.

There are nominally 50 patta-holders and all of them come under the head of non-cultivating landowners. The richest have no particular occupation. Many are Nambudiri Brahmans not resident in the village, and they have comfortable positions as priests, preceptors, etc. The biggest landowners, who almost monopolise the land, are two or three in number and they live in ease on the revenues of their lands.

The great body of tenants own no land; they simply rent it on kanom lease or are tenants at will. There may be one or two among the landowners who are also the kanom tenants of some other landlord. But as a rule the kanom tenant owns no land.

There is a growing body of landless agricultural labourers.

By the census of 1901 there were 383 landholders (tenants) in that year. This number declined to 258 in 1917, paying land-revenue as stated below (note that the superior occupier contracts with his tenants that the latter pay the kist).

Less than Re. 1	54
From Re. 1 to Rs. 5	100
" Rs. 5 to Rs. 10	49
" Rs. 10 to Rs. 20	22
" Rs. 20 to Rs. 30	10
" Rs. 30 to Rs. 50	19
More than Rs. 50	4
	258

Many especially of those paying under Rs. 2 hold only the plots of ground in which their dwellings are erected.

Classification of holdings according to ownership.

Pattadars paying an assessment of	Number.	Extent.	Assessment.
		ACS.	RS. A. P.
I. Re. 1 and less	2	0·26	0 15 0
II. Over Re. 1 and up to Rs. 10 (inclusive).	22	28·04	95 8 0
III. " Rs. 10 " " 30 "	7	26·44	129 . 6 0
IV. " " 30 " " 50 "	6	65·04	234 7 0
V. " " 50 " " 100 "	3	55·59	196 5 0
VI. " " 100 " " 250 "	2	106·97	301 4 0
VII. " " 250 " " 500 "	1	62·15	274 7 0
VIII. " " 500 " " 1,000 "	...	...	...
IX. Over Rs. 1,000	1	645·04	2,469 1 0

Thus the greater part of the cultivated land is owned by a single pattadar—a Nambudiripad, a very enlightened and sympathetic landlord who has a reputation for fairness and kind treatment. The majority of the other pattadars are also Nambudiris, very often holding the land as trustees of temples.

The following table shows the rate of assessment, area so assessed, with amount of assessment, of wet, dry and garden lands:—

—	I. Wet land.		II. Garden land.		III. Occupied dry land.		IV. Unoccupied dry land.	
	ACS.	RS. A.	ACS.	RS. A.	ACS.	RS. A.	ACS.	RS. A.
At Rs. 7-8 per acre.	108·49	813 11	...	..	...	...	...	...
" 6-4 "	194·87	1,215 15	...	...	...	...	...	...
" 6-0 "	0·09	0 9	0·03	0 3	...	...	..	...
" 5-0 "	109·06	542 11	2·28	11 6	...	...	...	...
" 4-0 "	39·21	157 5	7·09	28 6	...	...	...	...
" 3-12 "	7·69	28 15	...	...	...	...	...	...
" 3-0 "	93·37	280 1	14·28	42 14	...	...	...	...
" 2-0 "	128·00	256 13	36·43	72 14	3·23	6 9	43·53	87 0
" 1-8 "	...	...	..	...	61·87	92 5	122·82	184 3
" 1-0 "	...	...	49·48	49 14	98·84	99 0	288·66	288 11
" 0-12 "	...	...	...	...	38·57	28 15	643·77	482 13
" 0-10 "	...	...	...	...	3·42	2 3	148·42	92 12
Total .	680·78	3,296 0	109·59	205 9	205·93	229 0	1,247·20	1,135 7

The assessment under IV. Unoccupied dry is the potential amount, i.e., it would be levied if the whole area were cultivated. About one-third or one-half of it may have been at one time or another under cultivation, but the area cultivated in any single year is very small.

Rents are generally paid in kind, though of recent years there is a tendency in some cases (e.g., when the tenant lives at a distance) to commute it for money at current market rates.

The village is assessed for land revenue at a permanent charge of Rs. 3,759-3-0, to which must be added (to obtain the total revenue demanded upon the village, for the year) the charges on the 'unoccupied dry land' actually under cultivation in the year. This last will vary from year to year; the possible maximum is above Rs. 1,000. There is a local cess of 1¼ anna in the rupee of kist levied by the Taluk Board for roads, etc.

Agriculture—Area under principal crops.—The area under this head varies from year to year according as more or less of the unoccupied dry land is taken into cultivation. For the year ending March 1916, the following figures are given in the village accounts but they are less exact than they appear, being partly estimates by the village officials.

Paddy—First crop, 847·20 acres; second crop, 460·51 acres.

Pulses and grains		122·47 acres.
Oil-seeds, gingelly		155·89 ,,
,, castor		12·59 ,,
Spices, etc.		87·23 ,,
Fuel and timber trees		63·00 ,,
Betel leaves		5·00 ,,
Vegetables and garden products made up of—		
Vegetables	59·41	
Plantains and bananas	29·57	
Coconuts	17·00	
Mangoes	23·00	
Arecanuts	9·00	
Jack fruits	8·00	
	——	145·98

According to the 'A' Register the area of one crop wet land is 271 acres. In some years it appears that this area is smaller, because part of this is *potential* double-crop land, two crops can be raised on it under favourable conditions. But it may safely be said that some 150 acres of wet land yield only one crop. Such portion of the 'unoccupied dry' land which is cultivated in any year also yields but one crop—even that with difficulty, after lying fallow for one, two or more years.

The minimum available area of two-crop land is 409·73 acres. In some years (according to the weather and seasonal conditions) this may increase to some 525 acres. If irrigation could be extended more of the single crop area could be made to yield two crops.

Some fifteen to twenty-five acres may yield three crops, under favourable conditions.

All the wet land is utilized for paddy cultivation. Paddy is sown in May soon after the first rains. By the end of September or the beginning of October the first crop is harvested. The seedlings for the second crop are then planted and will be ready for harvest in December or January. In double-crop wet lands both crops are as a rule paddy. But a small area may be used for growing garden vegetables, and this is invariably the case in the three crop lands. Only one crop is raised in the dry lands actually tilled and this crop is determined by a rotation of crops, consisting of paddy, other grains and pulses, gingelly, etc. There is great variety in rotation. Usually the field lies fallow once in three years, often for two or three years continuously, according to the fertility of the soil. The importance of rain in due season for paddy cultivation cannot be over-estimated, the whole prospects of the village for the year may be altogether changed by even a slight failure of the monsoon at the critical stages in cultivation. In that case the local prices of paddy go up very suddenly, as now (August 1917).

Only one type of plough is seen—the usual old fashioned country plough, which merely scratches the ground. It lasts only for a year or two and costs only from ten to twelve annas.

Other implements are the levelling board, harrow (a long wooden hammer used by the hand), spade, kuzhi kutti (i.e., burrowing tool), jack-knife, etc. The levelling board costs about Rs. 2½ and lasts from 6 to 8 years; the spade costs Re. 1 and is worn out in a year. It has a blade set at right angles to the handle and is swung like a pick-axe.

Stock.—

	1914.	1910.
(*a*) Working oxen	296	250
(*b*) Cows	350	382
(*c*) Male buffaloes	256	286
(*d*) Cow buffaloes	6	10
(*e*) Young stock of above species ...	266	221
(*f*) Riding horses	2	...
(*g*) Donkeys and mules...	...	..
(*h*) Sheep	...	...
(*i*) Goats	201	285
(*j*) Pigs	...	...

The 1914 figures are approximately true in 1916.

Working oxen and buffaloes are better fed than others. They are given enough straw or grass, and hot conjee (gruel) mixed with oil-cake, bran, atc. Occasionally working oxen are given flesh (fowls). Cows and cow-buffaloes are given straw and conjee and bran water. They are led out to graze on the hill sides and pastures during the day. Their young follow them. The goats are allowed to stray and feed themselves as best they can. Their milk is used for medicinal purposes and is considered very nutritious.

There is no good pasture in the village, and the cattle are lean and bony. After harvest cattle stray over the stubbles, finding what food they can. The fields are often quite small, say 100 by 75 feet, and frequently there are considerable differences of level between adjoining fields, which is a difficulty in the way of proper irrigation.

Manuring.—About seventy-five per cent of the cattle dung is used as manure. The rest is dried in the form of thick cakes (called varatties) and used as fuel to supplement firewood, by the poorer classes, who go about picking the stray deposits of cattle-dung in the by-ways and streets. Perhaps a small percentage of cattle-dung is wasted. Yet it is the most important manure and an acre of land uses 100 to 150 baskets of it.

Cattle urine is not used, except by Brahman ladies to a very small extent, in growing kitchen vegetables in their backyards.

The refuse of goat-pens and of fowls (which are kept in most low-class and Nayar houses), as well as bone dust, is used in small quantities for growing garden vegetables.

All sorts of green manure are used. About fifty to seventy-five bales of green stuff are used on one acre of land. But green manure is not grown ; it is obtained from the neighbouring woods, and the shrubby undergrowth which is commonly found on almost every hillside and in the compounds of houses.

Wood-ash is commonly used, especially in garden cultivation.

Salt is used in coconut plantations.

Chemical manures are unknown in the village.

Garden cultivation is an important item, and very profitable too, though it is not yet carried on very extensively. About 110 acres of land are used for this purpose. Water is obtained mostly from wells, of which there is one or more in every garden. The chief products are coconuts (selling at Rs. 3 to Rs. 5 per 100), arecanuts used for chewing, etc. (Rs. 1½ to Rs. 2 per 1,000), plantains or bananas (Rs. 5 to Rs. 15 per 1,000), jack-fruits (2 to 6 annas each), mangoes, yams and various kitchen vegetables like pumpkins, brinjals, etc. These are cultivated in almost all gardens. Pepper and ginger, betel leaves and turmeric, are also cultivated in all good gardens. Pepper is very valuable and gives a good profit.

Coconuts being largely exported in the form of copra, have fallen 50 per cent in price, through shortage of freight, during the war. This has entailed great hardship on the large classes of coconut growers and workers in the Malabar Coast, this village suffering with the rest.

Insect-pests.—A kind of beetle sometimes does great damage to the crops—especially the new paddy crops and plantains. Small birds also carry away grains of corn. The usual method of combating them is to keep watch in the fields and drive them off—a very tedious and difficult operation. No help is got from the Agricultural Department, of whose very existence the village is unaware.

Cattle diseases.—Hoof disease is the commonest and most dangerous. Kerosene oil mixed with lamp black is the popular remedy. There is another disease—a sort of suffocation. A cholera-like disease is also heard of, accompanied by bleeding, etc. Snake-poisoning is another danger, a bite on the nose being supposed to be fatal. The villagers have their traditional methods of combating these. Charms and incantations are used to supplement medicine. No assistance is obtained from the Agricultural Department.

Wood is obtained from the neighbouring forests, as well as from the clusters of trees in the village. Building timber is often

PEPPER GARDEN IN MALABAR.

Photo by Agricultural College.

purchased from the nearest markets and brought in carts. Wood is getting dearer and dearer. It used to be very cheap.

The increase in price is due to the felling of trees without replanting, increased outside demand for fuel, as by the railway company and the Shoranur Tile Works; and the better appreciation and consequent increased demand for the local timber trees.

The village.—Strictly speaking there is no village-site. The houses are not built in street formation, but are scattered throughout the village. This is characteristic of most villages in Malabar and strongly contrasts with what obtains in other districts. The area of the village is 2,380 acres.

Localization of castes is not complete. Brahmans are located in the centre around the temple, with the Nayars, and the other higher castes surrounding them. The Thiyyas or Ezhuvas live farther apart and the depressed classes—Cherumas, Pariahs, etc.—live far out of the way of the higher castes on the outskirts of the village in hovels on hill sides, which are unfrequented by the other castes. Of course there are social prohibitions to their approaching the higher castes, much more to living near them.

There are a few fine houses: about 20 are tiled and have two storeys, about half of them belonging to the Brahmans. About 100 are one-storeyed thatched houses, almost exclusively owned by the castes. The rest are mere huts used by the poorer classes. There is no terraced house at all. Most of the houses are pretty old, but the tiled ones are mostly of recent construction. The houses are built more or less on a uniform plan and are often large without being convenient or comfortable.

The Pariahs and Cherumas live in thatched huts, miserable hovels one should call them, small, dark and exposed.

Almost every house has a 'garden' of some sort, with a few fruit trees like the coconut-palm, the mango tree, the jack tree, the areca-palm, plantain trees, etc. But very few houses have really good gardens. The gardens are watered from wells, which are found in every house. Whether there are fruit-trees on it or no, each house of the better class has a compound attached to it. This is sometimes used for growing kitchen vegetables.

The distance of cultivated lands from the home of the cultivator is never more than one mile. In the working season the ryot starts very early in the morning from his home with his oxen and agricultural implements so as to reach his land in time.

Field huts are almost unknown—except tiny watchmen's huts where watch is kept by a man at night when the crops are getting ready for harvest.

Subsidiary industries—Potters.—There are no weavers. There is a class of potters, of Telugu origin (as their language shows) engaged in making pots for household use, etc. They get the clay for their industry from the banks of the Bharata river (situated to the south of the village). Their wares find a ready market in the neighbouring villages, being very cheap and necessary. The lower castes cook in pots of burnt clay, while the better classes use bronze and other metals, such as copper. The art is the whole time employment of this class. But earnings are not very high, only just affording the means of subsistence. If the art is refined and improved to suit modern conditions and requirements it would be better paid. Some of these potters are employed by tile works producing pottery and glazed earthenware and are there paid Rs. 10 or so a month.

Carpenters.—There are five families of carpenters. There is steady demand for their labour, which is well paid. The occupation is hereditary and confined to the caste of 'Asaris', as they are called, a division of the Thiyyas. Full time is spent on the craft, which follows very old traditions. Earnings average about 6 annas a day. The carpenters go out to other villages for work.

Goldsmiths, blacksmiths.—Two or three families of each combine their traditionary crafts with agriculture, and are better off than most other low caste families. In the agricultural seasons they work morning and evening in the fields; and only at noon at their crafts. So they earn wages in money and in kind. The goldsmith earns Rs. 8 to Rs. 10 in this way per month; the blacksmith Rs 5 to Rs. 10.

Moulders.—There is one family making vessels of bell-metal for all sorts of uses—domestic utensils, temple bells, etc. They are very skilled workers and well paid, owing to the great demand for their productions. Some cups, bowls, etc., made by these are very beautiful and exquisitely designed and polished. Earnings Rs. 10 to Rs. 15 per month, according to state of business.

Basket-makers.—Baskets, mats, etc., are made out of the bamboo by the Pariahs. Very useful, but cheap. Only a local market and mostly made to order, as most business is in the village. Only spare time is spent in this occupation; it is miserably ill paid owing to weakness in bargaining. There is scope for development.

Umbrella makers.—Umbrella making is the hereditary occupation of the Panans. The umbrellas are made of palm leaves and bamboo, and much used in the village. Until recently imported umbrellas were not seen. The indigenous article costs only a few coppers and gives better protection against rain, but is unwieldy. The earnings of the Panans from this source are very low, and they are now taking to agricultural labour.

The Chettis make what are called *Pappatams*—the thin cakes to be fried in oil, for which Malabar is famous. The Chettis are also cartmen and take goods and passengers to neighbouring places. The *Paravans* make slaked lime for chewing. About half the adults chew a mixture of betel, areca, and slaked lime.

Village trade.—The village buys every year agricultural implements such as ploughs, spades, levelling boards, harrows, *kuzhi kutti*. Most of these are made to order by the village craftsmen. Some are bought at neighbouring fairs. Seed is usually preserved by the cultivator out of his produce, but sometimes he is forced by poverty to consume it and then borrows it or buys it with borrowed money. Live stock is bought at the weekly fair of the neighbouring village of Vaniamkulam.

The villagers buy the articles of ordinary consumption like salt, sugar, kerosene oil, gingelly and coconut oil, as well as the various grains and pulses at the village shop. Sugar is a luxury to all but the richest villagers. More than Rs. 600 worth of toddy is sold in the village, the Cherumas, Pariahs and Panans being the chief consumers. They pay in paddy, out of their wages. Clothing is bought at neighbouring fairs or in the nearest trading centre,

Sale of village produce.—Paddy, coconuts, bananas, plantains, arecanuts, pepper, vegetables, medicinal plants and roots are sent to market in larger or smaller quantities.

Paddy is not taken to the market, but traders come to the houses or the village shop to buy. Pepper is bought by Muhammadan traders early in the season, while not yet ripe, and afterwards sold at a great profit, often 100 or 200 per cent. All the other articles are taken by the producers to the market, chiefly to the Vaniamkulam weekly fair and sold at greater or smaller profit. A part of the produce is consumed in the village.

The trunk road from Palghat to Ponnani passes through the middle of the village. It leads to the two railway stations of Shoranur (the junction for the South Indian Railway and the Cochin Railway) and Pattambi, which are almost equidistant. The road also passes through Vaniamkulam, 6 miles east of the village, where there is the most important fair in Malabar. The town of Ottappālam (where there is a High School and a Munsif's Court) which is a small commercial centre, also lies on the road, some nine miles east of the village. Palghat is thirty miles east. Ponnāni, 22 miles distant, is a small coast town and a commercial centre and it is the western terminus of the road, which is also connected with Angadipuram, the taluk headquarters. The stream which passes through the village is full during the rains and is accessible to boats from the Ponnāni river. Some trade is thus carried on. Carts are the usual vehicles of transport. There are four in the village itself.

Village trade and consumption.—There is only one important shop in the village and it is therefore possible to get some idea of the amount of commodities bought by villagers from the accounts of the shop. The shop was started in 1892 and was at that time the only one in those parts. Since then a few petty shops have been started, but the business done by them is not very considerable. They deal mostly in those common articles of every-day consumption which are purchased in small quantities from day to day by the poorer classes. On the other hand the one important shop mentioned supplies the needs not only of the inhabitants of this village but of other villages as well. Some allowance must be made on this score when considering the consumption of commodities by this village, so that the total sales of the village shop may not be taken as representing the purchases of the inhabitants of this place.

The total sales of the shop amount in value to about Rs. 12,000 a year. The chief items are—

	RS.
Paddy	2,500
Salt	2,000
Coconut-oil	1,500
Iron bolts, bars, screws and other metallic articles	1,000
Kerosene oil	750
Tobacco	750
Gingelly oil	500
Dhall, grains, pulses, etc.	1,500
Betel leaves and nuts	500
Castor oil	250
Sugar	200

Of these paddy is mostly bought by outsiders and non-agricultural labourers, such as carpenters or blacksmiths. Most labourers indeed get their wages in paddy. Metallic articles are mostly bought by blacksmiths, both in this village (to a very small extent) and by outsiders. So, too, in regard to coconut oil, gingelly oil, tobacco, sugar and all other articles, large quantities are purchased by persons coming from other villages, where there are no shops. Probably about 50 per cent of the total sales are to outsiders.

As regards the quantities of these articles consumed, the shopkeeper says that there is no difference between what is sold now and what was sold 25 years ago when the shop was started. Only the prices have risen. One or two new articles of consumption have however been introduced, e.g., coffee, the sale of which is increasing. Iron and other metallic articles began to be sold some 15 years ago and the sales are increasing, though very little is consumed in the village. Besides the articles mentioned the shop deals in sundry small articles of consumption in the village, such as medicinal products, garlic and onions (consumed by the Cherumas and the lower castes), chillis, spices and the like. An important commercial product is pepper. The village produces about Rs. 2,000 worth of it and the shop buys about Rs. 1,000 worth from other villages. Very little of this is sold in the village. It is sent to the towns and commercial centres. The trade is very profitable and may be extended.

The commodities sold in the village are brought from the nearest towns or trading centres, like Palghat, Calicut, Trichur and Ponnāni. The usual means of transportation are bullock carts. It does not pay to bring small quantities by railway and there is also the risk of delay and damage. The villagers also sometimes buy their clothing and other articles in towns or at the Vaniamkulam fair. About a thousand rupees worth of vegetable and garden produce is also taken to the fair in a year for sale, with the proceeds of which the villagers buy cattle and implements or commodities for consumption. The local prices of commodities are 10 per cent higher than prices in towns, about 4 per cent representing cost of carriage and the remainder interest and profit. After deducting interest on capital invested at 9 per cent, the owner of the shop makes a fair sum as wages of superintendence and profits—about Rs. 400 per annum, excluding the profits from the pepper trade which are at least as much again as this. The shop also sells paper and other articles of stationery for the use of villagers at fair prices.

As regards the rise in retail prices in recent years, the village accounts show a general rise in prices of nearly 100 per cent—salt alone having fallen in price. The rise is most marked in foodstuffs and other articles of immediate consumption, and in metallic articles. Betel leaves have not risen much in price. Paddy, which used to sell at 2½ to 3 paras per rupee 25 years ago, now sells at 1·2 to 1·8 or 2 paras. Oils have generally risen at least 100 per cent in 25 years. So also sugar, tobacco and the like.

If one compares the total value of purchases by different classes, one will find that the many purchases of the few well-to-do persons and the few small purchases from day to day of the great majority of poor persons roughly equal one another. The Cherumas and other lowest classes pay in paddy for their purchases of salt, chillis, onions, kerosene oil and so on. Nearly 1,000 paras of paddy per annum are received in this way. The Cherumas probably spend about as much also in the toddy shop, and at least Rs. 600 worth of paddy is sold in the village to Cherumas, Panans, etc. The sale of paddy is not confined to the shop. The most important sales take place at the houses of the persons who have surplus paddy to sell. It is mostly purchased by Muhammadan traders and others from outside the village.

Economic condition.—Money wages range from three to six annas per day according to the nature of the work and the efficiency of the labourer.

The labourer cannot earn these wages regularly throughout the year, as employment is irregular and cannot be obtained at all during certain seasons. Though rice in the staple food, the poor cannot afford a full meal of solid rice a day; instead, they take it in the form of a thin gruel, occasionally supplemented by a better meal as after harvest or during the *Onam* festival, which is the great national festival of Malabar. In harvest time labourers get extra wages for reaping and threshing—usually 10 per cent of what they reap and thresh. A competent man then earns from one to one-and-a-half paras * of paddy a day for a few days.

When wages are paid in kind it is usual to give from three to five edangalis. † Agricultural labourers are paid less. There is a sort of agricultural serfdom, the Cherumas being the victims. Of course it is not legally recognized and is breaking up. These Cherumas who do the greater part of agricultural work, are paid from one and half to two edangalis of grain, supplemented by certain allowances during sickness, festive occasions, women's lying-in, etc. A sort of feudal or patriarchal relationship prevails between these and their employers. They are attached to certain families and get work, or at any rate are paid, throughout the year. The standard of life among them is very low and most of them drink the toddy made in the village. They live in miserable hovels, and are physically and mentally very inefficient. But they are, to some extent, looked after by their masters, to whom in spite of ill-treatment, they are often very much attached. I have heard farmers saying that if these Cherumas left them they would be ruined, since the success of their cultivation, i.e., its profitableness under existing conditions, depends, they believe, on their cheap labour. In very recent times some of these Cherumas have begun to emigrate to other places attracted by the higher wages and better conditions of work. But this is uncommon owing to the covert opposition of their masters.

The Muhammadan coolies, who are superior both in skill and strength to the Hindus, earn higher wages, both because their labour is worth more, and because they are more independent. But their usual wages cannot be stated, as they contract for each job. Such work as splitting rocks, digging wells, splitting logs, and

---

* [By Mr. Wood's tables (op. cit. p. 6), a para of paddy in this taluk weighs 22½ lb. Mr. Sundara Aiyar calculates it at 20 lb.—Ed.]

† [I.e., about 10 lb. weight of paddy, yielding about 7 lb. weight of raw rice.—Ed.]

other work demanding skill or strength is mainly done by them. They handle tools better than the Hindus. A strong Muhammadan coolie will carry sacks of grain of 8 paras weighing 160 lb. a distance of two miles half a dozen times in a day, a Hindu coolie will carry only half a sack.

Women's work.—In the better class families, especially the Brahman and higher Nayar families, women confine themselves to household business and looking after the children. Among the lower castes they work for their living. They help the men in agricultural work, such as transplanting seedlings, sowing, reaping and threshing. Rice husking is their special occupation, they also carry paddy from place to place on their heads. They are paid less than the men, three edangalis where men get four or five. Children also help in agricultural work and in looking after cattle, sheep and goats. Cheruma women work just like the men and get about the same wages. Some Nayar women go out to work in Brahman families.

Rice is the staple food, either by itself or in the form of kanji (a sort of watery gruel). Its price depends on that of paddy. The price of paddy is lowest after the first harvest in September, being 2 to 2½ paras (ten edangalis = one para) for one rupee. In about two months the price rises, and paddy sells at about 1¾ paras for a rupee. With the second harvest in December or January the price again falls, but rises gradually till July or August to its maximum height and grain is only 1·5 to 1·8 paras for a rupee. Towards the end of June 1916 it was only 1·6 for a rupee. Price fluctuations are greater or less according to weather conditions and outside demand. In August 1917 the price was 1·3 paras per rupee, and prices were still rising.

Not more than 5 per cent, or 20 families, mostly of the higher classes, have made savings.

Very little money is invested in agricultural or industrial capital of the productive kind except the ordinary farming stock. Some persons (foolishly) invest their money in Kanom land the value of which largely depends on the goodwill of the landlord. Few are rich enough to buy land in absolute ownership.

Savings bank accounts are unknown. No one apparently has any.

Loans to neighbours is a popular and common way of utilizing savings, especially loans to agriculturists for short periods on high interest, 12 to 24 per cent. Even higher interest is obtained by speculative loans on grain. Thus before harvest a poor peasant may borrow grain for a month, repaying 102 or 102½ measures for 100 measures borrowed.

Most saving families possess some jewellery and other movable goods worth about one-eighth to half of their total capital, an obvious attraction to thieves in former years. The amount of jewellery is deceptive as a test of prosperity.

Savings are utilized also for the purchase of houses, gardens, and increased consumption. Under this head should also be mentioned small investments in what are called 'Kuris' (chit-funds).

The majority of the villagers are in debt, for smaller or larger amounts. During certain seasons of the year many families actually go without the needed food and keep body and soul together as best they can. Well may economists and others speak of the power of resistance of the Indian peasant, his power of doing without! I wish I had some photographs of the living skeletons who call forth this praise!! But they are proud; they will never tell you the whole story. The village schoolmasters tell me that boys do not attend school regularly (though it is free) owing to actual starvation, cold hunger takes away all appetite for study. There are practically very few who do not owe something to the village money-lenders. Tenants are always in arrears with their rents; they sometimes even consume the grain reserved for seed. Villagers come begging for small loans just to tide over difficulties from day to day. The high rate of interest includes a large percentage of insurance for risk. Debts vary from a few rupees to hundreds. Exact information is not available.

Causes of indebtedness.—Poverty is of course the chief cause; other causes are want of suitable work, especially for women of the lower classes, the low rate of wages, due in its turn to inefficiency and weakness in bargaining, which exist side by side with improvident habits of the labourers, who are as a rule ignorant (though intelligent) and stoic; the growth of population without a proportionate increase in agricultural products and foodstuffs; the high, almost ruinous rates of interest, often as high as 36 per cent, which are both a cause and a result of poverty; an all round rise in prices, especially in foodstuffs; fast living and improvident habits among the richer—though this is rare—due to the desire to better their standard of life in response to western influences coming from cities. The Brahmans borrow largely to educate their sons and to marry their daughters. General extravagance is however unknown especially in food and dress. Many of the poorer villagers beg you to give them a meal or one of your old used up cloths.

Only a very small percentage, not more than 10 per cent, of the debtors have liberated themselves from debt. The tendency is for a perpetuation of debts. Debt is driving many villagers to other and distant places. When they have earned a small sum they return, but are soon forced into their old state. Of course provident habits do not always exist.

There is no co-operative credit society in the village.

There is no communal income of any sort in the village.

Selling prices of land.—Owing to the prestige and social importance of landownership, the landowning class never sell their lands even for good prices unless driven to it by necessity. This raises the price of land. The rights of ownership peculiar to Malabar, known as janmam, are very complete and thorough and not ordinarily found in ryotwari areas. Janmam land yields very low rates of interest on the price paid for it; prices are so high, having risen 25 to 50 per cent in recent times. Janmam land is usually let out on lease, usually for twelve years renewable at the option of the owner, if the due renewal fees are paid. Even Kanom tenure rights have risen in value, though they depend so much on the good will of the landlord, the tenants having no legal protection against eviction, or arbitrary enhancement of rents. Kanom lands are sublet to the actual cultivators, who are a rack-rented peasantry. The Kanom tenant, even when he does not himself cultivate the land, gets a higher return than the janmi on his capital; this is probably due to the insecurity of his tenure and his assumption of risks in relation to the actual cultivators. The renewal fees are heavy and many people contract debt to pay them. Some unscrupulous janmis or their agents arbitrarily enhance the rents payable by the Kanomdar and turn him out if he refuses to pay. The principal landlord of this village does not belong to this class.

The village spends between Rs. 150 and Rs. 200 annually on religious festivals. This is the common expenditure and is raised by subscription. It excludes small individual expenditures.

The village temple was built many years ago. No new one has been built.

Sanitary condition.—Malaria is unknown, but other fevers are occasionally seen. Cholera visits the village at rare intervals. Plague is unknown. Tuberculosis may be rarely met with. Small-pox also visits the village at rare intervals. From 125 to 150 out of every 1,000 children born die in their first year. Thus in 1915 while 81 children were born 10 died before completing one year. This is the figure given in the village register. It needs some correction and the figures should be slightly higher. The rate of infantile mortality varies with the seasons, etc. A few cases of snake-bites are recorded, but fatality owing to this cause is not high. I hear that sometimes the Hon'ble Moopil Nayar of Kavalappara (our representative in the Legislative Council) gives free medical help in such cases.

No reliable medical assistance of an effective kind is available. There are no English doctors in or near the village and few could afford to pay their fees even if they did exist. There are one or two ayurvedic physicians, whom one should more correctly call quacks.* They have no scientific knowledge and cannot properly diagnose. They take advantage of the simple credulity and superstition of the ignorant villagers and give an air of mystery to their art by the practice of superstitious rites akin to witchcraft. I believe there is much preventible disease in the village. Some remedy is badly needed. It would be a useful reform that the village officers and the village schoolmasters should know something of medicine, hygiene, and sanitation. Then they could at least instruct the villagers as to what ought not to be done in the care and treatment of the sick. There is a proposal now to found an ayurvedic college and laboratory at Shoranur, near our village. When it is accomplished a better state of things is hoped for, as the physicians would be really capable men and reliable, though practising the ayurvedic system, in which the people have faith.

Insanitary habits are rare. The Cherumas and other depressed classes drink. Chewing of tobacco and betel is common, but this can hardly be called insanitary.

* This remark does not apply to real students and practitioners of the indigenous system of medicine, but only to the unworthy representatives of the science in the village. There is high official and non-official testimony to the real worth of ayurveda as it *ought* to be practised, and as it is practised by many learned persons all over the country.

There is no infant marriage except perhaps among the Brahmans. Our girls are given away in marriage between the age of 10 and 12. Formerly it used to be younger. But strictly speaking this is only betrothal, the actual consummation of the marriage taking place only after the girl has attained womanhood at about 16 years of age. Our girls are very healthy and well developed so long as they remain at home. But their husbands take them away with them when they are old enough to the places where they are employed, e.g., there are three of them in Madras, and others nearer home. Boys are seldom married before 20 or 21 and the age is rising. Having to live away from home for their education their health is often impaired and they are less healthy and have less vitality and power of resistance than the girls, and are, in the writer's opinion, more subject to illness when away from home. Brahmans have to pay large dowries, whether they are able or no: the least sum being Rs. 1,000 for a bridegroom whose educational qualifications are measured by the Matriculation examination. Even 'ne'er-do-weels' get a high dowry owing to the unsatisfied demand for bridegrooms. We are groaning under the tyranny of an effete social system which is ruining us. Yet our elders protest against any change in our social system, such as post-puberty marriage. Something is sure to be done to remedy this state of things before long: the social conscience cannot long stand it.

Among other castes there is no infant-marriage, nor the system of dowries as it exists with us.

Among the Nayars there is a curious marriage ceremony performed when a female child is only a few days or months old. Some male person, not necessarily or ordinarily the future husband, ties the sacred marriage thread around the baby's neck. This ceremony is purely formal. Real marriages take place after puberty, and the girl may choose any man she pleases as her husband, this marriage being not at all formal, and great freedom, comparatively, is allowed to the wife. Polyandry, which once prevailed, has now disappeared.

The purdah system does not exist except among the Nambudri community of Brahmans. There are two families of Nambudri Brahmans in our village. Their females can never see the faces of any males except their husbands and near relations. They seldom go out to any distance, except to the temple, never travel by railway, and hide themselves, when going about, with huge umbrellas made of palm leaves and bamboo sticks. There is post-puberty marriage among them, and only the eldest son of the family marries. Marriages are often exchanges of bride and bridegroom (i.e., a brother and sister marry the sister and the brother of another family), and in that case dowries need not be paid. Otherwise heavy sums are paid. The Numbudri Brahmans are noted for their simple lives, their Vedic learning, and their intense conservatism, though one very enlightened and aristocratic family near my village owns a tile factory at Shoranur and a large part of a spinning mill at Calicut. They lack western education. This year one Nambudripad (i.e., a member of the Nambudri aristocracy) has joined the Presidency College in Madras as an extraordinary student, to get the benefit of the lectures and the college life. He belongs to the family mentioned above, who also own most of the cultivable land in the village. This family draws an income of rather more than 10,000 paras of paddy from the village, husking it in the village and using it to feed a vast household of Nambudri priests and students, and maintain a choultry. It employs a Sanskrit pandit, whose time, as the demand for Sanskrit teaching diminishes, is partly taken up with the recital to the young students of Puranic stories to which the unseen ladies of the household listen eagerly.

Water-supply.—The water-supply is abundant and is obtained from deep wells and tanks. Water from deep wells alone is used for drinking purposes. Owing to the rocky nature of the subsoil some wells are dry in summer. Each house has one or more wells; it costs about Rs. 20 to bore an ordinary deep well. The quality of well water is excellent and is an asset to the village. All people bathe every day in tanks, sometimes both in the morning and evening, especially Brahmans. The villagers are personally very clean and tidy.

Education.—One elementary school, started (very recently) and managed by the philanthropic Nambudri landlord of the place, gives free instruction to boys and girls of all castes up to the fifth standard. The school has two tiled buildings, one having an area of 72 by 20 feet, inside, and a verandah of the same length which is 9 feet broad, and the other having an area of 15 by 18 feet. Both are well ventilated and well situated and have a good appearance. There is a small flower garden in front. The school is provided with the necessary furniture, maps, and pictures, and is as far as it goes one of the best equipped of such schools. It teaches reading, writing and arithmetic, music, drawing and gardening. About the practical, as distinct from the cultural value of this education, one must say (like the Scotchman) "I have my doots." There are now no less than 5 "qualified" teachers; how one wishes that "qualified" meant much more than it does mean in educational language! They are so ill-paid (Rs. 7 to 15 per month) that it is hopeless to expect more capable men to be forthcoming or to take real interest in the work of the school. As it is, I know that at least one master is interested in the work. One hundred and twenty-six boys and 42 girls, I am informed, attend the school more or less regularly. These are drawn from all classes, except the very lowest like Cherumas and Paraiyas. The vast majority however are caste Hindus—all the girls are—and come from the Nayar and Brahman families. One could wish for greater regularity in their attendance. But they complain of having work to do at home, in assisting their parents, or they are sometimes too hungry to attend school. They are as a rule too poor to buy their own books or slates and these have to be provided by the school. Numerous prizes of books, slates, etc., are given by liberal villagers and the manager every year, to encourage the pupils to persist and to attract others. The school is steadily growing.

The average duration of school life is about four years. Many students leave before that period owing to the necessity of working for their livelihood.

About 18 per cent of the adults can read the vernacular. This includes hardly any females. Some 12 per cent can write the vernacular. Nearly one per cent can talk and read and write English. There are some ten pandits or others who have made a special study of grammar, logic and rhetoric, medicine, astronomy and astrology, all according to Sanskrit works. Two are able Sanskrit scholars, both Brahmans. All the Brahman scholars—some four in all—are well versed in Vedic lore. But no one cares nowadays for such learning, and in consequence their scholarship is miserably inadequately rewarded. They have given up the idea of bringing up their sons in their own fashion and instead send them to English schools. There is one boy in Madras in the Presidency College and some eight others in colleges in Calicut and Palghat, reading in the High School or college classes.

Most of the Brahman boys proceed to advanced schools; there are about ten such now. No Brahman girls proceed to higher schools. But with the advent of an elementary school in the village, they attend that. Formerly they learnt at home or in pial schools with boys. Social difficulties stand in the way of their advanced study. Non-Brahman boys also now go in small numbers to advanced schools. They number not more than a dozen, and none of them has reached a high standard.

One or two of the more advanced students get scholarships covering the school fees; all of them manage with great difficulty to defray their expenses, by borrowing money at high rates of interest, by starting what are called "Kuris," i.e., loans which are paid back by instalments; by selling any property they possess, etc. There is no one in the village who can easily maintain his son at school. Fathers, however, spend their all on their sons' education, hoping that they will get remunerative employment afterwards.

A few boys from the village who have passed through secondary schools have obtained small jobs; none has a good situation. Poorly paid schoolmasters, railway employees and clerks make up the list of the small number of such persons—not more than a dozen. It is more and more difficult for persons who have not got high educational qualifications to get suitable employment. Boys of the village who have received a secondary education and cannot proceed further complain of getting no satisfactory work and having to stay at home or return to their old occupations, which they have very likely neglected and forgotten during their school life. So farmers complain that such education is no good to their sons and we can say nothing in reply, unless we can guarantee situations for the educated. "What is the use of all this fine education," they ask, "if it does not procure a living and makes the boys unfit for what work they know? We would much rather keep them at home to stick to that work and earn a living." How can one urge the cultural and other benefits of education in the face of this practical argument? The quality and kind of education must be improved, made more practical and a better preparation for life.

There are some private libraries of Sanskrit books and palm-leaf manuscripts with the pandits numbering perhaps some 500 in all. The school has a little library where magazines (in the vernacular) and books (English and vernacular) to the number of about 100 are kept. Some of the more advanced students—there are only two or three—have small libraries of English books, text-books and general literature. Most Nayar families have Malayalam translations of the Ramayana, etc., which they read during the midday rest from work, i.e., one member of the house who can read, reads aloud to others. There cannot be more than a hundred Malayalam books. The Brahman ladies own a few song books and story books in Tamil.

Village administration.—There is no panchayat. There seems to be scope for one, and educated men are not wanting. The general administration of the village is in the hands of the village munsif or adhikari, who is assisted by the karnam. The adhikari represents the Government in all matters. The village officers can send for the police from the nearest police station—4 miles away. There is no regular police quartered in the village. But there is no need for any. The villagers are not prone to criminal acts and nuisances are not committed. The villagers are terribly afraid of the police too. Above the village officers is the Tahsildar of the taluk, who checks all their acts. Occasionally the Tahsildar or his deputy pays a visit to the village and is warmly welcomed by the prominent landlords. Revenue Inspectors and Land Records Tahsildars also visit the village to verify and check the village accounts. There has been no serious crime of any sort within recent years. Petty thefts are occasionally heard of particularly when corn is very dear and many of the poor actually starve.

Of late there is a growing tendency towards litigation, especially among half-educated people. Most of the cases are civil causes involving small sums of property. The object may be to recover unpaid debts, long arrears of rent, etc., or to establish claims to property where such are disputed. Most litigation has relation to the possession or tenancy of land and other property rights. The chief landlords have a power—resting upon their position, dignity and tradition—of settling small civil disputes between their tenants. The tenants dare not transgress their wishes. So arbitration by the janmi may settle many disputes, especially civil ones. Many cases are also settled amicably by the intervention of respectable and trustworthy persons of the village. The village munsif has jurisdiction in petty cases. But in all these cases the tendency is to resort more and more to the courts. But persons who have experience of them complain of the worries of litigation, even if successful in the end. This is a strong restraining influence.

History and prospects of village.—There seems to be clear evidence of economic deterioration, though in some respects there is slight improvement. Thus, many families which were once well-to-do have been reduced to abject poverty or very adverse circumstances. It is inconceivable that this is due, in all or most cases, to individual folly or vices. There is not a proportionate increase of persons of the well-to-do classes when compared with other classes. The head "others" in the Census report is steadily growing, while the numbers of landholders and labourers (i.e., agricultural workers) are decreasing.* This, in a village where

* [This is chiefly due to a change in the system of classification.—Ed.]

land is the chief source of a livelihood and industries do not exist. What is the conclusion? The increasing emigration to other places points in the same direction. The fact that the emigrants return as soon as they earn something shows that they are not likely to leave home unless hard-pressed. The increasing indebtedness of the villagers and the growth in the number of assignments and mortgages are other evidence. But population has increased only 7 per cent between 1901 and 1911. Wages are very low and have not risen in proportion to prices. Prices of food-stuffs have in many cases doubled within my own personal knowledge. Articles like milk, ghee, etc., have doubled in price within the last ten years. The price of grain has risen enormously in a generation. I have been told on good authority that some fifty years ago grain was four times as cheap as to-day. Only the land-owning classes and those who have surplus grain to sell have profited from this high rise. Many independent owners of land have been forced to sell their land to keep themselves free from debt and to pay the Government taxes. Taxation is much heavier: when the settlement was introduced into the village some twelve years ago the assessment was doubled and many villagers suffered. Against all this evidence of deterioration one must place the improvement in the standard of living of some classes and the growth of education, though unsatisfactory in many respects.

As for possibilities of economic improvement and the opportunities therefor, it may be said that the former are many, the latter few (as things now are) unless the villagers get help from outside—from the Government. In the sphere of agriculture improvement is badly needed, though the means of bringing it seem to be lacking, methods of cultivation could be improved and the use of scientific manure introduced. But all this requires capital and that is conspicuous by its absence. The advantage must be practically demonstrated to the cultivator and to the landlord, who alone can take the initiative herein. It seems to be impossible to introduce scientific farming so long as the system of scattered and strip holdings continues. The landlord must get his lands continuous; as it is as many as half a dozen landlords may have strips of land in one survey division of half a dozen acres. A man holding 10 acres may have it in 20 parcels, a distance of a mile from one plot to another is not uncommon.

About the possibility of extending the area of irrigated land only an expert could speak with confidence. As it is, out of a total area of 2,380 acres only 680·78 acres are wet land and 110 acres garden land—the rest coming under 'unoccupied or occupied dry.' It would be a very good thing if more of this could be brought under cultivation than at present. It does not appear that many more wells could be sunk with advantage. At present the wet and garden lands abound in wells, the 'dry' land being without any. It would not pay to sink wells in it and take out water according to the existing methods. If cheaper and more efficient methods are possible, then it would be worth attempting.

Something might be done—must be done, if the village is to improve—to ameliorate the general condition of the villagers and to free them from debt. Co-operation is worth trying. The Agricultural Loans Act might be made more accessible. The tenants need more protection in their holdings. *The burden of taxation must be lightened* and more equally distributed, so that the incidence of taxation may not be so heavy on the poorest class; the villagers are starving themselves to pay the taxes.* Any appearance of an improvement in the standard of living of the villagers is deceptive, being only on the surface and confined to the better classes. The condition of the Cherumas and other agricultural labourers is badly in need of improvement. The fundamental evil is poverty and debt.

The industrial position of the village must be strengthened. The existing industries (i.e., crafts) are languishing. To an able and enthusiastic industrialist there are further possibilities of profitable employment of capital and labour.

Garden cultivation can be extended, the cultivation of valuable commercial products like pepper, coconuts, etc., might be carried on on a larger scale on capitalistic lines. Plantain fibres, it is said, can be utilized for the manufacture of a kind of silk-like cloth, much in demand by certain classes, for certain purposes.

Bamboos abound and may be used in the manufacture of paper.

The cultivation of gingelly seed on dry lands might profitably be extended and the product crushed in the village oil machines worked by oxen. There seems to be scope for considerable development in this line. It is a question whether groundnuts and indigo cannot be introduced and cultivated in the village. The Agricultural Department might usefully depute one of its staff to make a tour of the district and examine the possibilities of extending and improving cultivation—of introducing new crops and an improved and more varied rotation of crops. *The quality and extension of village education is a serious and pressing problem.* The present system of elementary education is doing as much harm as good. Its first fruits are seen (in this village) in the unwillingness of the 'educated' boys to return to their old occupation; all sorts of vain notions and sentiments get into their heads and they are learning bad habits. It is certain that the 'educated' village boy has a supreme contempt for his uneducated parents and others and puts on airs of superiority and refuses to work in the field. Some of the boys are becoming regular scamps, good-for-nothing, and up to all sorts of mischief. Education of this sort is the last thing in the world to destroy the estrangement between the literary or intellectual tendencies of the higher classes and the practical labour of everyday life and industry. In actual fact the vices of the existing state of things tend to be perpetuated. It is high time to find a remedy.

---

* [The taxes referred to are the very small quit-rents charged as land revenue, averaging less than Rs. 5 per acre for wet land which mostly yields two crops per annum, less than Rs. 2 per acre for garden land and less than Re. 1 per acre for dry land. Mr. Sundara Aiyar explains that the janmi shifts the burden of paying the land revenue on the kanomdar, and makes this stipulation in writing; the kanomdar in turn shifts it on to the working tenant, who is a tenant-at-will. Including the kist the working tenant pays 50 to 60 per cent of the gross produce to the kanomdar, the kanomdar pays to the janmi about one-quarter of what he receives in addition to the kist.—Ed.]

EXPENSES AND PROFITS OF A WORKING TENANT.

Estimates for 1 acre under paddy.

Fertile two-crop land.—(On two-crop land the tenant pays the kanomdar the whole of the first crop, which is always more than the second crop, and averages about 60 per cent of the total of the two together, kanomdar paying kist.)

Cost of cultivation—

	Paddy. PARAS.		Money. RS.	A.	P.
Seed for first sowing	5				
Seed for second sowing	7				
Wages for sowing	15				
Manure, 125 baskets of cow-dung with ashes and green manure ...			3	8	0
Reaping and threshing wages (10 per cent)	13				
Allowances to village craftsmen ...	1½				
Allowances to labourers for festivals, child birth, etc.	1½				
Clothes to labourers			0	8	0
Use of oxen			5	0	0
Renewals of agricultural implements			1	2	0
Total ...	43	and	10	2	0

Estimated crop—190 paras—

Distribution of crop—

	PARAS.
Kanomdar's share, estimated at 60 per cent	114
Sub-tenant's share (gross)	76
	190

	PARAS.
Cultivation expenses in grain	43
Sub-tenant's grain surplus	33
	76

	RS.	A.	P.
Money value of 33 paras	22	0	0
Cultivation expenses in money	10	2	0
Sub-tenant's profit and wages of supervision ...	11	14	0

The working tenant also has the straw, and the wages that he may save by his own labour and that of his family.

Moderately good paddy land—

Costs—

	PARAS.		RS.	A.	P.
Seed for two sowings (7½ paras) ...	15				
Reaping and threshing wages	10				
Other expenses as before	18	and	9	6	0
	43	and	9	6	0

Product—150 *paras*—	PARAS.	RS.	A.	P.
Kanomdar's share	90			
Tenant's share	60			
,, grain surplus, 17 paras, worth ..		11	6	0
,, money expenses		9	6	0
,, money profit		2	0	0

Good one-crop land—

Posts—	PARAS.			
Seed	8			
Wages for sowing	8			
Reaping and threshing wages	6			
Allowances	2			
Money expenses		6	0	0
Total ...	24 and	6	0	0

Product 88 paras, tenant's share being 44 paras.

Grain surplus 20 paras, worth Rs. 14, leaving a money profit of Rs. 8.

Inferior one-crop land.—Here the produce falls to about 72 paras, of which the sub-tenant may get 36 paras. The money profit is Rs. 2.

A small share of the straw is paid to the kanomdar, but the working tenant keeps about nine-tenths. This is not much more than sufficient to feed his oxen.

A small extra rent, in the large Malabar variety of banana, is paid to the kanomdar in the *Onam* festival by each sub-tenant, of an estimated value of eight or nine annas, irrespective of the size of holding.

The annual budget of a typical well-to-do Nayar, a leading kanomdar.

Income—	PARAS.
The probable income from lands wet and dry together having an extent of 27 and 40 acres, respectively.	4,600 to 5,000
Expenses—	
Food for the family of eight members, two male servants and one female servant	700
Cherumas' wages for the year	950
Seeds	400
Bran, oil-cake and other food for cattle purchased in addition to what is found in the house	75
Janmi's michavaram (rent)	600
Government assessment at two paras for a rupee ...	400
Extra expenses such as salts, oil, etc.	90
Feasts in the temple	60
Charity, such as giving alms and pujari's wages ...	50
The village festivals	10
Sradhas (six in all) (dead relations)	30
Seven kuris	710
Interest on loans (calculated as above) on Rs. 1,500 ...	270

	PARAS.
Wages for the two servants and the servant maid ...	72
Payments to the carpenters and blacksmiths, Panars and Pariahs	25
Allowances to Cherumas on festive occasions	25
Washerman's and barber's wages	15
Clothing for a few members of the family	50
(The karnavan and the servants only are clothed by the family, the rest having their private money for the purpose.)	
	4,532

Fuel is got from their jungly lands for bringing which they manage with their daily labourers, Cherumas. They do not keep any strict accounts about their income from gardens which is usually spent in the family. If the harvest proves a success it may be possible to save something.

Budget of a middle class Brahman schoolmaster (for 1917).

	RS.	A.	P.
Income—			
Interest on Rs. 2,000 at 9 per cent	180	0	0
Income as interest on 700 paras of paddy at 15 per cent, calculated at 2 paras for a rupee	52	8	0
Salary	144	0	0
	376	8	0
Expenses—			
For food, etc., for man, wife and two children ...	144	0	0
Various kuris	112	8	0
Interest on loan of Rs. 225 at 6 per cent	13	8	0
Miscellaneous expenses such as sradhas, festivals, washerwoman's wages, thatching cow-shed, fencing, Government assessment, etc.	50	0	0
Brother's educational expenses, Rs. 250 (probable).	250	0	0
Expenses of mother in Madras	60	0	0
	630	0	0

So there is a deficit of Rs. 253-8-0 this year.

SUMMARIZED SURVEYS.

Kshetralapuram, Mayavaram Taluk, Tanjore District

[*By V. Venkataraman, Presidency College, Madras.*]

Kshetralapuram is a village in the Tanjore delta, bordering on the river Cauvery, on the main road from Māyavaram to Kumbakōnam.

Population—1881, 1,431; 1891, 1,511; 1901, 1,481; 1911, 1,545.

Average birth-rate, 1911—1916, 33 per thousand; death-rate 30 per thousand.

" A greater number of children die in Brahman families than in any other caste . . . the children in the Paracheri are all very healthy and they possess better physique than the children of other castes. They subsist upon mother's milk and kanji, and become inured to all sorts of hardships before they come to be five years old. In spite of the recklessness and negligence of many of the Pariah mothers, the children manage to survive and attain hardihood."

Land—Wet land 666·75 acres; dry 140·40 acres.

The river Cauvery is the sole source of water-supply for agriculture. Water for drinking and bathing is obtained from wells and tanks, the latter being fed from the Cauvery. When the river runs clear and is free from silt it is used also for drinking and bathing. (It is rich in cholera germs.—Ed.)

The assessment of wet land is as follows:—

	ACS.
At Rs. 9 per acre	34·10
" 8 "	140·50
" 7 "	342·75
" 6 "	96·99
" 5 "	52·39
Of dry land—	
At Rs. 4 per acre	·44
" 3 "	77·56
" 2–8 "	59·53
" 2 "	5·87

About 165 acres of wet land are cultivated by the pattadars; the remainder, 500 acres, of wet land and all the dry land is sub-let to tenants. The former holdings vary from 6 to 30 acres in extent. "It seems unprofitable to a pattadar to cultivate his land himself if it is less than 6 acres in extent, and it becomes rather unwieldy if it is more than 30 acres." Holdings in the hands of tenants vary from 3 to 25 acres.

Sometimes the land is leased to the sub-tenant, on condition that the latter pays all the costs of cultivation, except permanent improvements. The average rent of land so leased is 24 kalams of paddy, worth about Rs. 48, and a certain quantity of straw.

More frequently there is merely an unwritten agreement between the pattadar and sub-tenant. "The tenant keeps an account with the pattadar, who finances the tenant for buying oxen, etc., without charging interest. Manuring and other improvements will be effected by the landowner. The cultivation will have to be done under his supervision, the harvesting in his presence. The gross produce is then measured and the cultivating tenant is given one-fifth . . . the straw is shared, the landowner getting one-third." The average rent under this sort of tenancy is 26 kalams of paddy, worth about Rs. 52. It is less profitable to the pattadar immediately than the former, but is preferred as it prevents the tenant from exhausting the soil by want of manure.

In 1916–17 there were 679·42 acres under paddy, 63·79 acres under plantains, 29·44 acres in coconut topes, 4·97 acres occupied by other trees, 9·28 acres under ragi, and 3·12 acres under other crops. In plantain and coconut gardens the spade takes the place of the plough. About 5 acres of wet land can be cultivated per plough, or a little more.

Costs of cultivation.—(1) An acre of wet land growing paddy, land of average fertility carrying an assessment of Rs. 7 per acre, and yielding only a single crop—

Costs.	RS.	A.	P.	*Yield.*	RS.	A.	P.
Seeds	3	0	0	About 25 kalams of paddy selling at Rs. 2 per kalam	50	0	0
Ploughing	2	12	0	Straw	5	0	0
Transplanting wages...	2	0	0	Total ...	55	0	0
Weeding wages ...	1	0	0	Net income	28	12	0
Tilling and levelling...	3	8	0				
Gathering seedlings ...	0	12	0				
Cost of transportation to the place of transplantation... ...	0	4	0				
Harvesting	6	0	0				
Total ...	19	4	0				
Land assessment ...	7	0	0				

If the land yields two crops, the expenses will be about double, and the land assessment not less than Rs. 8 according to the quality of the soil. But the yield will be only 1½ times as great or a little more; hence the gross yield will be about Rs. 83 or 84, and the net income about Rs. 37 or 38.

(2) An acre of garden land growing plantains—

Costs.	RS.	A.	P.	*Yield.*	RS.	A.	P.
Tilling	20	0	0	Plantain bunches for 450 at Rs. 30 per 100 ...	135	0	0
Fencing	10	0	0	Leaves	50	0	0
Cost of young plants, 900 in number ...	40	0	0	By sale of young plants.	30	0	0
After planting, tilling three times a year, less thoroughly than before	18	0	0		215	0	0
Silt manure	20	0	0	Net income	95	0	0
Total ...	108	0	0				
Land assessment ...	6	0	0				
Water tax	6	0	0				

N.B.—The plant does not require renewal for a period of five years so that the cost of cultivation during the second year will not be so much as in the first. The cost of tilling, manuring, etc., will yet remain the same.

(3) An acre of dry land yielding two crops, but depending upon seasonal rainfall. The customary crops for such lands are ground-nut and gingelly. But such cultivation is very occasional and over only a small area in the village.

Costs.	RS.	A.	P.	*Yield.*	RS.	A.	P
Groundnut ploughing ...	4	8	0	15 kalams of groundnut at Rs. 1-8-0 per kalam	22	8	0
" Seed ...	2	0	0				
" Weeding (four times) ...	9	0	0	3 kalams of gingelly at Rs. 7 per kalam ...	21	0	0
" manure ...	4	0	0				
Gingelly ploughing ...	4	0	0				
" seed	0	8	0	Total ...	43	8	0
Land assessment ...	3	0	0				
Total ...	26	8	0	Net income ...	17	0	0

"About two years ago the villagers experimented in single transplantation of paddy. The result was satisfactory so far as the quantity of grain was concerned, but it led to a diminution in the quantity of straw . . . next year they silently returned to their old methods."

There are 200 working oxen, 13 male buffaloes, 150 cows, 145 cow-buffaloes, 197 young beasts of these species and 184 goats.

The dwellings.—"The Pariah huts and dwellings of other agricultural labourers are very narrow and ill-ventilated, and consist of mud walls and bamboo roofs thatched with the leaves of coconut palms and straw . . . But all the houses in the village have a small garden at the back, varying from 3 or 4 cents in the paracheris to about 30 or 40 cents in Brahman quarters, generally containing coconut palms and fruit trees . . . It is noteworthy in this place that very few of the labourers own the sites on which they have built their huts. These are owned by the 'mirasdars' of the village, mostly Brahmans, and the labourers pay a nominal rent of As. 8 or Re. 1 per annum, if the labourer is not in the employ of his landlord."

Fragmentation of holdings.—"The maximum distance of cultivated lands from the home of the cultivator is two miles . . . A cultivator who cultivates 10 acres will have his lands scattered about in ten places, on the average . . . The convenience of having land in a continuous area is well appreciated by the villagers . . . but the practice of exchanging to get this result is not very wide-spread . . . In the past ten years there have been only about ten cases of such exchange."

Subsidiary industries.—"In 1891, there were about 44 weaving looms in the village, which, by 1901, diminished to 1. At present there is not a single weaver . . .

"There are a number of persons weaving mattresses from a kind of thick grass grown in these parts called *korai*. There are about 51 looms used in this industry, and it is practised in one of the non-Brahman streets in this village, the female inhabitants of which have made this their sole profession, but not their sole means of subsistence. Their husbands are almost all of them country actors."

"A loom can be managed by a single person and she can turn out about ten mattresses per month. That will bring about Rs. 5, of which the net income excluding the cost of raw materials will be about Rs. 3. By my estimate, they spend only about four hours on the loom per day. The rest of their daily time is generally spent in rice hulling for the mirasdars and others in the village."

Padiyals or pannaiyals.—"There is a class of agricultural labourers, mostly of the Pariah caste, called pannaiyals, about 120 in number. Each, at the time of his employment, gets a sum varying from Rs. 15 to Rs. 35, which he enjoys free of interest as long as he serves under his master. If the labourer transfers his services to another master, the amount will be returned by the new employer; if the labourer runs away the mirasdar loses the amount. Sometimes some of them run away to the emigration depot at Negapatam. Otherwise, as they are not able to discharge their debts, they have to toil for their masters perpetually. There are families of these labourers hereditarily working under particular mirasdars.

"Their wages are generally paid in kind, two Madras measures of paddy a day during the summer months, when no cultivation goes on, and one Madras measure a day during the cultivation season. Calculated in money value this comes to 2 annas 8 pies and 1 anna 4 pies, respectively. They get in addition certain advantages, the fruits of which are enjoyed in the cultivation season; and hence it is that the regular wages are higher outside the cultivation season. They have regular employment throughout the year. Wages are paid once in three days. Each time the labourer gets an additional quantity of paddy for toddy and betels gratis. Each labourer enjoys the fruit of a small area of wet land, about 15 cents on an average. Each gets two kalams of paddy gratis in the course of the year. Their marriage and funeral expenses are borne by their respective masters."

Indebtedness.—"About thirty years ago, I hear, the whole village was full of debtors, Brahmans and non-Brahmans, landowners and tenants, all alike. Now about fifty per cent of them have liberated themselves from debt. About 15 families, most of them Brahman mirasdars, have made savings which I estimate at Rs. 75,000. There are also some of the tenant population who have made savings aggregating about Rs. 10,000. These savings are for the most part lent to neighbours at about 8 or 9 per cent interest, or as much as 12 per cent for loans less than Rs. 500.

"A considerable portion of the savings is utilised also in the purchase of land in the village. Despite the fact that the sellers are debtors obliged to sell to discharge their debts, the land commands a good price, competition being very keen among purchasers. The average price of an acre of wet land is about Rs. 1,000. Dry land fit for plantain cultivation sells at from Rs. 400 to Rs. 1,000."

Communal income.—"There is communal village property consisting of 6·32 acres of wet land, and 9·17 acres of dry land, the total income from which is, however, only about Rs. 300. This income is spent on affairs which relate to the village as a whole, as channel digging, putting up banks, repairing bridges, and so forth. There were times when these lands were well cared for and the income therefrom was spent for the common good in the best possible manner. But at present the administration is in a hopeless condition. No proper accounts are kept. The villagers are lacking in the spirit of co-operation.

"There are six old temples—three or four needing immediate repair,—altogether owning 13 acres of land yielding an income of about Rs. 450."

Progress.—"All the evidence that I can collect goes to show that the village has during one generation past improved economically. Even a few years ago, there were no non-Brahman mirasdars in the village. But at present there are about eight or nine of them holding land of about 50 or 60 acres. The ancestors of the majority of these were mere agricultural labourers some thirty years back. Again, in times past it was but rarely that one met with a tiled house in non-Brahman quarters. Now about ten or fifteen per cent of the dwellings of tenants are of tiled roofs. Some of these non-Brahman mirasdars are now bold enough to set at nought some minor Brahmans of the landholding class. The whole tenor of the social life of the village, the habits of the various castes, go to show that an advancement has taken place in the welfare of the people, except perhaps among the Pariahs. Lastly, until about two decades ago, not a single landlord in the village was free from debt. But most of them have now liberated themselves from it, have made savings and are living on comparatively better lines. But this advancement seems to have had an enervating effect on the physique both of the labourers and of the landlords of the village. People here now are not half so strong and hardy as they were twenty years ago. Such advance has not been followed by the development of social life on very wholesome lines. The atmosphere of the village was wholly of the rural type. The villages have now come into contact with the urban civilization that is daily developing outside their village. Such contact has made the villagers lose faith in the old time-honoured customs which still linger on. The inhabitants of this village and the life that they lead represents a type neither wholly modern nor wholly ancient.

"The village does not seem to possess much scope for further economic development on old lines. There is absolutely no possibility of extending the area of irrigated lands. Already too high a proportion of the total area of the land has been converted into wet land for growing paddy. There is no scope for garden cultivation except on small strips of land on the banks of the river. The villagers at present are too indifferent to give serious thought to such ideas. Curiously the landlords are not very zealous about improving the yielding capacity of their lands. For the present it seems that the only way of improving agriculture is for the state to take the initiative and train the cultivators in the improved methods of cultivation. A better ordering of the social life in the village and the development of the co-operative spirit among them will open a number of avenues for further economic development. In spite of all that people say regarding the remarkable development of co-operation in India during the past 10 years or so, I find that the villages hereabouts are disposed to misunderstand each other even in the most trifling affairs. It is on account of this fact that the administration and supervision of the communal and temple incomes are in a very irregular condition. Each villager tries only to appropriate for his own use as much as possible of the common property. The temples are usually looked after by a panchayat purporting to be elected by the villagers on the whole; in fact no such panchayat exists. The whole management rests with one person or a few. No regular accounts are kept. There is no one who has any power as of right to supervise these affairs. The result of all this is gross mismanagement.

"While such is the condition of affairs, I am not very optimistic regarding opportunities for further development in this village on the old lines. Some radical reform in the social life and the spirit of the villagers is needed before this village can take the path of progress on healthy lines."

General.—"In this place, I regret to state that I am not in a position to give any detailed statement regarding the occupations, income, etc., of individual families. The villagers, most of them, do not realize the necessity and the advantage of keeping regular accounts of their expenditure, and therefore most of them do not keep strict accounts. Hence it is that I am not able to give such information as can only be obtained from the family accounts of the villagers.

"It is however noteworthy that the non-Brahman castes in the village have attained to some degree of material betterment within the last 10 or 15 years. They have purchased lands from some Brahmans, who out of the necessity to discharge debts had to sell their lands."

Emigration.—"Emigration from the village to foreign parts has become fairly established. The pannaiyals of the villages, mostly of the Pariah caste, run away to emigration depots without the knowledge of their masters. Every year at least one or two cases of such escapade occur. The whole Pariah population of this village consists of persons who have migrated at least once to foreign parts, such as Penang, Singapore and Mauritius. All of them have returned after a stay of one or two years in those parts. Their idea before they migrated seems to have been that they could live better there, but they seem to have found out, after a stay of six months or one year, that life in those parts is absolutely intolerable, and that is the reason why they have returned. Except four or five persons who have permanently settled in Mauritius, all the emigrants have returned here, most of them afflicted by some deadly disease. Their report is that they could earn more in foreign centres, but they also say that somehow or other the climate does not suit them and that they are treated worse than here. Of course there is the usual complaint regarding the proportion of women to men. In most cases, that accounts for the diseases which they contract and which compel them to return. Having once returned, they do not entertain any idea of going out again. Their movement from this village to foreign parts seems to have had no effect on their economic, intellectual and social life, except for the fact that they get contented with their lot here."

NOTE ON PATTAMADAI VILLAGE, TINNEVELLY DISTRICT.

[*By P. S. Loganathan, B.A.*]

The population of the village of Pattamadai is gradually decreasing as will be seen from the following figures:—

Years of census.	Number of inhabited houses.	Males.	Females.	Total.
1881	936	2,040	2,290	4,330
1891	1,020	2,518	2,867	5,385
1901	1,078	2,155	2,617	4,772
1911	1,306	1,923	2,202	4,125

I questioned many villagers if they could explain the decline in the population of the village. The following seem to be some of the more reliable possible explanations that were offered to me:—

(*a*) The census figures were not entirely to be relied upon. People who actually took the census in the village in 1911, bore witness to the fact that many among the Panchamas and other illiterate people were unwilling to give the facts about the number of persons in their families.

(*b*) Another explanation is the prevalence of cholera in the village almost every year. It appears that about 15 years ago, cholera raged in the village to such an extent that it counted more than 50 victims every day; and it went on for more than a month and a half. The union office has from the year 1908 recorded the number of deaths due to cholera.

Month and year of attack.	Number of deaths.
December, 1909	6
November and December, 1911	13
December, 1912	3
January and February, 1913	6
January, 1914	12
January, 1915	45
1916	Nil.

From the above it can be seen that the village is yearly attacked by cholera, though it is doubtful if this can go any great way in explaining the decrease in population.

(*c*) The most satisfactory explanation seems to be the yearly emigration in large numbers of the Muhammadans and Panchamas to Bombay, Colombo, Rangoon, etc. The Muhammadans serve there as coolies or rickshaw-wallas. Others also do scavenging. Some of them return every year but usually the number of persons that return is less than of those who go away. From 50 to 75 persons go out from the village every year.

The causes of emigration are discontent at the low income they get in their village and better material prospects outside. Moreover the Muhammadans consider it beneath their dignity to work as labourers in the village, but have no objection whatever to working outside as coolies.

Regarding the subdivision of lands into plots, the 370 acres of wet land have been divided into roughly 780 plots, i.e., just less than half an acre on an average. There are plots of only 30 cents and a little above whilst there are others (though very few) having an area of more than an acre and a quarter.

The 370 acres of wet land have been classified as follows :—

Soil.	Taram.	Single or double crop.	Rate per acre.	Extent.
			RS. A. P.	ACS.
1. Ordinary black loam ..	4	Double ...	15 4 0	21·37
2. Good black loam	2	„ ...	19 12 0	40·80
3. Best black loam	1	„ ...	22 8 0	283·68
4. Good red sand	11	Single ...	1 4 0	24·28

Thus 283·6 acres have been classified under taram 1 and they yield a kist of Rs. 22-8-0 per acre. There are other lands in the Tinnevelly district classified also under taram 1, but which are far more fertile. However these are also among the best lands, and their selling price is Rs. 3,000 per acre now.

A cultivating landowner—a Brahman—owning 3 acres, gave the following account regarding his cost of cultivating the same.

	RS.	A.	P.
Services of one Paraiyan throughout the year, 1½ kotais of paddy (1 kotai = 112 Madras measures = 280 lb.).	15	0	0
Payment for watering expenses, 1½ kotais of paddy.	12	8	0
Services of two persons for six months in the fields to do miscellaneous work (ploughing expenses included), 2 kotais of paddy.	20	0	0
Cost of labour for harvesting 3½ kotais	35	0	0
Cost of labour for weeding and transplanting ...	18	0	0
Seed, 2¾ kotais (at Rs. 13)	35	0	0
Manure (48 cart loads)	48	0	0
Sheep manure, 1 kotai	10	0	0
Green manure	20	0	0
	213	0	0
Kist	68	0	0
	281	0	0

He got last year 35 kotais in the kar (first) crop and 24 kotais in the pisanam (second) crop, the total of 59 kotais * yielding an income of Rs. 590. Deducting cost of cultivation, he got a net income of Rs. 300 nearly and straw Rs. 15. But he told me that he

[* Nearly 2¼ tons per acre per annum, or about 90 bushels per acre per annum.—Ed.]

could very easily have got this same amount if he had left his lands to be cultivated by his tenants. That is the reason, he said, why so few Brahmans were themselves cultivating landowners. In the whole village there are only two Brahman gentlemen who cultivate their own lands. Land is productive substantially, only to those who can themselves work in the fields. In former days, even Brahmans did not hesitate to take ploughs in their hands and plough the fields. Now that is a thing of the past.

But it may be asked, how it is that tenants are able to pay a rent as high as can be got by actual cultivation? The only answer is that the tenants are the Pariahs and Pallans of the village, and they have to depend on agricultural work entirely for their livelihood. Hence anything that will just give them a return for their labour they accept with thanks. In fact labouring tenants get merely their wages and nothing more. They would even prefer to work as labourers throughout the year instead of as tenants; but this they cannot do because landowners prefer to leave the lands in the hands of the tenants for cultivation.

It must also be noted that when some of these Panchamas, themselves own a little land and cultivate it, they get good profits. A Pallan, for instance, owning half an acre of land, can get nearly Rs. 60 or 65 out of it without much difficulty. Even manure has not to be paid for, because he himself or his wife collects cow-dung and other manure and preserves it for use in the fields.

EXTRACTS FROM SURVEY OF NEERMAGA VILLAGE, MANGALORE TALUK, SOUTH KANARA DISTRICT.

[*By Joseph A. Pinto, Presidency College, Madras.*]

A Billava Household.—The *Billavas* like the *Bants* of South Kanara, and the *Nayars* of Malabar, hold land in joint families, and inheritance is in the female line of descent. This is locally called *Aliyana Santana*, or sister's son lineage. The administration of the family property is usually entrusted to the eldest man; but "the head of the family whose account I am giving is the second eldest brother, and the eldest brother is alive and living with him. The second eldest brother has been recognized as the head of the family since he saved the family from ejectment from the tenancy of the lands it holds for arrears of rent which the eldest brother was without means to meet, some forty years ago. . . . This family owns no land, but holds large tenancies under two landlords. It consisted till lately of 44 persons. They have now been reduced to 40, four brothers, the sons of a younger brother, having gone to a neighbouring village to claim their *Aliyana Santana* inheritance there. The forty people are divided into two homesteads about a furlong distant from each other. The expenses for the two homesteads, as given by the head of the family are:—

"Half a mura of rice per day. (One mura = 42 Mangalore seers, about 93 lb.)

"Five coconuts per day.

"Condiments to the value of Rs. 1-4-0 per day.

"In this family there is no restriction to the amount of rice eaten at meals; but in most Billava families definite quantities are allowed.

"Oil for the hair is supplied to each one; one sari to each woman per year and one bed-sheet to each man. The rest of the personal expenses of the able-bodied men and their wives and children have to be met by the proceeds of the growing of vegetables, for which each one is assigned a patch of ground. They also make a considerable sum from poultry."

"No dowry is given to a bride, but all the expenses of a marriage are met by the head of the family. He also generally presents the bride with a sari and some linen."

At a wedding "the friends of the parties are entertained with a grand dinner at the bride's house. The bride and bridegroom are seated and before them are placed two plates, one full of rice and one empty. The friends of the couple then sprinkle them with rice and place a gift, usually a silver coin, on the empty plate. The left hands of the bride and bridegroom are then placed one over the other, with palms upwards, by the *Gurkar* or head of the sept. He also fixes on the nose ornament of the bride. He then calls out the names of the fathers of the couple, and touching the joined hands with water, says thrice 'Purpokaidare.' The ceremony ends with a second grand dinner . . ."

"Flesh, other than beef, is eaten by the Billavas, as well as fish. Alcohol is not forbidden but rarely taken. Cock-fighting, as among the Bants, is the favourite pastime."

[COST OF CULTIVATING AN ACRE OF BEST LAND.]

	RS.	A.	P.
4 kalsis of seed at Re. 1 per kalsi	4	0	0
4 pairs of buffaloes for three days at 6 annas per day...	4	8	0
100 baskets of manure at 4 pies per basket	2	1	4
25 loads of ashes at 1 anna per load	1	9	0
Transplanting, 25 people for one day, at 2 seers of rice per cooly	6	4	0
3 men one day to carry at 2 seers each	0	12	0
Reaping, 12 people for one day	3	0	0
3 men one day to carry	0	12	0
3 men one day to beat the rice...	0	12	0
2 people half a day each to wet and boil the paddy and put it to dry	0	4	0
Husking the rice, 1 seer per kalsi, taking the yield at 10 muras	3	12	0
To tie up into muras of rice, at half a seer per mura...	0	10	0
	28	4	4

This shows the cost of cultivating paddy entirely by hired labour.

"If we regard 10 muras to be the yield of 1 acre, and the price Rs. 6-4-0, at which Mascati rice now stands in Mangalore, we find that there is a clear net yield of Rs. 37-3-8; and the tenant can pay an economic rent of 6 muras, more or less, at which the figure stands in Neermaga."

[14 seers of rice = 1 kalsi; 3 kalsis = 1 mura. The best two-crop wet land pays kist at the rate of Rs. 8-12-0 per acre.]

Arecanut cultivation.—" Nuts matured on the tree are preferred for planting. They are soaked in cow-dung for two or three days, or simply allowed to dry for ten or twelve days. They are then planted in a shady spot with the eyes uppermost, only just covered. This may be done from January to May. Till the rainy season they are watered once in four days. After one year they are replanted during the early monsoon in pits half a yard deep, and covered with manure and fresh leaves and watered once in four days if there is no rain. Sometimes young trees are replanted after two or three years in deep pits at a distance of one yard from one another. Once every year they have to be manured. After five or six years they bear fruit, and the nuts are yielded in three crops which ripen in succession from November to January. The yield from the best trees may be as much as 1,000 nuts, while the lowest may be only 25 per crop. From the fifteenth to the fiftieth year the crop is most abundant, and then diminishes, but the quality of the nuts improves."

Betel leaf cultivation.—" Well shaded spots are chosen for the cultivation of the vines. The tender vines are planted when the rains are well begun, about the feast of St. John (June 24th). Parallel rows are dug at distances of two yards. Cuttings are planted in the rows 4 inches from each other. If there is no rain they are watered once in three days. At first branches, later bamboo poles are placed for the vines to creep up. Manure and red earth is supplied when the vines begin to grow up the supports and again just before the rains set in. After nine months the leaves can be picked, but generally they are allowed to grow for a year. Plantains and sometimes arecanut trees are planted at intervals between the rows. If well cared for, the vines may thrive for six or eight, or in rare cases ten, years. Leaves are tied into bundles of twenty-five, known as *kooli*; four *koolis* make one *choodi*, and in selling the leaves are reckoned by the number of *choodis* for three annas."

Chilli cultivation.—" Big red chillis selected from the previous year's crop are preserved in pots covered with a coconut shell and entirely sealed with cowdung and placed on the loft above the fire place to keep dry.

" In April the seeds are taken out of the pots and soaked for about twelve hours and then tightly tied in a piece of cloth which is kept wet. Within six or eight days they sprout. They are then sown in rows in ground previously prepared and manured. They must be watered till the rains commence; they are then transplanted. Urine is poured in once in four days, and fresh manure, ashes and red earth added once a fortnight. About six weeks after transplanting the bushes bear chillis. A good crop will sell for about Rs. 1-4-0 to Rs. 1-8-0."

A typical house of a Roman Catholic family.—This house was built in the summer of 1917, and is up-to-date in style and material. It consists of two rooms, one 12½ feet by 9 feet, and one 8 feet by 9 feet. These face east; and on the east and south sides there is a verandah 4½ feet deep on the east and 8 feet deep on the south. The larger room has a door and two windows opening on to the verandah; the smaller room is entered from the bigger, the walls are 9 feet high. Above the rooms are lofts in which rice, coconuts, dried vegetables, etc., are kept. The walls are made of earth; the heavy beams and rafters are chiefly of coconut trees, the doors and windows jack wood, the framework of the roof principally bamboo. This is covered with coconut leaf matting and then thatched with straw. The whole house is whitewashed and looks neat. The landlord gave a jack tree to the tenant who built this house, worth about Rs. 8; the other expenses in building were:—

	RS.	A.	P.
Cutting into the hill and levelling site, one man 4 annas per day for 36 days	12	0	0
Labour for raising the walls	20	0	0
2 muras of lime	2	0	0
Labour for plastering the walls, two coolies at 6 annas per day and one seer of rice per day for both	20	0	0
Felling and sawing the jack tree	4	13	0
Carpenter, frames for doors and windows ...	13	0	0
Other carpenter's work	6	0	0
Screws and ten iron bars for windows	4	0	0
150 bamboos	26	4	0
Conveyance of bamboos by water from Mangalore	3	0	0
Do. road to house site...	1	0	0
Rope	2	0	0
300 coconut leaf mats	4	8	0
Straw	5	0	0
Roofing and thatching	5	12	0
Building with stone the outer verandah ...	2	0	0
Total ...	131	5	0

These expenses are in addition to the personal labour of the tenant and his wife.

Accessory sheds and the yard for threshing and drying paddy have yet to be added.

Much of the material has been given by the landlord. It has to be noted that the tenant by his labour and expenditure has acquired no legal right to the house, or to compensation if he is ejected from his holding, which he holds on an annual tenancy. This shows the good relations between the landlord and the tenant; and the confidence the latter has in a continual renewal of his tenancy.

A family budget.—The following is an estimate of the annual expenses of a family of four, husband, wife, and two small children:—

	RS.	A.	P.
Rice, 1¾ seers (3½ lb.) at 2 annas per seer ...	79	13	6
1 coconut for 3 days	7	9	8
Salt, 1 seer per week	3	12	8
Chillis, ½ seer per week	3	12	8
Other curry stuff	5	6	8
Betel	4	3	6
Snuff	1	14	5

	RS.	A.	P.
Toddy	2	0	0
1 sari for wife	4	0	0
1 jacket for wife	0	12	0
2 handkerchiefs for 3 years	0	9	4
1 jacket for husband	1	0	0
2 handkerchiefs for husband (for head-dress) for 3 years	0	10	0
1 good dhoti	1	0	0
2 small dhotis for rough use	0	12	0
2 handkerchiefs to be used as loin cloths ...	0	8	0
1 bedsheet	1	0	0
Church dues	1	6	0
1 bottle of kerosene oil for 10 days	5	11	3
1 bottle of coconut oil for 20 days	8	8	10
Total ...	136	7	2

If such a husband and wife lived entirely on their wages, these may be calculated at 4 annas for the husband and 3 annas for the wife, for a maximum of 300 days per annum. This would amount to Rs. 131-4-0 per annum, which is not quite sufficient to meet the above expenses, apart from *rent* and *fuel*. But a labourer without any tenancy of land, which would at least give him fuel and a house rent-free, is rare.

The actual daily expenses of the family that built the house described above are stated at Rs. 178-1-10, 2 seers of rice per day, 1 coconut per day, and a more liberal amount of clothing being allowed for.

Expenses of a house opening ceremony.—The following are the expenses incurred for the feast on the completion of the house described above :—

	RS.	A.	P.
Rice	19	12	0
3 pigs	31	0	0
Currystuff, dholl and vegetables	7	10	0
50 coconuts	3	0	0
1 bottle of milk	0	2	0
5 bundles of jaggery	1	0	0
400 plantain leaves (for plates)	1	0	0
Salt, 1 kalsi	1	0	0
Coffee, 1 seer	0	6	0
200 arecanuts	0	10	0
Betel leaf	0	3	0
Tobacco	0	2	0
Toddy and arrack	15	8	0
	81	5	0

About 350 people sat down to dinner. According to custom the head of the family received Rs. 40 to Rs. 50 in cash as presents.

Wedding expenses for the bride's family.—The following are the expenses recently incurred by a man reputed to have Rs. 4,000 in

Implements used in Godavari district.

Photo by Agricultural College.

land and cash at the marriage of a daughter. He has 10 children—3 sons and 7 daughters, of whom 1 son and 5 daughters are married :—

	RS.	A.	P.
Dowry	100	0	0
Bride's silk wedding sari, necklace and ring ...	150	0	0
Another silk sari, present to bride	24	0	0
Bride's underclothing and linen	30	0	0
Rice for wedding feast	52	8	0
Two pigs for the fourth day dinner only ...	13	0	0
Other provisions for wedding feast	49	8	0
Betel and tobacco	2	1	4
Total ...	421	1	4

Per contra, he received Rs. 175 in presents ; and presents were separately given to the bride.

NOTE ON TENKARAI VILLAGE, TIRUCHENDUR TALUK, TINNEVELLY DISTRICT.

[*By K. N. Krishna Aiyar, Christian College, Madras.*]

Village administration.—There is only one tank in this village, called the *Tenkarai kulam.* It is about three square miles in area. It is supplied from the Tambraparni river by means of a canal. As the Tambraparni river, rising on the western side of the Ghats and flowing eastwards, is in flood regularly twice a year, the south-west monsoon bringing very heavy rain to the west slope of the ghats, and the north-east monsoon such rain as comes to the east slope, the tank is full in June and July and again in November and December.

Fishing in the tank has been leased to a man for 30 years at Rs. 225 per annum. This sum is the chief factor in the common fund, which is chiefly used to keep the tank in repair. There is a village panchayat, consisting of all the pattadars. The richest man is elected president of the panchayat. He, with the advice of the members, administers the village fund ; he also settles disputes between pattadars and tenants. There is also a hereditary *munsif*, who settles minor cases, both criminal and civil. The *karnam* of the village collects the land-tax, and registers transfers of land. Under these are four *talaiyaris* and three *vettis*. The *talaiyaris* guard the cultivated land. The *vettis* work under the *talaiyaris*, run on errands and do some police work.*

There are many people in this village engaged in litigation, mostly in connexion with the recovery of debts. Some two years ago a Vaishnavite spent about Rs. 50,000, about half his money, on a religious dispute. He desired that holy water and flowers should be served him first in the temple, and the villagers would not

* [The *karnam* is a Government official ; the *munsif* is so also, though the hereditary tenure of his office must be due to ancient local custom. The rest of the village constitution may be taken as an example of extra-legal village organization.—Ed.]

consent. The case was decided in the High Court in favour of the plaintiff. A similar dispute is in progress now.

About half of the Brahmans are well-to-do. Most of them have no children. They adopt children. The wealth of the father and of the adoptive father goes to the son. Thus the properties of two persons go to one. Being well-to-do, they do not engage in work; but spent their time in idleness and gossip. Some engage in money-lending at usurious interest.

POTHAVARAM, RAZOLE TALUK, GODAVARI DISTRICT.

[*By B. Lakshminarayana Sastri, Christian College, Madras.*]

Population.—Brahmans, 8 families, 53 individuals; Sudras, 191 families, 948 individuals; Muhammadans, 5 families, 28 individuals. Birth-rate 44 per thousand; death-rate 35 per thousand.

"The Brahmans used to monopolize the land till recently and cultivate it through non-Brahman (Pariah) servants. But being far away from their land their property was not safe with the uneducated Pariahs. A sect of non-Brahmans called Kapus are now buying lands through their economy and industry and low standard of life. The Brahman having to maintain a high standard is slowly incurring debts. There is a chance of the non-Brahman Kapu sect in the village gaining the lands if they maintain their low standard of life and economical and industrious habits. While the non-Brahman always remains in the field or garden the Brahman stays for a major part of the day in the main village as he has to perform his daily religious ceremonies and social functions. The Brahman cannot live in such an isolation as the non-Brahmans. He cannot do hand labour and his supervision is inefficient.

"People buy land as a secure form of investment. The educated classes after saving money buy lands with it though they never cultivate it. It is the only form of secure investment with which they are familiar being ignorant of other safe investments. Moreover, land investment pays a man better and gives him some status among his neighbours. The emigration from this village is slow. Some are leaving for neighbouring towns for their sons' education while a few are emigrating to Burma for labour. The former rarely return except during vacations while the latter return after four or five years. This emigration once started catches fire, education is simply being undergone for appointments, there being a sort of respect and awe attached to this sort of life. Every average villager now eagerly wants to educate his son in spite of heavy debts and great inconveniences. Economically it is a loss though intellectually it may be a gain. Socially it is removing some of the superstitions of the villagers. The mixing with the educated villagers is removing many deep-rooted superstitions. The emigration to Burma of coolies is to a small extent an economic gain; but at the expense of family life and social intercourse. The husband has to part from his wife and friends for a very long time. He does not even become intellectually advanced and his earnings are spent on drink."

"Karim", water-lift used in Godavari Delta.

Photo by Agricultural College.

NOTE ON KODAGANALLUR, TINNEVELLY DISTRICT.

[*By K. Ramanchandran.*]

Of 2,628 acres of cultivable land, 2,620 are occupied, 606 acres wet land and 2,014 dry. The assessment by the latest settlement is Rs. 10,878. The rent for the use of one acre of land is 12 kotahs of grain if there is a good harvest. The average produce is about 18 or 19 kotahs, worth Rs. 180 or 190. The selling price of wet land ranges between Rs. 2,000 and Rs. 2,500 per acre.

The following figures show how rapidly the subdivision of holdings under the Hindu Law of Inheritance has been proceeding:—

There were—

	Holdings paying Rs. 10 and less in kist.	Holdings paying more than Rs. 100.
In 1882	112	22
1887	140	19
1892	173	18
1901	204	15
1906	239	14
1911	367	11
1916	366	8

The population shows a steady decrease. In 1881 it was 3,017, in 1901, 2,393, in 1911, 2,164. The number of oxen decreased from 300 in 1888 to 283 in 1910; that of he-buffaloes used in agriculture from 101 to 42; and the number of ploughs from 219 to 187. All the land was originally in the hands of Brahmans. Now more than half the pattas are in the hands of people outside the village. Though the Brahmans in the village depend wholly on the land yet no Brahman as yet tills his own plot. Many families have been obliged to sell their holdings to pay their debts, contracted either because (1) the holdings by subdivision became too small to support a family, (2) to pay for the education of sons, (3) (more frequently) to obtain husbands for daughters. The "bridegroom price" which was a few hundred rupees some years ago has risen to thousands.

While the Brahman's income has diminished his standard of living has not decreased but increased. Coffee and other drinks make a big hole in the pockets of many of the landholders, while the costly dress which their females now demand also takes away a great deal of money . . . The class that could be expected at first to be prosperous are the Panchama labourers, who get now very good wages, and in whose families all the members earn. But they are not prosperous either. In their case drink is the enemy. Corresponding to the rise in the wages of the labourer there has been a rise in the price of toddy and arrack, and I am told that all the earnings of the man go to the toddy shop, and that the family is maintained by the small wages earned by the woman. The one class that I have found to prosper is the cow-herds. They are industrious, thrifty, and frugal. They work hard, get good wages, and save much. They confine themselves to the old rice-water diet and invest all their savings in land which they cultivate with care.

NOTE ON GOPALASAMUDRAM, TINNEVELLY DISTRICT.

[*By K. Ramachandran.*]

At Gopalasamudram, 2 miles from Taruvai, there is a high school and hence the village is more busy. The people of the village are also more careful and thrifty than those of Taruvai. I was able to get the actual cultivation account of a person who owned 1·82 acres of the best land in the village which was worth Rs. 6,325.

Expenses.

	RS.	A.	P.
Kar—			
8 cart-loads of green manure	32	0	0
4 cwts of bones	17	0	0
28½ Madras measures of seed at Rs. 13 per kotah.	3	4	0
Nursery preparation	4	8	0
Ploughings	15	0	0
Transplanting	7	0	0
Side—repair	1	8	0
Weeding	17	4	0
Harvesting	14	4	0
Watering and minor expenses	5	9	0
	116	12	0
Peshanum—	80	0	0
	196	12	0

Produce.

	RS.	A.	P.
Kar, 19½ kotahs	195	0	0
Peshanum, 18 kotahs	180	0	0
Straw	34	0	0
	409	0	0
Expenses ...	196	12	0
Profit ...	212	4	0
Kist	38	0	0
Net profit ...	174	4	0 which works out at 2·7 per cent.

[As the local kotah is 112 Madras measures, and a kotah of paddy weighs about 280 lb. the cultivator gets a crop of nearly 5 tons of grain from 1·82 acres, or at about the rate of 90 bushels per acre per annum, as in Pattamadai (p. 213).—Ed.]

POLUR, NORTH ARCOT DISTRICT.

[*By C. A. Tirumalai, Christian College, Madras.*]

Population—

Census year.	Number of houses.	Total population.	Hindus.	Muhammadans.
1881	781	5,747	4,356	1,278
1891	1,070	7,743	6,006	1,548
1901	1,278	9,206	7,038	1,900
1911	1,216	8,799	6,811	1,764

"The drop in population between 1901 and 1911 was probably due to emigration. . .

"I am sure that the limit of self-sufficiency has been reached beyond which a further growth of population will surely entail an additional burden which the extent of land" (1,230 acres wet land, 878 acres dry, 26 acres watered by wells) "would scarcely bear even with improvements in agricultural practice."

"Twenty per cent of the cattle dung is used as manure, 80 per cent is used for varatties and domestic purposes. Firewood sells at 4 annas per head-load. Varatty making and selling is a profession . . . The people readily resort to ground-nut and other oil cakes together with tannery refuse in preference to green manure which is scarce and expensive. Night-soil is bought from the union and alluvial deposits are fetched when the tank is dry. The last accounts for the great fertility of the land."

Costs and profits of calculation.—"According to my calculation the maximum cost of cultivation of an acre of wet land is Rs. 25. The average produce of 800 measures will sell at Rs. 75. Deducting the expenses of cultivation, and also one-fifth of the gross produce for vicissitudes of season in accordance with the method of the Settlement Department, the net produce is worth Rs. 35, and the assessment (averaging Rs. 5-12-0 per acre of wet land) is one-sixth of the net produce. . .

"For dry lands the average yield is 175 measures of ragi fetching Rs. 15. Making the same calculation, allowing Rs. 3 for the cost of cultivation, the net yield comes to Rs. 9, which is five or six times the assessment (average assessment of dry land per acre Rs. 1-11-5).

"One recent improvement is the raising of a dry crop on wet lands as first crop in years of scanty rainfall, and the cultivation of Palidi rice, which is sown without the aid of irrigation and two months before the irrigation source can receive a supply of water. This is due to the influence of Arni Jagirdar's Home Farm, which is 16 miles distant from this place.

"For agricultural and other purposes the people depend in great measure upon cattle imported from Mysore and Nellore, in particular the latter place. Cattle are brought for sale to the weekly market, but they are not reared as they ought to be. People are so ignorant of stock breeding that even when they buy well-bred cattle they allow them to mingle with the ordinary cattle of the village. The price paid per pair varies from Rs. 100 to Rs. 250. The breeds of Nellore district are preferred to those of Mysore."

"The maximum distance of cultivated land from the home of the cultivator is two miles. . . There is not a single instance to show that the ryots have exchanged lands to get their lands continuous. Even in the case of partible succession the claimants would rather divide each plot among their whole number than each have a plot by itself."

Weaving.—"There are 80 weavers as compared with 255 in 1891. No. 20 yarn is used, and a weaver will earn on an average six annas per day, producing the common cotton fabrics worn by the lower classes. . . If the majority of the weavers co-operate, and leave off intemperate habits and adopt new methods there is a future for this industry . . . the tendency is to produce more finished goods than was the case formerly."

Wages—Wages in money.—"Brick-layers, carpenters, blacksmiths and painters, if first-class men earn 12 annas per day, if not, 10 annas. Brick moulders earn 8 annas; head coolies, 5 annas, ordinary coolies, 4 annas 6 pies, women 3 annas. After the workmen finish a job they expect presents in cloths and money from their employers.

"There are about 200 padiyals of the old type, and they are paid in grain at the rate of a kalam of paddy per month, which produces about 60 lb. of rice. They also receive Rs. 6 to 12 a year in cash and one pair of dhotis, and presents on special occasions. They are very generally in debt to their masters, but are on the whole well fed even in unfavourable seasons. Part of their income is earned by their wives and children who work for daily wages. Emigration recently took place in large numbers, but has been stopped. The Tahsildar sent 18 padiyals to Mesopotamia as gardeners. As these people are sending money to their relatives a large number of the latter are willing to go to Mesopotamia.

"Sixty per cent of the ryots are in a chronic state of indebtedness, 35 per cent are able to pay their way, and the remaining 5 per cent are in affluent circumstances."

Water-supply.—"People are strictly forbidden to wash or bathe in the village tank kept for drinking purposes, and for this purpose two watchmen * are appointed to see that nobody washes his clothes or bathes in the tank. But in the river Cheyyar people do not observe this rule. It has been maintained that as the water is running there can be no objection to drink it though it has been used for other purposes."

Past history.—"During the eighteenth century it is plain from the history of Southern India as a whole, that for the vast majority of the people—farmers, weavers, traders and artisans—the struggle for existence must have been a very hard one. This generalization must be particularly true of Polur, inasmuch as this was a place through which must have passed the English and the French and the rival Nawabs of the Carnatic, and later on the Mahratta horsemen and invaders from Mysore as well. Even in the absence of

* [I have seen a tank thus protected, but the watchman was asleep, and some people were bathing and others washing very dirty clothes in it.—Ed.]

the above troubled times, the oppression and exactions of the local *Poligars*, always heavy, but particularly so in times of turbulence, left the peasant but little of his produce and at times deprived him of life itself. Sometimes the whole crop was taken, and the cultivators were seldom allowed to retain more than from one to three parts out of ten instead of the usual four or five. Their share was, in fact, only what they could conceal or make away with. Thanks to the advent of the British Government, in 1801, when Mr. Strutton was the first Collector, the Poligars were deprived of their power, and considerable improvement was made; yet it had to be admitted that the condition of the ryot was far from satisfactory."

Prospects.—"The population is increasing and the price of land and food-stuffs is also increasing. This must be considered a blessing in disguise. The margin for extension of cultivation having been exhausted, the ryots are resorting to more intensive cultivation, and the construction of wells is being pushed on vigorously. The cultivation of traditional crops is giving way to the cultivation of the more remunerative only . . . the emigration which took place for some time, but which has now stopped, acted as a stimulus to labour-saving appliances . . . Lastly, the establishment of two rice mills has affected the economic condition of the village favourably. The selling of paddy from the village, as such, has been completely stopped, while people turn out more paddy than in previous years; and the mills also import paddy from distant places, as Cuddapah, Bellary and Kurnool, to the value of about two and a half lakhs of rupees, and export rice to Madras. The very idea of installing a rice plant will suggest the gradual introduction of improved methods and labour-saving appliances."

TRICHINOPOLY DISTRICT.

[*By S. Vaidyanathan, B.A.*]

Family Budgets—

(1) Family budget of a village munsif of the Lalgudi taluk. He is aged 50 and has to support a wife, two sons and two daughters-in-law.

	RS.	A.	P.
Income from land—			
240 to 250 local kalams (1 local kalam = 37½ Madras measures = 94 lb.) worth ...	750	0	0
Salary as Munsif	84	6	0
Total ...	834	0	0
Expenses, food—			
Rice	252	0	0
Salt	4	0	0
Oil	25	0	0
Castor oil	5	0	0
Kerosine	4	0	0
Vegetables	10	0	0
Spices, and other articles of food	32	0	0

	RS.	A.	P.
Other necessaries—			
Betelnut and leaf	5	0	0
Clothes	150	0	0
Sraddha (anniversaries of parents' deaths) ...	35	0	0
Servant (to look after cattle)	50	0	0
Miscellaneous—			
Land Revenue	110	0	0
Education	50	0	0
Total ...	732	0	0

One of this man's sons is a school master in a Board School at a village about 8 miles distant and earns about Rs. 15 per month. He keeps a separate establishment and indents upon his father for rice for the whole year.

(2) Family budget of a Brahman mirasidar, Ariyur village, Lalgudi taluk, aged 35 years. Members of household, wife 30 years, daughter 2 years, father 65 years.

The Mirasidar owns 4 acres of land, and has Rs. 1,000 in money. Each year about half the land gives two crops, and the other half one crop only. The land is leased for a definite rent paid in paddy.

Income from land 100 local kalams of paddy (of 37½ Madras measures per kalam), worth Rs. 300 per annum.

	RS.	A.	P.
Expenses, food—			
Rice	100	0	0
Salt	3	0	0
Gingelly oil	20	0	0
Butter, ghee and milk, etc.	50	0	0
Spices	35	0	0
Castor oil	10	0	0
Kerosine	4	0	0
Vegetables	10	0	0
Other necessaries—			
Betelnut and leaf	7	0	0
Clothes	40	0	0
Miscellaneous	10	0	0
Bedding, etc.	5	0	0
Sraddha	15	0	0
Miscellaneous—			
Kist, etc.	40	0	0
Medicine	2	0	0
Festivals	5	0	0
Total ...	356	0	0

His income from land, according to his own statement, is Rs. 300 (but it may be a little more) and from interest from his capital of Rs. 1,000 he may get something like Rs. 75 or 80, making up his total income to about Rs. 375 per annum.

In my opinion a normal family, consisting of a man, wife and two dependent children, can maintain itself in most villages in the districts of Trichinopoly and Tanjore on the produce of 5 acres of land without any other resources, and without working themselves. If they own less land, they require some additional income for decent maintenance.

Costs and profits of paddy cultivation.

The following account of the costs of paddy cultivation was given me in writing by a well-to-do and respectable gentleman of the village of Ranganathapuram, whose account is, I believe, likely to be more reliable than many others. He is the only person in the village who keeps accounts.

The account relates to the pannai system of cultivation and the accounts relating to the pannai cultivation are maintained separately wherever accounts are kept. All accounts relate to 1 acre area unless otherwise specified.

	RS.	A.	P.
Manure, 16 cart loads of cattle dung	2	0	0
Cart hire	2	0	0
Manure, goats	4	0	0
Ploughing charges, first crop	3	8	0
Labour charges, for Pallan	10	0	0
Transplantation	2	4	0
Ploughing charges, second crop	6	0	0
Labour charge	10	0	0
Transplantation	2	8	0
Total ...	42	4	0
An acre of single crop land will produce under normal conditions 20 kalams of paddy (1 kalam = 24 Madras measures = about 60 lb. of paddy). This paddy otherwise called the 'kar'; at the time of harvest ordinarily sells at Re. 1–10–0. Thus the total income from the first crop is	32	8	0
The second crop may produce about 25 kalams, each kalam of this paddy—samba—will sell for Rs. 2 ...	50	0	0
Total income for two crops ...	82	8	0
Government revenue on 1 acre — kist Rs. 15, water-cess Rs. 1–2–0	16	2	0
Other extra charges, local	2	0	0
	18	2	0
Cultivation expenses	42	4	0
Total costs ...	60	6	0
Hence the total cost of cultivation for 1 acre of wet land to a cultivator who works completely with hired labour and with no implements of his own is Rs. 60–5–0, and the net income from 1 acre of wet land (for a double crop) for a year will be only	22	2	0

Sugarcane planting.

The information on this subject was given to me in writing by an old and respectable mirasidar of about 65 years of age. He has himself been a sugarcane planter for many years and I believe his statement to be accurate.

Sugarcane crop demands separate treatment not because of the large area it covers in some villages, but because of the love of the villagers themselves for the crop as an agreeable change from the paddy crop.

The ploughing of the land begins by about the beginning of February or so, and eight ploughings are given with the country plough. On the whole 36 ploughs are necessary for completely ploughing 1 acre of land to make it fit for sugarcane cultivation.

The variety of cane grown in the villages I inspected is the long, thin cane of the Trichinopoly district known as 'Kuchi-karumbu.' The seed cane is either taken from the previous years' planting or bought from the surrounding villages. The cane is cut into pieces 1 foot long each with about two or three eye buds.' On the whole about 3,000 canes are necessary for planting an acre.

The harvesting and preparation of the crude sugar, and other products are done by the villagers themselves, but almost all labour required has to be paid for. One acre of cane will give 16 pothis of sugar (1 pothi = 400 seers = 800 lb. approximately). The refuse is used for boiling the juice and no fuel beyond this is either required or used.

With regard to the expenses and yield of sugarcane per acre we have the following statement:—

	RS.	A.	P.
Outgoings—			
Seedcane	24	0	0
Manuring (goats)	15	0	0
Labour charges—			
Ploughing	13	8	0
Harrowing and levelling, well-digging, etc. ...	7	0	0
Planting	2	0	0
Weeding	5	0	0
Earthing up, etc.	6	0	0
Harvesting and preparing the canes for crushing	10	12	0
Preparing sugar or jaggery	96	0	0
Marketing	10	0	0
Total expenditure ...	189	4	0
Income—			
Sixteen pothis of sugar or jaggery at average price of Rs. 16 per pothi will come to	256	0	0
Net income ...	66	12	0

This account shows a net return of Rs. 66-12-0 per acre to a man working on his own land with hired labour. The return, of course, stands very high relatively to other crops, but the necessary outlay is large and capital has in many cases to be borrowed; and, further, the crop is on the land for almost a year.

But it should be noted that sugarcane is a very reliable crop if sufficient and proper care be taken and the risk of failure in the market is very small, judging by the experience of the villagers themselves.

I believe that villagers generally make a better profit than that shown above, as in many cases they supply their own labour and materials for the work.

The pannai system and the economic condition of the pannaiyal.

This account of the income of the pannaiyal was given in writing by a respectable, wealthy and progressive young mirasidar of a village near Tirukattupalli, who is very popular with his pannaiyals. This is shown by the fact that he is the only man in the village who is able to cope with the discontent of the pannaiyals.

The pannaiyal must work for his master almost throughout the year, but he is on active duty only for a few months. His work begins on the 12th Chitrai or so (April—May) and continues for three months from that date. For this work he is paid at the rate of 1 marakkal per day for the three months.

For the next season, that is, from transplantation onwards, he works from Ani to Arpasi, that is to say, from June to November. He is paid at the rate of ¾ marakkal per day.

A Pallan and his wife can transplant for 4 acres of land. For this they are paid 8 kalams of paddy. If it is double crop land they must be paid 16 kalams.

The following are details of income:—

	Kalams.
Weeding, ploughing, etc.	4
Transplantation	2
Harvest season, first crop	4
In the course of the year	16
Second crop, harvest	10
Gleaning	4
	40

Computing the value of 1 kalam at the market rate of Rs. 2 per kalam, the total income of a pannaiyal for a year will be Rs. 80. Further, the pannaiyal may engage himself for short periods to work for any other master without prejudice to the work of the permanent master. My informant is clearly and emphatically of opinion that the pannaiyal will be able to earn in all at least Rs. 100 per annum.

The master has also to pay his servant for certain family occasions, marriages, deaths, and the more important festivals. At Dipavali and Sankranthi he gives presents of new cloths as well.

In fact a true master cares for his pannaiyal as though he were one of his family, as he very clearly realizes the value of such labour.

CONCLUDING OBSERVATIONS.

The poverty of South India.—In considering the light which this collection of village surveys throws upon the question of the economic condition of the people of South India, it is convenient to take note also of some of the statistical facts which bear upon the question. Those here selected as throwing some light upon the poverty of South India relate to the Presidency of Madras, and not to all South India, but that is not important as there is no striking difference between the standard of living of the bulk of the population of the States of Mysore, Cochin and Travancore and that of the adjoining districts of the Presidency. Efforts from time to time have been made to convey a general impression of the economic condition of the people of India by the statement that the average income is so many rupees per head per annum. Such statements are bound to be misleading, and it is unnecessary here to enter upon the discussion of any such estimates that have been put forward. It is easier to give a fairly accurate figure for the average income of the people measured in the most important commodities consumed, and also more illuminating.

The area of the Madras Presidency is a little over 91,000,000 acres, which compares with an area of 56,800,000 acres in Great Britain. The population at the census of 1911 was 41,405,404, and assuming that it continued to increase at the same rate after 1911 as in the decade 1901—11, it averaged some 43,000,000 in the year 1916–17. It was then, therefore, just a very little more than that of Great Britain.

In that year, by the statistics collected by the Agricultural Department and published by the Board of Revenue (Season and Crop Report), there were produced in the Presidency 9,024,946 tons of paddy. The Madras agricultural statistics, by the way, have attained (for India) a very high level of accuracy, and what error there is is pretty certainly on the side of understatement. The production of paddy was therefore not less than the amount stated. There was, in addition, both import and export, with a net export on balance, which must be allowed for. We have also to allow for the fact that on husking paddy loses one-third of its weight. We have further to allow for the amount of grain required as seed. Taking this last at the outside figure of ten per cent, and making the various corrections indicated above, we find the amount of raw husked rice actually retained in the Presidency for food was 5,299,942 tons. This was a very good year.

Dealing similarly with the other food-grains the total amount of food-grain retained in the Presidency in 1916–17 totals 10,638,000 tons, or 23,829 million lb. This gives 554 lb. per head of population, or a trifle over 24 oz. per head per day. Even for a population living almost entirely upon cereals this quantity is ample. No doubt a good deal is saved or wasted; it is well that it should be, otherwise there would be much illness arising from overeating.

To supplement the cereal food there is the milk and meat produced from the herds of cattle and buffaloes, numbering 21,760,000, or nearly three times as many as those possessed by Great Britain (7,288,000 in 1915), and the mutton produced by 18,192,000 sheep and goats, or about three-quarters of those possessed by Great Britain (24,598,000 in 1915). This, however, means practically very much less than would appear at first sight. The results of the enquiries I have made on the subject lead me to conclude that the average cow in the Madras Presidency cannot be estimated to produce much more than 40 gallons of milk per annum for human consumption, nor the average cow-buffalo more than about double that quantity. This works out at a little less than one gallon per head per annum. Nearly all the milk, butter-milk, and ghee is consumed by the Brahmans, and there are very few children of lower castes who get any. But the mothers usually suckle their babies till they are from 2½ to 3 years old, and the little toddlers who play about naked in front of their parents' huts look remarkably well and plump. At a later age their appearance is less satisfactory. With regard to meat, apart from the ban on beef, and the general sentiment in favour of vegetarianism, the amount annually available is extremely small considering the numbers of animals in the flocks and herds. Oxen are seldom slaughtered till they are past work, the worn-out cows die of disease or starvation; and the amount of mutton in the carcase of a sheep or goat is rather small. However, meat is an important item of food for many poor people in the City of Madras, and to a less extent elsewhere. Fish both from the sea and from tanks is more important. Turning to other produce of the soil, the yield of oil from 779,196 acres under gingelly in 1916–17 was supplemented by a considerable import, and a part of that of the area, 1,796,468 acres, under groundnut, was retained for consumption. There were 724,664 acres under condiments and spices, 210,644 acres under sugar, and 1,148,339 acres under coconuts, plantains, and other fruits and vegetables; and though some of the produce was exported, the greater part was consumed within the Presidency. The land under sugar, coconuts and plantains, and much of that under other miscellaneous crops, is extraordinarily productive.

With regard to clothing and shelter, a fairly accurate idea of the standard commonly reached can be gathered from the descriptions and illustrations in the village surveys; but it may be added, from the statistics of trade and production, that if the people of the Presidency of Madras absorb the same average quantity per head of cotton cloth as those of all India, their purchases of mill-woven cotton cloth amount to ten yards per head per annum. Actually they probably buy a little less, as their needs are less than those of North India. But they also buy annually an unrecorded amount of hand-woven cloth; some of these cloths being of silk, or silk mixed with cotton, or either silk or cotton mixed with gold thread. For almost all the year the garb of the men of the poorest classes is, in appearance at least, the most reasonable and satisfactory possible—a loin cloth, a turban, enough colour in the skin to prevent injury from the sunshine, and enough toughness in the soles of the feet to make shoes superfluous. The chief hardship arising from defect of clothing comes, I believe, from the want of sufficient warm wraps for the night during the dampness of the monsoon.

The fact that husbands go to the cloth merchants to buy silk saris and other festival attire for their wives, instead of letting the ladies go themselves, no doubt leads to economy in dress. But in any case jewellery and not clothes is the pet extravagance of India. India is known as the burial-ground of the precious metals. The net import of gold and silver in the five years ending March 31, 1914, exceeded £129,000,000. Diamonds, rubies, pearls and other precious stones, on the one hand, cheap glass bangles on the other, are sought for with similar eagerness. The reasons for this are mixed. Apart from the belief that the human form can be beautified by nose-rings, ear-rings, toe-rings, etc., there are the facts that pockets and purses, though increasing in use, are still only the possession of a small minority; savings bank deposits are still more novel and rarer. Then advertisements of quack medicines reveal the fact that many Indians have a firm belief in the curative qualities of gold and silver; and even where this belief has died out, there is, probably, a persistent association between the idea of gold, silver and precious stones worn on the person, and that of health and immunity from disease. Further, in a country where the great majority are eager borrowers, the use of jewellery as an encourager of credit is important. I had a talk with two ryots in a village in Ganjām. The elder, whose hair was turning grey, wore two apparently heavy gold rings in the lobe of each ear, another gold ring in the upper part of each ear, and a gold ring in one nostril. The other, a man in the prime of life, wore a thin gold chain round his neck, half hidden by his clothing. It was not vanity that made the difference. Actually the thick gold ear-rings worn by the elder man were hollow, and the value of the gold worn by each man was the same. But the younger man was clear of debt, while the elder owed more than he had any prospect of repaying. He wore that conspicuous jewellery to give his creditors confidence and an easy mind.

Of the various sorts of houses in use, brick or stone and tiles, mud walls and thatch, bamboos and palm leaves, the last is still the commonest; but the brick and tile dwellings are increasing very rapidly. The amount of furniture in the home of a cooly or poor peasant is extraordinarily small, little beyond a few earthenware pots made by the village potter, and perhaps one or two brass pots which are greatly treasured.

In one commodity the Indian peasant is rich, and I believe he values it highly, that is leisure. In one commodity, a commodity which he does not properly appreciate, he is very poor, and that is good drink. The country produces one excellent beverage, clear, cool, refreshing and agreeable, the "milk" of the tender coconut. But coconuts are valuable, and a man cannot always be climbing up a tree to fetch one whenever he is thirsty. Fermented toddy is stupefying, and alcoholic drinks generally are much disapproved. Both aerated waters and coffee are growing very rapidly in popularity, but these are too dear for the ordinary consumption of the working classes. The result is that the habitual drink of the great mass of the people is filthy water, water drawn from rivers and irrigation channels which are allowed to receive all sorts of impurities under the idea that running water cleanses everything with which it comes into contact; or from stagnant tanks which are little better guarded. I believe that one of the greatest benefits which could be conferred upon India at the present time would be to popularize the use of tea, the cheapest of all boiled water drinks. An effort to do this in the schools for half-timers and children of mill hands maintained by the managers of the Buckingham and Carnatic Mills in Madras, is one of the many excellences of their management.

Efficient and accessible medical aid is another matter in which South India is deplorably poor. A great deal of hospital building is at present in progress, and though this, in itself, will be far from meeting the need, it is a very important step forwards. The country also cries out for more roads and more railways. Education, of a sort, is rapidly spreading, but not much value can be placed upon elementary schools which teach village children little more than to read and write the local vernacular in its own script. In so far as there is a vernacular literature the enjoyment of it can be better obtained by such dramatic recitals as are described in the surveys of Vunagatla and Watakancheri. The European child who learns to read has the stores of the world's knowledge opened to him; it is far otherwise if the reading is in Tamil, Telugu, Kanarese, Malayalam, Uriya, or Tulu. Roads, medical aid, prevention of plague, cholera, malaria, elephantiasis, hookworm, small-pox, dysentery, enteric and the like, and effective education, either through the medium of English or the vernacular, all require money, and State money at that. But increased State expenditure means more taxation, and while the Government of India is extraordinarily reluctant to levy more taxes, the spokesmen of the Indian people commonly complain that even the taxes at present levied are excessive.

The incidence of the land revenue.—It has been maintained, by certain Indian writers, that the revenue collected from land in India is an oppressive tax, and a main cause of the poverty and indebtedness of the peasantry. Such statements as that the land revenue exceeds one-fifth of the gross produce of the land; that it is one half, or more than a half of the net produce, and even that it is in excess of a fair economic rent, are not uncommon. A considerable amount of light on the question of the actual incidence of this charge is thrown by the surveys in this volume. The view adverse to the land revenue was strongly held by one contributor, Mr. N. Sundara Ayyar, who says "*The burden of taxation must be lightened*; the villagers are starving themselves to pay the taxes." But when he comes to details of a particular holding, we find that his typical "kanomdar," who is a middleman supervising and financing the working tenants, draws from them an income of from 4,600 to 5,000 paras of paddy, out of which he has to pay in land revenue only 400 paras, or one-twelfth. With the help of the other information he gives we can conclude that the land revenue in this village drawn from paddy lands is about 4½ per cent of the gross produce.

The corresponding items of information with regard to other villages are as follows :—

Vadamalaipuram.—Ramnad district.

Gross produce and kist.—Value of crops raised by Narayanaswami Nayakar, Rs. 3,900; kist Rs. 150 = 3·8 per cent.

Value of crops raised by Alagaraswami Nayakar, Rs. 1,190; kist Rs. 70 = 3·7 per cent.

Value of crops raised by the clerk to the Co-operative Society, Rs. 1,000; kist Rs. 50 = 5 per cent.

Value of crops raised by Krishnama Nayakar, Rs. 580; kist Rs. 20 = 3·5 per cent.

Selling price of tenant right of wet land paying on an average Rs. 5 per acre kist, Rs. 600; of dry land paying on an average Rs. 1-3-0 per acre, Rs. 500 if irrigated by wells, Rs. 100 otherwise.

Gangaikondan.—Tinnevelly district.

Gross produce and kist.—Estimated gross produce of one acre of land under paddy, Rs. 70, average kist Rs. 5-9-0 = 8 per cent.

Estimated average gross produce of one acre of black land (dry) under cholam Rs. 60, kist Rs. 1-2-0 = nearly 2 per cent.

Estimated average gross produce of one acre of red sand (dry) under cholam Rs. 15, kist 4 annas = 1·7 per cent.

Actual produce of 20 acres of dry land under senna in 1916 Rs. 1,560, kist (if at the highest rate for dry land in the village) Rs. 22-8-0 = 1·4 per cent.

Gross produce obtained by Brahman cultivator Rs. 450; kist Rs. 45 = 10 per cent.

Net produce or rent and kist.—Customary rent for two crop wet land Rs. 60 per acre, average kist Rs. 6 = 10 per cent.

Rent for dry land for senna cultivation Rs. 28 per acre. Kist Rs. 1-2-0 = 4 per cent.

Estimated net yield of one acre of wet land Rs. 35-8-0, average kist Rs. 5-9-0 = 15·8 per cent.

Estimated net yield of one acre of black loam (dry) under cholam Rs. 40. Kist Rs. 1-2-0 = 2·8 per cent.

Palakkurichi.—Tanjore district.

Rent and kist.—Rent of best land Rs. 40 per acre, kist Rs. 6 = 15 per cent. Average rent of all rented land Rs. 30 per acre, average kist Rs. 4-11-0 = 16 per cent.

Dusi.—North Arcot district.

Rent, selling price and kist.—Rent of wet land Rs. 50 to Rs. 75 per acre, average kist Rs. 9-13-0 = 14 per cent.

Selling price of tenant right to wet land Rs. 1,500 to Rs. 2,000 per acre.

Vunagatla.—Kistna district.

Gross produce and kist.—Average crop Rs. 56 to Rs. 60 per acre. Average kist Rs. 1-10-0 per acre = 2·8 per cent.

Neermarga, Malabar district.—Average value of first crop on two crop land (under paddy) Rs. 53; average kist for same land Rs. 6. If *total* crop is worth Rs. 90, kist = 6·7 per cent of gross produce.

Kodaganallur, Tinnevelly district.—Crop raised from 1·9 acres of land Rs. 360, kist Rs. 38-4-5 = 10·6 per cent. Selling value of tenant right Rs. 2,600 per acre.

Gopalasamudram, Tinnevelly district.—Crop raised from 1·82 acres of land Rs. 409, kist Rs. 38 = 9·3 per cent.

Kshetralapuram, Tanjore district.—*Gross produce* of one acre of paddy land (one crop) Rs. 55, kist Rs. 7 = 12·7 per cent.

From two crop land, Rs. 83, kist Rs. 8 = 9·6 per cent.

From garden land under plantains, Rs. 215, kist Rs. 6 = 2·8 per cent.

From ordinary dry land Rs. 43-8-0, kist Rs. 3 = 7 per cent.

Net income from one crop paddy land Rs. 28-12-0, kist Rs. 7 = 24·4 per cent.

From two crop paddy land Rs. 38, kist Rs. 8 = 21 per cent.

From garden land under plantains Rs. 95, kist Rs. 6 = 6·3 per cent.

From dry land Rs. 17, kist Rs. 3 = 18·2 per cent.

Polur, North Arcot district.—Crop raised from one acre of wet land Rs. 75, kist Rs. 5-12-0 = 7·7 per cent.

Crop raised from one acre of dry land Rs. 15, kist Rs. 1-11-5 = 11 per cent.

Net income from wet land Rs. 50, kist Rs. 5-12-0 = 11·5 per cent.

Net income from dry land Rs. 12, kist Rs. 1-11-5 = 14 per cent.

These cases are, of course, too few to furnish any statistical basis for a calculation of the ratio between the kist and either the gross or net produce of land; but taking them as they stand the kist is on an average 6 per cent of the stated gross produce, which, in most cases, includes the grain only and not the straw, and 14 per cent of the stated rent or net produce. As a matter of fact the former figure is probably somewhat too high, the latter may be a little too low. The total land revenue for the Presidency appears from calculations based on the crop and price statistics to be about 3½ per cent of the gross agricultural produce, reckoned in primary products, i.e., including straw, and not making allowance for seed, but on the other hand not including any products from cattle or other animals. But this includes zamindari properties under permanent settlement on which the land revenue is based, not on the produce now obtainable and present prices, but on the conditions of a hundred years ago.* Taking ryotwari properties only the land revenue may be about 5 per cent of the gross produce.

If therefore, the ryot who is a pattadar, holding land directly of the State, is himself the cultivator of the land, he holds on an extraordinarily favourable tenure. He pays only a very small quit-rent for his land, a quit-rent which is only a small fraction of what in many cases he has been able to add to his income by accepting the advice and assistance of the Agricultural Department; and if he pays a local cess in addition it is ordinarily limited to one anna in the rupee of the kist. However large his income, he is exempted, on consideration of that quit-rent, from paying any direct taxation. If the pattadar does not himself cultivate the land he is in the position of a superfluous middleman intervening between the actual cultivator and the State, and exacting in order to maintain his own idle existence four or five times as much as the State receives to defend and administer the collective interests of the whole community. Nevertheless the pattadar, particularly the wealthy pattadar of the latter class, does genuinely believe that he is treated, not with unjust favouritism, but with unjust harshness. I must confess I found it hard at first to understand his point of view. When, for example, I was visiting the district from which the complaints are loudest, and a representative of the oppressed ryots sent his motor car to the station to meet me, and later visited me in the travellers' bungalow wearing very expensive diamond

* The application of permanent zamindari settlement to Madras Presidency dates from 1802.

earrings, the situation struck me as quaint. But there was no doubt about this gentleman's own conviction of the justice of his case.

Simply stated that case can be expressed in two propositions: (1) the poor cultivating pattadar cannot afford to pay *anything* to Government; (2) the rich non-cultivating pattadar is required to pay more than is equitable. We will consider these in turn.

According to the deeply rooted conviction of the great mass of the people of the Madras Presidency, the only proper way of living, unless you should happen to be born into a potter, or goldsmith, or thief or other specialised caste, is to live from the land, if possible by means of other peoples' labour, but if not, by your own. While a landholder lives, his children and grandchildren, in whatever numbers they may be, expect to receive maintenance from the holding as long as it is physically possible for them to get it. After he dies the holding, if and when divided, is equally shared among his sons, each separate plot of land being so divided for fear one might get a minute advantage over the others. Many hands concentrated upon one small holding naturally make light work, but many bellies waiting to be filled from its produce make light meals. As I was sitting on the bund of a tank a few miles from the plague-stricken town of Palni, one old gentleman explained his family circumstances to me. He was 60 years of age. Till he reached his 50th year he had no debts. He held four acres of good wet land and eight acres of very poor dry land. His family had latterly so far increased that, including sons, daughters-in-law, and grandchildren, it now numbered 25 people. As the children grew their wants increased, and already the point had been reached at which the whole of the paddy he raised was required to feed them, and nothing remained for kist or interest on debt. Some ten years ago he had begun to borrow, he said to buy cattle, and for "domestic reasons," which probably meant a wedding. Since then, by compound interest and by the knavery of his creditor who falsely denied receiving certain moneys from him, and who was believed by the court to which he took the case, the ryot's indebtedness had swollen to Rs. 4,000. He estimated the selling price of his tenant right at Rs. 7,000. It was pretty clear that he would not take the heroic step of selling out and paying off his debts, and betaking himself with his family to some district where employment could be had; and I have no doubt that he will continue to borrow, until his creditor forecloses and he is left destitute.

In its essential features this story is not unusual, and in such cases as these it is perfectly true that the pattadar cannot live and maintain his family on his holding, and also pay his kist. But it is clear that in such cases as these no real help can be given by reducing, or even entirely abolishing, the rent that he is required to pay to the State. This would only postpone the moment at which the attempt to maintain increasing numbers on a given small holding necessarily breaks down. The only solution to the problem must lie in increasing the opportunities for alternative employment, and increasing the disposition and capacity of the peasantry to seize such opportunities. This means practically improved means of locomotion, more effective education, the spread of improved methods of agriculture, and development of non-agricultural industries—and, as a necessary condition in the actual condition of India for such developments—more Governmental activity, and larger expenditure. To reduce the land revenue is therefore a sure way of intensifying and perpetuating destitution among the poorest class of pattadars.

The idea that even the rich pattadar has to pay more in land revenue to the State than is just, arises from the habit of thinking that the land which he holds of the State is entirely his property, or the property of his family, that the whole income accruing from the land is his income, and any portion that he has to pay to the State is a tax, which, in equity, ought not to exceed the taxes levied on salaries or incomes drawn from trade and manufacture. Thus "New India" (21st March, 1918), says:—

"An Anglo-Indian with an income of Rs. 25,000 has now to pay on that income at the rate of one anna in every rupee, which comes to only 6¼ per cent. The poorest of the pattadars in the Madras Presidency, with an income of even Rs. 50, has to pay to the Government not less than Rs. 25, which is just half or 50 per cent of his income. Is that fair?"

Again, the honorary secretary of the newly formed Madras Ryotwari Association, the chief object of which is to press for a revision of land revenue policy in the interests of ryotwari holders, said to me "We do not object to paying at the same rate as those whose incomes come from productive sources other than land."

But neither in equity, nor in law, nor according to ancient custom and tradition, is the pattadar, or other peasant, or any private person whatever, the full owner of the land he holds. Some sort of right of ownership of the peasant in his holding, or of a group of holdings, has commonly been recognized both by the British Governments and by their predecessors. At times the extent of this right as recognized by the ruling powers has been little more than that of tilling the land and living, or starving, on the portion of the produce which could be concealed successfully. Under the Emperor Akbar the State took one-third of the total crop as its regular due, and more in the case of necessity. It appears that there was a period before the Muhammadan invasions, when one-sixth of the gross produce during peace and one-fourth during war was considered the proper proportion of the crops for the State to take. But to what extent actual practice agreed with the ideal is a question on which no information is at present available. But indubitably it has been recognized continuously, from remote ages, that the State, as provider against collective perils and necessities, is a part owner of all cultivable land except where it has of its own accord granted away its rights, and that upon it rests the responsibility of determining the extent of that part ownership.

In the Madras Presidency when after the assumption of the Carnatic the officers of the East India Company had to enter upon the task of determining how much was due to the Company as the successor of previous rulers, it was recognized that the old rulers and zamindars had been in the habit of exacting something over and above a full economic rent, that the peasants frequently had to be prevented by force from fleeing from the land, and the cases were extremely rare in which the peasant's tenant right had any selling value. The policy of Sir Thomas Munro, which was adopted after the disastrous blunder of the Bengal Permanent

Settlement had been imitated wherever zamindars could be found and even in some places where they had to be created, was to moderate the demands previously exacted, to remove the fear of unexpected and arbitrary increases; to give confidence and hope to the peasants, and such a margin as would ultimately make the tenant-right valuable.

This policy has been pursued ever since, and even at the cost of sacrificing the rights of the community as a whole, for which the State is the trustee. The demand of the State has been abated greatly in theory, and still more in actual practice. The standing instructions to settlement officers, who have to revise the fixing of land revenue for particular districts at intervals of thirty years, are that the kist *must not be more* than half the net produce of the land, after allowing for cultivation expenses. But various deductions have to be made; and it is not easy to ascertain correctly the facts by means of which the value of the net produce has to be calculated. Where there is a doubt the pattadar gets the benefit. Further, rupee prices have long been rising, and with great rapidity since about 1890—in other words the real value of the rupee has been falling rapidly. Although during the thirty years' period of a settlement the number of rupees a pattadar has had to pay has remained the same, the quantity of produce which he has had to sell in order to obtain a given number of rupees has been reduced generally to about one half. At the end of the thirty years, therefore, in order at a resettlement to make the new demand bear the same proportion to the produce of the soil as the old one did when it was made, even if there has been no improvement in methods of cultivation, the demand should be doubled. Actually it will be increased only by about 25 per cent. In consequence the kist does not on the average exceed one-fifth of the rent which a pattadar can get from a tenant without sinking any capital himself in the improvement of his holding.

In case a particular holding is capable of yielding an economic rent of Rs. 50, by law and by custom the income of Rs. 50 is partly the property of the State and partly the property of the pattadar. By ancient custom the greater portion belongs to the State. By the theory of the law Rs. 25 belongs to the State and Rs. 25 to the pattadar. Actually the State gets only Rs. 10 and the pattadar gets Rs. 40. The pattadar thinks that the Rs. 50 is his income, and that the State is taking 20 per cent of it in taxation, and that that is too much. Really the State is taking none of the income that belongs to the pattadar, but instead is allowing him to appropriate, in addition to the Rs. 25 which is the utmost to which he had any equitable claim, a further income of Rs. 15 which by right belongs to the people of the country in their collective capacity.

But the more the State allows the pattadar to appropriate the more convinced the pattadar naturally becomes that he is by right the full and not the part owner of the land he holds. This is a phenomenon not peculiar to India. It is part of the natural history of landlordism from the times of Jeshurun onwards. The continual diminution in the percentage of the rental or net income of the land taken by the State, a movement accelerated in very marked fashion in recent years, has naturally greatly increased the selling price of the pattadar's tenant right. It has (1) caused funds to accumulate in the hands of many of the larger pattadars, which they know of no profitable way of investing except buying more land, (2) increased the disinclination of those who hold land to part with it, (3) it has given the purchaser a well grounded expectation that he will obtain, not merely a certain income from his purchase, but an increasing one. When it is remembered also that the purchaser of land buys with it a social prestige which is valued extremely highly, it is not surprising to find that land (or rather the pattadar's tenant right) on being sold will fetch anything from twenty to thirty years' purchase of its annual value or even more. The large pattadar is frequently either buying or selling small portions of land. He estimates the value of his entire holding according to the prices realized at such sales, and then compares that total with his annual income, and then exclaims "I get only 3 per cent on my capital. What a shame to tax me more highly than the mill-owner who gets 10 per cent on his!" He does not see that in the case of the mill the income that accrues is created by the capital spent on creating the mill, whereas the selling value of his tenant right is the effect, and not the cause, of the income from rent which he enjoys. To put the matter in a few words, the partial failure of the State to do its duty as the trustee of the whole community has handed over an unearned income to the pattadar; but because it has also handed over to him a proportionately greater unearned increment to the sale value of his property, he thinks he is unjustly treated, and a still further unearned increment of income ought to be given to him.

The problem of the poor cultivator.—It has been necessary to discuss the question of land revenue at some length, because the persistence and vigour shown by Indian publicists in the expression of the views which have just been analysed has kept the real problems of the economic condition of the actual cultivator of the soil in obscurity. The present volume to some extent indicates what those problems are. The conditions vary from district to district; there is some indication here how complex they are, and a more extended enquiry would make the complexity still more evident. But at least we can attempt some classification which may help to make the further collection of local facts of service.

1. *Exploitation.*—The question of the economic exploitation of the actual worker on the soil is curiously intertwined with the question of caste privilege. The separation between castes attains its greatest intensity on the west coast, and there the condition of the caste which is traditionally occupied with the cultivation of the soil was actual slavery until, and long after, the establishment of British rule. On the east in the districts of Tanjore and North Arcot, where the hold on the land of the Brahmans is strongest, and a large proportion of the agricultural workers are Pariahs, these are frequently *padiyals*, debtors whose condition is practically one of slavery, since they are bound, and their children after them, to work for the creditor for a bare pittance of food, and are liable to be transferred from one owner to another, under the disguise of a transference of the debt. On the other hand in villages where nearly all the people are Sudras there is likely to be much equality of economic status also, many small peasants cultivating their own holdings, and comparatively few landless labourers.

The connexion, however, between caste inequality and economic inequality, is probably indirect. The districts where Brahman pattadars and Pariah padiyals most abound are districts of ancient renown for wealth and dense population, with ancient and sacred cities, like Conjeeveram and Kumbakōnam, full of great temples and centres of industries, like silk-weaving, which cater for the needs of the well-to-do. The districts where the nearest approach to social and economic equality is found are those where there has been in recent times a considerable development of the resources of the country, as in the Gōdāvari delta, through the development of irrigation, or in the Black Cotton Earth districts, through the development of the export trade in cotton. On the West Coast the conditions are peculiar. There is both a very dense population, and much uncultivated land. The backwaters, lagoons fed by rivers and separated from the sea by sand banks covered with coconut palms, appear to be one of the world's original cradles for navigation; the low lying paddy fields bear their two crops per annum regularly, and wonderfully few coconut palms will support a family. Rubber plantations have been established with great success. Spices are grown for the world's markets. But to extend the area of cultivation into the jungle, with its wild beasts and malaria, is only possible by heavy toil, and the life of such dwellers on the hills as the Nayadis is extraordinarily primitive. The high caste people in the West Coast, the Nambudri Brahmans, the Nayars, and the Syrian Christians for example, are the handsomest people in South India; the Nayadis among the most repulsive. The striking geographical features of the country, the coast line with its long tradition of distant trade, trade with Lisbon, with Baghdad, with Rome, with Babylon, the wild mountains and forests, and in between the strip of rich land and ancient cultivation, make the extraordinary intensity of caste prejudice intelligible if not justifiable. Even here, however, conditions are changing, and the Cherumas are demanding with great determination the right to walk along public high roads, and to visit the same bazaars as are used by the higher castes, and they have found some champions among the Brahmans themselves.

It would be out of place here to attempt to discuss the problem of the depressed castes, and too great a task even to attempt to disentangle its economic aspects, but I may permit myself one observation.

It is the rule of the Government when dealing with extension of cultivation, to offer the tenancy of land hitherto uncultivated in the first place to the holder of adjoining cultivated land, and, if he declines it, to other landholders, so that no landless agricultural worker can get it unless all the landholders refuse it. Where the cultivated land is held in many holdings, and these are too small to fully employ the holders, this rule is obviously a good one. But in such districts as North Arcot, where land is held by rich pattadars and cultivated by Pariah *padiyals*, it is obviously unjust. The pattadars will even take it in turns to pay rent for the new land and hold it without cultivating it, merely to prevent the padiyal from having a chance of emancipating himself by its means. A reform here seems desirable.

While in many cases the actual cultivator is thus exploited by non-cultivating landholders, where the cultivator is himself the landholder, he is frequently exploited just as mercilessly by the money-lender. A number of observations on this subject are to be found in this volume. Needless to say they rather suggest the need of investigation along certain lines than point to any definite conclusions. Legitimate banking may be said, in India, to be distinguishable from usurious money lending by the test that in the one the lender hopes that the borrower will be able to repay both principal and interest, and in the other he hopes the contrary; he lends in the hope of foreclosing and seizing the borrower's land. Following the guidance of Sir Frederick Nicholson the various governments of India are trying to cast out the usurer by the co-operative credit bank. The results so far are hopeful and encouraging, but the establishment of a credit bank in a village may mean little or nothing. I found one case in which the secretary of the bank was himself one of the chief usurers in the village, and he has his system of managing the bank to his own advantage. It is a doubtful point whether the actual indebtedness of the villagers to private money-lenders is not steadily increasing in spite of the progress of co-operation, the amount of debt rising *pari passu* with the sale value of the pattadar's tenant right.

II. *Local congestion.*—In the Ganjām district, in the extreme north of the Madras Presidency, Mr. A. P. Patro has raised the question whether the holdings are not in general becoming too small and too numerous, and many villages becoming so congested that even apart from failure of crops, there is insufficient food raised to feed the population adequately. I went with Mr. Patro to visit certain villages in this district. Perhaps the most striking example of local congestion was the zamindari village of Sirisola, which lies in a hollow surrounded by low rocky spurs of the neighbouring hills. According to the information which we received on the spot the population is 1,024, of whom fifty families, of about 450 individuals, are not cultivators but labourers and artisans. Curiously enough there are no less than sixteen families of the goldsmith caste in the village, and they are said to do pretty well. If so they can scarcely derive a large part of their income from Sirisola itself. To feed the 670 people who subsist upon agriculture there are 240 acres of cultivated land, of which sixteen acres grow a double crop of paddy, and the rest single crops of paddy or ragi, with perhaps an occasional additional crop of gingelly. Much of the land under rice is only rainfed. The average crop is said to be 1,800 lbs. of paddy, or 1,200 lbs. of rice per acre; but out of this the zamindar takes half. There remains, it will be seen, not much over 200 lbs. of grain per head per annum to feed the people, and there is a cultivating population of nearly three persons per acre of tilled land. The people did not look starved or miserable, though very many were marked with small-pox, of which there was an epidemic eight years ago killing eighty people, with the result that the village now believes very strongly in vaccination. But if the people did not look starved their cattle did. The village cowherd had charge of seventy of the most miserable cows I have ever seen. Three or four of them only were said to give a little milk for human consumption. The chief escape for the peasantry here from this condition of local congestion is ordinarily emigration to Rangoon.

Attention has been drawn to this problem of the congested village in other parts of India. Legislation has been suggested both in Bombay and in Baroda, with a view to checking the indefinite subdivision of small holdings. The proposal put forward by the Baroda Commission on the subject was that when a holding below a certain limit of size was inherited by two or more co-heirs, they should not divide it, but auction it among themselves, the highest bidder taking it, and the price bid being equally divided among them. It is not by any means certain how this will work; and nobody has recommended any similar measure for the Madras Presidency or the States of Southern India with any confidence. There is nothing in the law at present to prevent such an arrangement being made between the co-heirs if they choose to make it; and, if they dislike it, forcing it on them might not lead to satisfactory results. Nevertheless I find a widespread opinion in favour of the principle of some check on subdivision.

There is, however, much difficulty in laying down any defined rules to determine in which cases division of holdings is undesirable. The mere size of the holding is, in itself, no sufficient test, even if in defining the size there is a careful classification of the sorts of land, whether wet or dry or irrigated by wells, and how fertile. Whether it is a bad thing to divide between two or three brothers a holding which is just large enough to support one family depends on the other opportunities for employment in the village which are available. If the labour of all the brothers is needed in the village, it is good that each should have his home and plot of land. Even supposing all the brothers but one must leave the native village and go to some distant town for employment, it is doubtful whether it is a bad feature that they should, as commonly happens in India, retain some interest in the land in their native village, and return to it if possible at the busiest season of the agricultural year. Nor is it easy to ascertain whether a village is in fact congested. When the population reaches three per acre of cultivated land in a purely agricultural district (1,920 per square mile!) it would appear at first sight that it is too dense, and some of the people ought to leave to make room for the remainder. Yet villages can be found which have reached this extreme of density, but which nevertheless are obliged to import labour during the busiest agricultural season, which is the time of paddy transplantation.

So far as Madras Presidency is concerned, it appears to me that the first thing to be done is to collect a great deal more information in order to ascertain for villages of different types what is the critical agricultural operation, that is the one which there is most difficulty in getting completed in the time available, whether ploughing and sowing, or transplanting, or harvesting; and, with regard to that critical operation, over what area the work can be done by a given labour force in a given time, and, as exactly as possible, how much time is ordinarily available. In wet lands I believe paddy transplantation is always, or almost always, the critical operation, but the time available in different villages varies very considerably. If it is very short, and comes at approximately the same date over all the villages in a particular area, a large local population may be necessary, and any reduction of the population by emigration, instead of increasing the prosperity of those remaining, would only decrease the area under cultivation.

Such a village obviously cannot reach a high pitch of prosperity by the cultivation of its main crop. It requires either a large proportion of its land under other crops which demand labour at another time, or some subsidiary industry or industries of a non-agricultural character. Otherwise nearly all the labour time of the village is wasted, and the normal condition of the whole population is what is termed by English economists "chronic under-employment." That a condition of chronic under-employment does exist on a very great scale in South India I am convinced; how widely, and in what degree in different districts, is an enquiry which I am anxious to encourage.

Fragmentation of holdings.—Dr. Harold Mann, as a result of his exhaustive examination of the village of Pimpla Soudagar, in the Bombay Deccan,* suggested that what he called the "fragmentation of holdings" was as serious an evil as that of excessive subdivision. By this he means the arrangement, or lack of arrangement, by which holdings, large or small, consist of separate plots of land scattered more or less over the whole village area, perhaps in all directions from the home of the cultivator. Prof. Stanley Jevons of Allahabad was so much struck by the same phenomenon in the United Provinces, that he brought the subject before an agricultural conference of all India held at Poona in December 1917, and advocated a policy similar to that embodied in the English Enclosure Acts, the valuation and redistribution of holdings, so that each property might form one compact block, roads be laid out, and water channels planned scientifically, to economize both water and space.

It will be noticed that questions were inserted in my questionnaire to elicit the facts bearing upon this. That considerable inconvenience and loss results from such fragmentation within the Madras Presidency is certainly the fact, though the evil does not appear to be so marked as in the United Provinces. Plots of land are sometimes found in the paddy fields so small that it is impossible to get a plough into them; and as each of these is completely surrounded by an earth mound, the waste of land is considerable. Sometimes a man who would sink a well if he had several acres together in one spot refrains from doing so because, though he may have, say, 10 acres in all, they are scattered in ten different places. Sometimes a poor man has a small plot of land in the midst of land belonging to a rich and unfriendly neighbour, and is at his mercy in the vital matter of water-supply. Sometimes adjoining plots belonging to different owners are at slightly different levels, and each peasant spends much of his time watching his neighbour, to see that he does not bale water surreptitiously into one plot out of the other, either to increase his own supply of water when water is wanted, or to get rid of a surplus. But while such inconveniences as these are admitted to exist, and while the villagers agree that it would be an improvement if the intermixture of holdings were abated, the inconveniences do not seem to be considered a matter of much importance. It is, in fact, largely a question of waste of time; and waste of time does not matter much

* University of Bombay Economic Series, Vol. I.

unless it is at the critical period, the period of the critical operation, of the agricultural year. One ryot told me, when questioned on this point, that he had recently gone to great expense to buy an extra bit of land to serve as a seed bed to the lands he had adjoining. In that way he would save time for the critical operation. But very seldom are villagers willing to make the smallest sacrifice of area or value in order to have their lands continuous instead of scattered. I can only account for this by supposing that the fragmentation in actual practice makes less difference than might be supposed. With regard to this question also, the only definite conclusion I have come to is that more information is required.

Some urgent reforms.—But while it is advisable to wait for further information before embarking on such heroic measures as altering the law of inheritance or throwing villages into the melting pot, at least in South India, there are many reforms concerning which no more discussion or enquiry is needed. To stop starving the Agricultural Department is one; to stop starving the Industrial Department another. Extension and improvement of roads and railways is urgently needed. There appears to be no reason for delay in giving the medical service the powers it requires in order to stamp out plague and to utilize fully its knowledge of the best means of combating cholera. That accomplished, the serious organization, with adequate resources, of the campaign against malaria, hook-worm and the other great pestilences should naturally follow.

Further, there is an intimate connexion between agricultural progress and educational reform. The idea that elementary education should develope the capacity for facing the problems of life intelligently and with determination, has not yet been acted on in India very completely or very successfully.

A smaller matter, but still one of sufficient importance, is the clearing up of the unimaginable chaos of Indian weights and measures. Decades ago the first step was taken towards the adoption of the metric system, by fixing the statutory weight of the seer at one kilogramme. But nothing has been done to make people understand that a seer is a definite weight. While India has seers innumerable—in the same district the seer may vary from 22 to 180 times the weight of a rupee—I doubt if a true seer can be found outside French territory. Side by side with the seer or kilo, we want the "Sirkar Measure," which should obviously be the volume of water which weighs a seer. The Government itself muddles up all its statistical statements by wandering about between seers and pounds, tons and maunds. If it started by working out its own arithmetic in true seers and Sirkar measures, and imposed the same on the railways, kept sample weights and measures in all police stations, post offices and schools, and arranged for the supply at cheap rate of certified weights and measures to all who wished to purchase, the establishment of the metric system in weights and volumes would be accomplished without difficulty. Metres could follow. The boon to India would be great; the indirect benefit to the whole British Empire might be greater.

GILBERT SLATER.

GLOSSARY.

A

Abhishekam (Sanskrit) anointing, or the act of pouring any liquid over the image of a deity.

adappan (adiyappan). Both anthrax and hæmorrhagic septicæmia are given this name.

adhigari village headman (otherwise called munsif, monigar, or patel), from *adhigaram* (Sanskrit) authority.

aggi-jadyam, literally 'fire disease'. A term applied to the change of colour in paddy from green to red due to an early attack by the paddy stem borer.

agraharam, Sanskrit *agra* chief, *hara* a separate allotment. A royal donation of land to Brahmans, or the village or village-site thus given.

Aiyangar an honorific title used as a caste name by Tamil Brahmans of the Vaishnavite sect.

Aiyar (Ayyar, Iyer) an honorific title used as a caste name by Tamil Brahmans of the Saivite sect.

Aliyana Santana v. *Marumakkattayam.*

Ambalavasis, literally 'dwellers in temples.' A West Coast caste intermediate in status between Nambudri Brahmans and Nayars, whose specific caste occupation is temple service. They follow the 'Marumakkattayam' system of inheritance, i.e., inheritance through the female line of descent.

Amildar (Hindustani) = tahsildar (q.v.), a Revenue officer.

Ani v. *Tamil year.*

anicut a weir across a river or water channel to regulate the flow of water for irrigation.

Arpasi v. *Tamil year.*

arrack a spirit distilled from toddy (q.v.) or sugar-cane.

Aruppampuchi, literally 'harvest insect'. Probably a number of species are included.

Asaris. In most parts of the Madras Presidency the term Asari may denote any of the five artisan castes (carpenters, goldsmiths, blacksmiths, masons, braziers). On the West Coast the term is confined to carpenters, who can enter the houses of the higher castes without polluting them.

athalai wild croton or castor.

avarai. In Kanarese this word means the country bean, *Dolichos lablab*. But in Tinnevelly the name is given to a wild shrub, the leaves of which somewhat resemble senna and are used as an adulterant of senna, as well as a green manure.

ayacut the area of land watered by a given source of irrigation.

Ayanar (Aynar). The worship of this god is very widely spread over Southern India. He is associated with the horse, and his temple usually consists of a tiny shrine with two horses in front, built of bricks and mortar plastered over with smooth cement. The horses are more than life size ; each horse is held by a human attendant less than life size. In contrast with the village goddesses who are malignant, Aiyanar is a benevolent and protective deity. His cult appears to be very ancient, being part of the religion of the depressed castes. No blood sacrifices are made to him, his offerings being roughly constructed hollow images of horses. In Kumbakonam the statues sacred to him are a horse and elephant of equal sizes, instead of two horses.

B

Balijas the chief Telugu trading caste, found all over Madras Presidency. Many are landowners and cultivators. They forbid the remarriage of widows, but not the use of meat or alcohol. Their usual caste name is Nayudu, but sometimes they take that of Chetti.

bandaikkai ladies' fingers *(Hibiscus esculentus)*. The unripe fruits, which somewhat resemble small cucumbers, are eaten as a vegetable.

Bants. The word Bant means soldier, and the Bants are the chief landowning and cultivating caste of South Kanara. Their language is Tulu, but their customs closely resemble those of the Nayars (q.v.). They are fond of out-door sports, and specially addicted to cock-fighting and buffalo racing. The racing buffaloes are yoked in pairs and draw modified levelling boards over a muddy paddy field. Each pair races over the course separately, and the spectators award the prize, marks being given for speed, style, and especially for the height and width of the splash of mud and water.

Bestas a Telugu caste whose hereditary occupation is fishing and hunting, but who have largely taken to agriculture.

Bhagavathar one who recites the attributes of God. *Bhagavan* (Sanskrit) means dispenser, gracious lord ; and, as applied to the deity, this term connotes six divine attributes. *Bhagavat Gita* = the song of the god.

Billavas the Tulu-speaking toddy-drawers of South Kanara, and the most numerous caste of that district.

Boyas, or *Bedars*, a caste of hunters and soldiers of Mysore and neighbouring districts, from whom Hyder Ali's armies were largely recruited. Many of the Poligars, local military chieftains of South India, belonged to this caste. They have largely taken to agriculture, but still are frequently skilful hunters. They are also fond of wrestling.

C

cumbu = *kambu*, q.v.

Chakkiliyans the leather workers of the Tamil districts ; and in these districts the most despised of the depressed castes. They eat meat, even beef, drink alcohol, allow post-puberty marriage and remarriage of widows.

Chaitra Pournami full moon in the month of Chitrai, the first month in the Tamil year, beginning about the middle of April.

chalidomma black water (also called quarter evil and black leg). An infectious cattle disease accompanied by one or more swellings most frequently occurring on the hind quarter. The course of the disease is rapid and few cases recover.

chamulu (Samulu), Samai (Panicum miliare) a variety of millet grown on about a million acres in the Madras Presidency.

chavadi a small building used for the office of a village officer, or resting place for travellers.

chazhi a beetle paddy pest. It appears in the Malabar paddy fields usually about a fortnight before the harvest, and unless blown away by the wind does great damage.

Cherumas, called Pulayas in North Malabar, are a numerous caste of agricultural labourers on the West Coast. They were slaves before British rule was established, and continued to be bought and sold openly as such till the Penal Code of 1862 came into force. This made slave dealing punishable with seven years' imprisonment. They are short of stature and dark-skinned. A Cheruma hut near Trichur is shown in illustration. They pollute superior castes at a distance of 30 feet.

Chettis. The word Chetti (Tamil) means merchant; and it is both the name of a distinct caste, and also a title used by many people of other castes (e.g., weavers, oil pressers) to indicate that they make their living by trade. Among the true Chettis there are many wealthy money lenders.

Chitrai v. *Tamil year.*

chodi the Telugu name for ragi, q.v.

cholam, in Hindustani *juari* (*Sorghum vulgare*) the great millet. It is grown over about five million acres in Madras Presidency, and is the most important food crop in the Presidency next to paddy. It is also grown as a fodder crop.

country plough. A heavy country plough is shown in the illustration of "Implements used in Gōdāvari district." This is exceptional; over nearly all southern India the plough used is the light one also shown in the same illustration, and again in "Agricultural implements used in Thettupalli." I have seen a man of medium physique carrying two ploughs without apparent difficulty.

D

daffadar (Urdu dafēdār), head peon.

Desamma v. *Gangamma.*

dhall (dholl) red gram (*Cajanus indicus*), a very important food for vegetarians who adopt a rice diet (e.g., Brahmans) as it remedies the deficiency of rice in proteid.

dhobi washerman.

dikshadar one to whom land has been granted on specially favourable terms on account of sanctity or learning. There is a settlement of some 3,000 Brahman *dikshadars* at Chidambaram, South Arcot, who own the temple and are considered specially favoured of the gods.

District a division of the Presidency in charge of a Collector. The districts of Madras Presidency are:—Ganjām, Vizagapatam, Gōdāvari, Kistna, Guntūr, Kurnool, Bellary, Anantapur, Cuddapah, Nellore, Madras, Chingleput, South Arcot, Chittoor, North Arcot, Salem, Coimbatore, Trichinopoly, Tanjore, Madura, Rāmnād, Tinnevelly, Malabar, South Kanara, the Nilgiris.

domma sometimes a name for anthrax. In the text hoven or tympany, a form of acute indigestion among cattle accompanied by much fermentation in the large stomach.

Dommaras a tribe of tumblers and mountebanks, some of whom wander about the country, while others have become agricultural labourers, and others again make wooden combs. They are great drunkards and of dissolute habits, and eat all sorts of animals.

donthi a wooden harrow, with about 20 teeth, about 5 inches long, drawn by hand; used in paddy cultivation.

E

edangali (edangari, edangazhi). One *edangali* = 4 nalis, one Madras measure = 7 nalis. One Madras measure = 108 cubic inches or 62·5 fluid ounces. Hence one *edangali* on the West Coast may be said to be nearly a pint and three quarters. But like all other Indian weights and measures it varies from village to village.

Edigi-Gandlas (Ganigas) the oil pressers of the Telugu and Kanarese regions.

Eluvas (Ezhuvans), generally called Tiyyas, q.v.

F

Firka a division of a taluk (q.v.) in charge of a Revenue Inspector, comprising 15–25 villages.

G

Gangamma. Village goddesses are worshipped throughout South India under a great variety of names, of which Gangamma, Desamma, Poniamman and Mariyattal occur in the text. By some all these names are regarded as names of Kali. Whether this view be correct or not, the goddesses all have a similar character. They may be termed goddesses of calamity, as they are worshipped with bloody sacrifices, either periodically, to ward off famine or pestilence, or when these are actually present.

gingelly (Sesamum indicum), called *til* in North India. It is the most highly esteemed vegetable oil in South India, and is used in cooking, for food and on the body and hair. The oil pressers and merchants adulterate it largely with ground-nut oil.

gorru a seed drill; v. illustration "Agricultural implements used in Thettupalli" on the right.

gramam a village—not connected etymologically with *agraharam.*

ground-nut the 'monkey nut' of England, and 'pea-nut' of America. It is a leguminous plant, which requires little rain and is a profitable crop to combine or alternate with a cereal. It very seldom fails. Its cultivation was spreading very rapidly in the Madras Presidency, owing to the introduction of the Mauritius variety, up to the outbreak of war. It was grown for export to Marseilles, where it was pressed in successive processes, first cold, then with heat. The first pressing yields an oil used as a substitute for olive oil, the second an oil used in the manufacture of margarine, the third one used in soap making.

gundasala hæmorrhagic septicæmia, otherwise called buffalo disease, and malignant sore throat. It affects buffaloes more than cattle. Of animals obviously affected 75 to 90 per cent die, but those that recover are immune for life.

guntaka. This word was spelt *guntava* by Mr. Krishnamurti, but altered on advice. But it is doubtful whether these are not two distinct words, as *guntaka* means a sort of broad hoe, drawn by oxen, and *guntava*, as defined and described by Mr. Krishnamurti, is a sort of rake drawn by oxen. It is shown on the left of his photograph "Agricultural implements used in Thettupalli."

guru a teacher.

H

hook worm an intestinal parasite extraordinarily common in South India, especially among the lower castes. Probably the majority of the population of the City of Madras are affected. It ranks next to malaria as a cause of anæmia and debility. It greatly enhances the death-rate, both by facilitating infection by other diseases, and by reducing the power of resistance. Cure is easy, but seldom availed of.

I

Idayans the great shepherd caste of the Tamil country.

Inam lands lands granted on specially favourable terms to particular individuals, or to persons holding particular offices or performing particular services.

J

Jack a tree needing a wet climate, common on the West Coast. It yields good timber and produces a green fruit about the size of a vegetable marrow, which grows on a thick stem from the trunk or large branches.

jadi madu highly bred ox.

K

Kaikolans an important Tamil caste of weavers, specially numerous in the suburbs of Conjeeveram. According to tradition they are descended from nine heroes who assisted the god Subrahmaniam to destroy certain demons. One girl at least from each Kaikolan family should be dedicated to temple service.

Kailasanathaswami one of the names of Siva.

kainoi foot and mouth disease.

kalai bull.

kalam a measure in common use in the Tanjore delta and adjoining districts. It varies from place to place. In Madura 1 kalam = 48 Madras measures (a kalam of paddy being therefore about 120 lb.), in South Arcot it is, officially, 24 Madras measures, near Palur 36.

Kallans a Tamil caste, traditionally thieves, marauders and cattle lifters or burglars, largely employed in the Madura district as watchmen, and still subsisting in many parts on blackmail and robbery; but in others now agriculturists.

Kallasaris workers in stone, the occupational name in Malabar of a section of the great artisan caste of Kammālans, q.v.

kambu spiked millet *(Pennisetum typhoideum)*; v. also *sazzulu.*

Kammas originally a soldier caste, now landowners and cultivators, and very industrious and intelligent agriculturists.

Kammaralas (Kammalas, Kammalans). The great artisan caste of the Tamil and Malayalam countries, divided into five sections, Tattans (goldsmiths), Kannāns (braziers), Tachans (carpenters), Kal-Tachans or Kallasaris (stone masons) and Kollans or Karumāns (blacksmiths).

kanaga the bastard rose-wood *(Dalbergia lanceolaria).* An oil is extracted from the fruit which is used as an illuminant and on the hair.

kanjurnoi, Tamil, literally "dry disease." A name given to various plant diseases.

Kapus, or *Reddis,* the largest caste in Madras Presidency, numbering over two millions. They are Telugus but are numerous also in Tamil districts; almost invariably they are landowners or cultivators. The word Kapu is said to mean watchman, and Reddi king.

karuppukittinoi, Tamil *karuppu* black, *kitti* approaching, *noi* disease; a plant disease, not specifically identifiable.

karugal a plant disease, involving a blackening of the tissues. Not specifically identifiable.

Karuvans (Karumans) blacksmiths, a division of the Kammalan caste, q.v.

kathakali, literally 'story-entertainment.' A form of dramatic entertainment peculiar to the West Coast. The subject is always mythological, and the gods appear in grotesque forms, the actors wearing masks. Similar entertainments are common in Tamil districts, but without the grotesque conventional get up.

kattukuttagai (Tamil, *kattu* tie, *kuttagai* rent) a defined fixed rent, or the letting of land for a defined rent.

kazhichal ordinary diarrhœa.

keppai = *tenai*, q.v.

kilipuchi (Tamil) literally 'parrot insect.' A name given to various insect pests from a fancied resemblance to a parrot's beak; in text, the locust.

kist the word ordinarily used to denote the land revenue payable to Government, but sometimes used also for the rent paid to the landholder under Government.

kol fields are lands on the West Coast which have been partially reclaimed from backwaters for paddy cultivation. During and after the rains they are under water; in the hot dry season they are kept partially dry by pumping.

komari foot and mouth disease.

Komatis the great Telugu trading caste of the Madras Presidency, corresponding to the Tamil Chettis. They are very widely scattered.

kondapurirogam. *Kondapuri* is a Telugu name for a variety of paddy cultivated on high lands, *rogam* is Telugu for disease.

koraladappan (Tamil, *koral* throat, *adappan* swelling) hæmorrhagic septicæmia.

korra Italian millet.

kota (kotah, kotai, kottai) the measure of grain commonly used in the extreme south, the districts of Rāmnād and Tinnevelly. It may be 90, 96, 112 or 120 Madras measures.

Kshatriyas the kingly and warrior caste according to the Laws of Manu. In South India various people term themselves Kshatriyas, though their descent from any true Kshatriya caste is doubtful.

kudirai-val horse gram *(Dolichos biflorus)*, a small-grained pulse grown over about 2,000,000 acres in Madras Presidency, the regular feeding stuff for horses, also used for cattle food and for human consumption.

Kummaras the Telugu and Kanarese caste of potters.

kunaivandu literally 'hunch-back weevil.' In the text the cotton pest referred to is *Atactogoster finitimus*, but the same name is applied generally to weevils having prominent beaks.

kunnal a term used for ordinary fever in cattle, and in some places for black quarter.

Kunparars = Kummaras, q.v.

kurama anthrax.

kuruthupuchi, literally 'shoot insect', the stem borer caterpillar, *Chilo simplex*.

kuthakai (kuttakai) a lease of land.

L

lingam a phallic symbol found regularly in connexion with Siva temples, usually about 3 feet high, and carved out of very hard and durable stone.

M

Madras measure = 108 cubic inches = 8 ollocks ; 8 Madras measures = 1 marakkal = 500 fluid ounces.

mahimai (Urdu) a tax for religious or charitable purposes ; village octroi.

Malayalam a Dravidian language closely related to Tamil (q.v.) but with a larger accession of Sanskrit words, spoken on the West Coast, in the States of Travancore and Cochin, and the district of Malabar.

Malayas a Malabar caste of devil dancers or professional exorcists, who eke out their living by singing and begging.

malli coriander. Grown chiefly in Tinnevelly for its seeds, but the leaves also are used as a vegetable.

mamoti a short handled broad bladed hoe, used instead of a spade, or shovel, and for a great variety of purposes. There is one in the foreground of the illustration "Agricultural implements used in Thettupalli."

mamul custom, hence a customary payment (as to a village blacksmith), hence a bribe or illicit fee extorted by a village official, minor Government official, or station-master.

mandapam (Sanskrit) a porch, hall, or cloister—usually a pillared shelter for pilgrims.

mandravadi one who chants *mantrams.*

manjanathi morinda tinctoria, a common shrub, used for green manure. The bark of the root yields a yellow dye.

Mannans (Vannans) a caste of washermen in Tamil and Malayalam countries. On the West Coast they also act as priests of Bhagavati (a goddess of the Gangamma type) and as devil dancers.

mantrams hymns, prayers or spells recited with magical effect.

Mappilas (Moplahs) the Muhammadans of the West Coast, originally the descendants of Arab traders and native women, but with their numbers swollen by accession of converts from depressed castes of Hindus, who by conversion escaped from slavery and degradation. They are physically vigorous, but turbulent and disorderly.

marakkal usually 8 Madras measures, but 2 in Tanjore and Trichinopoly, 4 in Tinnevelly, and 3 in parts of Rāmnād.

Maravars a numerous caste in the Southern districts of Madras Presidency, originally robbers and marauders, more recently cattle thieves, village watchmen, and black-mailers, now partially converted to agricultural pursuits.

margosa, called also neem, *azadirachta indica*, a very common tree yielding hard, durable timber. The seeds yield oil, the leaves and bark yield a febrifuge.

Marumakkattayam the custom of inheritance through the female line, from mother to daughter, that prevails among the Nairs, Bants, Billavas, Tiyyas and other castes on the West Coast. As the property is usually held by large undivided families, and administered by the eldest male, who is succeeded in the management by a brother or nephew, it is called in North Malabar *Aliyana Santana*, or Sister's son inheritance.

maund a variable weight. A railway maund is 82·28 lb., a Madras maund about 25 lb.

melkanam (melcharth). *Mel* means over, above. *Melkanam* is the payment and receipt of an extra *kanam*, or fine on renewing a lease, in excess of that paid by the actual *kanamdar* or leaseholder, to secure a transfer of the lease.

minnai oil, commonly called *pinnai* or *punnai* oil, extracted from the fruit of the common poon (*Calophyllum inophyllum*, Linn.), which is also called the Dilo oil tree or Domba oil nut tree.

mirasidar (mirasdar). In Tanjore, Trichinopoly and North Arcot districts, where the ryotwari lands are generally held by Brahmans, the *pattadar* who holds direct from Government is frequently termed a *mirasidar*. This is an honorific title, and the mirasidar is usually very unwilling to do the actual work of cultivation.

mochai the country bean, *Dolichos lablab*.

monigar = *munsif*.

munsif village headman.

musara rinderpest.

Musaris Malayalam brass and coppersmiths, a division of Kammalans.

Mysore breed of cattle. Great attention was paid to the improvement of cattle for draught by Hyder Ali and Tippu Sahib, and they established systematic cattle breeding, using the best of the animals they captured. To their success was due the rapidity of their marches. The well-bred Mysore ox is a good sized, strong and active animal, allowed to run wild when young, and very hardy.

N

Nachiyar a non-Brahman lady who through extreme devotion to the worship of Vishnu became a goddess and one of Vishnu's mistresses.

nali (nari, nazhi) a West Coast measure, one-fourth of an edangali, q.v.

nalupujadyam. *Nalupu* blackness, *jadyam* sickness. In the text probably refers to malignant oedema.

Nambiyars a section of Nayars, q.v.

Nambudri (Nambudiri) Brahmans the Brahmans of the Malabar Coast. They have the highest reputation of all Brahmans for piety and Sanskritic learning.

Nayadis a hunting tribe living on the forest-covered hills of the West Coast. They are considered the lowest of the untouchable castes, and pollute a Brahman at a distance of 300 feet. Owing to the operation of the Arms Act and the shrinking of the forests, their occupation is largely gone, and while living mainly on small wild animals and roots, they often serve as watchmen, guarding crops from wild beasts at night, and sometimes do agricultural work, but they rely more on begging for subsistence.

Nayakars a Telugu-speaking caste of agriculturists numerous in the Rāmnād, Tinnevelly and Madura districts, closely akin to the Nayudus of Tanjore, and to the Kapus or Reddis.

Nayars (Nairs). The name means a leader or soldier. The military skill and valour of the Nayars was highly praised by various travellers of the seventeenth and eighteenth centuries, and by Camoens. It was the ancient custom for their chieftain, the Zamorin, to cut his own throat after reigning 12 years. This was modified at an unknown date, and during the seventeenth century the Zamorin instead held a great 12 days feast every twelfth year, at the close of which young men were invited to fight their way through the Zamorin's guards, and kill him, with the prospect of succeeding to the throne if successful.

Nayudu a title assumed by certain Telugu castes. The Nayudus described in the text are Kapus or Reddis.

Navuri (*na* tongue) lampas, a swollen condition of the bard palate in cattle, a symptom of various diseases, not a specific disease.

Nellore breed of cattle, also, and more correctly, called the Ongole breed. They are the largest and heaviest breed in South India, the oxen being slow, but suitable for heavy work, and the cows the best milkers of the native breeds. They are bred in the Guntūr district and adjoining parts of the Nellore district, Ongole being about the centre of the area, and they pass through the town of Nellore on their journey southwards. The soil in the locality is rich in lime, which favours the growth of bone. The cattle are fed on private pastures and certain bulls are dedicated to the gods and set aside for breeding, but these are not necessarily selected for any good quality.

nilams the name given to paddy lands in the Malayalam country.

O

Oddars a Telugu-speaking caste of navvies and earthworkers, who originally came from Orissa. They have relatively good physique, eat meat, are very fond of toddy, and allow polygamy and free divorce. Women are only restricted from changing husbands after having had eighteen. This limit does not apply to men.

Omum the crude drug from which thymol is extracted.

Onam the great annual festival of the Malabar Coast, held early in September or at the end of August, lasting about four days. At this time the god Parasurama, according to some accounts, revisits Malabar; according to other local traditions it is the local god Mahabali, a Dravidian deity, whose visit takes place.

P

Pachalai the green plant bug *Nezara viridula.*

Padiyals from *padi* a measure; one who receives a defined quantity of grain from his master.

Paliath Atchan. 'Paliath' is the name of a tarvad originally supplying hereditary prime ministers to Cochin, and still the richest jenmis in the State. Each member of the tarvad is called 'Atchan,' an honorific term meaning father.

paliki-guntaka, or, perhaps more correctly, *paliki-guntava* (v. *guntaka*), a twelve-toothed rake, drawn by oxen, similar to the six-toothed implement shown in the illustration "Agricultural implements used in Thettupalli."

palikimanu levelling board, more correctly spelt palakamānu; *palaka* means plain, level; *mānu* wood.

Pallans the great caste of agricultural labourers of the south of the peninsula, almost entirely engaged in the cultivation of wet lands, and once slaves, and now practically in serfdom, though partially emancipated by conversion to Christianity and the increased demand for their services caused by the need for labourers on Ceylon tea and rubber estates.

Panans a depressed caste of the West Coast, devil dancers and umbrella makers. They have paternal descent (father to son) of property, and are said to practise fraternal polyandry.

Panchamas, literally the fifth caste, a general name for all untouchables, as Pallans, Paraiyans, Cherumas, etc.

panchayat, literally an assembly of five men, actually a small committee of five or more or fewer men, either elected or nominated, to attend to the common affairs of a village or caste or other small aggregation of people.

pandaravaka from *pandara* Sirkar, government, *vaka* sort or kind (Malayalam).

Pandarams a section of the Vellala caste which performs priestly functions.

pandluminu a wooden harrow, with about 24 wooden teeth about 3 inches long, drawn by hand.

Panikkans. This word means teachers or workers, and is variously applied in the Malayalam country to barbers, fencing masters and craftsmen.

pannaiyals serfs, from *pannai*, home farm or demesne land.

paracheri the collection of huts occupied by the Paraiyans of a village. While the Paraiyans are not allowed to enter the caste village, Brahmans are not allowed to enter the paracheri, even if willing to do so. The Paraiyans hold that disaster would follow the entry of a Brahman.

Paraiyans, commonly termed Pariahs, a large untouchable caste, numbering about two millions, mostly living in the district immediately to the south of Madras. Like the Pallans they are very largely agricultural labourers on wet lands, and practically in serfdom. The domestic servants employed by Europeans in Madras are mostly of this caste.

parambas (Malayalam) cultivated lands under any crop other than paddy.

Parasurama the god Vishnu in one of his incarnations, in which he created the land between the Western Ghats and the sea (p. 146).

parivarthanai (Sanskrit) exchange or barter.

patel = *munsif* village headman (Kanarese).

patta the title-deed to ryotwari land granted to the peasant individually by the revenue officer.

pattadar the holder of a *patta*. His tenure is for life, and on his death the holding is divided among his heirs according to the custom of his community, i.e., if he is a Hindu, equally among his sons, if a Muhammadan, two-thirds of it between the sons, one-third between the daughters. He can mortgage or sell his rights.

pattu a horse disease, probably surra. Surra is caused by a protozoon allied to that which causes sleeping sickness, and produces general debility.

Poligars marauding chieftains established in the seventeenth and eighteenth centuries over many districts of South India, carrying on wars with one another, with the more settled native governments, and, latterly, with the East India Company. The present localization of great numbers of people of Kallan and Maravar and similar castes of criminal traditions is the permanent consequence of this political condition.

Pongal a harvest festival held early in January, the first three days of the Tamil month Tai.

Poniamman a village goddess of the Gangamma type.

poramboke land in a village reserved for purposes other than cultivation.

pothimuzhungunoi (*muzhungu* devour, *noi* = disease) not identified.

Pulayas a division of the Cheruma caste.

Punganur breed of cattle. There was a breed of cattle peculiar to the zamindari village of Punganūr, of short stature. not over 36 inches in height, but esteemed for the milking qualities of the cows, and the excellence of the oxen for draught. The pure breed is extinct.

puravaka (*pura* outside, *vaka* sort) land in Cochin over which Government's rights have been transferred to private owners, as contrasted with *pandaravaka* 'government sort.'

putti (pothi) a variable weight, usually about 500 lb.

R

Ragi (Eleusine coracana), an important crop, usually a dry crop, but sometimes irrigated. It very seldom grows with anything like the luxuriance shown in the illustration. It is grown on about 2,500,000 acres in Madras Presidency.

Ramayana. The version of the Ramayana of the poet Kamban is the great epic of the Tamil language, and is asserted by some to be far superior in literary quality to the Sanskrit version. A similar claim is made for the Telugu version of the Mahabharata.

S

Saivites worshippers of Siva and followers of Sankaracharya, the religious leader who flourished about A.D. 800, whose teaching superseded Buddhism over most of India. The 'Saivites' and 'Vaishnavites' are the two great Hindu sects. The Saivite symbol is white cowdung ashes smeared on the forehead.

sambal literally 'ashes,' an unidentified plant disease.

samooham Sanskrit for an assembly.

sandai (shandy) a village fair or market.

santhadappan haemorrhagic septicaemia.

Saradambal, or Sarasvati, the Hindu goddess of learning.

sarvamanyam from (Sanskrit) *sarva* entire and *manyam* gift. A gift of land free of rent.

Sastrigal a reciter of Shastras, or sacred hymns, or a Brahman who performs religious ceremonies. The word Sastri is used as a caste name by some Tamil and Telugu Saivite Brahmans.

Sathanis a Telugu caste of temple servants supposed to have originated in the time of the Vaishnavite reformer Ramanujacharya (cir. A.D. 1100).

sazzulu the Telugu name for spiked millet, *Pennisetum typhoideum*, called *kambu* in Tamil and *bajra* in Hindustani. Grown on about 3,000,000 acres in the Madras Presidency.

seer by statute one kilogramme; on the railways 80 tolas, a tola being the weight of a rupee (= 2·05 lb.), in Anantapur 21 tolas, in many parts of the Presidency 24 tolas (about 10 oz.).

sendal (*sendalai*) literally 'red leaf,' a reddening of the cholam leaf through the attack of mites. It is sometimes very destructive.

Shanars the great toddy drawing caste of the Tamil country, specially numerous in the extreme south of the Peninsula, where there is a considerable area where the palmyra is the sole means of subsistence. They call themselves Nadars, and claim to be by origin a landowning and soldier caste worsted in war by the Madura monarchs. They have been regarded by some other castes as Panchamas, and their right to enter Hindu temples disputed; and there is a bitter feud between them and the Maravars. Great numbers have become Christians, and they are rapidly rising in education, wealth and social status.

shanbhog Kanarese for *karnam*, village accountant.

Smarthas Tamil-speaking Saivite Brahmans.

Siva the supreme god worshipped by Saivite Hindus. Combined with Brahma and Vishnu in the Trimurti, or Hindu trinity, Siva is conceived as embodying the destructive function of the deity. But as the supreme god of the Saivites he is fundamentally the god of life and procreation, his symbol being the lingam. His consort is Parvati, his sons the elephant-headed Ganesa, and Subrahmaniam, who rides on a peacock.

soap-nuts (concinna) a species of bean. The outer cover of the seed is boiled or pounded into powder, and used to rub over the skin and hair after taking an oil bath to remove the greasiness.

Sraddha a day of mourning for a dead father or mother, on which two Brahmans are fed. It is celebrated every month for one year, and afterwards every year on the anniversary of the day of the death.

suruttai curling, rolling up. Any leaf disease or plant blight that curls up the leaf.

Swadesamitran, literally 'friend of one's own country.'

Syrian Christians. According to strong local tradition, disputed but not improbable, this church was founded by St. Thomas the Apostle. Little is known of it up to the arrival of the Portuguese, since when it has had a chequered history, mainly owing to the efforts of the Jesuits to bring it within the Roman fold.

T

Tahsildar the Revenue officer in charge of a taluk.

talaiyari a village watchman.

taluk a division of a district (q.v.) comprising 3 to 5 *firkas*. There are usually 8 to 10 *taluks* in a district.

tamarind a large evergreen tree, the heart wood of which is very durable, and used for the mortars of oil mills, shafts, axles, etc. The fruit is sour and laxative and is regarded as a necessary article of food.

Tamil the most highly cultivated Dravidian language, possessing a large poetic and grammatical literature. It shows the transition from the agglutinative to the inflected stage of development. It has no relative pronoun, instead the use of participles is wonderfully developed. It is extraordinarily difficult for a European to learn, as there is no accent, the words run into one another and the pronunciation is very rapid, the syllables being slurred over. The versification is very elaborate, being based on quantity, and using rhyme and alliteration.

Tamil names. Surnames proper are not used in Tamil. The caste name follows a man's own name and that is preceded by two initials, the first standing for the name of the place where he was born, the second for his father's name. The former of these is sometimes omitted. His own name is ususally one of the names of Siva, or of Vishnu, or the incarnations of Vishnu (Rama and Krishna), or Subrahmaniam. *Tiru*, holy, is a frequent prefix, and *Swami*, deity, a common affix.

Tamil year. The Tamil year has twelve months, Chitrai, Vaigasi, Ani, Adi, Avani, Purattasi, Arpasi, Kartigai, Margazhi, Tai, Masi, Panguni. April 12th, 1918, was New Years day, 1st Chitrai, of the Tamil year 1841. The months are solar. Each day (of 24 hours) is divided into 60 'naligas.' A month does not begin at any particular hour of the day.

taram class. Each field in a village is classified for revenue purposes according to the colour, texture and fertility of the soil, facilities for irrigation, and distance from village-site. The fields so classified fall into a series of classes, or *tarams*, each class being assessed at an appropriate money rate. There is a separate series for 'wet' and 'dry' lands.

Telugu the most widely spread Dravidian language, spoken, according to the Census of 1911, by 22,543,000 people, Tamil being spoken by 17,129,000, Kanarese by 10,526,000 and Malayalam by 6,792,000. It contains a larger proportion of Sanskritic words than Tamil, and is less subtle and precise, and there is an even wider severance between the literary and popular forms of the language. It has a considerable poetical literature, the Telugu version of the Mahabharata being asserted to be far superior in literary quality to the Sanskrit version. It is more euphonious than Tamil and has been termed "the Italian of the East."

thada an inflamed condition of the throat in cattle, a symptom, not a specific disease.

thalpuchi (Tamil) *thal* stalk, *puchi* insect.

tharvād (tarwād) the undivided family of the Nayars. As inheritance follows the female line, while a man has a right to maintenance during his life from the property of his *tharvad*, he transmits no right to his children. The desire to do so is frequently very strong, and the whole system of *tharvads* and *marumakkattayam*, though it has great advantages, appears likely to fall into decay.

Thattans (Thattars, Tattans) the goldsmith division of the Kammalan or artisan caste.

thellachida (Telugu) *thella* white, *chida* pest.

Thiyyas (Tiyyas) the toddy drawing caste of the southern portion of the Malabar coast, corresponding to Billavas further north, and to Shanars in the south-east. Like the Nayars, Bants and Billavas, they follow the *marumakkattayam* system of inheritance. They are advancing in education, wealth and status.

tirumanjanam, tiru (Tamil) holy, *manjanam* (Sanskrit) anointing.

Tirunal (Tamil) *tiru* holy, *nal* day.

toddy is extracted from coconut palms, date palms, and palmyras. It is a sweet juice which ferments immediately unless fermentation is prevented with a view to conversion into jaggery and sugar. It is usually drunk the day after it is gathered, being then a somewhat stupefying intoxicant. The next day it becomes vinegar, and then speedily decomposes.

tola the weight of a rupee, ·4114 oz.

Tolkollans leather workers and dyers of the Malabar coast.

tondaipuchi literally "throat insect," the paddy stem borer, *schoenobius bifunctifer*, a serious paddy pest.

Tondaman the family name of the Raja of Pudukkōttai, the head of the Kallan caste, and the name of a sub-caste of limeburners, supposed to be a section ot the Kallan caste which migrated to Tinnevelly from Pudukkōttai.

U

Uralla, presumably from *ūr* village, and *āl* headman.

V

Vainoi foot-and-mouth disease.

Vaishnavites worshippers of Vishnu, and followers of Ramanuja, the Vaishnavite religious leader and reformer, who flourished about A.D. 1100. The badge of the Vaishnavite is a trident shaped white and red mark on the forehead.

vakil a lawyer, who may act indifferently as a legal adviser or advocate. Lawyers entitled to plead in the High Court are termed High Court Vakils. The title 'Barrister-at-law' can only be acquired by studying in the United Kingdom.

varagu kodo millet ***(Paspalum scrobiculatum)***, a cereal inferior both as food and fodder, but very hardy and a useful famine reserve, grown over nearly two million acres in Madras Presidency.

varam share.

vekkai (Tamil, hot) rinderpest.

vellaithal (Tamil) *vellai* white, *thal* stalk.

Vellalas the great farmer caste of the Tamil country, corresponding more or less to the Telugu Kapus or Reddis, and ranking, among Tamils, next to Brahmans.

verpulu, literally "root worm." Any sort of worm or grub that attacks the roots of plants.

verumpattam tenancy at will. (*Verum* unqualified or unfavourable, ***pattam*** lease.)

vethupu rinderpest.

Vettis the lowest class of village servants, whose duty is to watch the burning-ground set aside for disposal of the dead.

Vinayaga Chaturti. Vinayaga, another name of Ganesa. *Chaturti* is the fourth day after new moon and full moon.

Vishnu the supreme deity worshipped by Vaishnavite Hindus. Vishnu underwent a series of incarnations in animal and human form. As Rama he is the hero of the epic Ramayana, as Krishna he is a character in the Mahabharata, and utters the Bhagavat Gita, the most sacred exposition of Vaishnavite ethics.

viss a variable weight. In Madras 1 viss 120 tolas, or about 3 lb., in Ganjām 1 viss 400 tolas.

W

Wariyar one section of the Ambalavasis, q.v.

Y

yetham-bana the bucket of a picottah.

Z

Zamindar (Zemindar) a local chieftain or revenue officer recognized by the East India Company in parts of Madras as well as in Bengal as a landed proprietor. The Zemindari properties of Madras Presidency are under permanent settlement as in Bengal, but in practice an important difference arises from the fact that they have mostly been brought under the Impartible Estates Act, so that no large class of poor but idle zemindars has been created.

Zamorin the title of the ruling princes of Malabar, of great importance at the time of the Portuguese arrival in India and later (v. also Nayars).

[*Note.*—Thurston's "Castes and Tribes of Southern India" and R. C. Wood's "Notebook of Agricultural Facts and Figures" have been used largely for this Glossary.]

INDEX.

R

S